# Dostoevsky

## WORKS AND DAYS

*Dostoevsky the convict. From a sculpture by S. T. Konenkov*

# Dostoevsky

## WORKS AND DAYS

BY

## Avrahm Yarmolinsky

## FUNK & WAGNALLS

New York

PICTURE CREDITS: Columbia University, Butler Library, 1, 2, 3; Dostoevsky Museum, Moscow, 7; New York Public Library, Slavonic Division, frontispiece, 6, 11, 12.

To  Babette

Some other books written or edited by
AVRAHM YARMOLINSKY

Author of
*Turgenev—The Man, His Art, and His Age*
*Road to Revolution*
*Literature Under Communism*
*The Russian Literary Imagination*

Editor of
*The Works of Alexander Pushkin*
*The Portable Chekhov*
*Russians Then and Now*
*Two Centuries of Russian Verse*

# FOREWORD

THE increase of more moderate writing on the subject of that immoderate man, Fyodor Dostoevsky, is gratifying. But if the rhapsodic note has been muted to a degree, he is still the victim of farfetched interpretations. They are exemplified in several recent studies listed in the bibliography. His personal history and his writings alike are marked by extremes. It is hoped that the sober treatment accorded them in the pages which follow will give the reader a more compelling sense of the drama and pathos of Dostoevsky's life, a more critical view of his performance as preacher and publicist, and a juster estimate of his power as an artist.

The present work is larger and more comprehensive than the second edition of a book on Dostoevsky, by this author, issued more than a dozen years ago. Its foreword opened thus: "A revised edition of a book published in 1934 on a subject as compelling today as the phenomenon of Dostoevsky scarcely requires an apology." Though the time span between that second edition and this larger volume is shorter, the author likes to believe that, similarly, no apology is needed for the book in hand.

The new material that has come to light includes all the notes for *A Raw Youth,* as well as the fourth and final volume of the novelist's letters—owing to the Stalinist terror, it had to wait a quarter of a century to be published. Recent contributions to scholarship and criticism, including fruit of the researches of American students, have been taken into account. Naturally, Soviet work received due attention. Furthermore, some sources have been re-examined. The effort has been to look more closely at characters and situations of special interest in *The Double* and *Notes from the Underground,* and in the major fictions, especially the most complete and resonant novels, *The Devils* (*The Possessed*) and *The Brothers Karamazov.** Pains have been taken not merely to eliminate inadvertent errors, but, in dispensing with dubious speculation, to accord nicer precision to matters of fact. As a result of second thoughts some of the text has been re-arranged, some rewritten, most of it altered in certain particulars.

The chronological table has been expanded, while the bibliography has been changed in order to serve the general reader and the student who has little or no Russian.

The author is greatly indebted to his wife, Babette Deutsch, for generous help in the preparation of this book.

A. Y.

*January, 1971*

---

* Constance Garnett's translation of the first title, under which it is generally known to the English-reading public, may be due to a misunderstanding. The Russian is *The Devils,* by which it is referred to hereafter. It is clear from the second epigraph to the book (Luke VIII: 32–7) that the reference is not to the sick man, but to the devils by whom he is possessed, and whom Jesus exorcises, giving them leave to enter into the swine. English-speaking readers have accepted Constance Garnett's translation of the second title, which preserves the word order of the original.

# CONTENTS

Illustrations following pages 166 and 324.

# CHRONOLOGY

The dates in this table, as throughout the book, except for those relating to Dostoevsky's sojourn in Western Europe, are Old Style. Being of the nineteenth century, they are twelve days behind those reckoned by the calendar now in general use. Dates for the works are those of publication.

| | |
|---|---|
| 1821, October 20 | Fyodor Mikhailovich Dostoevsky born in Moscow |
| 1833–37 | Attends boarding schools in Moscow |
| 1837, February 27 | Mother (born in 1800) dies |
| May | Leaves for Petersburg |
| 1838, January 16 | Admitted to the School of Engineering |
| 1839, June | Father (born in 1789) killed by his serfs |
| 1843, August 12 | Fyodor graduates from the School of Engineering and is enrolled in the Corps of Engineers as a draftsman |
| 1844, October 19 | Retires from the government service with the rank of lieutenant |
| June–July | Translation of Balzac's *Eugénie Grandet* |
| 1845, autumn | Joins the Belinsky circle |
| 1846, January 15 | *Poor Folk* |
| February 1 | *The Double* |
| 1847, early in the year | Breaks with Belinsky |
| spring | Starts to attend Petrashevsky's Fridays |

| | | |
|---|---|---|
| 1849 | | *Netochka Nezvanova* |
| | April 23 | Arrested and imprisoned |
| | December 22 | After preliminaries to public execution by shooting, last-minute reprieve and announcement of actual sentence |
| | December 24 | Deported to Siberia in irons |
| 1850, January–February | | A convict at Omsk |
| 1854 | | |
| 1853 | | Periodic epileptic attacks begin |
| 1854–59 | | Military service in Semipalatinsk |
| 1856, October 1 | | Obtains officer's commission |
| 1857, February 6 | | Marries Marya Dmitrievna Isayeva |
| 1859, March 18 | | Permitted to retire from the service |
| | March | "Uncle's Dream" |
| | July 2 | Leaves Siberia for Tver |
| | November–December | "The Friend of the Family" |
| | | Settles in Petersburg |
| 1860 | | First edition of collected works |
| 1861, January | | First issue of *Vremya*, a monthly, under his editorship |
| | January 16 | *The Insulted and Injured* |
| 1861–65 | | Acquaintance followed by intimacy with Polina Suslova, and foreign travel in her company |
| 1861–62 | | *Notes from the House of the Dead* |
| 1862, summer | | First trip abroad |
| 1863, February–March | | "Winter Notes on Summer Impressions" |
| 1863, May 24 | | *Vremya* suppressed by the Czar's order |
| | August–October | Trip abroad |
| | | Contracts gambling fever, which plagues him intermittently for some eight years |
| 1864, March 21 | | First issue of *Epokha*, a monthly, under his editorship |
| | March–April | *Notes from the Underground* |
| | March 15 | Wife dies |

| | |
|---|---|
| July 10 | His brother Mikhail dies |
| 1865, March–April | Acquaintance with Anna Korvin-Krukovskaya and her sister, the future Sophie Kovalevsky |
| June | *Epokha* discontinued |
| July–October | Trip to Germany |
| 1866 | *Crime and Punishment* |
| | *The Gambler* |
| 1867, February 15 | Marries Anna Grigoryevna Snitkina |
| April 14 | Goes abroad with his wife |
| 1868 | *The Idiot* |
| March 5 | Daughter, Sonia, born in Geneva |
| May 24 | Infant dies |
| summer | At Vevey, winter in Florence |
| 1869, July | Returns to Dresden |
| September 26 | Daughter, Liuba, born |
| December | Plans *The Life of a Great Sinner* |
| 1870 | "The Eternal Husband" |
| 1871, July 8 | Returns to Petersburg with family |
| July 16 | Son, Fyodor, born |
| 1871–72 | *The Devils* |
| 1872 | Summer at Starya Russa |
| 1873 | Edits *Grazhdanin,* a weekly |
| 1874, April | Resigns as editor of *Grazhdanin* |
| | Winter at Staraya Russa |
| 1875 | *A Raw Youth* |
| 1875, August 10 | Son, Alexey, born |
| 1876–79, 1880–81 | *A Writer's Diary* |
| 1877 | Elected corresponding member of the Russian Academy of Sciences |
| 1878, May 16 | Alexey dies |
| 1879–80 | *The Brothers Karamazov* |
| 1880, May 23– | In Moscow for the unveiling of the Pushkin monument |
| June 10 | |
| June 8 | Delivers the Pushkin address |
| 1881, January 28 | Dies in Petersburg |
| February 1 | Buried in a cemetery attached to the Alexander Nevsky monastery |

# Dostoevsky

## WORKS AND DAYS

# 1

# A CHILD

HE is at church in the arms of his mother, who has lifted him to receive the sacrament. It is summer. Suddenly a dove flies in through a window and darts out through one on the other side. In attributing this reminiscence to the hero of *A Raw Youth* over a half-century later, Dostoevsky will add that the child, about to kiss the chalice, is startled and cries out, "A dove, a dove!"

He is bigger now: he has turned three. Nurse has just brought him into the parlor to show off her charge to the company. He kneels, facing the icon in the corner, and before them all he says his bedtime prayer: "All my hope I place in thee, Mother of God; shelter me under thy mantle." "What a clever little boy!" the guests exclaim.

These were Fyodor Dostoevsky's earliest memories. They were of a kind natural to a child born into an Orthodox household established in the hallowed city of Moscow. Religious observances were a matter of course both to that unhappy army doctor, his father, and that good woman, his mother. Church attendance belonged to the daily routine. The family had but a step to go: a chapel, named for Saints Peter and Paul, was attached to the hospital where his father served on the staff and where they had their living quarters. Indeed, it was in this chapel, accustomed to the hasty funerals of the poor, that little Fyodor was baptized on a November day under the sponsorship of four godparents, one of them his mother's wealthy sister, Aunt Kumanina, who stood godmother to all his brothers and sisters. The children were also taken—and these were memorable occasions—to the great cathedrals of the city and to the sanctuaries behind the red swallowtail ramparts which wall in the Kremlin heights. The aged little churches with their glowing domes, their chimes filling the quiet lanes in which they nestled— the peace of these was to be shadowless in remembrance. Each summer, up to the time Fedya was ten years old, his mother bore her little flock on a long, leisurely pilgrimage to the shrines of the ancient monastery of the Holy Trinity, forty miles away. Besides pious memories, they brought back from the trip, which lasted nearly a week, toys of peasant make. It may well have been at the monastery that the boy saw possessed women exorcised at mass—a fearful and touching scene. Always at church the poor crowded at the entrance. He felt curiously drawn to these ragged men and women who bowed so low and prayed so humbly, earnestly, fully aware of their low state.

Perhaps it was in these early years that some scene deeply colored by emotion came to be associated for him with the enchantment of the sunset hour. It may have been his mother's holding him out to the icon while she prayed on her knees for the Virgin's protection of him, one still summer day as the sun was sinking—a memory that he was to bestow on Alyosha Karamazov. Fedya's first experience of having been touched, as a child of eight, in a peculiarly intimate way by religious feeling, while listening to the recital of the Book of Job in church, is incorporated in the story of his childhood years told by the elderly monk, Zosima, in *The Brothers Karamazov*. As related in the novel it was the Monday of Passion Week and the boy was at mass with his mother. Incense was eddying upward and melting, as it were, in the sunlight that streamed through the windows. A youth placed an enormous book on a lectern and read: " 'There was a man in the land of Uz whose name was Job; and that man was perfect and upright and one that feared God and eschewed evil. . . .' " The three thousand camels, the Lord talking with Satan, and other details of the tale stirred the little boy deeply, filling him with awe, wonder, and elation. A pillar of Orthodoxy, the monk will draw from the book lessons of piety and spiritual serenity. As for Dostoevsky, if Job's faith touched him, Job's rebellion must also have had an echo in his heart. At all events, the boy grew into a man who could not read those pages without "morbid rapture." The curtain was never wholly to close for him on the drama of God and man.

# ( II )

The children came in two sets: Mikhail was the eldest; one year later, on October 30, 1821, Fyodor was born; the next year Varvara came, and in 1825, the last of the elder group, Andrey. Four years later twin girls were born, Vera and Liubov. The latter lived only a few days—the children were not spared the sight of the little coffin. In due time there were two more additions to the family: Nikolay and Alexandra.

Fyodor was inseparable from Mikhail, and "Little Tail," as they nicknamed Andrey, was generally allowed to tag after them. The band was captained by Fedya. Though not a well child, he was full of high spirits. "I am not surprised, my dear, at Fedya's mischief," his mother wrote to his father, apparently in reply to a report about the boy's behavior, "for that is what we have to expect from him." He was the inventor, the explorer, the mime. Whenever the family went on a trip, he was in a fever. He would perch aloft on the coachman's box until they came to a station and then he would be poking his snub nose everywhere at once. After seeing a trapeze artist at a public entertainment play the part of a Brazilian ape, Fedya came home and was an ape for weeks. Once at a festival he saw a runner racing with a handkerchief between his teeth, and for days afterward he raced through the hospital park, a handkerchief fluttering from his mouth. Little encouragement as there was for it, he liked to imagine himself an athlete. In his eagerness he would cheat at cards when, on the great holidays, especially at Christmastime, the family indulged in a game. The little gambler persisted in it, although he was invariably caught red-handed. "A perfect flame!"—that was how his parents spoke of this sensitive, fidgety, boisterous son.

The flame burned in a close atmosphere. The sizeable household, which included seven servants, was confined to an apartment of three rooms and a large kitchen. The nursery, a windowless alcove of the spacious, dark pearl-gray foyer, was presided over by Alyona Frolovna, an old maid who called herself "Christ's bride." A mountain of a woman, she was forgiven her bulk, her prodigious appetite, her habit of taking snuff, because of her limitless devotion to the family. The living quarters were no brighter for being situated in a wing of a charity hospital attached to an institution for illegitimate children and foundlings.

What also clouded the air of home was the father's morose and irascible disposition. The elder Dostoevsky had made his own way and had had a rough road to travel, which had not sweetened his temper. His family's pedigree has been traced to Danilo Irtishch, a boyar in the retinue of a Russian prince whose father had fled to Lithuania in 1456. The boyar is believed to have descended from a Tartar chieftain who had emigrated to Muscovy from the Golden Horde. Thus, in Dostoevsky's case, as in Turgenev's, the adage about scratching a Russian holds good. In 1506 Danilo received from his prince a vast land grant, which included part of the village of Dostoevo, near the town of Pinsk. In the sixteenth and seventeenth centuries the Dostoevskys, as his scions called themselves, belonged to the Lithuanian-Russian upper class. Later on they came down in the world, settling in the Ukraine and entering the ranks of the clergy. The lineage was not without black sheep, whose misdeeds—pillaging, murder—are recorded in the documents of the period. In view of the novelist's intense animus against the Poles and the Roman Church, it is noteworthy that some branches of the family became Polonized and embraced Catholicism. Others, like the one from which he stemmed, clung to their Russian identity and to the Orthodox or Uniate faith.

The son of a priest with a parish in a town of the province of Podolia, the boy had been sent to divinity school as a matter of course. He had not remained there, and it is said that at fifteen he left home and that he never spoke of his early years. It is certain that in 1809, at the age of twenty, he entered the Imperial Medico-Surgical Academy in Moscow. He was in his senior year when Napoleon's army invaded the country, and he was forthwith put to work taking care of the wounded and, later, fighting an epidemic. He remained an army doctor until 1820, when he retired from the service, having, the previous year, married the daughter of a Moscow merchant, of pure Russian stock and in moderate circumstances, and settled down to civil practice as physician in the dispensary of the Mariinsky

Hospital for the Poor. In the parlor hung a gilt-framed pastel portrait showing him in his gold-braided uniform. Fedya usually saw his father, however, in the black frock coat, the white vest, and stock, which was the professional attire of a doctor, and wearing a decoration. He had the Orders of Saint Anne and Saint Vladimir and the rank of collegiate assessor, which enabled him to regain the status of hereditary noble (*dvoryanin*) that his forebears had lost when they became members of the clergy.

Mikhail Andreyevich, as his associates and few friends called him, was a sickly, moody man with a habit of fretting and complaining. His sullenness and self-righteousness would give way to self-pity and self-abasement. At once sentimental and mean, he was a prey to jealousy and groundless suspicions. When his wife was carrying her last child, he chided her because she was suffering from heartburn—a condition she had not known in any former pregnancy. She gathered that the symptom had roused his mad suspicion of her infidelity, and for the sake of his peace of mind she solemnly swore that she had been faithful to the vow that she had made at the altar sixteen years previously. It took all her tenderness to cheer him during his attacks of hypochondria and depression. Her letters to him overflow with assurances of boundless affection. She argued that they were happy in each other and in the love of their children, and that they had nothing more to desire, certainly not wealth. The children's love of their father must have been tinged with fear and perhaps resentment. Not seldom their mother or the nurse had to shield them from his uncontrollable rages. And although he spared the rod, he was a stickler for discipline and a believer in hard-and-fast rules, which did not lighten the oppressive puritanical atmosphere that he created in the home. The earliest extant note, signed by the four eldest children—Fedya was then in his eleventh year—reads: "All of us attest our deepest respect for you, dearest Papinka, and kiss your hands."

The mother was a kindly, devout, not uncultivated woman with a good deal of practical sense which she may have inherited from her father, the merchant, and with so delicate a constitution that she was able to nurse only the eldest of her children.

Fyodor was deeply attached to his mother. "When you left us, beloved Maminka" (she had gone with the younger children to spend the summer in the country), he wrote, at the age of thirteen, with real feeling and the scantiest punctuation, "I became exceedingly sad and now whenever I think of you I am overcome with such sadness that I can't chase it away at all if you know how much I want to see you I can't wait for that joyful moment. Every time I think of you I pray God for your health. Let us know, beloved Maminka, if you have made a safe journey kiss Andrushenka and Verochka for me I kiss your little hands and remain you obedient son F. Dostoevsky."

As long as he lived, he kept a miniature which had belonged to his mother. It represented an angel in flight and bore the inscription:

> *J'ai le cœur tout plein d'amour,*
> *Quand l'aurez-vous à votre tour?*

O heart! When will you be filled with the love which alone is man's salvation? This was the question that Dostoevsky, overflowing with bitter hatred and equally bitter compassion, would never cease to ask.

# ( III )

The day, which began early, was filled with set labors and staid pleasures. As soon as breakfast was over Fedya and his brothers were at their lessons in the canary-colored living room, where the family also took their meals. By nine o'clock the doctor had made his rounds in the wards, at twelve he returned from visiting his private patients, and at one dinner was placed on the table. The father took his after-dinner nap of two hours in the parlor, with Andrey by him to chase away the flies with a freshly cut linden branch, and woe to the boy if he was inattentive! At four in the afternoon tea was served, after which the doctor went out again, to see the hospital sick. The long winter evenings were spent by the light of tallow candles (wax tapers were reserved for company, lamps the doctor disliked) in the cobalt-blue parlor, over a volume of Karamzin's patriotic history or a novel, read aloud by the father. If it was a romance by Ann Radcliffe, at least one of the listeners, thrilled with delicious horror, would dream feverishly of it afterward. Promptly at nine o'clock the family went in to supper, and then the children said their prayers before the icon, bade their parents good night, and so to bed.

Rarely did Fedya's parents, by going out of an evening, release the spirit of boisterous fun which thrives in a large family but which here the father's presence tended to subdue. Visitors were infrequent. Among those who came to the house, mostly during the day, were the doctor's colleagues and, chiefly, the relatives. There was Grandfather, who came to dinner once a week. There was Great-Uncle, a genial and cultivated old gentleman who taught materia medica at the University of Moscow. There was Uncle Mikhail, who, like his sister, played the guitar and who left one of his instruments at the house, so that there were duets on his regular Sunday visits. But his appearances ceased abruptly, for a reason that was not divulged to the children. He had tried to seduce one of the chambermaids, and on being reprimanded for it in his sister's presence by the doctor, had spoken to her disrespectfully, whereupon the doctor gave him a slap which ended their relations. There were the cousins and the aunts, especially Aunt Kumanina, who would drive up in style, with a postilion in front and a footman behind to help her with all the packages of fruit and goodies that she would bring. Having no children of her own, she was all the more devoted to her poor sister's family, and until Fyodor was in his late teens played an important part in his life. All these relatives were on the mother's side, a fact that Fyodor must have noticed.

The monotony of the daily pattern was relieved by the holy days, and then there was the eighth of November to prepare for: the solemn occasion of the father's name-day. That day the doctor put aside his cares, devoting it, as he claimed, first to God, his "sole consoler in this grievous life," and second to himself. The two elder boys would recite their felicitations in French, after having handed their father the scrolls on which these were written in their best penmanship. The hero of the day, pleased by the performance, would melt and embrace his sons with warmth.

Another outstanding event, impatiently awaited, was the visit of one of the peasant women who had been wet nurses to the children. She would come on a winter morning and be shown into the parlor. After a short prayer before the icon she would greet the mistress of the house and kiss the young ones, among whom she would distribute whey cakes she had baked for them in her village home. Then, since lessons must not be interfered with, she would retire to the kitchen.

She reappeared in the unlighted dining room when dusk shrouded the birchwood chairs upholstered in green morocco, on each of which a small and eager occupant perched, waiting for her stories. A spell lay over the hour. The silence was so complete that one could hear plainly the scratch of the doctor's pen as he sat in the next room entering prescriptions on his patients' charts. Not to disturb the parents, the nurse would talk in a whisper, spinning out, with a gusto no less naïve than her listeners', the old stories in which the Fire-Bird and Blue-beard and that cunning son of a priest, Alyosha Popovich, played their wonderful or fearful parts. The more terrifying of these tales, muttered in the shadow-filled room, must have heightened Fedya's fear of the dark. There was, too, one old woman who told them stories from the Arabian Nights, and of course there were tales about holy men and holy places. Cheap editions of fairy tales, printed on coarse gray paper and illus-trated with crude colored pictures, lay about the nursery, so the children did not have to depend solely on the nurses' lore.

One especially memorable occasion was a performance of Schiller's *Robbers* which Fyodor witnessed at the age of ten. On certain holidays and regularly during Carnival Week the children made long visits to their great-uncle, who had no off-spring of his own. He and his wife lived near the Smolensky marketplace, so that from their windows they could see the No-vinsky Boulevard, a park where street fairs were held, with their bands and dancing bears, clowns and strong men, puppet shows and Indian knife-jugglers, "Russian mountains" (slides for tobogganing), and swings. It was specified in the bond that he would be allowed to take them there, although the doctor must surely have considered the entertainment vulgar.

Summer brought the young people a measure of freedom. The garden attached to the hospital was their natural playground. They were not, however, allowed to go there without a nurse or some other guardian—indeed, until Fyodor was sixteen he was not permitted to leave the house unaccompanied. The doc-tor had definite ideas about the proprieties. He would not let the children indulge in any games except "horses" and handball, the use of bats being proscribed as dangerous and unseemly. Here and there, strolling along the paths or seated on the benches,

were figures clad in loose gowns of camel-colored wool or tick-
ing, according to the weather, with white bonnets and slippers
without heels. These were the convalescent patients, and among
the many prohibitions that hedged in the children, none was
more rigid than that which forbade them to address these people. Fedya could not keep himself from violating this rule. The
seamy side of life fascinated him from the beginning.

On a fine summer evening the family would march in full force
to a neighboring park, which was known as Mary's Grove. As
they passed the gates of the Alexandrovsky Institute for Girls,
a kopeck or a groat would be tossed at the feet of the sentinel
who was standing there, gun in hand. The way led through
crazy streets and alleys, and the doctor improved the occasion
by discoursing to his sons on acute and obtuse angles, curves,
and broken lines. Even when they were beyond the city limits
the children had to walk sedately and a scamper or a romp
among the birches was out of the question.

Dostoevsky's second wife remembered his having spoken of
his "happy and placid childhood." Looking backward late in life,
he said that, in spite of "all deviations," his parents had
earnestly striven to be among the "best" people in the highest
sense of the adjective. Again, he mentioned, with a flash of
pride, his having come of "a Russian and pious family." One
fancies that the actuality was not as decorous as it appears both
from his remarks and from his brother Andrey's smug reminiscences. The fact that neither hide nor hair of the father's relatives was to be seen, and that no mention was made of them,
must have given Fyodor the feeling of living in a lopsided
family. Certainly the personality of the father was not condu-
cive to an atmosphere of serene gentility. One suspects that as
a child Fyodor looked upon things that do not belong to the
life of "a Russian and pious family."

# ( IV )

The doctor's income was small, as his salary was probably not
much more than the six hundred rubles a year that he had been
paid as an army doctor, and his private practice modest. Nevertheless, he was intent upon becoming the owner of a piece of

land in the country as behooved a *dvoryanin*. Real estate agents began to haunt the flat, and one fine summer afternoon when Fyodor was nine the doctor, having taken leave of his wife and kissed the children, seated himself in a covered *troika* and drove out of town to look over a bit of land with a view to purchase. Within an hour or two the family was dismayed to see him back again; he had forgotten his passport, without which it was not permissible to travel. He got his papers and set off again. The incident was considered an evil omen, a notion that seems justified in the light of later events. The immediate result of the journey was that, in 1831, he became the owner of Darovoye, a village in the province of Tula, a distance of a hundred miles from Moscow. The acquisition was solemnized by a mass in the Iberian Chapel.

The following year, after Easter, the mother, accompanied by the elder children, made the momentous journey to Darovoye, and took the management of the estate into her capable hands. Forthwith a fire razed the village to the ground; moreover, the new landowners found themselves involved in litigation. To safeguard their interests, they rounded out the property by acquiring a tiny neighboring hamlet, which went by the name of Cheremoshna or Chermashnya. The entire holding cost twelve thousand rubles. In the 1930s Darovoye became a collective farm named for Dostoevsky.

It must have relieved the elder Dostoevsky to think that now he could pass on to his heirs not merely his name and his noble rank, but also an estate of some thirteen hundred acres and nearly a hundred "souls," *i.e.*, male serfs. But the purchase put a great strain on the family resources. To swing it, the doctor must have spent his wife's dowry and gone heavily into debt. After the fire at Darovoye money had to be advanced to the peasants to enable them to put up new huts, and some of the loans were never repaid. The property proved a liability rather than an asset. Henceforth the doctor often found himself in dire straits. At one time, having taken five rubles in advance on his salary, he had not a kopeck to look for when they were spent— an experience with which his son Fyodor was to be painfully familiar. This was all the harder for the doctor to bear, as there was a streak of the miser in him. Like many a thwarted man, he would quibble over small expenses, so that his wife had to plead with him to buy a pencil box for Mikhail, who seems to have been reduced to begging from his schoolmates. In her

absence the doctor would write to his wife for an exact accounting of the silver left in the town apartment, and she would list
everything meticulously, from the tray, the milk pitcher, and the
slop basin, down to the broken silver tablespoon and the two
battered saltcellars in the chiffonier. He is perturbed. He can
find only five of the six spoons she mentions and the broken one
is nowhere to be discovered. Perhaps she is mistaken; he believes
he has had no more than five spoons since she left. As for the
broken spoon, she should try to remember whether she hadn't
locked it up elsewhere. For he keeps the keys by him constantly.
He also wants an inventory of everything in the storeroom, from
the bottles of brandy to his wife's dresses, blouses, and caps that
she may have left at home. One can't be too careful with thievish
servants about.

When he complained of being short, as he frequently did, his
wife replied soothingly: "Don't worry about sending me money.
As it is, I have left you with nothing. Get along as well as you
can, my dear. For the time being I am not in need, and should
I be so, I hope to have some oats left to sell." She was an
excellent manager, knew how to deal with her serfs, a rough lot
who had the reputation of horse thieves, and so meticulous in
her accountings to her husband that he described her letters as
"business records." She would report to him that God had given
them increase in the shape of a peasant lad and a girl as well,
since a son had been born to their Nikita and a daughter to their
Fedot; that the sow had presented them with five young; that
the ducklings were thriving, but that the goslings were being
depleted by the uncertain weather, and that only one hen was
setting.

From now on the summer was a season of release for the children, who spent it in the country with their mother. The doctor
came out rarely and for short periods. The summer residence was
the Darovoye "manor house," a four-room cottage made of
plaited boughs stuccoed over. The children used it chiefly as a
dormitory. The house was surrounded by venerable lime trees
under which they took tea, and beyond it was an orchard and a
thick birch wood which climbed up and down ravines. Fyodor was
so much attached to this place, with its green darkness, its steep
gullies, and its silence broken only by the rustle of leaves underfoot and the abrupt soft crash of a squirrel leaping overhead, that
they called it "Fedya's Grove." Not that Maminka liked them
to play there: she was constantly warning them about snakes and

rumored wolves. To keep the children occupied, she had a pond dug where they bathed, fished, and boated.

Each of the brothers had a *troika,* a three-horse team, of his own, consisting of peasant boys and girls. They would save up part of their dinners and, when the meal was over, take it to the stables, which were located under some bush. Imitating the horse dealers whom they watched at the fairs, they would look into the creatures' mouths, lift up their legs to examine the hoofs, and so on. Sometimes savages, armed with bows and arrows and fiercely feathered, prowled in the shadows of the lindens, and tents were pitched in the darkest part of the copse. Actually, there was only one tent, the feathers had once been worn by tame geese, and under the war paint the pale features of Fyodor and Little Tail were plainly visible. It was Mikhail who daubed the faces and even the bodies of the tribe, and it was Andrey who was destined to record its adventures in sentimental retrospect, but it was Fyodor who led them when they raided the enemy's stronghold in the birch wood, and indeed on most other occasions. When Fyodor was not chieftain, he was Crusoe, in a game of his own invention, with Little Tail for Man Friday.

There was an ancient wooden chapel near the cemetery beyond the lime copse. Entering it one day through the door which was never locked, they took the icons from the shelves and formed a procession. Carrying the images and chanting canticles and prayers, they marched along as they had seen the priests do, "blessing the fields."

Fyodor would hang about the peasants at work and would run errands for them, while they would let the little master put his hand to the plow or hold the reins. The raw clods crumbling under the harrow, the uncouth figure of a peasant merging into his field, the tangled thatch roofing a gray hut—such elements of the rural scene must have found lodgment in the boy's mind. But the impressions that remained with him for life were rather of the folk than of the landscape. He was always to remember a moment of sharp panic and the comfort he received from one of his father's plowmen. It was a clear, windy August day, and he was going to the birch grove to gather mushrooms, when the cry of "Wolf!" tore through the midsummer hush. Screaming with terror, he ran straight to a peasant who was walking behind his plow. It was their serf Marey.

"Hearing my outcry," Dostoevsky tells the story, "he stopped his mare in surprise, and when I caught, on the run, the plow with one hand and his sleeve with the other, he noticed my fright. 'A wolf!' I cried out, panting. He threw up his head and looked around. 'Where is the wolf?' 'Shouted . . . someone just shouted: "A wolf!" ' I stammered. 'What are you talking about? What wolf? You imagined it, my boy. There aren't any wolves hereabouts,' he mumbled, trying to reassure me. But, my whole body shivering, I tightened my hold of his *zipoon* [coat]. I must have been very pale. He looked at me with an alarmed smile, apparently worried about me. 'See how frightened he is—oh, oh!' he shook his head. 'Enough, sonny. A child, eh?' he stretched out his hand and suddenly stroked my cheek. 'Well, enough, sonny. Christ be with you, cross yourself.' But I did not cross myself; the corners of my lips trembled, and this seems to have struck him particularly. He gently put out his large soil-stained finger with its black nail and gently touched my quivering lips. 'A child!' he smiled at me with a long, motherly smile." The boy was at last reassured and, after Marey had made the sign of the cross over him, went away.

In a sense, Dostoevsky clung to Marey's *zipoon* all his life. *Narod*, that is, the populace, chiefly the peasantry, was to him the vessel of grace and the source of salvation. There may have been times, however, when he felt, like a leading character in *The Devils*, that he was placing laurel on lousy heads.

# 2

# SCHOOL DAYS

THE doctor believed that instruction could not begin too early, and when Fyodor was four years old, he was set to learning his letters, literally at his mother's knee. He was not as quick as Mikhail, a fact of which he was made painfully conscious by the family's mockery. His primer was a book illustrated with quaint lithographs and entitled *One Hundred and Four Histories Chosen for the Benefit of the Youth from the Old and the New Testament, by Johann Hübner, accompanied by pious reflections.* The first lesson concludes with these reflections: the power of God is immense; the wisdom of God is infinite; the loving kindness of God is ineffable.

Later on two tutors were called in. The deacon taught the older children "God's law." The card table would be opened in the living room and the four of them, together with the ecclesiastic, would sit at this worldly piece of furniture to recite their lessons from Metropolitan Filaret's *Principles*, which opened thus: "The one God worshipped in the Holy Trinity is eternal, that is, He hath neither beginning nor end to His Being, but ever was, is, and shall be." Having reviewed the assigned portion of this edifying text, the deacon would give the better part of his time to telling Bible stories. Of the flood, of Joseph and his

brethren, of the Nativity he spoke with so much gusto that even
Maminka, who sat near by, dropped her knitting to listen.

Monsieur Souchard taught the children French. This émigré,
after changing his name in an excess of patriotism to the Russian
form of Drashusov, eventually opened a small preparatory
school, which was attended by Fyodor and Mikhail. In one respect the establishment resembled Dotheboys Hall: the staff consisted of the members of the master's family. Since none of them
had any Latin, that language was not in the curriculum. Dr.
Dostoevsky took it upon himself to make up the deficiency. The
lessons, which were given in the evening, were an ordeal. The
pupils did not dare to sit down or even to lean against the table,
but stood for the whole period, as Andrey remembered, "like
little idols," spouting their declensions and conjugations. At the
slightest mistake the doctor would fly into a rage and call them
"lazybones" and "dolts." He never struck them. His worst
punishment was to stop the lesson.

The doctor liked to repeat that he was a poor man and that
after his death his boys would have to shift for themselves. He
was, however, prepared to make heavy sacrifices to provide his
sons with the education of gentlemen. At the age of thirteen
Fyodor, together with his inseparable companion, Mikhail, was
entered at Chermak's, one of the better boarding schools in
Moscow. Instruction here was offered by teachers from the university, and if the curriculum was rather stiff, the atmosphere
was homelike. The pupils took their meals with the headmaster
and his sons, and if a boy had a sore throat he was dosed and
coddled by Mme. Chermak. Fyodor made himself somewhat
conspicuous by protecting the newcomers against the tyranny of
the older boys. The presence of his brother must have contributed to his comfort. It is doubtful if he had any chums at school,
in spite of the fact that secretly his heart hungered for friendship; his touchiness and sensitiveness stood between him and
his companions. He seems to have been, in words that he used
of another boy, "doomed to solitude," a nature flung back upon
its "own resources and dreams."

Every Saturday morning the doctor's carriage, driven by one
of his serfs, came to fetch Fyodor and Mikhail home for the
weekend. The two free days were crowded. The father, a
practical-minded man, had the older boys give lessons to Andrey,
Fyodor's subjects being history and the Russian language. Then
there was church attendance. And there were always books and

magazines about that Fyodor wanted to read. Books had been his refuge from the beginning. On one occasion the boys appealed to their parents for arbitrament as to who was the greater poet, Zhukovsky or Pushkin. Family readings in the evening had long been an institution, the father and mother taking turns at the book. Mikhail, who was himself given to verse writing, cared more for poetry and Fyodor for prose, but both had an unlimited admiration for Pushkin. Fyodor had a special liking for literature that took him away from his surroundings—the novels of Walter Scott, the plays of Shakespeare, or books of travel. In his daydreams—the boy indulged his fantasy—he journeyed to Italy or the East and thought seriously of running away to Switzerland.

At home he had practically no visitors. The father, besides being a disciplinarian, was something of a snob. One of the reasons his sons lacked friends was that he rigidly censored their contacts with their contemporaries. Once or twice, it is true, the Dostoevskys gave an evening party for the young people, but this was not much of a diversion. Decidedly, the brothers lacked the social graces and they had to be all but driven to the dancing floor. Fyodor especially had a shy and reserved manner. Only when he felt completely at home would he express his uncompromising opinions. Then he would speak hotly and sharply. Often the doctor would be moved by his son's fiery outbursts to a warning which was more prophetic than either guessed: "Eh, Fedya, enough! You won't get off with a whole skin! Mark my words: you will yet wear a red cap!" He meant the cap worn by privates in the Siberian regiments, which were recruited partly from convicts who had done their term.

# ( II )

And now the two elder boys were in their middle teens, and it was high time to begin thinking about what to make of them. There was no question of consulting their inclinations. It was only natural that the army doctor should decide upon a calling having to do with the army. He resolved to place them at the military engineering school in Petersburg, an exacting and exclusive institution. When the decision to send them there was taken, their mother was far gone in consumption. The disease had developed rapidly. Toward the end she looked almost a stranger, not only because of the ravages of illness: too weak to comb her own hair and considering it indecent to let others do it, she had it cut. Mikhail and Fyodor had to part from her even earlier than they had feared. She died, at the age of thirty-seven, before they left.

Several weeks earlier, in the northern capital, another death occurred which was a fresh blow to the two brothers. On January 29, 1837, Pushkin died of a wound received in a duel. The news only reached the Dostoevsky household a month later, at the time of the mother's funeral. Fyodor kept repeating that if he had not been wearing mourning for his mother, he would have asked his father's permission to put on black for Pushkin. An elegy on the poet's death was so often on the brothers' lips that Andrey was to remember every word of it forty-five years later. Was it that Fyodor concentrated his attention on the less personal bereavement in order to take his mind off the deeper pain? The loss of his mother grieved him all the more because his relations with his father were not intimate and probably not happy. Now there was no one to stand between him and his sullen, despondent parent who loved but was apt to antagonize his children.

It was only meet that the orphaned boys should not leave home for the strange, rather terrifying, and fascinating place which the school must have meant to them without again visiting the shrines that had hallowed their childood. Escorted by their Aunt Kumanina—for who was closer to them than she?—they made a pilgrimage to Troitzkaya Lavra. There was now a sacred place for them nearer home: their mother's grave. The brothers had been allowed to select the inscription for the stone, and had chosen an epitaph from Karamzin: "Rest, dear dust, until the joyous morn."

At last came the day of departure for Petersburg. It was then May, for they had been delayed by a stubborn affection of the throat that attacked Fyodor. A solemn mass was served, and the boys occupied their places in the *kibitka* beside their father, who was going with them to the capital.

It took them nearly a week, traveling, as they had to do, by coach, to cover the four hundred miles which separate Moscow from Petersburg. On their recent trip to the monastery, the boys had relieved the more tedious stretches by reciting verses to their aunt. The widower was probably not in the mood to respond gratefully to this sort of thing, but Mikhail pleased himself and his brother on this more momentous journey by maintaining his habit of writing three poems a day, while Fyodor kept composing mentally a novel of Venetian life. The *kibitka* jolted along the dust-padded road across a bare, monotonous landscape, but he was drifting in a gondola that ruffled the colored shadow of palaces under a proud sky. En route the boys decided that on arriving in Petersburg, they would make it their business to visit the site of Pushkin's duel and also find their way to the dead poet's old quarters, to behold the room in which he had breathed his last. Dr. Dostoevsky had seen to it that his sons' heads were packed with theorems and dates as their luggage with necessaries, but there were things tucked away in Fyodor's mind of which he had little inkling. Peculiarly sensitive to all the mean and sordid aspects of his surroundings, the adolescent boy fled to an ideal world, which may have seemed nearer now that he was at the entrance to a new life, in a new city, among new people.

Before he reached his destination an ugly incident took him out of his dreams. One evening when they were waiting at an inn for their horses to be watered, fed, and rested, Fyodor, looking out of the window, saw a *troika* halt at the steps of the posting station across the street. A tall, corpulent man with a purple face, wearing the gaily-plumed tricorn of a military courier, leapt out of the vehicle and dived into the building. A moment later a fresh *troika* pulled up, and the driver, a peasant lad in a red shirt, carrying his coat on his arm, jumped onto the box. The courier came out at once and took his seat, but without giving the driver time to start, he rose and began striking him with his great fist. The lad hunched forward and lashed the middle horse with all his might. The team leapt ahead, but the courier was not satisfied. As long as Fyodor, watching greedily, could see them the courier kept on beating the coachman, who never stopped flaying the horses. The picture, which with time took on a symbolic character, remained with him.

# ( III )

Once in Petersburg the doctor placed his sons with a coach who was preparing a group of boys for entrance to the engineering school, and after six weeks of paternal supervision interlarded with sightseeing, went back the way he had come. They never saw him again.

Months of hard work were in store for the two brothers. In addition to cramming mathematics, fortification, artillery, they had to study mechanical drawing and take an intensive course in military drill, a subject of major importance at the school. It was only on Saturdays and Sundays that they could snatch time to write home. On his return from Petersburg the doctor had retired from the service, given up his practice, and settled at Darovoye, taking with him the younger children. In one letter the drudges speak wistfully of the occupations that engage their brothers and sisters in the country. They take occasion to remind Varenka of her promise to study and read Karamzin, and Fyodor hopes that his quondam pupil, Andrusha, is not as careless of his history as he used to be. In the autumn it will be his turn to enter Chermak's. "So for a long time yet you will have to look out for your children's education: you have so many of us," they tell their parent, adding with chilling reasonableness, "Judge for yourself, then, how earnestly we pray to God that He should preserve your health, which is so precious to us." Their joint letters home, apparently written by Mikhail but signed by both, indicate interest in affairs at the farm—the crops, the new wing which is at last under way—and they abound in expressions of piety and filial regard.

When September came and examinations with it, they wrote home: "Time itself can't keep pace with us. We're always poring over a book." With the Lord's help, however, they hoped to come through. They worked harder than ever, and when they visited the Kazan Cathedral, they did not neglect to say a prayer. Their industry was calculated to please their father, but he must have frowned over the news that in order to be presentable at the examinations, the boys had been compelled to buy new hats, at the shocking price of seven rubles apiece. He wrote to them not to discard any old clothing they could no longer use, but he seems to have been as generous as his limited means allowed, and for the time being the boys were in funds.

But soon real troubles commenced. Mikhail, who had always been considered the stronger of the two, was turned down by the school doctors on the grounds of poor health. His own explanation was that this was a pretext so that both brothers should not be an expense to the government. And then Fyodor, who had come through the examinations brilliantly—indeed, practically at the head of the list—was assigned twelfth place because, for one thing, some of the boys had bribed the authorities. Fyodor had nothing with which to grease their palms and would have been ashamed to buy priority in any case. He was serving his monarch, not these grafters. The injustice of it galled him. To make matters worse, he was refused the scholarship on which his father had counted. Preference had been shown to those boys whose fathers could better afford to pay tuition. "Where can we get 950 rubles? . . . What will become of us?" they wrote home, adding: "We will pray to God." Their prayers were answered. Aunt Kumanina, on hearing the news, volunteered to pay the tuition for both boys, should her brother-in-law swallow his pride and permit it, which he did.

It was not until January 16, 1838, that Fyodor found himself a member of the company of *conductors,* as the students in the lower grades were called. Among other formalities he had to take an oath of allegiance to Emperor Nicholas I, for he was now in military uniform. After some delay Mikhail entered a military school at Reval (now Tallin). And so Fyodor lost the companion from whom he had been inseparable since the beginning, just when he needed him most. In commenting on this misfortune, he wrote to his father that blind Fate played with man as with a toy, but that perhaps God ordered everything for the best. His circumstances at the time were not calculated to strengthen the latter sentiment. He was making his way alone in an unfamiliar, hostile world.

# ( IV )

There was something oppressive about the very look of the place: the Cyclopean walls, the huge portals flanked by obelisks, the vast chambers massive with bronze and marble, the chilly statues and somber historical canvases, the granite stairways leading to long drafty corridors. The school was housed in that cross between a palace and a fortress which the mad Paul had built for himself and in which he had met his violent death. It was said that one of the oval rooms had been the scene of weird rites, performed in secret by an outlawed mystic sect, which in the early part of the century was fashionable in high places. The boys doubtless pointed out to newcomers the hidden passages, the secret staircases, the chambers where the throne had once stood, where the Emperor had dined, and the one where, it was whispered, he had been strangled one night by one of his own courtiers.

A harsh spirit governed the school. The boys could expect no leniency here. In addition to the academic work, there were lessons in singing, dancing, and fencing, as well as sentry duty and the eternal drill. It was only during the summer, when the students went camping as part of the training course, that there was some relief from the routine. The boys lived in tents pitched just outside Peterhof (now Petrodvoretz), the old Imperial residence. The constant drill was hateful to Fyodor, and the out-of-door life bored him then as it always would, but at least the absence of classes allowed more leisure for reading. It was natural that there should be martinents among the instructors. When the bayonets quivered because the class faced the sun and was dazzled, one drill sergeant would shout in a rage: "Attention! Never mind the sun! There is no sun on parade!" During his first term Fyodor had to take part in five parades within three months, all of them reviewed by the Grand Duke Michael and the Czar. May was marked by the agony of the gala parade reviewed by the entire Imperial family. Since the Polish insurrection of 1830–1831, which had revealed Russia's need for fortifications, the Emperor had taken particular interest in military engineering and he had kept a fond eye upon the school, which responded to his frequent visits with every mark of fervent devotion.

The strict discipline and the strenuous work were perhaps less hard for a sensitive boy to bear than the conscienceless cruelty and the rigid conventions of his schoolfellows. In the first letter Fyodor wrote home after he entered school he said that he was beginning to get used to the routine but that he could say nothing good about his companions. A newcomer, who was contemptuously referred to as a "hazel hen," was victimized as a matter of course. He was subject to a protracted hazing process. The unfortunate would undergo severe beatings, and when he was ready to creep into his bed, might find it flooded. He would be required to lick up ink, and if he gave signs of squeamishness would be forced to repeat obscenities. A hazel hen would suffer in silence, for complaint rendered him a pariah. An immemorial feud raged between the upper and the lower classmen. On one historic occasion a member of the senior class considered himself slighted by a younger boy and there was a fight in the course of which some youths ran for their rifles. The commander of the company checked the hostilities before the guns were brought into action, and assembling the whole contingent and lining them up, commanded reconciliation by shouting the order: "Kiss to the right! Kiss to the left!" It was only in such extraordinary cases as this that the authorities intervened. During Fyodor's second year at school there occurred a mysterious scandal, so grave that five students were transferred to the army as privates and for a time all outgoing letters were censored. Apparently what happened was that one night a *conductor,* suspected of having squealed, was beaten within an inch of his life.

The hazel hen who answered to the name of Dostoevsky, a plumpish, sallow-faced, fair-haired boy, with freckles on his snub nose and an inward look in his small deep-set gray eyes, wore the military uniform of a *conductor* as though it were a misfit. And indeed, in this training school for builders of fortresses, he was a misfit. Not that the raw-skinned daydreamer was a softy. There was a strength in him that his fellows respected in spite of themselves. But he did not join in the fun, and for the most part kept his own company. He formed the habit—which was to last his lifetime—of working late into the night, long after everyone else in the house was asleep. A proctor making his rounds would notice a lonely blanketed figure hunched over a desk beside a drafty window in the light of a single tallow candle. The quiet, the half-darkness, he would explain, disposed him toward work. He impressed his schoolmates as a solitary, who never laughed and seldom spoke, who would customarily be seen carrying his equipment as though it were an ascetic's irons and striding along in his jerky fashion with a concentrated stare. They nicknamed him "Photius," after the recently deceased archimandrite who had had the reputation of saintliness in court circles, and twitted the awkward, retiring boy with being "a mystic or idealist."

He was good in all the academic subjects except mechanical drawing, of which there were four kinds, but he did not get on with his teachers as well as he might have, at least in the beginning. When the first year was over, he found that he had not been promoted, in spite of the fact that by his own account he had passed the examinations with flying colors. He blamed this misfortune on certain of his instructors who disliked him—the algebra teacher was particularly hostile, holding his rudeness against him, he wrote to his father. He took the blow so hard that he was ill in bed for several days. Another whole year to be spent in this beastly class! That he should be left behind, while, through favoritism, nonentities were advanced! O meanness of man! O harshness of Heaven! Such was the tone of his reflections on the event. "Oh God," he exclaims in the same letter, "what have I done to bring down Your wrath upon me? Why do You not send me Your grace, that I might rejoice the tenderest of parents? Oh, how many tears this has cost me!" He goes on to beg his father not to take it to heart. This by no means implies that he will be expelled. Surely he is not altogether lacking in ability! Writing to Mikhail, he confesses that in his mortification he wanted to crush the world with one blow. Never before had he known what it meant to have his *amour-propre* injured. When he said this, he was forgetting the previous occasions on which his self-esteem had been wounded. His relations with his teachers improved with time, but the taste of humiliation remained.

Mikhail, too, wrote home in an effort to comfort his father and perhaps to shield Fyodor from paternal wrath. The doctor indeed needed solace: on getting the bad news he had collapsed and only a copious bleeding had saved him, he believed, from a fatal stroke. By way of balm Mikhail offered such reflections as that "whom the Lord loveth He chasteneth," that, conversely, "all these physical joys and all this filthy happiness in which the heart and the mind lie swaddled in a pitiful stupor are merely the mockery of Fate . . . ," and that "in misfortune man becomes more man and thereby nearer to the Divine ideal." In thus exalting suffering, Mikhail sounded a note which was to become a major motif in his brother's thinking.

# 3

# A RAW YOUTH

AT school Fyodor lived in a turmoil of thought and emotion, dominated less by the adolescent's ecstasy than by the adolescent's despair. "I don't know if my sad thoughts will ever cease," he writes to his brother the first summer. "It seems to me that the world has taken on a negative meaning." The idea of suicide is not far from his mind: "To see nothing but the hard shell under which the universe languishes, to know that one explosion of the will is enough to break it and allow one to merge with eternity, to know this and yet live on like the lowest of creatures—how terrible! How faint-hearted man is! Hamlet! Hamlet! When I think of his wild, tempestuous speeches in which resounds the groaning of a numbed world, then neither sad vexation nor invective wring my heart. My soul is so oppressed by sorrow that it fears to fathom this lest it rend itself to pieces." A prostscript to the letter suggests a singular way of escaping from responsibilities and harassments: "I have a project; to go mad. Let people rage, let them doctor me, let them try to restore me to sanity."

As time goes on he does not cease to indulge in this melancholy mood. "Brother," he writes in the autumn, "it is sad to live without hope." The present depresses him, the future horrifies.

He is breathing a chill, sunless air. Often his state is that of the
Prisoner of Chillon after the death of his brothers:

> *I had no thoughts, no feeling—none—*
> *Among the stones, I stood, a stone. . . .*

It is long since he has known "an explosion of inspiration." He
is not visited any more by "poetry, the bird of paradise." His
dreams have abandoned him, and "the marvelous arabesques"
that his fancy used to trace "have shed their gilt." The thoughts
that used to kindle his soul have lost their heat.

Again, he breaks off his complaints to plunge into muddled
philosophizing. Mikhail's remark to the effect that to know more,
one must feel less, is dismissed by his brother as "delirium of the
heart." Love, the soul, Nature, God, can only be known, he
insists, through the heart, not through the intellect, which is a
"material faculty," a machine set into motion by "the spirit's
fire." Thought generates in the spirit. Thoughts are whispered to
the spirit by the heart. Philosophy is not merely an equation in
which Nature is the unknown quantity. It is poetry that appre-
hends the ultimate, which is the proper object of philosophy.
Fyodor would have his brother know that poetic and philosophic
ecstasy are the same, and philosophy is but the highest degree of
poetry. Some of these antirationalist notions, fragments of a
romantic system of ideas, will be the anchorage of his mature
thinking.

He had few companions to whom he could open his heart as
he did to Mikhail. Only three or four of his schoolmates fell
under his influence. Yet if he was backward at forming personal
relationships, he attached himself with violence to those friends
whom he made. He knew the transports of friendship as celebrated by the romantics. One object of his amical passion was a
minor official five years his senior whom he had first met at the
inn where they stopped on arriving in Petersburg. During the
weeks of tutoring, after their father had left them, this Ivan
Shidlovsky had been in the habit of visiting the brothers every
Sunday, looking after them like a fond relative, and accompanying them to church. When he was alone, Fyodor clung the more
closely to the companionable youth. Of a winter evening he would
make his way through the snowy streets to the humble lodging
of his friend and they would spend exquisitely melancholy hours
together. The spirituality of Shidlovsky, his sensuousness, his

literary talent—he wrote poems expressing the desire to leave the vale of life and settle in a cloud, to govern the universe, and gossip with God—his golden tongue, his ready tears, his easy ecstasies, his sufferings as a victim of unrequited love—everything about this tall, ascetic-looking youth enchanted the lonely boy. Here was "the proper image of a man," such as Shakespeare and Schiller had painted.

Shidlovsky was also friendly toward Mikhail, with whom he exchanged fervent letters. In one of them he explained that he loved his correspondent, firstly, as a confidant, and secondly, as a poet with a serene view of the world. His own view, at least at the moment of writing, was that "God is good, or He would not be God, that the universe is the visible, palpable beauty of this goodness, and that their essential identity is truth." On another occasion he told Mikhail that he envisioned the laurels awaiting him, in the same breath invoking Werther and Chatterton, and declaring that the bottom of the Fontanka Canal beckoned to him as the nuptial bed beckons the bridegroom. "*Ach,* why weren't you with us?" Fyodor wrote to his brother on New Year's Day, 1840, as he counted over the precious memories of the past year in which Shidlovsky loomed so large. "I remember how tears flowed from his eyes as he read your poems. He knows them by heart." During the summer Fyodor saw little of this comrade, who was making ready to leave the capital. They spent their last evening together walking the streets of a Petersburg suburb, recalling the past winter, which had been peopled by the shades of Homer and Schiller, and discoursing of Mikhail, of themselves, of the future.

Then Shidlovsky stepped out of Dostoevsky's life, but not out of his memory. He had strengthened his young friend's notion that writing was the only worthy occupation, since it furnished an avenue of escape from sordid reality. Years later this odd fellow entered a monastery, but soon retired to his estate without taking off his cassock, and divided his time between drunken orgies and fits of piety. He would be seen preaching the Gospel to a crowd of awestruck peasants near a tavern, and he made pilgrimages to various shrines, but in the end the bishop forbade him entrance to the monasteries on the ground that he corrupted the monks.

Shortly after he became intimate with Shidlovsky, Fyodor found himself involved in another violent friendship, which he surrounded with mystery, perhaps because he considered it too precious to expose to vulgar comment. It seems to have consumed itself briefly and intensely upon a plane where life merged into literature. In his New Year's Day letter he was telling Mikhail: "I had a comrade with me, a creature whom I loved so much! You wrote me, brother, that I hadn't read Schiller. You are mistaken! I learned Schiller by heart, I talked him, I dreamed him, and I think that Fate has done nothing more fitting for me than to let me know the great poet at just this period of my life: at no other time could I have responded to him so fully. Reading Schiller with my friend, I verified by him the noble, ardent Don Carlos, the Marquis Posa, and Mortimer. This friendship brought me so much sorrow and joy! Now I shall be silent about it eternally. But Schiller's name became for me a cherished, magic sound, calling up many reveries; they are bitter, brother; that is why I said nothing to you about Schiller! . . . I am pained when I hear his name."

This friend, he confessed, had been closer to him than Mikhail, for whom, he went on, he had never had any real brotherly feeling, although he loved him for his verse, the poetry of his life, and his misfortunes. But in the same breath he laid balm to Mikhail's soul by enlarging on the joy that a letter from him brought with it. When one arrived, he looked at it, turned it over in his hand for a minute or two, fingered it to find out how ample it was, and then, having thoroughly examined the envelope, he put it in his pocket unopened, and spent a "voluptuous" quarter of an hour before he eagerly picked the treasure's lock, a way he was to have with precious letters.

The mysterious friend vanished, to be heard of no more. Mikhail remained. Whatever he may have felt about Fyodor's temporary disaffection, he must have warmed to the praise of Schiller. He had himself once written to their father: "Let them take everything from me, leave me naked, but give me Schiller, and I shall forget the whole world." Dostoevsky was ultimately to revolt against Schilleresque idealism, and yet something of it always remained with him.

There were other authors whom he was reading avidly, and both brothers took their literary opinions sufficiently to heart to quarrel over them seriously. The first season at camp Fyodor read prodigiously. He devoured, among other things, the whole of that weird fantast Amadeus Hoffmann, almost all of Balzac, Goethe's *Faust,* as well as his lyrical poems, and a great deal of Victor Hugo. He dipped with equal relish into the older writers and into current books, nor did he neglect native authors. His enthusiasm is as violent as his taste is eclectic. He prizes highly *The Confessions of an English Opium-Eater*. Of Balzac he exclaims: "His characters were created by the intelligence of the universe. Not the spirit of an age, but the struggle of millenniums has prepared for such a dénouement in the soul of man." Racine commands his admiration. *Phèdre* is the quintessence of truth and poetry: it matters little that this Shakespearean theme is executed "in plaster of Paris rather than in marble." As for Corneille, he is "almost a Shakespeare." Only offended angels speak as Auguste does in *Cinna*. "Have you read *Le Cid*?" he asks his brother, who had dared to disparage the French classics. "Read him, you wretch, and lie in the dust before Corneille." He has the highest praise for both Homer and Hugo.

Already it was clear to him that his true pursuit was not the building of fortresses, but "the meaning of man and of life." He was, he wrote Mikhail on August 16, 1839, making sufficient headway with this study, since he was spending his best hours with great writers "freely and happily." For all his moodiness he had moments of serenity and self-confidence. Thus, in the same letter he wrote: "Man is a mystery. It must be unriddled, and if you spend your whole life unriddling the mystery, do not say that it was wasted time; I devote myself to this mystery because I wish to be a man."

# ( II )

In addition to his metaphysical ache and the difficulty of adjustment to the uncongenial environment, there was another hardship that beset the raw youth. From the beginning of his stay at school he felt the pinch of penury, which was to fret him practically to the end of his days. At home he had done without pocket money because, in his father's opinion, a gentleman's son required none. Living as he now did in a boarding school, his needs were nominally provided for. Yet there were all kinds of demands on his purse. When a review was in prospect, the boys, most of whom came from well-to-do families, bought new apparel, and he had to do likewise or risk being remarked by the Emperor. And then there were paints and brushes to be got, and the French circulating library—he simply must join it. On October 30, 1838, he was writing home: "Send me something without delay. You will pull me out of hell. Oh, how terrible it is to be in this extremity!" Such modest sums as he received he found hard to keep. Money burnt a hole in his pocket, and being frequently without a groat, he fell into the habit of borrowing. The unseemly situation was calculated to wound his pride deeply. He borrowed to pay the priest's fee when he took communion. He borrowed the price of a stamp to send a letter to his father, and sometimes he had to enclose a missive to Mikhail with that of a friend. Soon he was in debt to the tune of fifty rubles. "Save me," he wrote to his father. "Send me sixty rubles. . . . My God, I know that we are poor. But Heaven is my witness, I do not demand anything excessive."

Six months later he repeated the same cry, which was to sound in his letters to relatives and friends so often throughout the years to come. "I have a head, I have hands," he tells his father. "If I were free and thrown upon my own resources, I would not ask a kopeck from you. I would put up with iron poverty." He recognizes that the parents' want "must be fully shared by their children." But he is in the service, and, as he says plainly, must either conform to the standards of his fellows or be outlawed. Camp opens early in June, and that means extraordinary expenses. He is willing to forego tea and sugar, although if one has to spend hours in a canvas tent in the rain or when one comes in from practice tired and cold, these are no luxuries. Indeed, the previous year at camp he had been taken ill for lack of them. But what he must have is two pairs of plain boots, since the government does not supply enough, and a chest in which to keep his belongings, particularly books. "For how," he adds, "how can I pass the time without books?" Moreover, the tent holds only cots—bundles of straw, covered with sheeting—and so the orderly must be paid to find a place for the chest. Nor can he be expected to do without bootblacking and such things as writing paper and stamps, and all that costs something. He requires at least twenty-five rubles besides the fifteen he has on hand. "And so send me this sum by the first of June," he writes, "if you wish to help your son in his terrible need. I dare not demand; I am not asking too much, but my gratitude will be boundless." Fyodor was perhaps moved less by actual need than by a fear of being looked down upon by his more prosperous companions. At least one of his schoolmates managed without any tea of his own (the school provided tea morning and evening), without extra boots, being content with what the government supplied, and without a chest, although he claimed to be as great a reader as Dostoevsky.

The doctor, who had no way of checking his son's statements, in reply to his pitiful plea pointed out that he had had a succession of ruinous seasons on the farm: after a long and bitter winter, during which they had had to sacrifice the very thatch of the roofs to keep the cattle from starving, there had been a spring drought which spelled famine; further, he hadn't ordered a new suit of clothes in four years, and was without a groat. Nevertheless, he enclosed a remittance for ten rubles more than his son had requested.

This was the last letter that Fyodor received from his father. Wrapped up in his own troubles, he probably knew little of what was going on at home or of how wretched an existence the widower had been leading since his retirement. Living alone on the farm, without his customary occupations and contacts, he rapidly went to pieces. Like thousands of isolated provincial gentlefolk, he tried to drown his loneliness in his cups, and for want of better company took a sixteen-year-old housemaid for his mistress. His old fits of rage came upon him more frequently and with greater violence. It is vaguely reported that he suffered from peculiar seizures. He would be heard talking aloud to his dead wife. As time went on he was practically never sober, and behaved like one half mad.

One June day in 1839, a fortnight after having written to Fyodor, he was killed by his Chermashnya serfs. The identity of the murderers was known to the local peasantry and even to the priest. Nevertheless, there was no trial. It is said that the Moscow relatives, arriving on the scene, easily learned the true story, but succeeded in persuading the police to see the death as the result of apoplexy. Since a number of men were involved—was Marey among them?—bringing the culprits to justice would have meant sending them all to Siberia. The family argued that this would only result, on the one hand, in the loss of so many workers to the heirs, and on the other, in a blot on the family 'scutcheon. In any event, the scandal was hushed up so carefully that no breath of it reached the general ear until over eighty years after the tragedy.

Under these circumstances gossip, embroidering upon rumor, gave rise to several versions of the way in which the doctor had met his death. According to one, his anger had been roused as he was inspecting the work that some of his Chermashnya serfs were doing in an outlying field, and he let loose on them. One of the peasants answered him impudently and then, in fear of a flogging, rushed upon the master and with the help of his fellows did him in. It was said that for two days the body lay at the mercy of the weather and the crows. Another version has it that the murder was a premeditated one in which over a dozen men, practically the entire male population of Chermashnya, took part. Dostoevsky's daughter reported that her grandfather had been suffocated by his coachman with his own carriage cushions. But though the tale varies there is no doubt that it was one of those acts of vengeance against a brutal master which were ominously on the increase at the time. Long years afterward his ugly disposition was still remembered by the old inhabitants and contrasted with his wife's kindness. One aged peasant, upon being told that Fyodor Dostoevsky had become famous, observed that it could not be true that he was a great man: from such a one as his father nothing good could come.

Fyodor seems to have been the first to learn the dreadful news. He passed it on to Mikhail. Later Mikhail recalled that on the night of June 8, apparently the fatal date, he had seen his father in a dream sitting at his desk, his hair all white, and that looking at him thus, he became so sad that he began to cry, and then went over and kissed his father without being noticed. He had waked with fear in his heart. In his letter to Mikhail of August 16, 1839, which has already been mentioned, Fyodor wrote: "I have shed many tears over our father's death." Oddly enough he goes on to say that he has faith in himself and in his future, and a growing sense of being at peace with the world, that he is free from the turbulence which had agitated his soul, that "now there is calm in it, as in the heart of a man who hides a deep secret." One gets the impression that the disaster was in the nature of a release for the boy.

One can only speculate about his feeling for his father. Is it here that one must look for the matrix of that emotional ambivalence, the love-hate motif, which he will eventually erect into a law of the heart? His letters home abound in emphatic expressions of filial devotion, but sometimes the emphasis rings false: "My God, how long it is since I last wrote you, how long it is since I tasted those moments of true, cordial bliss, true, pure, exalted . . . bliss which is experienced only by those who have someone with whom to share the hours of rapture and sorrow, who have someone in whom to confide all that goes on in their hearts! Oh, how greedily I now drink in this bliss!" There is no doubt, however, that occasionally Fyodor felt a pitying tenderness for the unhappy, hysterical, narrow-minded, spasmodically generous man who was his father. "I am sorry for our poor father!" he had once written to Mikhail. "A strange character! How many misfortunes he has sustained! It is bitter, even to tears, that there is nothing to console him with. And do you know, Papasha completely lacks knowledge of the world. . . . But he is deeply disappointed in it—this seems to be our common lot." In any event, the eighteen-year-old Hamlet must have brooded long over the murder, a murder hedged about with secrecy and unavenged. One suspects that he carried the scar of the crime to the end of his days.

And now what was to become of the family? Of the seven children, at least five still needed parental care. Mikhail conceived the idea of settling in the country and bringing up his brothers and sisters, and Fyodor applauded this generous impulse. It remained, however, a pious wish. Mikhail stayed on at Reval, where, as he had written his brother, he was "plucking the flowers of love," the reference being doubtless to his infatuation with Emilia Ditmar, who was before long to become his wife. Meanwhile there was the matter of guardianship to be decided immediately. Mikhail begged the Kumanins to undertake this responsibility, but although they were ready to do a good deal for the children, particularly the younger ones, they declined, and eventually the office was entrusted to Varvara's newly acquired husband. This Piotr Karepin, to whom the Kumanins had been at pains to marry off the eldest of the Dostoevsky girls, was a substantial citizen in the government service in Moscow. He was a widower, already past forty, while his bride was a girl of seventeen. Although Fyodor, being away at school, was not present at the wedding, the marriage, with the grave discrepancy in the ages of the couple, seems to have made a shocking impression upon him.

# ( III )

Fyodor spent, or as he would have said wasted, more than five years at the engineering school. He never really managed to make an adjustment, and at the end of his stay there he was much the same retiring, self-absorbed daydreamer that he had been at the beginning. His mind was of the sort that could draw but small sustenance from the scientific subjects which prevailed in the curriculum. Mathematics—analytical geometry and calculus were included—he could not bear. It was a subject so useless, he had once written to his father, that it was positively foolish to study it. When not put to practical use, it was a mere zero, a soap bubble. His school record was good. He cursed and crammed—and passed. But in the end all this laboriously acquired information dropped away from him as water rolls off a duck's back. The chief effect of his training seems to have been to cultivate in him a distaste for the sciences. His abilities as a military engineer may be gauged by the fact that at the final examination he is said to have submitted a plan for a fortress without providing for gates. The friend who tells the story says that the Emperor's scrawled comment: "What fool did this?" so rankled in Dostoevsky that he finally decided to leave the service.

As time went on he chafed more and more under the yoke of his uncongenial duties. He had been at school less than two years when he wrote to Mikhail that his sole aim was to be free. He was depressed by the thought that he was engaged in work unworthy of him. "How sad life is, and how burdensome its moments," he reflected, "when . . . you feel that the soul's flame is being beaten down and extinguished by God knows what; when the heart is being torn to shreds—and why? Because of a life worthy of a pygmy rather than of a giant, of a child, not of a man." In his isolation, he told his brother, he had grown brutish. Left alone after a brief visit from Mikhail (he came in January, 1841, to take examinations for promotion to officer's rank), Fyodor was plunged into deeper despondency. He had nothing to hope for except that he might win a million rubles. The gambler's demon was already at his elbow.

Now and then, however, he was filled with the prescience of limitless power. The future was his. There was a kind of fire in his soul, in which he firmly believed. Freedom—that was the thing!—freedom and one's calling! The mere thought of such happiness made his soul expand, allowing it to grasp the greatness of life. He approached this longed-for freedom when, in August, 1841, he received the rank of ensign.

As a commissioned officer he could have his lodgings outside the school and taste something of independence. There were now many afternoon hours to devote to reading and—what was perhaps more necessary to him—writing. It is certain that he had obeyed the literary impulse even while he was still an inmate of the school. At least some of those nocturnal hours that he spent wrapped up in his blanket beside his candle must have been given to setting his fancies down on paper. Although he shared Mikhail's passion for poetry, he did not try his hand at verse, lacking, according to one friend, the requisite patience. When Mikhail, having taken his examinations, was leaving Petersburg, Fyodor gave a farewell party at which he read passages from his plays: *Maria Stuart* and *Boris Godunov*. He was still at work on the first-named play in 1842, attracted to the subject both by his passion for Schiller and because he had seen Lily Loewe in the title-role of the German drama. Nothing of these early efforts, including the piece *Jacob the Jew,* has been preserved.

In the autumn of the first year that Fyodor was living in his own quarters, Andrey came from Moscow to stay with him and be tutored by him for entrance examinations to the school. He found Fyodor sharing a gloomy apartment of two rooms with a schoolmate, Adolf Todtleben. Eventually the two brothers set up housekeeping together in a roomier flat. Here some of Fyodor's friends would drop in after dinner, and the evening would often end with a card game, played for such stakes as they could afford, and much relished by Fyodor. There were other amusements, too, in the form of the theater, the ballet, and concerts by such artists as Liszt and Rubini. The small allowance he received from the family guardian was of course inadequate, and as usual he was frequently reduced to borrowing. His creditors included Andrey, who was getting an occasional remittance from the Kumanins. Nevertheless, he managed to send a respectable sum to Mikhail when, early in 1842, at the age of twenty-one, the impecunious if enterprising young man married his Emilia. That year Fyodor passed his examinations successfully, and was promoted to the upper section of the school, known as the engineering academy, and was given the rank of sub-lieutenant, next above that of ensign. The school rated him as very zealous in the service, good as regards his mental capacities, his morals, and the care of his equipment, and proficient in "God's law" and the art of laying mines, among a score of other subjects.

Now there was only one more year of this drudgery. There was little but the hope of speedy release to distinguish it from the preceding years. One change was the absence of Andrey, who, having been admitted to the School of Architecture, was living in a dormitory. The petty, matter-of-fact person that his younger brother had turned out to be was no companion for Fyodor, and he was rather relieved to be free of him. As for the rest, there were the same dull classes, the same worries over making ends meet. He had a remarkable faculty for getting rid of money. It almost seemed as though he were striving for the penury that he found so distressing. His health was rather poor and, whether out of carelessness or despondency, he refused to take care of it. Books were as ever his meat and drink. The year brought him at least one new book that was to prove a source of endless interest and delight. It was Gogol's *Dead Souls*. Here was the Human Comedy in Russian terms and, moreover, a work that the ambitious author planned as the first part of a Divine Comedy.

Dostoevsky marked the great occasion of the passing of his finals in June with a dinner in the private room of a fashionable restaurant. In spite of the wine and a piano, the night was probably less festive than he could have wished, for he had dragged the friend who was his sole guest out of a sickbed to help him celebrate the end of his servitude. The following day he set off for Reval to visit Mikhail. His month's leave over, he returned to Petersburg, carrying with him a complete wardrobe, including linen, such things being cheap in the prosperous Baltic city. He may also have taken back with him the distaste for everything German which was one of his many pet prejudices. He was within two months of his twenty-second birthday when, in August, 1843, he was graduated and forthwith entered the government service as a draftsman in the Petersburg Engineering Corps.

# 4

# THIS IS FAME!

HE did not intend to follow the profession for which he was trained. Literature, not military engineering, was to be his life work. And yet there he was, stuck in the service. His circumstances were as uncertain as ever, in spite of the fact that now, being a draftsman in government employ, he had a small salary in addition to the income from the estate. During the winter he shared living quarters with a friend, a physician by the name of Alexander Riesenkampf. Mikhail had made the arrangement in the hope that the orderly German would have a steadying influence on his brother. The association did not last and failed of the desired effect.

As before, Dostoevsky lived from hand to mouth. The arrival of money from home—Moscow was still that to him in a vague way—was a great event. His voice gained assurance, his step became jaunty. He paid his creditors, he feasted, he tried his luck at billiards and cards. But a brief day or two of riotous living saw him back again on a diet of bread and milk got on credit or paid for with money borrowed from friends and usurers. He was plagued not so much by lack of money as by the inability to spend it sensibly.

It may have been at this time that he became so intimately

acquainted with the shabby taverns of the city and noted, as he never noted the details of the natural scene, such smells and sounds as the reek of burnt fat and greasy napkins, the stuttering air from *Lucia,* the shouts for the waiters, the clicking of billiard balls, the songless nightingale pecking at the bottom of its cage.

He had long ago conceived the notion of giving up his share of the inheritance in exchange for a lump sum, but the guardian would not hear of it. Sometimes a few of his rubles found their way into the pockets of Dr. Riesenkampf's patients, who were mostly poor folk. Dostoevsky was attracted to them much as he had been to the inmates of the charity hospital where he had lived as a child. He hung around the waiting room. He drew them out over a glass of tea. He studied them. He sank himself in the pinched, warped lives of the penniless and ailing. Here was the stuff for his pen.

For himself, he was not content to remain poor. He was full of grand moneymaking schemes, half commercial, half literary. In collaboration with Mikhail and a friend he would translate a thriller by Eugène Sue, they would publish it themselves, and reap a profit of four thousand rubles. Or they would get rich by issuing a complete Russian Schiller. There must be a public for these sublime writings! Then there were George Sand and Balzac to translate. He hoped to get at least a hundred rubles for his version of *Eugénie Grandet,* but he had no cash with which to pay for the copying of the manuscript. If only Mikhail would lend him ten rubles for the purpose: he swore by Olympus, by his just finished play, by his future mustache, that his brother would get half of the proceeds. One could so easily fail to hook a fortune for want of a few rubles' bait. In the summer of 1844 this translation found a place in a magazine, the others all coming to nothing. Still, translation seemed a road to ease. Mikhail must go on with Schiller. *Don Carlos,* issued on their own with an introduction by him and a paean in verse to the dramatist by Mikhail, was bound to be a hit. And then there was money in writing plays. Why not toss off a popular melodrama? But no, potboilers be damned! He would write only what was worth writing, and that as well as he could.

The service was as distasteful to him as school had been. It was, indeed, intolerable. He compared it to a diet of potatoes. He had endured only eight months of it when he spoke of retirement as a foregone conclusion, and indeed in August, 1844, he tendered his resignation. Why, he argued, waste one's best years? Besides, he wrote to Mikhail, they wanted to assign him to a post in the provinces. And what on earth would he do without Petersburg? How he was to make a living did not worry him. He would find a crust of bread somehow.

The step he had taken deprived him at once of a dignified position with a chance of advancement, and of a salary which, though small, was steady. He knew that he would have to justify himself in the eyes of the Moscow relatives, particularly his brother-in-law, who as guardian held the pursestrings. In the letter that he addressed to Karepin shortly after he had sent in his resignation, he said that he had been forced to resign because of his debts. He had been assigned to a distant post and, to save his honor as an officer, would have had to settle with his creditors before leaving the capital. He named twelve hundred paper rubles as the amount of his indebtedness, although he later confided to Mikhail that it was no more than eight hundred, a large part of which he owed to his landlord: he had rented a rather expensive four-room flat because he liked the looks of the owner, and to save firewood was occupying only one room. Furthermore, he told Karepin, he had no clothes, no food, and would soon have to vacate his unpaid-for rooms and be reduced to living on the street or sleeping under the colonnades of the Kazan Cathedral. "For three years," he wrote, "I demanded, begged, implored to be given a lump sum in lieu of my share of the inheritance. Nothing availed, I was tormented, humiliated, mocked. I bore everything patiently, incurred debts, endured shame and sorrow, illness, hunger, and cold." Now his patience was at an end. His demand must finally be granted. He would be content with a payment of five hundred silver rubles down and another five hundred in small monthly installments.* Then he would clear off his debts and start life anew. He wound up with the threat that if his plea remained unanswered, he would sell his share in the estate to a stranger.

Not hearing from the guardian, Fyodor wrote to him again, reiterating the plea he had made in the previous letter. He admitted that he might have acted rashly in resigning, but declared that he would rather rot in debtors' prison—he would have to go there without trousers, he told Mikhail—than re-enter the

---

* Both paper and metal currency were in use. Sometimes a sum is named without indication which currency is meant. In 1843 the government fixed the value of a silver ruble at three and a half paper rubles.

service before his affairs were in order. As to giving up his share of the inheritance for a lump sum, that was positively his duty now, in order to reassure the family that, being unemployed, he would not become a charge on it. At any rate, he was writing for the last time.

Two days before this message was dispatched Karepin had sent Fyodor fifty silver rubles and a long missive. Therein he had some hard words to say about his ward's arrogance, selfishness, greed, and irreverence toward the memory of his parents. The estate, he wrote, provided an annual income of no more than seven to eight hundred paper rubles for each of the four brothers, but during the last three years he, Fyodor, had received much more money than his co-heirs. As for exchanging his share of the inheritance for a lump sum, partly paid down, or selling his claim to a stranger, Karepin continued, either transaction was out of the question for legal reasons. Followed a homily on the rewards of diligence in performing useful and respected labor, on the advantages a young man might gain by heeding the opinions of his elders, the pleasure of discharging one's duty successfully, the joy of being approved by one's superiors. Apparently bearing in mind his brother-in-law's literary ambitions, Karepin indulged in a muddled tirade to the effect that "Shakespearean reveries," sophistical and voluptuous, were but an insubstantial "bubblelike image." He ended by urging Fyodor to withdraw his resignation and, indeed, ask for an assignment to a post as remote as possible, for an officer in military uniform must not think about "soft featherbeds and a Lucullan kitchen."

Dostoevsky replied with a communication that he described to Mikhail as "a model of polemics" and, like his other letters, "an epistolary masterpiece." He did not mince words. He accused the guardian of having invented the legal obstacles to the arrangement that he had pleaded for. "What has Shakespeare done to you that you cry him down so?" he asked. "Poor Shakespeare!" He told Karepin to spare himself the trouble of offering him unsolicited advice and admonition. His debts he blamed on the loansharks with whom Petersburg was overrun— no other city, he wrote, had so much business favored by Bentham, the allusion being to Jeremy Bentham's *Defense of Usury*. Toward the end of his missive he opened his heart to this man, of whom he had an unprintable opinion, by announcing that the study of people's lives was both his prime purpose and diversion.

In conclusion he indicated that his resignation would be accepted by October 1 and that he was down to his last groat.

Apparently galled by this letter, Karepin left it unanswered. On October 19 the resignation was accepted, and Dostoevsky informed the guardian of it without delay. This time he refrained from rudeness; indeed, he ate humble pie. "I am left alone," he wrote, "without hope, without help, exposed to all the calamities, the sorrows of my terrible situation: destitution, nakedness, disgrace, shame. . . ." In addition to everything else, he was ill. If the arrangement that he had suggested in previous letters was impossible, he would sign an IOU to the family for the sum he would receive. Wouldn't that be satisfactory? It would be his salvation, would even enable him to re-enter the service. If there was no ready cash, why not borrow? And couldn't he at least, for heaven's sake, get a statement about his financial expectations that he could show his creditors? If he didn't get the five hundred rubles, he would be forced to turn over his share of the estate to the sharks to whom he was in debt.

These dealings with his brother-in-law strengthened any unflattering impression of him that Dostoevsky may have had. "Karepin drinks, f . . . s, shits, swills vodka, has a rank in the service, and believes in God. Has accomplished all this on his own." Such is the thumbnail sketch of the man that he draws for Mikhail. "Clearly," he wrote to his brother on a later occasion, "Karepin is a son of a bitch and a scoundrel of the first degree." According to Andrey, Karepin was "the kindest of men, not simply kind, but angelically kind."

Although it was months before Dostoevsky finally pocketed the five hundred silver rubles, he had not had to go to prison. Given to exaggeration, he was as readily depressed about the sad state of his purse as about that of his body. Nevertheless, it is certain that when his resignation made him, at the age of twenty-three, a free man, his circumstances were dismal. He was making his start in life under the most inauspicious auguries.

# ( II )

What kept up his courage through all his troubles was one great hope. While he was parading his misery before Karepin, he was writing to Mikhail that he was finishing a novel. Here was something definite to build on. He would sell it to a magazine or, better yet, he would publish it himself with part of the money that he expected from the guardian. But when at long last he did get the coveted five hundred, they were not enough to pay his debts, so that publishing his book was out of the question. Besides, much as it had pleased him while he was working on it, he had no sooner finished it than he decided to rewrite it completely. He cut, he added, he polished. It was only in March of 1845 that he considered the job done. By then it was too late in the season to issue the novel in book form. Should he hand it over to a magazine for a song? No. He was writing, as he told Mikhail, not for glory, but for bread. Not that he would, for the sake of the money, do less than his best. He would follow in the footsteps of Pushkin, of Gogol. Those supreme craftsmen were sure of their monuments, and of their money, too. No, he would tighten his belt, arm himself with patience, lay aside three hundred rubles, even if he would have to go into debt again, and in the early autumn when people returned to town hungry for something new, he would stake his last chance on publishing the thing himself, and either be ruined or make a pile of money. Should the novel fail, he would probably hang himself. He concludes the letter by telling his brother of an article he had been reading about German artists who had died in penury, committed suicide, or gone mad: "I am still terrified. One must be a charlatan."

Five weeks of tormenting worry go by, and he is forced to a fresh decision. He is now apparently sharing two rooms and a kitchen with his old schoolmate, Grigorovich. They stoke their samovar and get their meals themselves. These are often extremely frugal, sometimes consisting of rolls and barley coffee. At least he has clothes enough to last him for two years. The money that was to have been saved up for the publication of the book has vanished. Besides, well-informed people have assured him that it would be bad business for him to issue the novel on his own. And so he will submit it to *Otechestvennye zapiski* (*Fatherland Notes*), a monthly which has the enormous circulation of twenty-five hundred copies. If the thing is accepted, his future is assured. He has new ideas that before long will increase his fame threefold. He has put away childish things. When he does not write, he reads. He can fairly feel his mind expanding, his powers growing. He has revised his novel again, greatly to its advantage. This, he assures Mikhail, is absolutely the final revision. He won't touch it again. If the book is accepted, he will have the heart and the time to undertake the translations of Sue and Schiller. If it is rejected, he will probably throw himself into the Neva.

Dostoevsky's entrance upon the literary stage was a piece of crude melodrama, of the sort in which both his art and his life abound. The manuscript of *Poor Folk* did not, after all, land upon the desk of the editor of *Fatherland Notes*. Instead, it found its way, through Grigorovich, to whom the author had read it, into the hands of a pushing, prodigiously active young man who was then little more than a hack, but with a sound business head on his shoulders: Alexey Nekrasov. Dostoevsky had read his first collection of verse, a thin little book in pink covers, while still at school. The man was now a publisher in a small way, and was on the lookout for manuscripts for a miscellany that he was planning to issue. In this enterprise he was to have the help of Belinsky, the arbiter of the intellectuals of the period. This critic had gathered about him a group of young men who formed the nucleus of the left wing of the so-called Westernists. For the most part sons of the gentry, they were liberals in an age of reaction, chafing against the autocratic regime of Nicholas I and dreaming of a Russia rebuilt on the European model.

Was there anything in *Poor Folk,* after all, to recommend it to a critic of Belinsky's caliber? So much depended on the fate of this story! All Dostoevsky's faith in his performance could not quiet his fears as to what was to become of it and him. The late spring was ushering in the short, luminous "white nights" of the North. Restless with the knowledge that Nekrasov had his tale, Dostoevsky left his rooms to spend an evening with a former schoolmate. They passed the time together re-reading Gogol's *Dead Souls*. Dostoevsky returned home in the small hours.

The night was too rare for sleep. He opened the window and sat beside it, breathing the mild, disturbing air. Suddenly the bell rang. It was just four o'clock. The door opened and in burst Nekrasov arm in arm with Grigorovich. They rushed up to the dumbfounded watcher of the dawn and put their arms about him. From their incoherent words Dostoevsky made out that Grigorovich had started to read *Poor Folk* to Nekrasov in the evening, that when, late at night, he had reached the finale, both of them were reduced to tears, and that the novel had stirred them so deeply that they had to come to the author at once. Suppose they found him asleep—they would wake him up. They had to tell him.

Here was an hour to savor and remember. They talked not only of his story, but of truth and poetry; they quoted Gogol, and every second word was Belinsky. Vissarion Belinsky, he would see the manuscript that very day, Nekrasov promised the young author, shaking him by the shoulders. And then they left him, with the absurd injunction to sleep. For a long time Grigorovich, lying on the divan in the adjacent room, heard him pacing back and forth.

At first Belinsky proved skeptical about "the new Gogol" that his fellow editor was pressing upon his attention, and two or three days passed before he touched the manuscript. But he too stayed up all night to finish it. In the morning he clamored for the author. And so Dostoevsky was brought before the great critic. There was something solemn about the tone and bearing of the slight, frail man. Dostoevsky, awed as he was, could yet discern the nature of this solemnity. It was not that of a pompous, self-important person, but that adopted by a man of stern integrity about to say grave and weighty words. What Dostoevsky heard, in substance, was that he had written a great book, a book that reached depths beyond the grasp of the author himself. As Belinsky proceeded, his excitement mounted, and as usual on such occasions, his voice grew shrill, while his assumed dignity melted into enthusiasm.

Dostoevsky came away from the interview intoxicated. He stood still on the street corner overlooking Anichkov Bridge, near which Belinsky lived, and stared at the bright day, at the sky, at the unaware pedestrians. In all his dreaming he had never figured to himself anything like this. He was on the threshold of a new world. His whole being was buoyed up by "timid elation." He was not worthy of this glory. Well, then, he would make himself worthy. He too would become part of the circle of which Belinsky was the master. He would be faithful. This was the greatest moment that he had known or, indeed, was ever to know.

# ( III )

The exaltation could not last. A man of his unstable temper was bound to suffer more than most from the dejection that follows intense excitement. Besides, there were enough worries to cancel those high moments. The summer brought a breathing spell in the form of a trip to Reval to visit Mikhail whom he had not seen for two years. He returned to Petersburg by sea, and as the boat was crossing the stretch of water between Kronstadt and the capital, he was assailed by a weariness of the spirit not a little complicated by a weakness of the flesh. He was seasick. He was thinking miserably of having left behind him, for an indefinite period, his brother and his new sister-in-law who, however badly situated, had each other to comfort them. The flat, lifeless landscape, as the dirty little steamer churned up the Neva, depressed him hideously. He was overwhelmed by a sudden dread of the future and a reluctance to go on living.

He came back to his empty, expensive, unpaid-for flat, had a brief interview with his creditors, bought paper and pens, and was in such bad humor that he could not make up his mind either to sit down at his desk or to visit the one friend who was in town. He would have been undone by melancholia if he had not been distracted by money troubles. And yet these very difficulties interfered with his work, which was of the sort that must mature slowly. "What a pity," he wrote, "that one must work to live!" Still, there was something to be said even for his spleen: it had given him two new ideas and a fresh situation for the new story, or, rather, novelette, *The Double,* with which he was busy. The spleen persisted. It was not merely that he was penniless and had to live on credit. He was, as was frequent with him, a victim of the mood that begins with depression, passes into apathy and self-neglect, and goes on to a self-contempt that is an equal mixture of fury and despair.

Early in October money matters took on a fairer complexion.

Nekrasov paid down part of the sum agreed on and promised to settle the account shortly. He had bought the novel for a hundred and fifty rubles, but now in a fit of compunction, he voluntarily added another hundred. Here, in advance of publication, before it had even come back from the censor, half the town was talking about *Poor Folk*. Grigorovich was his self-appointed *claqueur*. It was also a matter of general knowledge and satisfaction that he had begun work upon another piece. He had become the darling of the Belinsky circle. In his paternal tenderness the little man, forgetting that he was shorter than Dostoevsky, would tell everyone: "He's a little bird," adding as he held out his hand three feet from the floor, "but he has sharp claws." Belinsky's affection for him, as Dostoevsky told his brother, was due to the fact that the critic saw in his writings the justification of his own views. But Dostoevsky's understanding of the matter could scarcely lessen his pleasure. And there was something else in the offing. He was to be one of the editors of a satirical paper, to be called *The Wag*, which would poke good-natured fun at everything offensive to the group. Dostoevsky projected for the paper a serial to be called *A Valet's Memoirs of His Master*. It was a good scheme and would mean a fair monthly income.

As the season progresses he is lifted to the pinnacle of glory. He is an habitué of the favorite haunt of the Belinsky coterie: the drawing room of Nekrasov's young mistress, Mme. Panayeva. The great critic loves him to distraction. Arriving fresh from Paris, Turgenev, a poet, an aristocrat, handsome, rich, keen, has become enamored of him. But his fame is by no means limited to literary circles. Wherever he goes, he says, he is treated as a wonder. Whenever he opens his mouth, people repeat to each other: Dostoevsky has said this, Dostoevsky thinks of doing that. He would run short of paper, he tells Mikhail, were he to enumerate all his successes. He has met a lot of very fine people—in fact, he is in high society. Prince Vladimir Odoevsky has begged for the pleasure of a visit from him. Count Sollogub is tearing his hair because he cannot get hold of this genius everybody is talking about. As a matter of fact, the Count went so far as to call on the author, in an effort to lure this prodigy into what he called his "menagerie." The young writer seems to have been thrown into confusion by the appearance of his titled and loquacious visitor, himself a popular novelist. The latter carried away with him the impression of a sickly-looking, abashed, yet withal attractive young man, possessed of a great deal of reserve and *amour-propre*.

Success did not seduce Dostoevsky into resting on his laurels. He had no end of ideas. In a single night he wrote a complete story and sold it in the morning for thirty rubles. Read aloud in Turgenev's room before the whole company, it caused a furor. Now Belinsky felt sure of him: he could handle such a variety of subjects. The story in question is entitled "A Novel in Nine Letters." It is a humorous piece in the manner of Gogol, deriving comedy more from the style than from the situations. The plot, in which shady business dealings and cuckoldry play a part, is a rather farcical one.

There were still days when he was without a kopeck, and, of course, the debts had not been wiped out. But that no longer worried him. Money was sure to come. An editor, hearing of his straits, begged him please to accept the loan of five hundred rubles. He needed the money. "The Minnas, Claras, Mariannas," he wrote to Mikhail on November 16, 1845, were "prettier than ever, but frightfully expensive." Perhaps he liked to boast a bit about these exploits, as about his infatuation with the clever and beautiful Mme. Panayeva. Turgenev, he declared, joined Belinsky in scolding him for the irregular life he was leading. Belinsky kept watch over him in the most fatherly fashion. "These people," Dostoevsky writes, "don't know what to do to show their affection for me, they are in love with me, one and all."

The miscellany, with *Poor Folk* in it, was out. It appeared on January 15, 1846. Forthwith Belinsky wrote a lengthy review of the novel. He stressed the originality and profound humaneness of Dostoevsky's talent. "Honor and glory," he wrote, "to the young writer whose Muse loves people in garrets and basements, and says of them to the denizens of gilded mansions: 'These, too, are human beings and your brothers!' " *Poor Folk* is the literary topic of the day. He has, Fyodor tells Mikhail, thrown a bone to the public. Let the pack fight over it. The fools are making him famous. They are taken aback by a work from which the author has completely effaced himself. And then too there is the novelty of his analytical approach, of his probing. As for his own set, they are agreed, and Belinsky along with them, that he has outstripped Gogol himself. "My future, brother," he sums up the matter, "is a most brilliant one."

*The Double,* too, is out. It took longer to write the novelette than he had thought, but it was a matter of three or four days between the setting down of the final period and the printing of the piece in *Fatherland Notes* a fortnight after the appearance of *Poor Folk*. It is, the author informs Mikhail, ten times better than *Poor Folk*. The clique declare it a work of genius and say that there has been nothing like it in Russia since *Dead Souls*. Further, the story brought in more than twice as much as its predecessor. And he was in receipt of other moneys as well. In fact, in the course of some six months he has spent a small fortune.

# ( IV )

The winter months flash by. There are so many impressions crowding upon him, so many new contacts, that he has no time to collect himself. Ideas swarm about him. His pen never stops. In two months he counted thirty-five mentions of him in various articles. This is fame! Yet there are flies in the ointment. His friends, after praising *The Double* extravagantly, have on second reading found it sorely wanting. The larger part of the public, too, has dismissed it as prolix and dull, though he has also heard praise too fulsome to be repeated. "The idea that I have botched what could have been a masterpiece was killing me," he wrote to Mikhail shortly after the publication of the story, adding: "Now the thing disgusts me. Much of it was written hastily and when I was tired. . . . Alongside of brilliant pages there is vileness, trash, nauseating unreadable stuff. All this temporarily made life hell for me, and I became ill with misery." And he has money difficulties as well. He has been rash enough to accept two hundred and fifty rubles for "goods" that he had not yet produced. Now the cash is spent, and he is again without a groat.

He is busy with several new projects. There are two stories, very terse and with thrilling tragic plots, for a miscellany planned by Belinsky, also a trifle for *Fatherland Notes* and a novel for Nekrasov. Although a number of new writers have appeared, supremacy is still his and he hopes it will remain so indefinitely. Never before had his mind been so furiously active.

His elation was short-lived. By May he was sunk in a mood of mixed apathy, anxiety, and the feverish expectation of some change for the better. Again he spent part of the summer with

Mikhail and his family in Reval and returned armed with the resolution to live modestly and write slowly. He manages to get along, but works badly, and has no prospects. To escape from the impasse in which he finds himself he conceives the idea of running away to Italy. On what? Well, he will publish on his own a collection of his writings and make a thousand rubles on it by the first of the year. In order to tide him over, he could, of course, get an advance on an unwritten story, but that is just what he is trying to avoid. He has been doing that sort of thing too long; to keep it up would only be to continue slavery. He is resolved to achieve his emancipation. The thousand rubles will permit him to pay off his debts and keep him in Italy for eight months. To find himself in that land of romance had been his dream since childhood. There he will start a novel, at which he expects to work two years. The plan is ripe in his head. At last he will be able to write something to please himself, without being hurried or hounded. Also he will be in a position to dictate his price. On his return, he will find himself in clover, what with the second part of the novel ready for publication and another volume of collected short pieces, both old and new, to be put on the market.

The grandiose plan fell through. He postponed the trip until the autumn. The delay fretted him. He was not prepared to resign himself to half portions either of fame or of wealth. He busied himself meanwhile with his story "The Shaved Whiskers." He would dangle it before the hungry eyes of the magazine editors, watch them scramble for it, and fling it to the highest bidder. Of course, if he could publish it separately, that would be even better. Alas, he had followed the bad example of Aesop's milkmaid. A few weeks pass, and all his projects are so much spilled milk. The edition of his collected stories is a vain dream and so is the Italian journey. Furthermore, when he had reached almost the end of "The Shaved Whiskers" he was suddenly overcome by the feeling that he was merely repeating himself and jeopardizing his reputation. "In my position," he wrote to Mikhail, "monotony is ruin." He must bring forward something fresh, new, startling, or he was lost. The manuscript of "The Shaved Whiskers" has not been preserved. He must have destroyed it in disgust. What did appear in the October issue of *Fatherland Notes* was the short story "Mr. Prokharchin," at which he had "slaved the whole summer," as he put it.

Early in 1847 he decided that he had been rash in dismissing

*The Double* as a failure. "Some people say," he wrote to Mikhail, "that it is an unrecognized marvel, that it will play an enormous role in the future, that it would have been enough for me to have written that story alone, that it is more interesting than a novel by Dumas." And he added: "How nice to be understood." What heartened him also was that he was at work on another story, which was going splendidly. Once that piece is finished (it was "The Landlady"), he will take off a whole year to write the novel that is tearing at his vitals. But one must live. So he would publish *Poor Folk* and *The Double* as separate volumes, and only issue his collected writings two years later: "This will be extremely advantageous, for I will take in money twice and make myself famous." If only he had the capital with which to be his own publisher! The book-publishing industry, be it said in passing, then in its infancy in Russia, was suffering from the business depression the country was feeling at the time. He offered Mikhail one fourth of the profits of the undertaking for the loan of two hundred rubles, which would make him independent of printers and booksellers. Booksellers were scoundrels. But this time Mikhail, who was often in straits himself and who had a growing household to support, failed to respond as usual, and the publishing venture was indefinitely postponed.

# ( V )

To make matters worse, in the second winter of his fame Dostoevsky had a falling out with Nekrasov and, indeed, with the entire circle. When he had first appeared in Mme. Panayeva's drawing room, where the group met so often, the fair-haired youth with the restless gray eyes and the nervously twitching lips struck his hostess as pitifully ill at ease. Turgenev described him as a mole who had crawled out into the light of day. He had moments of abysmal shyness. His eyes would hide behind their lids; his head would seem to withdraw like a turtle's; his words would come in gasps. But as his visits became more frequent, his bashful manner gave place to a tactlessly forward one, which these clever literary people failed to interpret as another sign of shyness. They saw merely that he was obstinate and cocky and that his fame had gone to his head. Indifferent to the fact that they had to do with a thin-skinned youth who had been too abruptly pulled out of his dark self-communings into the public eye, they behaved like a crowd of schoolboys baiting an offensive newcomer. Led by Turgenev, who was generally the life of the party, they would encourage Dostoevsky in his contrariness and amuse themselves with the spectacle. Instead of laughing off these attacks, he took them seriously, seeing himself as the victim of envy, and fairly choked with gall.

One evening Turgenev was making sport of a man he claimed to have met in the provinces who imagined himself a genius. Dostoevsky, trembling in all his limbs and white as chalk, ran out before the story was finished. He never came back. The one member of the circle whom he continued to see, reported that he spoke of them as envious, heartless nonentities. Their own tongues were not quiet. The very hands that had set him on a pedestal now none too gently took him down. His erstwhile admirers had become his detractors. They circulated a rumor that the young author had demanded a special decoration, some said a gold border, on the pages of the miscellany containing *Poor Folk*. An epigram, tossed off by Turgenev and Nekrasov and dedicated to Belinsky, described Dostoevsky as a new pimple glowing on the nose of literature, assured him that the Sultan was about to send his Grand Vizier for him, and referred to his having fainted when introduced to a society belle at a fashionable soirée—an actual occurrence. The gold border figured here too.

Nekrasov was just then starting a new magazine, *Sovremennik* (*The Contemporary*)—its first issue appeared on January 1, 1847—or rather reviving an old periodical by that name which had been launched by Pushkin, and the quarrel lost Dostoevsky this market. According to Nekrasov, Dostoevsky had come to him to demand that a certain critical article about him be withheld from publication; he had mentioned the epigram, fumed, and threatened, until the editor had concluded that the man had gone out of his mind. One unpleasant aspect of the break was that Dostoevsky was obliged to refund the sum he had accepted as an advance. The result was that he agreed to work the entire winter for *Fatherland Notes,* and in return, Krayevsky, the editor of that periodical, was to pay all his debts. So here he was again, enslaved as before, with no prospect of escape.

He continued to see Belinsky for several months after his break with the rest of the coterie. And then that link, too, snapped. Not long afterward Dostoevsky was to blame the estrangement on their failure to agree on the proper function of literature. He may indeed have objected to the critic's emphasis on the writer's moral and didactic mission, seeing it as a brake on the freedom and spontaneity of art. But the fact that Belinsky had grown cool to his work is more likely to have proved fatal to a friendship which, to begin with, was pitched in too high a key, particularly for one as touchy as Dostoevsky. The previous year Belinsky had been praising him unreservedly. Here, he had said, was a genius who must make his way slowly and whose fame would be at its zenith when talents that might temporarily eclipse him were forgotten. But in his survey of the literature produced in 1846, he found "monstrous defects" in *The Double* and deplored the fantastic element in it. "In our time," he opined, "what is fantastic occurs only in insane asylums and comes under the jurisdiction of physicians, not fiction writers." He rejected "Mr. Prokharchin" because of an obscurity scarcely illuminated by sparks of talent. In his review of the literary output of the following year he dismissed "The Landlady," which had appeared in the autumn, as utterly false and, moreover, unintelligible. In a letter to a friend, dated February 14, 1848, he was even more outspoken. " 'The Landlady' is awful rubbish," he said. "He [Dostoevsky] has turned out other work since, but every new piece of his is another failure. In the provinces people can't stand him, and in the capital they speak with hostility even of *Poor Folk*. How we have fooled ourselves about this genius! . . . I, the foremost critic, acted like an ass raised to the second power."

He had hailed the author of *Poor Folk* as the hope of what was known as the "New" or "Natural School," of which he was the chief champion. This group, which took shape in the mid-forties, was made up of writers who portrayed realistically the life of the poor, both urban and rural, in a spirit critical of the existing order.

Belinsky died shortly after dictating—he had been too weak to write—the letter just mentioned. Dostoevsky's relationship with the critic lasted less than two years, but it left an indelible mark on his thinking. At school he had been an enthusiastic reader of George Sand and thus may have caught a whiff of socialist ideas. In the early forties they were beginning to seep into Russia, in spite of the rigid censorship set up by Nicholas I. By 1843, in Petersburg, the works of the French exponents of socialism were, in the words of a contemporary, "the object of

study, ardent discussion, questions, and all manner of hopes."
The doctrine had gone to the head of Belinsky, among others.
Several years before Dostoevsky came to know him he had announced in a letter that for him socialism was "the alpha and
omega of faith and knowledge." His socialism was a humanitarian credo, at once ethical and emotional, involving summary
rejection of the Establishment, emphasis on the importance of
the external conditions of man's life, and concern for the physical
welfare of every human being here and now. But people are
so foolish, he said to himself, that you have to get them into
Eden by force. "Fierce Vissarion" was not one to consider doing
things by halves. "To make even a small fraction of mankind
happy," he wrote to a friend, "I am perhaps ready to destroy
the rest by fire and sword." He adopted the motto: "Sociality
or death!" and applauded the eighteenth century for guillotining
"aristocrats, priests, and other enemies of God, reason and
humanity." His devotion to reason and humanity never flagged,
but under the influence of Ludwig Feuerbach's ideas he turned
against the Deity. Shortly before he discovered Dostoevsky he
was writing to a like-minded friend: "In the words 'God' and
'religion' I see darkness, chains, and the knout. . . ." While for
some of his contemporaries socialism conjured up the vision of
a new Christianity destined to regenerate mankind, Belinsky saw
it as a scheme of secular meliorism based on a humanistic outlook.

Many years later Dostoevsky recalled that after meeting him
the critic had tried to convert him to his own faith. Of this
Dostoevsky gave a somewhat incoherent account. According to
him, Belinsky began to initiate him into his credo by inveighing
against religion. He also exalted socialism and communism, apparently using the terms interchangeably. Himself a good husband and father, he rejected as immoral such props of society
as the family and property rights. Socialism, he held, placed "the
freedom of personality in unheard-of grandeur upon a new and
adamant foundation." It would become "the law" of the sacro-
sanct communist society in the renewed world that was to come.
Curiously enough, during his last months, Belinsky, remaining
the ardent idealist, turned away from socialism, declaring that
Russia was to gain most by developing a strong middle class.

"At this time" (1846), Dostoevsky wrote, "I passionately
accepted his entire teaching." The accuracy of this reminiscence
is questionable. On one occasion the preceptor conceded that if
Jesus had lived in the nineteenth century he might have headed

the revolution, yet this did not prevent him from making disparaging remarks about the Savior. When he did this, he told a friend, his disciple would pull a face as if he wanted to cry. It may have been during the long talks with the critic that the nodus between socialism and atheism was established in Dostoevsky's mind.

# 5

## A SICK SOUL

DOSTOEVSKY'S quarrel with the *Sovremennik* circle coincided for him with a brief period of well-being. "Never," he wrote Mikhail in the same letter in which he announced his break with Nekrasov, "has there been such abundance and serenity in my life, so much evenness in my character. Never have I known such physical health." New images were crowding into his mind as never before. "Work for Holy Art," work done in "the simplicity of the heart"—that was his ideal. He believed that he was actually undergoing both a moral and a physical regeneration. This amazing change he attributed to the influence of a group of new-found friends centering around three young men—the Beketov brothers.

With these, the eldest of whom had been a schoolmate of his, Dostoevsky set up a kind of communal ménage on Vasilyevsky Ostrov in an outlying section of the city. "They cured me," he wrote, "with their company." He was as eager for comradeship as only a solitary who found sociability difficult could be. Even when he was in the midst of pressing work, he wanted someone near him. Here with the Beketovs there was no lack of companionship. There were Dutch-treat dinner parties and an occasional picnic. Of an evening there would be ten or fifteen people at the house, gathered, one fancies, around the samovar and bubbling over with talk. It was not unlike that in which the Belinsky coterie indulged. Here was the same animus against oppression, the concern for social justice, the Westernist orientation, the tendency to think of the human condition in naturalistic terms.

The communal household was not only of spiritual benefit to the young man: it had as well the advantage of economy, the expenses not exceeding thirty-five rubles a month per person. "So great," he exclaims, "are the benefits of association." The term meant co-operative living and was prominent in the socialist vocabulary of the day. The arrangement did not interfere with his privacy. He had a room of his own where he spent much time at his desk. He was at work on a novel: *Netochka Nezvanova.* Occasionally he broke off at seven o'clock to divert himself with the Italian opera, choosing, for cheapness, a gallery seat. He needed distraction, for writing was a strain, although, strangely enough, he wrote best and fastest when his nerves were at their worst. He felt as though he were being tried by the editors, the critics, the public, and he hoped to win the case with his novel, to the undoing of his enemies. His main problem was to deliver enough copy to Krayevsky to work off his debt by the time summer came. Other periodicals offered better rates, but since he had taken an advance from Krayevsky, he was under the man's thumb.

He would not publish what he was writing until the whole thing was finished. He would keep at his job even if the sky came crashing around his ears. He knew the measure of his ability and would not go astray. Meanwhile, being pinched in pocket, he had to depend on the help of "kindly people." He would "perish" if it weren't for them. Besides the novel, he was writing a story: "The Landlady." It was in the manner of *Poor Folk,* only better. "My pen," he blusters, mixing his metaphors, "is guided by a spring of inspiration that leaps straight from my soul." The novel will appear at the end of the year and will wipe the floor with his former friends of the *Sovremennik* set, who are now trying to bury him. Once he has published this novel, he will issue it separately at his own expense, and *Poor Folk* and *The Double* as well, and then perhaps Fate will smile upon him. Meanwhile, life, what with poverty, the constant sense of being driven, the unbearable fatigue, is the same hell that it has been ever since he first achieved his "doubtful fame."

When he was thus complaining of his circumstances, he was no longer sharing quarters with the Beketovs, who had moved away from the capital. There was no trace of the euphoria that had resulted from his association with the group, and he was again in the thick of his anxieties and distresses. In his loneliness he began pleading with Mikhail more earnestly than ever to retire from the service and come to settle in Petersburg. He would be sure to find work. Perhaps he would make a literary career for himself as a translator. Everybody was doing it. Dostoevsky hinted that he might even make peace with Nekrasov for Mikhail's sake. At least they would be together, and so they would gain courage and their strength would be doubled. In ten years they would have three hundred and fifty thousand rubles. The benefits of association—the word is never far from his penpoint —would be theirs.

Mikhail succumbed to his brother's enthusiasm. Yes, he agreed, association was a great and sacred thing. He would tender his resignation and move to the capital, with the expectation that his Emilia and their three children would join him there later. What with selling the furniture and borrowing, he might bring with him as much as two hundred rubles, and this would be the foundation of their future fortune. They would want accommodation for a servant—one of their serfs—and they must have a lodging with firewood supplied. In the autumn of 1847 Mikhail arrived in Petersburg, to the great joy of his brother and the regret of all those wishing to inquire closely into what Dostoevsky was doing and thinking during the two or three years that followed, for with Mikhail in the same city he had no need to pour himself out in letters to this his sole confidant.

# ( II )

To add to the difficulties that beset the young author, his health was wretched. A sedentary life and long periods of overwork must have aggravated a condition due to more fundamental, if obscure, causes. When he resigned from the service he had talked vaguely of being ill. He had been in the habit of neglecting himself and avoiding doctors. Now just the contrary was true. The months that had followed his initial success had been filled with

more definite complaints. He suffered from nervous spasms of
the throat. He feared "nervous fever." If he failed to have sea
bathing in the summer, he didn't know what would become of
him. "It often seemed to me that I was dying," he told a friend
in later years; "really, death would come and then would leave.
I was also afraid of morbid lethargy." At the end of April,
1846, he explained his silence to Mikhail on the grounds of
having been at death's door. "I was terribly sick, suffering from
an irritation of the entire nervous system, and the ailment attacked the heart, causing it to become congested and inflamed—
a condition which was barely checked by leeches and two blood-
lettings." He was by then out of danger but far from recovered.
In his doctor's opinion the illness had been developing for three
or four years and recuperation would be a correspondingly long
process. He was to diet and lead an orderly, quiet, and utterly
lean existence, and perhaps have a change of scene. This grave
illness is never mentioned again.

That summer an advance received from Krayevsky enabled
him to have a visit with Mikhail at Reval. But before he left
town he had to undergo more doctoring. On a May morning
in 1846 he went to a certain young medico named Yanovsky,
recommended to him by a recently acquired friend, to be treated
for a minor complaint. The doctor, being a man of literary
interests, must have been somewhat flattered to be consulted by
the celebrated author of *Poor Folk*. Looking at this patient with
a more attentive eye than usual, he noted that his visitor was
below medium height (actually, he measured five foot six), but
broad-boned, especially in the shoulders, and with remarkably
large hands and feet, that his fine soft hair was blond to the point
of whiteness, that his forehead was unusually well developed,
his pale gray eyes small and restless, and his lips thin and compressed, giving a look of concentration to the face. The doctor
was surprised to see that the patient held himself not like the
graduate of a military school that he was, but rather in the
slouching fashion of a divinity student. His black jacket was of
excellent cloth, his vest of black cashmere, his linen fine and im-
maculate, and he carried a topper—indeed, he looked almost
fashionable, except for his shoes, which were shabby.

The examination showed that there was no trouble with the
vital organs, except that the heartbeats were irregular and the
pulse uneven and "remarkably compressed, as with women and
people of nervous temperament." To a very marked degree the

patient exhibited the traces of having suffered from such diseases of childhood as rickets and scrofula.

While he was treating Dostoevsky for the local disorder, which he did not choose to name—was it an unmentionable ailment?—the physician came to suspect that in addition his patient was probably suffering from an obscure affection of the nerves. He was led to this notion partly by Dostoevsky's account of a nervous condition to which he had been subject in childhood, partly by what he saw of the man's disposition and constitution. As the doctor may have known, Dostoevsky's heredity, too, was bad: he was the son of a consumptive and a dipsomaniac who had strange seizures. That the family tree bore bad fruit may be seen from the fact that one of his brothers became a hopeless drunkard and one sister a psychopath. A few weeks' treatment was sufficient to cure the patient of the local ailment, but the nervous trouble persisted. The doctor was soon to recognize its true nature.

Dostoevsky's character was in itself indicative of his affliction. He was irritable and suspicious, given to magnifying trifles and distorting ordinary facts. There were times when he behaved paradoxically: he adored his little godson, Mikhail's firstborn and his own namesake—he was cross with him about nothing; he admired and respected his brother's wife—he was rude to her; he looked up to his brother—he treated him as an inferior. "Sometimes when my heart is swimming in love," he wrote to Mikhail, "you can't pull a kind word out of me." Extraordinary circumstances, he claimed, could sometimes bring him to show his true feelings, but too often his ill temper and sullenness caused him to be misjudged by those around him. He gave as a reason for his behavior that his nerves refused to obey him, and rightly connected with his illness the discrepancy between the way he felt and the way he acted.

Another symptom was his hypochondria. He complained of palpitations of the heart. His condition threw him into a panic. The projected trip to Italy was planned, he told Mikhail, not for his pleasure, but for his health. Should he try Priessnitz's cold water cure? He must do something. He also spoke vaguely of inflammation of the brain. He came to believe that the climax of his illness was something like temporary insanity. It was of this period that he said: "For two years on end I suffered from a strange moral ailment. I fell into a hypochondriac state. There was even a time when I lost my reason." He was past middle life when he wrote reminiscently to Dr. Yanovsky: "You loved me and looked after me, mentally deranged as I was (now I know that that was what was wrong with me). . . ." Toward the end of his life he wrote Pobedonostzev that in the late forties he had had an ailment due to "abdominal plethora," which in some cases led to "moral and mental derangement and limitless hypochondria." He said that one of his brothers had suffered from the same ailment.

Sometimes Dostoevsky was afraid to go to bed. Suppose he were to fall into a sleep resembling death? Spending the night with a friend, he begged that they would not be too quick to bury him, should they think him dead, and he pictured the horror of waking in the grave. He would leave a note on his bedtable to the effect that he should not be buried too soon. Now and again he felt as though death were paying him a call—a loathsome and terrifying experience. He may well have been remembering his own sensations when, in *The Insulted and Injured,* he described the mystic terror of his hero: the dread of an inconceivable and impossible something turning into a horrible, ruthless reality, a dread no less harrowing because the mind is divided between an understanding of its folly and an inability to reject it.

He fell into the habit of dropping in at Dr. Yanovsky's bachelor apartment every day and sometimes spending the night. If he came early, he would not breakfast before glancing at himself in the mirror and having the doctor look at his tongue and feel his pulse.

He turned to Yanovsky for more than relief from his hypochondriac obsessions. Here was a man who knew the secret workings of the body, the diseases of the flesh and the mind. There was so much to be learned about the nervous system, about the brain, about insanity. For one who felt himself always trembling on the verge of a nervous breakdown, there was something of both fascination and terror in the subject. He would pump the doctor. He would borrow medical tomes. What especially caught his attention, as it did that of so many of his contemporaries, was phrenology. Assiduously Dostoevsky felt his own bumps and discovered, not without satisfaction, that his skull was shaped like that of Socrates. He had the same development of the frontal bone over the perceptive and reflective organs, the same jutting superciliary ridges, the same absence of projections in the supraoccipital bones where the lower instincts and sentiments were located, amativeness among others. This he found truly remarkable. Yanovsky must have seen for himself that he was "no petticoat chaser." What he was fond of was not the petticoat at all, but the cap: the kind worn by his friend Maikov's mother, Yevgeniya Petrovna. Indeed, according to his friend and physician, Dostoevsky had never shown signs of a passionate interest in women. Riesenkampf, who had known him earlier, also found him indifferent and even hostile toward them. Barring his brief infatuation with Mme. Panayeva, one finds no sentimental involvement of the slightest consequence. On the other hand, the young man did not lack sexual experience, as is evident from the letter to Mikhail referring to the "frightfully expensive" Minnas, Claras, and Mariannas. It remains true, however, that his early writings are curiously sexless. Only in his mature work does passion find its voice.

# ( III )

In addition to his physical distresses, his irritability, his hypochondria, his "moral ailment," Dostoevsky came to show symptoms of a more specific and far more alarming character. About the time when *Poor Folk* was on the stocks he was subject, if Grigorovich's testimony is to be credited, to seizures, which were usually followed by two or three days of mental misery. On one occasion the two friends were walking together and met a funeral procession. Dostoevsky wanted to beat a retreat, but before he could go any distance he had a "fit" so violent that he had to be carried to the nearest grocery, where with great difficulty he was restored to consciousness.

Another friend saw him in a mild attack in the summer of 1846 or '47. It was late at night, a small party was drawing to an end, when Dostoevsky's face changed queerly and a frightened look came into his eyes. A few moments passed and then in a hollow voice he asked: "Where am I?" and ran to the window for air. When his host came into the room, after seeing the other guests off, he found him sitting on the window sill, his face twisted, his head bent to one side, his body shaking convulsively. He doused him with cold water, but Dostoevsky, without coming to himself, ran out into the street. The alarmed host dashed after him, but could not keep pace with him, and jumped into a cab.

When he caught up with him at the gates of a hospital, a couple of blocks away, Dostoevsky was in a calmer state and allowed himself to be taken home. He explained that he had run to the hospital with the vague notion of finding help there.

Dr. Yanovsky saw him in the throes of a serious attack three times. The first of these occurred in July, 1847. One day the doctor was drawn like one hypnotized to Saint Isaac's Square, although he had no business there, a fact that Dostoevsky afterward adduced as proof of the significance of forebodings. As he was crossing the square, he ran into his patient clutching the arm of a military clerk. Hatless, his coat and vest unbuttoned, his cravat untied, Dostoevsky was shouting that he was dying and calling for Yanovsky. His pulse was pounding away at the rate of more than a hundred, his head was thrown back and held rigid, and his body was beginning to shake with convulsions. The doctor took him home, opened a vein, drawing coal-black blood, and kept him at his apartment for several nights.

In the case of the second attack witnessed by Yanovsky, just as in the instance reported by Grigorovich, it was something that had to do with death which appears to have touched off the paroxysm. It was caused by the death of Belinsky. When Dostoevsky brought the news to Yanovsky one May morning in 1848, he was in such a state that the doctor insisted that he remain with him. All went smoothly during the day, but at three o'clock in the morning the doctor heard heavy stertorous breathing in the room where Dostoevsky was sleeping. He went in to him and found him lying on his back in convulsions, with open eyes, foaming lips, and protruding tongue. The third attack occurred in the early spring of 1849, also late at night, after an unpleasant incident at a meeting of a discussion group of which Dostoevsky was a member. Again he ran to Yanovsky for help when he felt the seizure coming on. The doctor describes it as "violent and characteristic," adding that his patient also had many light attacks.

Not that Dostoevsky understood the nature of his trouble. He called it humorously "*kondrashka* with a little breeze"—the "breeze" was apparently his way of describing the premonitory sensation as of a current of air experienced before an epileptic attack, and *kondrashka* is the popular term for a stroke.

At the time Yanovsky recognized that Dostoevsky was suffering from epilepsy, which in his opinion first showed itself in 1846, if not earlier. Grigorovich would have it that the malady was already apparent in his school days. Another friend, A. S. Suvorin, said that Dostoevsky had suffered from the disease "since his childhood," and accounted for it thus: "Something terrifying, unforgettable, tormenting, happened to him in his childhood, the result of which was his falling sickness"—an opinion in which Dr. Yanovsky concurred when he was in possession of most of the facts. "It was precisely in his childhood," the physician then wrote, "that Dostoevsky had a dark, gloomy experience such as never passes without leaving a scar, even if it occurs in maturity, and which so affects the temperament as to lead to nervous diseases and consequently to epilepsy." It is clear from the context, however, that the doctor was referring not to a specific trauma but to the oppressive atmosphere which the father's tyrannical behavior created in the home.

That Dostoevsky's illness was caused by a shock and that this occurred early in his life is the story related by Orest Miller, co-author of the first biography of the novelist. He was told by a person "very close" to Dostoevsky that his malady dated from his "earliest youth" and was connected with "a tragic event in their family life." Unable to corroborate this statement, the biographer discreetly withheld all details. If this "tragic event" was the assassination of the father, his reticence is intelligible, since mention of the matter was forbidden by the relatives. It may be noted that Dostoevsky's daughter, in her unreliable life of him, mentions a family tradition that the news of the murder brought on the first epileptic seizure. That Dostoevsky had Smerdyakov, in *The Brothers Karamazov,* contract epilepsy at the age of twelve is perhaps of some significance.

These suggestive, if meager and uncertain clues, together with scraps of evidence derived from Dostoevsky's writings, have led to the formulation of a psychoanalytic theory of the origin of his trouble. Unlike lesser lights, Freud himself, realizing how scant and dubious the information is, was not dogmatic on the subject. He was strongly inclined to see in the ailment not an organic affection, but rather the symptoms of a neurosis. "The most probable assumption," he wrote, "is that the attacks go back far into his childhood, that the symptoms were mild to start with, and did not assume epileptic form until after the shattering experience of his eighteenth year, the murder of his father." The key with which he tried to unlock the mechanism of Dostoevsky's neurosis was the familiar one of the Oedipus complex.

The Freudian theory sees the boy as a creature torn between love and hatred of his father, the hatred being all the more intense since it was hidden from his pious and filial self. On the one hand, in the inmost depths of his heart he longed for the satisfactions of a tender union with his father; on the other, he feared him, broke out in revolt against him, and unconsciously wished his death. The news of the slaying comes as the tidings of fulfillment, both joyful and terrible. Are not his hands stained with his father's blood? Did he not commit the murder, in will if not in deed? Henceforth his sense of guilt will be heavier than ever and find a dozen subtle ways of shaping his life. His epileptic attack, with its premonitory moment of bliss, due to the granting of the death wish, its period of unconsciousness and subsequent distress, is then a punishment meted out to him by his own conscience and at the same time a fond identification of himself with his dead father. The psychoanalyst sees a special meaning in the fact that the attacks were released by such experiences as the sight of a funeral procession, the news of the death of Belinsky, the man who had stood to him *in loco parentis*. It is perhaps of significance that the theme of a child believing itself responsible for the death of its parents is touched upon in two of Dostoevsky's early tales, and that the father-son relationship and the crime of parricide play an important part in his major fiction.

His epilepsy has also been diagnosed as genuine, one physician opining that it was due to "an endocrine abnormality." When doctors disagree, the layman must remain in doubt. One thing is certain: Dostoevsky's attacks manifested themselves at least as early as 1846, when he was twenty-five, and plagued him for the rest of his life, while his supersensitive, misanthropic, unstable disposition, marked by hypochondria, a strong religiosity, and a tendency to take refuge from reality in a dream world, answers to the description of the epileptic personality as presented in medical literature. An eminent authority on the disease has stated that it develops in most cases when the patient is in his teens and another physician maintains that the epileptic make-up is discernible from earliest childhood. Exactly what caused the malady, and what its true nature was, will probably always remain open questions.

# 6

## REBELLION?

OF a Friday evening Dostoevsky would occasionally make his way—sometimes taking Mikhail along—to a small frame house on Pokrov Square, walk up a stairway lit by an ill-smelling lamp in which hempseed oil burned smokily, and emerge into Petrashevsky's rather dingy drawing room. Dostoevsky had made his acquaintance in the spring of 1846—the man, a complete stranger, accosting him in the street and, without any preliminaries, saying: "May I ask what is the idea of your next tale?" It was the following year, around Lent, that he first appeared at one of Petrashevsky's Fridays—they had started some two years earlier. Like the opera, the circus, and Nilsen's sermons, the gatherings in the rooms of this translator in the Foreign Office were then one of the institutions in Petersburg about which visitors to the capital would write home. Dostoevsky found there, wrapped in a fog of tobacco smoke, about a score of people: officers, government clerks, teachers, literary men, university students. There were some habitués and not a few transients, including tradesmen; and the host, a short, thickset young man, wearing the beard and mustache on which the authorities frowned, and with lively black eyes and nervous gestures, darted from one group to the next, too intent on having the minds of his guests meet to bother about their being properly introduced to each other. The names of some Dostoevsky never learned.

The samovar would be purring, the piano might be opened, and before the company broke up in the small hours the table would be spread with a modest supper. Cards were banned. The place was a cross between a social club and a debating society. What chiefly drew the men together was the talk. It was of the kind that could not but attract a disciple of Belinsky. Ideas were touched upon, sentiments were voiced that scarcely befitted faithful members of the Orthodox Church and loyal subjects of the Emperor. Domestic and foreign news was discussed, official measures freely criticized, the antics of the censors and other abuses denounced; serfdom was attacked, the family and religion questioned. Quite a few of Petrashevsky's guests were freethinkers or, indeed, like himself, atheists. He had once described Christ as "a well-known demagogue who ended his career rather unsuccessfully." He seems to have regarded man as capable of developing Godlike attributes—an idea that Dostoevsky would eventually reject as diabolical. The group included some professing Christians. Ensign Konstantin Timkovsky, who declared his readiness to be the first to lay down his life "for the sacred cause of liberty," volunteered to prove the divinity of Christ "purely scientifically." An excerpt from a Church Slavonic translation of *A Believer's Words* by Robert de Lamennais was read at one meeting when Dostoevsky was present. Lamennais was a Catholic priest who broke with the Church and became a champion of the poor and oppressed in the belief that they alone obeyed God's will.

Dostoevsky contributed little to the conversation. Reserved and taciturn, he gave the impression, when he did speak, of possessing the earnestness and ardor that make a good propagandist. On one occasion he moved the company deeply by describing from hearsay the flogging of a corporal who had avenged himself on a brutal officer—a punishment that he was to witness more than once. An acquaintance had it that at the spur of the moment he was "capable of appearing on a square with a red flag."

After the revolutionary events which marked the year 1848 in the West the tone of the gatherings became somewhat more formal. At times there would even be a chairman who wielded a bell, which was in the form of a hemisphere with a handle representing Liberty. Occasionally a speech would be delivered on a definite topic, such as social reform or the principles of political economy. Dostoevsky gave a talk in which he dealt with a theme that is the subject of several of his stories: the dwarfing of personality. Again, a man might read a manuscript, perhaps a story with a purpose. The host had no stomach for pure art. He insisted that literature was merely one of the means to the noble end of regenerating society.

A born proselytizer, he had attempted to spread his ideas by taking part in the compilation of a dictionary of loan words (1845–46). In defining "Negrophile" he managed to attack serfdom; under "opposition" he defended civil rights and the jury system; "odalisque" offered him a chance to champion women's rights. Under other terms he smuggled in summaries of democratic and socialist teachings. Of course, the copies of the book were confiscated by the police. This led him to concentrate on oral propaganda. In the hope of making converts not only among the educated, he is said to have joined a workmen's dancing class.

In addition to holding at-homes he had organized a small cooperative lending library, which included forbidden foreign publications. Both Fyodor and Mikhail used it. Such bootleg literature was smuggled over the border in quantities. Among the books circulated by Petrashevsky a prominent place was occupied by works of the French social philosophers and their disciples. One suspects that the Russians prized these authors perhaps more as critics of the established order than as planners of the perfect society that would usher in the Golden Age. The Belinsky circle, to which Dostoevsky had belonged, was acquainted with the ideas of Saint-Simon, Cabet, Fourier. Not a few of those who attended the Fridays embraced the doctrine formulated by the last-named. A megalomaniac who was given to wandering off into quaint nonsense, this Utopian socialist was nevertheless an exceptionally keen and bold thinker. He called for a revolution more radical than Marxism in liberating the individual from the evils of a civilization gone wrong. Just at the time when the Fourierist colonies that had sprung up in New York, New Jersey, Pennsylvania, Wisconsin, and on the shores of Lake Ontario were falling into decay, the seeds of the faith were sprouting on the cold banks of the Neva. A few Russian heads were giddy with Fourier's shining vision of a society that instead of repressing man's natural drives (*"passions"*), gives them free rein. Mankind will then be freed from "political imbecility," with its states, armies, wars, and people will be enabled to live happily and securely as members of small productive communities (phalansteries) from which pauperism and drudgery will be eliminated, while exploitation, injustice, hatred, envy, become things of the past.

Unlike the Americans, who were free to test out their theories, the Russian radicals, under the stern paternalism of Nicholas I, had to confine themselves to idle discussion. Since there was no chance of carrying out their schemes, there was no limit to their extravagance. On a certain Friday in December, 1848, Dostoevsky listened to a proposition, advanced by Timkovsky, that the world be divided into two halves, one to be given to the Fourierists, the other to the communists, for social experimentation. "Let them live as good neighbors," the speaker is reported to have added, "and borrow from one another the good things each has." To this the host took exception. There was nothing, he argued, that the Fourierists could borrow from the communists, except perhaps atheism. A devoted follower of the French reformer, he looked forward to living in a phalanstery himself, and it is said that he attempted to induce his own serfs to form one, but that they burned down their Eden.

On April 7, 1849, eleven men met at dinner to celebrate Fourier's birthday.* The occasion they were marking, the first speaker declared, was bound to accomplish "the transformation of the planet and of the human beings that inhabit it." After setting forth the master's doctrines at some length, he touched on matters nearer home, saying: "My fatherland is in chains, my fatherland is enslaved." He ended, however, on a note of confidence in the triumph of the cause, exclaiming: "Transfiguration is at hand!" There was general applause and two men embraced him. Petrashevsky, who rose next, extolled Fourier's system as the only one capable of harmonizing society with human nature, but did not underestimate the difficulties of planting the seed of socialism in "the savage soil" of Russia.

The third speaker was the most grandiloquent. He painted the life around him in the blackest tones, but wound up with a proud rhapsody. "We have come here not to lament and tell pitiful tales; on the contrary, we are full of hope, triumph and joy. . . . Man is waiting for his crown, he deserves it and will soon take it, set it on his tormented head and appear as the king of the earth.

* Because of the difference between the Western and the Russian calendars, the event should have been solemnized eleven days earlier.

. . . We must remember the greatness of the cause for which we are fighting. To rehabilitate the laws of Nature, trampled upon by the teaching of ignorance; to restore God's image in man in all its grandeur and beauty; to set free and organize the lofty, harmonious passions now restrained and crushed; to destroy the capitals and cities and to use all their materials for other buildings, and to turn this existence of torments, disasters, destitution, shame, and disgrace into joy, material plenty, happiness, and to cover all this indigent earth with palaces and embellish it with flowers—that is our great goal, than which there is no greater on earth. . . . We here in our country will begin the transformation, and the whole planet will bring it to completion."

Dostoevsky was not present at the dinner. He knew Fourier's plan for the perfect society at second or third hand, but he was strongly attracted by the spirit of radical libertarianism that animated the man's ideas. He was also comforted to find that, like many other of the French reformers, Fourier was a believer. The *"passions,"* he took it for granted, were divinely ordained. In Petrashevsky's co-operative library there was a treatise (Paris, 1848) by Considérant, Fourier's leading disciple, with a supplement entitled "Jesus Christ Before the Army Councils" by another Fourierist, who argued that should Jesus walk the earth again, He would be immediately court-martialed because His teachings were akin to the most subversive doctrines of the times. Belinsky, as has been noted, had once spoken to the same effect.

Fourier held that his scheme of things could be introduced anywhere on earth without infringing on the powers-that-be and without the use of force. Petrashevsky agreed with the master in this as in all else. The belief that a new social order could be established by peaceful means was not shared by all whom he had drawn into his orbit. Harsh facts broke in on utopian dreams. Among the frequenters of the Fridays there were those who had a less feeble grasp on Russian realities than that of the man who had attempted to form a radiant phalanstery with brutalized serfs. Violence was already exerting its lure upon a few men who by temperament were not prone to follow the counsels of moderation and gradualism. It appears that Dostoevsky was involved with a handful of potential militants who were planning to act in defiance of the law.

# ( II )

As has been said, the coterie that centered around Petrashevsky had none of the earmarks of an organized body. There were those in the company who came to feel the need of setting up something in the nature of a formal association. One of them, an army officer, Nikolay Mombelli, was the author of an essay in which he suggested that the Czar be put on the diet of the Vitebsk peasants for a few days—their bread looked like dried horse dung mixed with straw. He and another man conceived the idea of establishing what they vaguely called "a brotherhood of mutual aid." The matter was discussed privately by half a dozen people, including one Nikolay Speshnyov.

Among Petrashevsky's guests this man, who was of the same age as Dostoevsky and survived him by a year, stood out as a strikingly handsome figure and a magnetic personality. A substantial landowner, he had lived abroad a good deal. There was a touch of the Byronic about him, something at once splendid and sinister. It was rumored that during his stay in Dresden he had had at least two desperately romantic affairs with Polish ladies. Bakunin called him a gentleman from head to heel; Petrashevsky called him a man of masks. While abroad, he may have come under the influence of the early communists. At one of the Fridays he made a speech to disprove the existence of God. He seems to have begun by declaring his intention to spread by word of mouth "socialism, atheism, terrorism, everything, everything good in the world," and advising his hearers to do likewise.

There was general agreement that "the brotherhood" should be a secret society run by people of republican views. One man suggested that its rules include the threat of death to any informer. The purpose of the projected organization was moot. Speshnyov cut in on the hemming and hawing by indicating that he favored "a purely political society," engaged in propaganda and preparing for "insurrection." This bold word was seldom heard at the Fridays, and then only when talk turned to the condition of the serfs.

Speshnyov was to insist later that he had mentioned insurrection in order to bring the discussions of "the brotherhood" to an end by frightening the participants. The matter was in fact dropped. Nevertheless, Speshnyov, for one, apparently did not abandon the idea of a secret society working for a violent upheaval. He believed that a revolution might occur in Russia within a few years. There was nothing fuzzy about his socialism. He favored nationalization of the land and government control of both agriculture and industry.

It was Speshnyov who for a while seems to have exerted a strong influence on Dostoevsky's thinking. There is something enigmatic about their relationship. "Now I am with *him,* and I am *his.* . . . Do you understand, I have a Mephistopheles of my own?" Dostoevsky told Yanovsky, if one is to credit the doctor's reminiscences set down many years later. Yanovsky has it that his friend was referring to having borrowed no less than five hundred rubles from Speshnyov. "I'll never be able to pay back this sum," Yanovsky quotes Dostoevsky as saying, "and besides, he won't take just money—that's the kind of man he is." Was there another element in the situation? Among Speshnyov's papers the police found a pledge to the effect that "the undersigned" had joined "the Russian Society" and had obligated himself "to take part openly and fully in the uprising and fight, when the Committee has decided that the time for rebellion has arrived," and also to enlist other members and have each sign a like pledge. Speshnyov assured the authorities that the paper was nothing but a draft, without significance, and that it had not been signed by anyone nor indeed been shown to anyone. To account for Dostoevsky's feeling that he had sold his soul, it has been suggested that he actually took this pledge, but there is nothing to support the conjecture.

By the winter of 1848–49 some of those who had been attending the Fridays were also meeting elsewhere. A number of men, Dostoevsky among them, drawn together by a plan to issue a literary miscellany, had decided to start "a salon" of their own. The group met at the lodging of the poet Pleshcheyev and later at the apartment of another minor writer, one Durov, each member paying three rubles for his share of the refreshments and the rent of a piano. The explanation was that they had grown tired of serious talk and wanted to have intimate literary-musical evenings.

According to Speshnyov, however, the real reason for the secession was the suspicion that undercover agents had been planted at the Fridays. As a matter of fact, in March, 1848,

Petrashevsky was placed under surveillance and in March of the following year a secret service man who succeeded in gaining his confidence began to frequent the meetings. In his report to the Minister of the Interior a police officer has this to say about Petrashevsky's guests: "Most of these young men are, as it were, in radically bitter opposition to the existing order. . . . Under the influence of West European Utopians, they imagine themselves called to bring about a rebirth of all social life, to make over all mankind, and they are ready to be apostles of and martyrs to this unfortunate delusion. Such people will stop at nothing, for they hold that they act not for themselves, but for the entire human species, not for the present moment, but for eternity."

At a gathering in Pleshcheyev's room Speshnyov urged the authors present to send him manuscripts that were sure to be barred by the censor, saying that he would have them printed abroad and smuggled into the country. During the very first meeting at Durov's, Mombelli again harped on the necessity for "people of advanced views" to form a close association. A student by the name of Filippov proposed that the group make a systematic study of conditions in Russia, each member dealing with some phase of the subject, and that the results be circulated among "discreet people." Dostoevsky's essay, which like the rest never materialized, was to be on socialism. Filippov urged further that they secretly reproduce their manuscripts by lithography. This was a daring proposal. But everyone knew Filippov. Hadn't Dostoevsky seen the daredevil munch a cluster of green rowanberries the previous summer in the midst of a cholera epidemic, just to prove that he was afraid of nothing? Half of those present, not wishing to be taken for cowards, held their peace. When people finally broke into speech, it was to raise objections, cite difficulties. Two of the musical members of the company changed the subject by taking up their instruments. Nothing further was done about the matter except to inquire into the cost of a lithographic stone.

It is a fact that seven men, including Speshnyov and Dostoevsky, resolved to establish a clandestine press for the printing of subversive literature. Parts of the machine were bought in several stores at various times and taken to the lodging of Mordvinov, a member of the circle. One evening early in 1849 Dostoevsky, greatly agitated, called on his friend Apollon Maikov and asked leave to stay the night. He had an important matter, he declared, to take up with his host: he had been delegated to invite him to join the group that was setting up a secret press, for the purpose of bringing about a revolution in Russia. Everything, he said, was ready. They had left Petrashevsky out—he was "a fool, an actor, a chatterer," while in this business reticence was essential. That Maikov should have been approached with this request is odd. Though an occasional guest of his old acquaintance Petrashevsky, he was not politically-minded, and just then he was absorbed by a love affair and by a novel that he was writing.

Naturally, he balked at the idea. It meant certain ruin; further, he argued, the two of them were writers, impecunious, impractical men, while politics was an eminently practical matter. "And I remember," he wrote thirty-six years after the event, "how Dostoevsky, in a red nightshirt open at the neck, sat like dying Socrates before his friends, and enlarged, at the height of his eloquence, on the sacredness of this undertaking, on our duty to save our fatherland, and so forth. . . ." The argument lasted late into the night, but Maikov was adamant. The next morning Dostoevsky went off, having charged Maikov not to breathe a syllable about the matter. The setting up of a secret press in the Russia of Nicholas I was an undertaking tantamount to planting a bomb. All Dostoevsky's other acts against the constituted authorities were trifling by comparison.

If the press was actually set up, it certainly remained idle, though not for lack of suitable copy. A number of subversive pieces were passed from hand to hand. One of them, written by Filippov himself, was a commentary on the Ten Commandments in which the Czar who does not side with the people against the masters and officials is described as "a ruler whose authority is not from the Lord but from Satan." It was read at a dinner given by Speshnyov and attended by Dostoevsky along with other members of the Durov group. A story, entitled "Soldiers' Talk," from the pen of an army officer who was occasionally seen at the Fridays, was to be officially described as "revolting" and "intended to undermine the private soldiers' devotion to the Throne and obedience to their superiors." There was great demand for copies of another piece: the lengthy letter addressed on July 3, 1847, by the outraged Belinsky to Gogol on the publication of the latter's obscurantist book, *Selected Passages from Correspondence with Friends*. The missive was a vehement philippic against the bureaucracy, the Church, the institution of serfdom. For a government, Belinsky wrote, Russia had "a huge corporation of thieves and robbers." As for the Church, it had always been "a prop of the knout and a toady to despotism," and had nothing in common with Christ, who "was the first to instruct mankind in liberty, equality, fraternity." The Russians were fundamentally a level-headed and "a deeply atheistic people." They needed civilization, enlightenment. The first necessity was the freeing of the serfs, abolition of corporal punishment, respect for the existing laws. Dostoevsky received a handwritten copy of the epistle from Moscow and read it at Durov's, as well as at Petrashevsky's and elsewhere. The letter aroused "universal rapture," and it was decided to make several copies of it. This document, the last testament of his former mentor and the manifesto of Russian liberalism, was to become for Dostoevsky one of the chief instruments of a hostile fate.

But before doom fell he was to know the stimulus of ideas, fantasies, beliefs, tapped from many minds. For a writer there was even more pabulum in the faces, the voices, the gestures, the minutiae of personality that these various contacts offered. Not that everything was seized upon and used at once. In the writing that he was doing at the time these concerns and impressions found no resonance. There was a laying-up of treasure, a perhaps only half-realized hoarding.

Young Dostoevsky's associations were by no means confined to radical coteries. The group that centered around Dr. Yanovsky was of a conservative temper and so were the Maikovs. On Sunday evenings he would often repair to the spacious apartment near the Blue Bridge occupied by that family. Headed by a veteran of the Napoleonic wars who was a painter with academic laurels, it included four brothers. One of them, Valerian, a critic who crossed swords in the press with Belinsky himself, was drowned in the summer of 1847 at the age of twenty-four. Another, Appollon, a poet, was to be Dostoevsky's lifelong friend. At these gatherings he was bound to be exposed to the anti-democratic, nationalist ideology which was just then taking on the character of a political program. But it was not only here that he ran into it. By this time the discussion of these theories had gone beyond the Moscow salons and penetrated into the public prints of both capitals. Most young men in touch with their times were familiar with the Slavophile point of view: Russia was totally different from and superior to the West; the latter emphasized individualism, Russia was prone to collectivism; Europe was mortally sick, Russia was bursting with health; while in the West the State, being based upon conquest, must live by violence and remain merely a formal, legalistic institution, the Russian body politic, having been founded by amicable compact between the people and their sovereign, could develop organically and peacefully; the Czar's rule rested firmly on the loving submission of his subjects; while Rome had imposed upon Western Christianity a stifling rationalism, the Orthodox Church had preserved a quickening spirituality which made it the sole vessel of true Christianity. Some of these ideas were the unacknowledged foundations on which the world of Dostoevsky's childhood had rested. There was something reassuring and protecting about a philosophy that exalted the ancestral order and the familiar faith, that saw in the Czar the image of the Father who by the mere fact of his existence established and preserved the social framework. But at this time Dostoevsky was not ready to accept these views. He was to endure much travail of body and mind before they would become his rod and staff. In a feuilleton that he contributed to a Petersburg newspaper in 1847 he dismissed Slavophilism as "a dead letter." Now he was responsive to ideas of a different order.

# ( III )

Dostoevsky's discontent with the state of public affairs may well have been aggravated by his private harassments. Mikhail's arrival in Petersburg did not bring all the blessings expected of it. Certainly it brought no money. The sum of Dostoevsky's published work for the year 1847 was the short story called "The Landlady," aside from that bagatelle, "A Novel in Nine Letters," and several feuilletons. True, *Poor Folk* appeared separately, but *Netochka Nezvanova,* the novel upon which so much had been staked, failed to materialize and indeed nothing is heard of it until two years later. The situation was desperately discouraging. The brothers shared quarters until Mikhail's family—his wife and three young children—came to join him the following Easter. On Good Friday, when Dostoevsky had to prepare some sort of reception for the newcomers, his creditors were all at his throat.

In 1848 he was more prolific, perhaps because of the sustaining influence of his brother's presence. Mikhail, too, in addition to a good deal of translating, did some original work. Dostoevsky came out with four long stories and two lesser pieces. One of the latter, "Polzunkov," appeared in the miscellany edited by Nekrasov, who went out of his way to secure it—he could more easily give up a friend than a contributor.

The winter of 1848–49 was one of penury and general wretchedness. Yanovsky offered him fifteen or twenty rubles of his own and told him to borrow some cash from the alms box into which he and his friends dropped their spare five-kopeck pieces for beggars too proud to accept the free meal tickets then in use. The friends had also, at Dostoevsky's suggestion, started a small co-operative loan fund. A drawer in the doctor's desk was the bank, the same drawer containing the rules of the institution written in Dostoevsky's hand. But he rejected Yanovsky's offer. It was not twenty or fifty rubles that he needed, but hundreds.

By New Year's Day his distress was acute. There was no getting along with him at all. He was more irritable than ever, more easily offended, and ready to make much of trifles. He complained more frequently of attacks of vertigo. He felt that he was going to pieces. And he owed money to everybody. As usual he borrowed from Peter to pay Paul.

The enormous sum Speshnyov had lent him was no more a solution of his present difficulties than the sum he had received from the guardian had been. His original debt of four hundred rubles to Krayevsky had almost doubled. He felt as though he were in peonage to the man. The worst of it was that he was forced to botch his work. In order to pay off the debt, he told the editor, he was endangering his health, poor at best, and what was worse, injuring his name, his "sole capital." He began to look upon his work as drudgery that did not even yield bread. A mood of what he called "self-belittlement" took possession of him—a mood that gave way to self-assertiveness when he addressed Krayevsky. He wrote to the man that the advance made him had been in the nature of a business risk, rather than a personal favor, that his vogue had been steadily increasing throughout the previous year, and he must be genuinely gifted if he could overcome "beggary, slavery, the fury of the critics who were solemnly burying [him], and the prejudice of the public." It was criminal to make a man so talented do less than his best.

He had previously agreed to turn over to Krayevsky practically everything he wrote in return for fifty rubles a month, the subsistence minimum. He was now faced with an unforeseen expense. One way of taking care of it would be to write a story for another review, but this would interfere with his work on *Netochka Nezvanova,* the first two parts of which had recently appeared in *Fatherland Notes.* It was essential to keep at it so that at least the first six parts could appear in successive issues. Besides, he wasn't writing for money only. "I love the novel. . . . It's more precious to me than the whole of *Fatherland Notes.* I wouldn't spoil it for one thousand rubles a signature," he declared roundly.

The point of this outburst was that he wanted one hundred rubles at once. Let it be considered an advance on the third and fourth parts of *Netochka*—still unwritten—the remainder of the sum that will be coming to him for those two parts to go toward the amortization of his debt. He promises to deliver the third part of the novel by the fifteenth of February. He must have the money, though he knows that to accept it is against his own interest, since it prolongs his slavery, and furthermore, after all that has passed between him and Krayevsky, is indecent.

Dostoevsky received the hundred rubles that he had begged for. Not that he delivered the third part of the novel by the middle of February, as promised. He was only just finishing it by the end of March. He was then in fearful straits, and wrote again to Krayevsky, begging abjectly for ten rubles so as to throw a sop to his landlady, whom he had not paid for two months. On the last day of March he was telling the editor without a trace of compunction that he hadn't turned in the third part of the novel earlier because he had spent a month trying to write a story that would bring him an additional fifty rubles. He hadn't succeeded: in fact, he had only acquired a headache and ruined nerves, in addition to three magnificent subjects for big novels. Krayevsky must have felt that he had hold of an author who, whatever else was lacking, had all the reputed irresponsibility of genius.

Without taking a moment's rest, Dostoevsky insists, he is now plugging away at part four. It can't be delivered before April 8. But how can he go on writing at all? When he accepted the money in February, he swore to himself that he would never take another advance. But he can't help himself. Easter is only three days off. The remittance that should have reached him from relatives in Moscow will only arrive after the holiday. This is one of the two periods in the year when creditors refuse to be put off. "I will come to you on Saturday," he announces. "For God's sake don't send me away without a hundred rubles. I'll never ask another kopeck of you. My brother is my witness. Ask him." If he doesn't get the money, Krayevsky will have no further installments of the novel to offer his readers, for Dostoevsky will have to turn his hand to something that will bring an immediate return. After seven years of living on credit he is at the end of his tether. He must put a stop to this system of working off debts. He still remembers Good Friday of the previous year when, in addition to everything else, he had to prepare against the arrival of his brother's family. He can't face it again: he'll have cholera. And what of literature them?

Krayevsky did not send him away without the hundred rubles, but before the date set for the delivery of the fourth and fifth parts he was writing to the editor again. This time he needs only fifteen rubles. He is fighting his small creditors as Laocoön fought the serpents. The fourth part of the novel, which he has not yet delivered, he promises a second time for the middle of April. But he must have fifteen rubles. Only fifteen rubles. "What are fifteen rubles to you? But for me they're a great deal. For a week I've been without a groat. Literally nothing. If you only knew to what I've been reduced. It's shameful to write about it. And what's the use? Isn't it disgraceful," he adds, with something between humor and pathos, "that the contributors to *Fatherland Notes* should be so destitute?" Whether or not he got the fifteen rubles is not known, but Krayevsky never received the fourth part of the novel.

# ( IV )

On the twenty-second of April, Dostoevsky was on his way to the usual gathering at Petrashevsky's. It was an unseasonably warm evening. Drenched to the skin by a sudden shower, he stopped off at Yanovsky's to change his clothes and borrow fare for a cab. The doctor's pockets were as bare as the proverbial cupboard and the drawer with the loan fund held only large bills. Yanovsky, rather than see his friend go out into the rain on foot, persuaded him to draw on the alms box. Dostoevsky took six five-kopeck pieces and let. He never paid back the money. The following morning he was roused out of his first sleep—he had come home in the small hours after stopping off at another friend's—arrested, and committed to prison in the Fortress of Peter and Paul.

# 7

## PRISON

SUDDENLY the hand of that sternest of fathers—the Czar—was heavily upon him. He had sinned against him, and here was retribution. He was roughly pulled out of his familiar, if harassing, existence and thrust into a vacuum. He was stripped of his clothes, his books, his manuscripts, his very name. This Number Seven, this thing in the filthy gray prison gown and felt slippers, locked up alone in an ill-lighted cell, treated by the silent guards and the examining magistrates as a creature set apart from men by the unnatural ways of the criminal—was he not a terrifying stranger tenanting the body of Fyodor Dostoevsky? But what nonsense! Come, he must get a grip on himself. If only he were writing, this nightmare would lift.

But writing was not to be thought of—he was not allowed paper and pen. The first days were particularly hard. Except for the few visits of the guards—they would bring him his meal of watery soup and boiled meat heavily seasoned to disguise its age —there was nothing to divert him. No human voice reached him, indeed no sound, save the grating creak of keys in locks and perhaps the muffled chime of the cathedral clock measuring off his hours.

What, after all, were the charges against him? What penalty

might he expect? He did not know. He could perhaps reason himself into something like courage in the daytime, particularly if the upper part of the high window—the lower panes were chalked to opacity—showed a blue patch of sky. Yes, he had listened to wild talk against the constituted authorities, the established order, the Czar himself, against property, the laws, the family, against God and the Savior—he had contributed to it himself. But he was a writer, not a conspirator, and at heart a Christian and a patriot. Yet there were other times when everything looked black. At nine o'clock lights were put out, and as he lay on his straw pallet in an agony of sleeplessness for what seemed interminable hours he must have touched panic. He had been reading forbidden books. He had been associating with hotheads. He had read Belinsky's letter at gatherings more than once and had it passed on to be copied. Of course, they were bound to find out about his part in setting up the secret press. He was without question a criminal.

The present was empty. The future did not bear thinking of. His mind naturally turned to the past, though that too was dangerous ground for a man in his situation. Only a few days ago he had been running about, trying to get a few rubles from Krayevsky—trying to squeeze blood out of a stone—trying to keep on his feet in spite of wretched health, trying to get on with *Netochka Nezvanova,* and all the while feeling at the end of his rope. And then came the night that had changed everything and made all that preceded it seem almost a lost paradise.

It was four o'clock in the morning when he had been awakened by the clank of a saber and a soft, friendly "Get up, sir!" The weapon belonged to an awkward gendarme stationed at the door, the gentle voice was that of a major of the gendarmerie. In the uncertain light Dostoevsky also made out the figure of a police captain with superb sidewhiskers. While he dressed himself with unsteady fingers, the two men searched his room, looking over all his books and papers. The police captain went so far as to rake over the cold ashes in the grate with Dostoevsky's pipe, and had the gendarme climb to the top of the stove to see if anything forbidden was concealed there. Noticing a bent silver coin on the table, he eyed it suspiciously and ended by placing it with the books and papers that they were confiscating. The last things that struck Dostoevsky as he left his disordered room were the scared face of his landlady and the stupid solemn look in the eye of his servant, frightened but also impressed with the importance of the proceedings. Then there was the trip through the morning streets, and the headquarters of the political police near the Summer Garden. The doors of the detention room kept opening to admit more sleepy-eyed prisoners under the escort of men in blue uniforms. Before the morning was over nearly two score people had been rounded up. Among them Dostoevsky was astonished to encounter his irreproachable brother Andrey, who had been arrested by mistake. One literal-minded gendarme brought along with his captive the woman found in that gentleman's bed. Most of the men knew each other, and the day dragged on not too disagreeably, what with the companionship and the fine dinner capped by good cigars.

It was late in the evening when Dostoevsky made the long trip across the Neva to the Fortress of Saints Peter and Paul. In the guardroom he changed to prisoner's clothes and then crossed the little drawbridge connecting the main fortificaion with the Alexis Ravelin. Excitement had delayed the fatigue of a sleepless night, and anxiety waited until he had entered the squat old prison, walked through a dark vaulted passage and down a half-lighted corridor to find himself in this shadowy, bare, ill-smelling cell. Rumor had it that men left this northern Bastille either for the grave or the insane asylum.

At the end of a fortnight he was summoned to appear before the investigating commission that was at work examining papers and grilling the prisoners. He was interrogated about his education, income, personal contacts. Four weeks passed before he had another hearing. In addition to being examined orally he was given pen and paper and requested to make a general deposition and to answer specific questions in writing.

In his affidavits he admits having gone to Petrashevsky's on an occasional Friday. But he asks: "Who has seen my soul? Who has measured the degree of perfidy, wickedness, and rebelliousness of which I am accused?" If he made a speech once or twice, it was not on a political subject. Perhaps he did sometimes express himself with excessive heat, but that was momentary. Not that free and frank discussion, within limits, can displease the authorities. His own reputation is that of an uncommunicative person. He has few friends and little leisure for them.

Like everyone else, he writes, he talked about such things as censorship at home, the course of events in Western Europe. A breathtaking drama is unfolding there, an age-old order is breaking up. Was it a criminal offense to have felt concern about what is happening in the land that gave Russia its culture? The crisis in France is perhaps an historic necessity and may lead to happier times. That makes him no enemy of autocracy. "There never was anything more absurd to me," he declares, "than the idea of a republican régime in Russia. . . . All the good things in Russia since Peter the Great have come from the Throne. . . ." As for censorship, no one who loves literature can avoid discussing it. The differences between the writer and the censor are the result of misunderstanding, and all he ever said on the subject was in an effort to bring the two together. What was the use of having given him an education if he is denied the right to have opinions of his own?

Yes, he read aloud Belinsky's letter, but he also read Gogol's reply. And not by so much as intonation or gesture did he indicate his own bias. Indeed, he is definitely out of sympathy with Belinsky's ideas. That letter is too bizarre, too soaked in gall, too full of wild assertions to lead anyone astray. It is obviously the product of a mind embittered and distorted by illness. He read it partly because it is something of a literary document, partly to clear himself of the suspicion that he still bore a grudge against this late friend with whom he had quarreled. Besides, he owed respect to a man who had admirable qualities and was remarkable for his time. He admits, however, that he had made a mistake in reading the letter. As regards the mad suggestion for lithographing subversive pamphlets, made by Filippov—a lovable youth, but so hot-tempered and impetuous—it was because of his, Dostoevsky's, dissuading voice that the proposal had been rejected.

He was not, he points out, intimate with Petrashevsky and knew nothing of any plans he may have had. The Fridays were informal gatherings. The group lacked unanimity, he wrote, there was constant wrangling, no three men could agree on anything. If the chatter sometimes exceeded the bounds of propriety, it was because the guests felt that they were among friends, *en famille* as it were. At all events, he thought Petrashevsky was a ridiculous rather than a dangerous character. Consider: he was an ardent Fourierist, and where? In Petersburg! Now Fourierism is a "peaceful system that bewitches the soul with its elegance, captivates the heart with Fourier's love of mankind, and amazes the mind with its simplicity." It does not infringe upon government, property, religion, the family. In France it may prove harmful, for there the starving proletarians in their desperation grasp at any means and are ready to use it as a banner. But "one need walk no more than twenty paces in a Petersburg street to realize that on Russian soil Fourierism can exist only in the pages of an uncut book or in a soft, gentle, dreamy soul." For his own part, he is devoted to the study of history and economics, and so he has investigated socialism in all its ramifications, but he has never been a socialist. Not that he can wholly condemn it. It is a false science, like alchemy, but just as out of alchemy issued chemistry, so out of socialism there may arise for the common good "something harmonious, rational, and beneficent."

It is clear that Dostoevsky did not recant and abjectly plead for mercy as did so many of his fellow prisoners. Nor did he try to shift the blame for what he had said or done to other shoulders. That he was not quite candid and that he concealed certain facts is equally plain. He was obviously at pains to represent the whole affair as a matter of venial indiscretions and, by the same token, to minimize his own guilt and that of his comrades. Many years later, long after he had repudiated his radicalism as youthful folly, he pictured the "Petrashevists," including himself, as far from impetuous but well-meaning innocents.

The investigating commission sat through the summer months, the official wheels grinding out in leisurely fashion what the government was pleased to call justice. Meanwhile, Dostoevsky lay in prison. There were moments when he felt that he had never known any other life and did not look forward to any other. Time, here as elsewhere, flowed unevenly. He marked off each day as it passed on an improvised calendar, but the end of the trial seemed as unimportant as it was remote. His appetite was poor, he was living on castor oil, sleeping about five hours a night, waking repeatedly, and suffering from abominable dreams. He had spells of dizziness when the floor swayed under his feet; he suffered from throat spasms again, and from a variety of pains and aches. Yet the horrors of the first weeks abated. In some ways life here was not unlike what it was outside. He even managed to borrow ten rubles. A few letters from Mikhail reached him. In July he was permitted paper and pen and so was able to write to his brother. He could unburden himself of the stories that he had composed and that he had had to keep locked up in his head. This was a great relief, but in the absence of diversions, the strain persisted. If only he had books! The prison library held a few edifying tracts that could offer no distraction. And the confirmed city-dweller longed for the sight of green leaves.

In August he was permitted a short daily walk in the prison courtyard. Trees grew there, unhealthy-looking things, shaded as they were by prison walls, but they were green, and they reminded him of the park at the engineering school and of the visits to Mikhail in Reval when early summer was crowding the squares with green. The same month he was allowed a candle at night. Occasionally Mikhail managed to smuggle in to him money and cigarettes. And then books drifted in—Schiller, Shakespeare, the Bible, and even magazines. In the May issue of *Fatherland Notes* he found the last installment of *Netochka* that he had sent to Krayevsky in those almost unimaginable days before his arrest. It was unsigned: the authorities could not allow the name of a political prisoner to appear in print, but at least his story was there. Could he ever again take up the thread of the unfinished tale?

# ( II )

The investigating commission discovered nothing aside from the fact that there had been meetings at Petrashevsky's and elsewhere at which "pernicious" opinions and doctrines, especially Fourier's system, were freely aired and subversive manuscripts read. Both Speshnyov and Filippov confessed that they had tried to set up an illegal printing press, but the authorities failed to find any trace of the press. It had been spirited away from Mordvinov's quarters after his arrest and presumably disposed of. No evidence was discovered of the existence of any organized secret society or of any attempts at revolutionary propaganda or action. At worst the whole affair was a "conspiracy of ideas." Nevertheless the high commission recommended that twenty-eight of the prisoners be court-martialed. Dostoevsky was among them, as one of "the most important" culprits. Accordingly, the Emperor appointed a special tribunal presided over by a general. It was then the end of September.

Dostoevsky was brought before the judges and asked if he

had any statement to make. This is what he wrote: "I have never acted against the government with malice prepense. What I did was done without premeditation and much, so to say, inadvertently, as, for example, the reading of Belinsky's letter. If I ever spoke freely, it was only in the circle of my close intimates, who were in a position to understand me and knew in what sense my words were intended. But I always avoided disseminating my doubts."

Followed more weeks and months of solitary confinement. He anticipated the cold season with dread. A slit of bright sky seemed a guarantee of cheerfulness and health. The coming of winter aggravated his aches and pains. For two and a half months he was forbidden either to send or receive a letter. His purely cerebral existence, without impressions from the outside to feed his mind, was beginning to tell on him. He had the sensations of a man sitting in a chamber from which the air was being pumped. He was living entirely in his head, and his writing was squeezing the last juices out of him. And yet, strangely enough, he knew that at bottom all was well with him. Beneath the surface worries which fretted him there ran a strong undercurrent of contentment. He was conscious of an inexhaustible store of vitality. He was at peace with himself and the world. Eventually he came to believe that his arrest had saved him from insanity. His curious serenity fits in with the theory that he unconsciously accepted this punishment as an atonement he had long craved. Here was assuagement for any sense of guilt that may have been lurking in some subterranean corner of his mind, disturbing gravely both his bodily well-being and his mental poise.

He did not know that the court, after six weeks of deliberation, had condemned him, along with fourteen others, to capital punishment by shooting. In due time the verdicts were reviewed by the highest judicial body, known as the Auditoriat General. These jurists opined that since, in political crimes, no distinction was made between ringleader and follower, fully twenty-one of the twenty-three prisoners were legally liable to the supreme punishment. In view of the prisoners' youth, however, their repentance, and the fact that they had not translated their designs into action, the high judiciary recommended to the monarch that terms of hard labor of varying length be substituted for the death sentence. In the hierarchy of guilt Dostoevsky occupied the tenth place, the list being topped by Petrashevsky, who received a life term.

Dostoevsky's sentence was to be eight years of hard labor in a Siberian fortress and the loss of all civil rights and privileges. The counts against him were as follows: participation in criminal designs, the circulation of a private letter full of insolent expressions against the Orthodox Church and the Supreme Power, and the attempt to circulate writings against the government by means of homemade lithography. The part he had played in setting up the secret press remained unknown to the authorities.

A summary of the report drawn up by the Auditoriat General was submitted to the Emperor on December 19. The fate of the prisoners was now in the hands of Nicholas. He decided not to treat them quite as harshly as he had the Decembrists, whose abortive rebellion he had so ruthlessly crushed on his ascension to the throne. He confirmed the commutation of the death sentences, and in some cases reduced the term of hard labor. Opposite the paragraph relating to Dostoevsky he wrote: "Four years [of penal servitude] and then into the ranks with him." The severity of the sentences could be accounted for only by the hysteria which seized the Russian government as it watched the thrones of Europe rock in the revolutions of 1848.

The Emperor had a weakness for theatrical effects, in addition to immense self-righteousness. He gave orders that the death sentence should be announced to the prisoners in a public place in the presence of the populace and the troops, and that only after the men had gone through all the preparations for their execution were they to be informed at the last moment that the Czar in his ineffable charity had made them a present of their lives.

# ( III )

On the morning of December 22 Dostoevsky was aroused before daybreak. Something unusual was going on in the prison. He was given the clothes he had worn when he was arrested eight months earlier, except that he was handed warm socks, and thus scantily protected against Christmas weather he was placed with a guard in a closed coach. There were more coaches containing other prisoners, and when they started on their way, each vehicle was escorted by mounted gendarmes with sabers drawn. From

the window he could see crowds of people walking in the same
direction. He did not know where he was being taken. Though
they went at a trot, the trip of three or four miles seemed endless. When he alighted, it was into freshly fallen snow. Just
above the horizon a huge red ball was glowing dimly through
the morning mists. The biting air seemed to pierce through his
light clothing to his bones. Yet it was intoxicating. Glancing
eagerly about, he found himself in a familiar place—Semyonov
Square, with its orange barracks and the cupolas of the cathedral
veiled in haze. But the parade ground had an unusual look. It
wasn't merely the crowds nor yet the troops lined up in square
formation. It was that structure right in front of him, a railed
platform, draped in black, its three sides framed by soldiers.
Dostoevsky did not know that the height of the platform, like
the speed of the horses that had brought him there and every
other detail of the drama that was to follow, had been determined by the authorities with the approval of the Emperor.

More coaches kept arriving, bringing more men, some of them
total strangers to him. Dostoevsky shook hands with the fellow
prisoners whom he knew, exchanged a few words with them,
stared at their terribly changed, emaciated, bearded faces. The
general who seemed to be master of ceremonies put an abrupt
end to these exchanges and had them line up. Then a priest, in
the vestments appropriate to a funeral and carrying the cross
and the Gospels, approached the prisoners and bade them follow him. They tramped after him in the deep snow, past the
long line of troops, which had been chosen from regiments in
which some of the prisoners had served as officers. Dostoevsky
walked briskly. The men ascended the scaffold. Here they were
rearranged and stood in two unequal rows. In a whisper—they
were forbidden to speak—Dostoevsky told his neighbor the plot
of a story he had written in prison. He was now in that state of
calm that extreme nervous tension sometimes produces.

Answering the short command "Present arms!" came the re-
verberant clanking of rifles. A court clerk stepped forward and
stood between the rows of prisoners. They were ordered to bare
their heads. Calling on each of the men by name, the clerk read
off the verdicts. As he mumbled in the fashion peculiar to his
kind, much of what he said was lost on his hearers, but not the
identical phrase which recurred at the end of each verdict. Dostoevsky heard it like a refrain: "Petrashevsky . . . condemned
to capital punishment by shooting." Other names were called,

and finally, like the name of some stranger, his own: Fyodor Mikhailovich Dostoevsky. The mumbling went on as before and ended as before, with the incredible words: "condemned to capital punishment by shooting."

The reading lasted an unconscionable time. In his light clothes, his head uncovered, he shuddered with cold. Suddenly the sun, which had been hovering behind the mists, broke through, and somehow it came over him that they were not going to be executed. He said so to Durov, who was standing beside him. But Durov pointed out a cart covered with a mat which hid, he thought, their coffins.

The clerk finished his reading. With a kind of vacant intensity Dostoevsky watched his gestures as he carefully folded up his paper and shoved it into his side pocket. The clerk's place was taken by the priest. Choosing as his text St. Paul's judgment "The wages of sin is death," he preached briefly to the condemned. In a voice that shook he told them that with bodily death all was not over and that through faith and repentance they would inherit life eternal. He urged them to confess their sins and make their peace with God. Only one man was shriven. Dostoevsky, with the others, knelt to kiss the cross. One guesses that he did so like the condemned criminal in *The Idiot,* who pressed his lips to the cross greedily, as though in a hurry to possess himself of something he might need badly. With that act he knew himself abandoned by all men, beyond help, alone.

The gold-laced master of ceremonies dismissed the priest, who was lingering, saying abruptly: "There is nothing further for you to do here, Father." Therewith the guards helped the condemned perform their last toilette: to remove their outer clothing and get into hooded white linen shirts with long sleeves —their shrouds. Petrashevsky, who could still joke, asked: "How do we look in this attire?" And then, in silence, he and two of the others were led away from the scaffold to three gray posts and bound to them. They faced a firing squad of fifteen soldiers standing fifteen paces off.

For ten, for twenty, perhaps for forty minutes—how could he tell?—Dostoevsky had now been living with the thought, the excruciating certainty, that he was about to die. It seemed impossible that these staring thousands, their faces red blurs in the frost, their eyes fixed upon the condemned, would go on living, while he must cease to exist, and now. He was the sixth. He must go with the next lot. So soon?

"Someone condemned to death," reflects Raskolnikov in *Crime and Punishment,* "says or thinks, an hour before his death, that if he had to live somewhere on a height, on a rock, and on a ledge so narrow that he had only room to stand, and around him, abysses, the ocean, everlasting darkness, everlasting solitude, everlasting tempest—if he had to remain standing on a square yard of space all his life, a thousand years, eternity, it were better to live so than to die at once! Only to live, to live, and to live! To live, no matter how!" In *The Iidiot* the emotions of a condemned man just before his execution are described in detail. With five minutes left, he feels that there is an infinity ahead of him, that with so much intervening time there is no need yet to think of the final moment. He sets aside time for a last farewell to his comrades: two minutes; he allots a period to his last thoughts: two minutes; the remaining minute is for looking about him the last time. As he says good-bye to one of his comrades he asks him a trivial question and is deeply concerned over the answer. The two minutes come that he set apart for thinking to himself. "He knew beforehand what he would think about. He wanted to realize as quickly and clearly as possible how it could be that now he existed and was living and in three minutes he would be *something*—someone, or something. But who? Where? He meant to decide all that in these two minutes! Not far off there was a church, and the gilt cupola was glittering in the bright sunshine. He remembered that he stared with terrible persistency at that cupola and the rays flashing from it; he could not tear himself away from the rays. It seemed to him that those rays were his new nature, and that in three minutes he would somehow merge with them. . . . The uncertainty and feeling of aversion to that new thing which would be and was coming at once was frightful." But there was a more dreadful sensation. He was tortured by the thought of what life would be if it were given back to him, of the eternity that would stretch out before him, of all that he would pack into it, of the fullness with which he would live it. At last the thought made him so furious that he wished they would shoot him at once.

Inevitably one imagines that Dostoevsky was here transcribing emotions that he had lived through. At the last a feeling of utter indifference came over him. He was not sorry to die. Perhaps the sheer intensity of his experience brought him momentarily to the point of emotional exhaustion. Everything seemed insignificant beside the terrible moment of transition to the unknown, to darkness. He embraced Pleshcheyev and Durov. There was momentary comfort in the warm contact. He had some five minutes more to live. He thought achingly of Mikhail.

Meanwhile the men tied to the posts had their hoods shoved over their eyes. Dostoevsky watched them with a kind of composure. A sense of the inevitability of the end blunted his agony. The command rang out smartly: "Ready. Aim!" Fifteen rifles swung into position. There was a rumble of drums like doom. But at the sound the rifles were tilted upward, the men at the posts were unloosed, a government courier leapt from his carriage with a paper in his hand. The terrible comedy was over. It was a reprieve.

Capital punishment was commuted to terms of hard labor in Siberia. At the news two of the men threw themselves on their knees in prayer, one of them crying out: "The good Czar! Long live our Czar!" Grigoryev, who had just been unloosed from the posts, was raving. One man said bitterly: "It would have been better if they had shot us." Several others felt so too—the blow to their human dignity implied in this sham execution was crushing. Dostoevsky was incapable of either joy or indignation. The stupor of indifference still held him. He had lived through something so terrible that now nothing mattered.

Two men in bright kaftans came forward and broke a sword over the head of each of the prisoners who was of the nobility, in token of the loss of the rights and privileges pertaining to their rank. Dostoevsky knelt with the others to suffer the disgrace. This over, the guards busied themselves with the convicts. They aided the men in removing their shrouds—Dostoevsky kept his as a souvenir—and gave each a convict's cap, a stinking sheepskin coat, and a pair of felt boots. In the biting cold the warm clothing was a godsend. Petrashevsky was clapped into irons right there on the platform with his own help, and after, stepping awkwardly in his shackles, he had embraced and kissed every one of his comrades, was sent off directly on his long journey to Siberia. The rest were taken back to prison. When Dostoevsky found himself again in his cell, whole and alive, he was at last able to surrender himself to the joy of resurrection. He strode back and forth, now and then actually breaking into song.

# ( IV )

So this was what he had to face—four years of hard labor in Siberia. And then, for an indefinite period, the black lot of a soldier in the ranks. But he would not look so far ahead. The main thing was that he was alive, a human being among his kind. Life was a gift, a single moment could be like the widow woman's cruse. He felt conscious of an untapped reservoir of spiritual energy. It fairly seethed in him. Not to be brutalized, to remain a human being under the most degrading circumstances—he must stick to that now. He had come to an end, but that meant actually a beginning. He would be reborn. The head that had been busy with ideas and images, that head was off his shoulders. To love, to suffer, to pity, to remember—wasn't that enough? The hopes of youth were torn out of his heart. He was done with writing. But was he really? Perhaps when he had served his term there would be a chance for it yet. But for years the images that he had conceived and nourished would either fade out of his mind or, dying there, fill him with the poisons of decay. Yes, he will go under if he can't write. And even if his spirit holds out, won't his body go to pieces under the strain? No matter! He had been about to die: he was alive. What had he to fear?

He poured out his heart thus to Mikhail in a letter that he wrote the day of the reprieve, after permission to see his brother was refused. He charged him to live quietly, with prudence and foresight. His commissions were few. Mikhail would probably receive his books and papers, the draft of a play and of a novel and the manuscript of *A Fairy Tale for Children*—all he had written in prison. He should make certain to return to the old lady Maikov her own copy of her late son's book, which Dostoevsky had borrowed. Mikhail would find the right words in which to give that old friend his last greeting. He should press the hands of the young Maikovs, of the good Yanovsky, kiss brother Kolya, send a word to Andrey, to their sisters, to Uncle and Aunt. He assured him that there was no bitterness in his heart, and that all he wanted was to be able to embrace some one of his own people.

This wish was finally granted him. He was allowed to see his brother two days later, a few hours before his departure for Siberia. It was Christmas Eve. With Durov he was taken to the commandant's house, where the investigating commission and the court-martial had held their sittings. In a large room on the ground floor, lighted dimly by a single lamp, he saw a familiar figure. Dostoevsky was wearing a sheepskin coat and felt boots in readiness for his long journey. Of the two brothers, it was the convict who was the calmer and it was his part to comfort the one who remained at home.

The farewells were over quickly and Dostoevsky went back to his cell. Shortly afterward he left it again for the last time. It was precisely midnight, the hour that ushered in the birthday of his Savior, when he was clamped into irons. They weighed ten pounds and made it hard for him to walk. It was usual for convicts to tramp the long trail to Siberia. Dostoevsky, with his comrades, was spared this ordeal. He left the fortress seated beside a gendarme in an open sleigh. There were two more sleighs, holding Durov and another convict, with a courier leading the way.

It was mild and clear, and the air must have throbbed with the booming of innumerable church bells. The holy night was upon Petersburg. Dostoevsky's heart was heavy; small anxieties pricked him. But the fresh air and the swift soft movement were easing the aches and longings. A kind of calm elation filled him. He looked with steady intentness at the houses that he knew by heart, each lit for the holiday, at the streets that were part of the life that he was leaving behind: they were familiar and strangely different. He said a mute good-bye to each. His way lay past Mikhail's lodgings and Krayevsky's apartment. Behind those gaily lighted windows were Mikhail's wife and children—they had been invited, his brother had told him, to the Christmas party. His heart was cruelly squeezed as the sleigh glided past the house. Now it was out of sight.

# 8

## CONFESSIONS

SUPPOSE the reprieve to have arrived too late and Dostoevsky to have been cut off from life at the age of twenty-eight. He would then have been known as a minor writer, having to his credit a handful of stories, two novelettes, and an unfinished full-length novel—the fruit of half a dozen years of feverish labors. These early writings deserve attention, not only because they hold intimations of his later achievements, but also in their own right.

The influences that helped to shape the young Dostoevsky's work are fairly clear. Discernible there are traces of Gothic and sentimental foreign fictions of which he was an avid reader. It is harder to find evidence of the eighteenth-century French classics that were among his idols. He may have read Diderot's *Le Neveu de Rameau,* which was in the library of the Petrashevsky circle. He could have known nothing of Hegel's comment on it, to the effect that the immoralist who is its hero has a consciousness "torn to pieces, which is a consciousness of absolute perversity." Lately a Soviet scholar has found resemblances between the nephew in Diderot's dialogue and characters in many works by Dostoevsky, beginning with Polzunkov in the story of that title.

The style and subject matter of his early narratives bear the marked imprint of Amadeus Hoffmann, the Gothic fantast, and of Gogol, the grotesque humorist, both romantic and realist, who ushered in the age of prose that followed Pushkin's death. It should be remembered that at the time Turgenev was the author of some verse and several short stories, while Tolstoy was occupied with the studies and amusements of an undergraduate. In a recent work Donald Fanger has shown that Dostoevsky had a lifelong admiration of Balzac and Dickens. The numerous similarities among certain themes, situations, characters in his fiction and those in the work of the two foreigners were due, we are told, not to mimesis but to affinity. Perhaps subconscious memory, too, contributed to the parallels.

Dostoevsky opened his career with *Poor Folk,* a short novel about a minor official, like the scores of tales, largely the progeny of Gogol's "The Overcoat," which appeared during the forties. Devushkin, a gentle middle-aged copyist in a government office, takes upon himself the role of guardian of a young girl whom he might have married had he been less miserably circumstanced. He is utterly lost when the girl, in her weakness and despair, becomes the bride of a well-to-do, coarse, tight-fisted landowner, able to give her the creature comforts that are beyond the poor clerk's power to provide. George Moore summed up the situation thus: "Makar [Devushkin] is one of life's convicts, Varvara [the girl] is the mouse that comes for crumbs, and the end is the same: a better filled hand is extended to the mouse, and the mouse returns no more to cheer the cell's loneliness." While the book indirectly condemns the social system responsible for the misery portrayed and also calls attention to the "little man's" worth as a human being with a mind of his own, its chief appeal is to the reader's compassion. These pages must have brought tears to the eyes of many of its early readers.

*Poor Folk* lacks the autobiographical cast common to first novels. The hero is not a projection of the author's self, nor is the milieu one that he knew from experience. The characters live the life not of the senses but of the sentiments. This is a work of pathos rather than of passion. For a love story it is curiously sexless. The attitude of the poor clerk toward his correspondent—the tale is told in letters—is half avuncular, half maternal. A contemporary reviewer thought he saw in the tale the hand of a young lady.

Dostoevsky followed up *Poor Folk* with a narrative of a totally different cast: *The Double.* Of the two, the second tapped

a deeper level of the author's mind than its predecessor and
is clearly prophetic of his powers. *The Double* is incomparably
the more original piece. It is a study of psychosis. Dostoevsky
was to be occupied with morbid characters all his life. Golyadkin,
the protagonist, is a middle-aged minor official, a rung or two
above Devushkin on the bureaucratic ladder. He has some sav-
ings, rents a tiny flat instead of a corner of a room, as does
the central character of *Poor Folk,* employs a servant. Yet he
is haunted by a paranoid feeling of insecurity. Everywhere he
sees enemies spreading ugly rumors about him, plotting to destroy him "morally." He himself spurns intrigue, always, he
insists, keeping to the straight path. On guard, he is prone to
efface himself, to pretend that he is someone else looking
strangely like him. He is uncertain of his own identity. Repeatedly he does the opposite of what he has decided to do, as
if compelled by an outside force. He calls himself "an old rag,"
which does not deter him from claiming to be as good as the
next man. "Everyone ought to be satisfied with his position,"
he opines, but as a matter of fact he is not without giddy
ambitions. The very day that the story opens he tries to crash
a magnificent dinner party given by a high-ranking official to
mark the birthday of Clara, his nubile daughter. Perhaps Golyadkin thinks of himself as her suitor. Not that he is in love;
he regards a wife as merely a conventional appurtenance. Refused admission, he steals into the ballroom, only to be uncere-
moniously ejected.

After this catastrophe he rushes home through a blizzard in
the dead of night. "He looks like a man wishing to hide from
himself, to run away from himself, as it were." On the way he
encounters his double, clearly an eerie hallucination of his. R. D.
Laing, a leading British psychiatrist, relates the "double" to
"Golyadkin's own secret intention *not to be himself.*" The following day—the second of the four allotted to the story—the
double materializes, fraudulently manages to insinuate himself
into the good graces of the authentic Golyadkin, and by evening
has become his guest. Forthwith Golyadkin becomes the butt and
victim of the fraud he had befriended, is made game of, cruelly
baited, gulled, wiped the floor with by the impostor. The double
is in many respects the image of what the real Golyadkin wishes
to be: a free and easy fellow, able to ingratiate himself with
his superiors, to toady and fawn, to gambol and frolic, to make
himself liked by all and sundry. Yet at the same time, what with

his unscrupulousness, viciousness, depravity, the usurper is a rascally replica of the protagonist.

Golyadkin comes to believe that the blackguard is the chief tool of his enemies. The impostor seems to have a hand in playing the practical joke which, after many complications, some of them murky, brings the narrative to a close. He receives a letter from Clara to the effect that she loves him ardently, and is resolved to elope with him, at 9 P.M. sharp, from the family residence. He is appalled by the prospect of taking a step which is clearly forbidden by law and which may cost him his berth. No, he will not get involved, he will merely be an onlooker and so remain free from any blame. This is another way of escaping from himself.

Of course, he keeps the tryst. He assures himself, without believing it, that all will be well and slips into the shadow of a woodpile in the yard within sight of the mansion occupied by Clara's family. Then, instead of the love-smitten maiden, the odious double emerges from the house and persuades him to enter the drawing room. It is packed with distinguished guests, each of whom gazes at him with sympathy and unaccountable concern. Overcome by a wave of emotion, he is ready to become reconciled with everyone, even his double, who, strangely, no longer looks like one, although there is still something sinister about him. Golyadkin offers no resistance to being led out of the room—he is scarcely aware of what is happening—and helped, with the double's aid, into a carriage which takes him to a lunatic asylum. Just before he leaves the house he has a momentary hallucination that an endless stream of his doubles is bursting in at every door. He had previously had a dream in which he was endlessly duplicated by exact replicas until the entire capital was chock full of them. One is tempted to read this as a premonition of the nightmare of depersonalization that haunts mankind in our time.

Golyadkin's thoughts and states of mind are conveyed with remarkable understanding and brilliant effect in tongue-tied language. The young author has an uncanny knowledge of the working of the diseased psyche. The theme of a man victimized by his double may have been suggested to him by his reading. Yet introspection surely played a vital part in his treatment of the subject. He spoke of the story as "a confession." It has been indicated that in his estimate of it Dostoevsky vacillated between enthusiasm and disparagement. At heart he knew that in this

novelette he had hit on a subject of signal originality and importance. After his return from Siberia he planned to revise it.
He did not carry out his intention, but variations of the theme
run through his mature work.

Psychopathology reappears in "Mr. Prokharchin," his next
story. It is a lugubrious, phantasmagorical piece, couched in
stuttering, unintelligible language. The character around whom
it revolves is a petty clerk, an utterly insignificant, utterly lonely
creature. Ostensibly he owns nothing but a chest with a German
lock. It contains only rags, but his dirty mattress is stuffed with
coin. His hoarding grows out of a morbid fear of want, money
being doubly precious to him as a crutch for his tottering ego.
He is a victim of other fears. Malicious waggery on the part of
his fellow roomers throws him into a panic about the little
security that he has. He falls into a delirium, his reason goes,
and death follows his mental breakdown. The clink of coin is
seldom absent from Dostoevsky's tales. As he was constantly
plagued by the need of money, so too he was haunted by the
idea of its peculiar power, here for the first time a dominant
note.

Shortly after the completion of "Mr. Prokharchin" Dostoevsky, as will be recalled, attempted a new story, which he called
"The Shaved Whiskers," but gave it up in disgust as a mere
repetition of what he had previously done. In the spring of 1847
he tried his hand at journalism, publishing four feuilletons in
the daily *Sanktpeterburgskie vedomosti* (*St. Petersburg Bulletins*). The genre, then flourishing in France, was becoming
popular in Russia. What attracted him to this type of writing
was its informal, intimate tone, its easy freedoms, the opportunities it offered for setting down random opinions, observations, fantasies. He was to go back to it in later years, enlarging its scope.

# ( II )

When he returned to fiction, it was to start on a new tack. His
next work, "The Landlady," is, like *The Double,* an experimental
piece, quite different from his previous writing in its departure
from the realistic approach. It is a tale abounding in murder,

madness, mystery, and couched in an affected style. Ordynov, a young recluse who lives with his books and his dreams, is drawn out of his self-communings by a weird amorous adventure. Katerina, the ravishing beauty who inspires his ecstasies, is under the powerful spell of an evil old man of Tartar stock who is her father or her husband, perhaps both. He is gifted with occult powers and subject to epileptic seizures. She too has strange fits, caused by her belief that she is responsible for the death of her parents. As for Ordynov, he passes from one sinking spell to another. Is the wild story of her life, as she relates it to the half-delirious young man, his dream or the fantasy of a madwoman? Is the Tartar her dead mother's quondam lover and her father's assassin, as she indicates? Did he really try to shoot Ordynov and did Ordynov actually attempt to knife the old man? The author does not answer these questions. The story concludes with the parting of the young people. Katerina apparently decides that Ordynov is a feeble reed and chooses to stay with the old man. Ordynov is abruptly thrust back into the state of brooding in which he was first found. He sinks into a deeper shadow from which he vainly seeks escape in prayer.

Belinsky said, truly, that the story was "a monstrosity" and that every word in it was false, stilted, artificial. In this strange narrative, however, one finds here and there a hint of power, a token of startling insight. There is something at once original and authentic in the description of Ordynov's delirium. One is brought up short by the girl's confession that at bottom she cherishes her shame—an attitude of which more will be heard later—and by the old man's casual remark: "Give freedom to a weak man, and he himself will tie it up and bring it back." This is an idea to which Dostoevsky will return.

The author was shrewd enough to recognize that the Gothic features in "The Landlady" were not what the critics admired. His next story, "Polzunkov," is a character study of a man who habitually makes a clown of himself in order to borrow a few rubles from the people he amuses. At the same time he feels shame for those from whom he calls forth this ugly laughter and snatches eagerly at any fig leaf that will cover his moral nakedness. His effort, while making a butt of himself, to win a grain of respect from those who jeer at him, is a disturbing and pathetic spectacle. He may have been modeled on the drunkard who haunted the Petersburg suburb in which Dostoevsky spent the summer of 1847. When other sources failed, the wretch would canvass the cottages, offering to flog himself for a consideration. Dostoevsky took up a collection for him.

In the tale that followed, "A Faint Heart," the main character is once more a humble copying clerk, a young man with a gentle spirit and a sad flaw in his make-up. Feeling himself a nonentity, he is literally overwhelmed with gratitude for what he conceives to be undeserved good fortune and by his inability to express that gratitude. His mind breaks under the strain, not of suffering, but of happiness.

"An Honest Thief," the story which appeared next, deals with a man of the people. The tale is told by a veteran who has turned tailor to support himself in his old age. It has to do with a drunken derelict whom the tailor has taken in and allowed to live on his charity. The wretch repays this kindness by stealing a pair of riding breeches his benefactor has made for a customer, and does not confess until remorse brings him literally to his deathbed. Here is another broken soul that has no power to mend itself. In the original version the narrator appends a moral to the tale: that the death of the poor devil attested to the human dignity he had all but forfeited by his crime, and that vice is not a native element in human nature. Dostoevsky wisely omitted this postscript in the later editions of the well-rounded and moving story. As for its successor, "A Christmas Tree and a Wedding," which exposes the ugly character of a schemer who manages to marry an heiress young enough to be his daughter, one might be inclined to neglect it altogether as a bagatelle were it not that these few pages carry, however lightly, the suggestion of that sexual interest in a child on the part of an adult which recurs not infrequently in the novelist's mature writings.

"White Nights," the last of his early stories, if one excepts the piece he wrote in prison, presents a situation similar to that detailed in "The Landlady." The difference is that here the action is within the range of the usual and the characters are within the range of the normal. The hero, as in the other story, is a daydreamer, unfitted for life, who falls in love with Nastenka, only to lose her and retire again into himself. During the brief period of his happiness it is as though the mists of fantasy have melted from before his eyes and he feels himself at last a man among men. The ghost, having as it were drunk of human passion, is about to take on flesh. But no! The girl is beginning to reciprocate his feelings, yet she loves another. He has left for Moscow in the hope of improving his circumstances so that he can marry her. He had solemnly promised to return exactly one year after their parting. Now the year is over and she knows that he has been back in town for three days but has neither shown himself nor written to her. The daydreamer, instead of pressing his own suit, goes out of his way to help his rival. The laggard lover appears and carries Nastenka off. What had had the heat and color of reality proves a mirage. The experience leaves the young man sadder but not bitter, and the last note is one of gentle resignation that is in key with the wistful tone of the entire story.

# ( III )

If that winter morning on Semyonov Square had been Dostoevsky's last, we should have had no full-length novel from his pen but only the torso of one, the ill-fated *Netochka Nezvanova*. He began to hatch the plan for a big novel soon after the publication of *The Double*. Before long he was speaking of a work in four parts that was ripe in his mind and that he expected to write in Italy. It gave him no rest. The final issue of *Fatherland Notes* for 1846 carried an announcement that "*Netochka Nezvanova*, a novel by Dostoevsky," would run in the magazine the nex year, and indeed he obligated himself to deliver the first installment on January 5, 1847. It did not materialize, and the final issue for that year again contained a notice promising it to the subcribers the following year. The first installment, which included two parts, did not appear until 1849, and at the time of his arrest he was up to his neck in the writing of another installment. The third part appeared without his signature while he was in prison awaiting sentence and he read it in his cell with some misgivings, since he had not seen it through the press. There were to be at least three more parts but, presumably since too much had happened to him in the interim, when he returned to literature he did not take up the work where he had been forced to drop it. Nevertheless, he included a revised version of the unfinished novel in the two-volume edition of his works issued in 1860. The revision was chiefly a matter of cutting—indeed, an entire episode was omitted from the text.

In *Netochka Nezvanova* Dostoevsky attempted an ambitious work with a complicated plot. It is a loose-jointed affair and even in its abridged form contains three distinct themes. The first is the tragic story of a possessed soul, a violinist with a rare, innate talent who lets it go to waste while clinging to the mad dream that he is the greatest musician in the world. In the end he destroys himself too, dying of "acute insanity" when he discovers that his mania of grandeur is an absurd delusion. The second theme is the childhood of his motherless little step-daughter, Netochka, who is morbidly attached to him and who, after he dies, is adopted by an aristocratic family in which she develops a passionate feeling for the small princess who is the daughter of the house. The third has to do with the consequences of a suspected infidelity on the part of the lady who is tenderly bringing up the waif. Here for the first time Dostoevsky uses a mysterious letter as part of the machinery of the plot. The procedure is clumsy, and in every respect the third part is the weakest.

The tale is chiefly remarkable for the illumination of the emotional and imaginative life of children, its intensity, sensuality, and paradoxical ambivalence. Netochka, as a little girl, loves her stepfather with a strange passion grounded in pity. All her joy is to think of him. She imagines him to be a harassed sufferer, abused by her mother, and accordingly conceives a deep hatred for that unfortunate woman. The child is driven in upon herself, gradually loses contact with reality, and moves in a world of fantasy. Her relation with the proud little princess, like that with her father previously, is in the nature of a love affair having all the tokens of adolescent passion. The little princess, too, adores her own father, has strained relations with her mother, and has a violent affection for Netochka, although this love for some time disguises itself as hatred.

Originally Dostoevsky intended to give Netochka a male counterpart. The passage in which this character was introduced figures only in the text of the novel as published serially. Like Netochka, he is a poor orphan, a crushed, terror-stricken little creature rescued by the prince from a life among hostile strangers. With great difficulty Netochka wins his confidence, and he tells her that at the bottom of his misery is the unbearable thought that he is partly responsible for the death of his parents

—they died within a few days of each other. He confesses to Netochka that out of sheer selfishness he had practically tormented his father and mother to death, but the little girl sees more deeply into the situation. She understands that he really loved his parents, but out of a desire to realize fully their devotion to him he perversely made them suffer on his account. At the same time his confession awakens her to the consciousness of the suffering that she had caused her own mother and arouses in her a like feeling of guilt.

At the outset Dostoevsky had called the novel, as he did *The Double*, "a confession." It is possible that he was unburdening his heart of the tangled emotions that belonged to his own early years. Certainly he could not draw upon observation. While he was writing the story he was living outside a domestic circle and most of his friends were young unmarried men like himself. He saw little of Mikhail's children and had been separated for years from his own small brothers and sisters. It is hard to see how he could have written some of these pages without an extraordinarily clear retrospective view of his own childhood.

*Netochka Nezvanova* reveals such an interest in and understanding of both childhood and early adolescence that it is not surprising to find "The Little Hero," the piece he wrote in prison, dealing with a similar theme. "The Little Hero" is the story of an eleven-year-old boy's first experience of falling in love, an experience which, alike in its raptures and its agonies, held a troubling foretaste of maturity. A wistful note steals into the narrative toward the end, but the setting is a country house where elegant ladies and handsome men are gathered for a festive occasion, and a brightness appropriate to the tale, if unusual with the author and in sharp contrast to his situation when he was writing it, lies on the story like a bloom.

# ( IV )

Looking closely at these stories, one discovers now and again settings and situations that the author knew at first hand. The swollen, gleaming field of the frozen Neva; the black canals with the lean lampposts along the embankments; the Petersburg streets in all seasons and weathers but chiefly at dusk, especially when the granite is wet underfoot and the grimy houses loom bulky and dark; damp, filthy, ill-smelling stairways leading to rooms with sooty green walls which exude a putrid odor—these made the background of his days. It is not implausible that the match in *Poor Folk* had some distant connection with his young sister's marriage to the middle-aged Karepin. Ill health, particularly in the form of a nervous ailment, is the lot of several of his characters, as it was his own. Ordynov, in "The Landlady," who "did not miss a single impression, looked with thoughtful eyes into the faces of passers-by, and watched the characteristic appearance of everything around him"—this *flâneur* walked in Dostoevsky's shoes. The narrator of "White Nights" who knows some houses in Petersburg so intimately that they seem to him almost human is also none other than Dostoevsky. He is said to have walked miles just to see a particular building in a certain light.

Yet less of the stuff of his personal history found its way into these narratives than is often the case with a beginner's work. He naturally kept out of these pages the ideas that were bandied about at Petrashevsky's as well as elsewhere. These could not get into print. Yet as a disciple of Belinsky he manages to express, if covertly, his sympathy for the underdog, his resentment of social injustice, his concern with the public good. In one of the previously mentioned feuilletons he attacked his compatriots' proclivity for building castles in the air. He incorporated an anatomy of daydreaming into "White Nights." The dreamer, the narrator of the story has it, is a solitary who lives in a world ruled by fantasy. Mercurial, febrile, it seizes upon a hint, a nothing, and spins a cobweb in which the dreamer is caught like a fly. Soon the web is replaced by another gossamer net. Space vanishes, time abdicates. Thrilled and soothed by his reveries, the dreamer craves more of them without becoming aware of the poisons his self-indulgence is distilling or of the terrible price that he will have to pay for it. Intoxicated by the bewitching scenes that his imagination conjures up, he looks on reality with disdain. He walks through life with averted eyes, dreading every new situation, fearful of having to meet the world on its own terms. Fancying himself in a golden nook, the haunted troglodyte does not see that he is leading an inane existence in a dusty, dingy corner.

Several pieces are cautionary tales. The dreamers who figure in them are horrible examples of the consequences of addiction to idle reverie. They are men shipwrecked on the coast of dreams. Such is the central character of "The Landlady" and that of "White Nights." According to a badly jumbled quasi-reminiscential passage in "Petersburg Dreams in Prose and Verse" (a feuilleton that Dostoevsky contributed to an early issue of the monthly he began editing in 1861), he himself had been a victim of daydreaming. An incident that occurred in his early youth had freed him from the obsession. On a bitter January day, he wrote, he had halted on the Neva embankment to get a quick view of the frozen river glistening in the sunset's fading crimson. Giant pillars of smoke rising from every roof were building an airy city above the substantial one. At this twilight hour the world took on the semblance of a dream. And it was then that a wholly new world which had previously been known to him by "vague rumors and mysterious signs" was opened to his eyes. From that moment he dated what he called "the beginning of my existence." He went on to say that before the incident—he termed it "a vision"—he had been living among ghosts, fancying himself a Pericles, an ancient Roman general, a Christian martyr, a knight riding into the lists, a character out of Walter Scott; he had wanted to flee to Switzerland, to Italy. And abruptly men and women swam into his view, ordinary people leading humdrum lives, but about whom there was something strange and fantastic.

The description of the "vision" is muddled and the account of its effect is illogical. The feuilleton goes on to suggest vaguely that by "the beginning" of his existence Dostoevsky meant his birth as a writer. Be that as it may, the question arises: did the epiphany beside the Neva really occur? Dostoevsky's recollection of it is not supported by his correspondence. Furthermore, the description of the incident is lifted bodily out of a passage in the penultimate paragraph of "A Faint Heart." There the experience is attributed to Arkady, a friend of the anti-hero, and the reader is told that as a result Arkady understood what made the faint-hearted copyist lose his mind. In fine, there is no reason to doubt that in his youth Dostoevsky was given to daydreaming, but the years *gradually* and tardily brought him a sense of reality—a reality not devoid, however, of a mysterious, fantastic quality, on which he would eventually expatiate. As late as 1847 he warned Mikhail of the danger involved in a surrender to fantasy and dwelt on the necessity of establishing a balance between the inner life and that in which one must cope with the actual world. In admonishing his brother he was also admonishing himself.

The stories allow a place, along with the dreamers, for souls flawed in another way—humble, submerged, degraded individuals. Their infirm egos readily break down under a strain. It is conceivable that in identifying with these dwarfed, stunted creatures, Dostoevsky was gratifying his sense of his own deficiency. From the first, one suspects, his writing was for him a form of veiled, ambiguous confession. It has been noted that he used the term in speaking of *The Double* and of *Netochka Nezvanova*. Did he see himself as another Golyadkin? There was a time when Belinsky, for one, got the impression that his disciple shared at least one of Golyadkin's weaknesses: the illusion that the world was in league against him. Possibly in portraying the inner life of Netochka, of the little girl to whom she was attached, and of the little boy who was to be the hero of the tale, the author was unburdening his heart of the mixed emotions of his own childhood. It was as though in trying to understand himself, he was moving up the stream of his memories to its source.

# 9

## PENAL SERVITUDE

THE slow frosty dawn of a brilliant winter day was just breaking as the little caravan of sleighs approached the town of Schlüsselberg. The travelers had made the forty miles from Petersburg in a night. The trip in the open air had given a sharp edge to Dostoevsky's appetite and he attacked his breakfast as though he had gone without food for a week. The heartache he had felt on leaving Petersburg had somehow been eased by the journey, and the brisk weather and the glimpses of Christmas trees cheered him. The sun shone on the clean snow and brought out the color in the scarlet sashes of the gray-kaftaned drivers— they changed at every station. What with the holiday, food at the roadside inns was plentiful, and through the generosity of the government courier, a friendly old soul, they were provided with good meals. The sleighs glided on, past snowbound villages and forlorn towns, first in a southerly direction, and then straight east, against the sun. Choosing the less-frequented roads, they followed virtually the very route traversed a quarter of a century earlier by those aristocratic convicts, the Decembrists. As the days wore on, the cold became unendurable, and they were transferred to covered sleighs. In spite of this, Dostoevsky froze "to the heart." One night in the province of Perm they struck forty degrees below zero (centigrade). He did not know how he lived through it.

As he put home farther behind him, his mood sagged. The party was in the Ural Mountains, crossing the borderline between the two continents, marked by a post bearing the inscription "Europe" on one side and "Asia" on the other, when it was caught in a snowstorm. The sleighs stuck in the drifts and the convicts had to clamber out—a clumsy job, what with the heavy irons on their legs. While the drivers were struggling with the horses and the vehicles, Dostoevsky stood still and peered into the tossing night. Behind him lay Europe and his past, before him stretched Siberia, as dark as his future. His eyes filled.

He did not get a taste of the life that awaited him until, on January 9, he reached Tobolsk. The Tobolsk prison was a cross between a clearing house of crime and a hostelry for transient convicts. Before being assigned to their respective places of confinement or exile, all the condemned spent a brief period in these vile, congested, dilapidated cells. Dostoevsky and his two comrades were first taken to a large chamber, crowded with prisoners of both sexes and all ages. Some were having half of their heads shaved, as was prescribed, some were being clapped into irons, others, ready for the march to their final destination, were being chained in groups to an iron rod. In the foul air, against the grimy walls, these grotesque heads, these branded brows, these brutish snouts, were frightening to behold.

There was little time for reflection. Dostoevsky and his companions were searched, a process during which he was relieved of all the money he had on his person, and then the three of them, half frozen and dog-tired, were locked into a cold cell together. Durov lay down on the bench that served as a bed. Dostoevsky and the other man, Jastrzembski, crouched on the dirty floor. It was a black hour. Jastrzembski spoke of suicide. Dostoevsky tried to put heart into him—of the three he was the least depressed. Finally, solace came in the shape of hot tea and a candle. Jastrzembski had been deprived of the rum he had bought at Kazan, but Dostoevsky still had a few cigars in his pocket, and what with the hot drink and the light and the tobacco there was a kind of conviviality in the foul, narrow room.

The half dozen days that he stayed here were not utterly bleak. Some of the Decembrists had settled in this Siberian town with their families, and the womenfolk, who with such high fortitude had followed their exiled husbands into the wilderness, made an opportunity to mother this new generation of political prisoners. Dostoevsky, like the five or six other members of Petrashevsky's circle who were temporarily confined here, received food at their hands and warm clothing, of which he was in sore need. Above all, these contacts gave him the feeling that there were people beyond the walls to whom the prisoners were still human beings. These ladies—they were the wives and daughters of aristocrats —engineered a meeting with the prisoners at the warden's house. They tried to encourage the men, offered them practical advice, and gave each a copy of the New Testament, the only book permitted in prison. They took occasion to warn Dostoevsky—together with Durov he was to do his term at Omsk—that the warden there, a Major Krivtzov, was an ugly customer whose viciousness was as limitless as his power over the convicts and who was the autocrat of the prison. It was a cheerless prospect, and such glimpses as Dostoevsky caught of the men with whom he was to spend the next four years of his life chilled him to the bone.

One of the ladies who was especially kind to the Omsk convicts was Natalia Dmitrievna Fonvizina. She had high connections, being related to the Governor-General of Western Siberia, and was therefore in a particularly favorable position to help Dostoevsky. When the time came for him and Durov to set out for Omsk, Mme. Fonvizina, with a friend, saw the two of them off. It was an irregular procedure, but the ladies made sure that the escorting gendarmes should be complaisant. One of them was to transmit a letter from Mme. Fonvizina to an influential friend at Omsk in which she begged him to take an interest in the two prisoners. In a bitter frost the two women waited on the highroad, several miles from the town, having taken care to leave their sleigh a good distance behind them, so that there should be no witness to the meeting. The *troikas* bearing the convicts halted, and with some clanging of irons the men climbed out to say their last farewells. Durov's black beard was covered with icicles. Dostoevsky, in his heavy sheepskin coat and fur cap with earlaps, looked rather homely, frail, slight, and young.

# ( II )

When for the first time he lay down on the bare planks that for
four years were to serve him as a bed, covering himself as best
he might with his short sheepskin coat, he was fairly sick with
the impressions of the day. It was afternoon when they had
driven into the town of Omsk, a week's journey from Tobolsk.
They had at once been taken before the major of whom they had
been warned. The pimpled purple face with eyes that glared
maliciously through spectacles made Dostoevsky think of a spider
about to pounce on a fly. The man was all he had been painted.
Before dismissing them he promised them the lash for the slightest misdemeanor.

At the guardhouse a barber shaved Dostoevsky's beard, half
of his mustache and one side of the head in the fashion prescribed for civilian convicts. All his own clothes were taken away
from him—the major had told him plainly that a convict had no
property—and he was given a particolored suit of gray and
black with a yellow diamond on the back, a soft visorless cap,
and a new sheepskin coat. He was to change his linked fetters
for irons made of rods, which were worn under the trousers and
were less clumsy for work, but this was to wait till the next
morning.

The short winter day had already turned to dusk when he
passed through the sentinel-guarded gate and found himself
within the high prison enclosure. The convicts were returning
from work under escort and falling in preparatory to rollcall.
A bewhiskered noncommissioned officer opened the door of the
prison barracks, a long, low log house, and Dostoevsky got his
first sickening whiff of prison air. All at once the low-ceiled room,
dark except for the light of a few tallow candles, filled up with
men and the stench thickened. Then the doors were locked for the
night. Dostoevsky, like everyone else, had three planks on which
to stretch his sore body, soaked with iodine and mercury. Until
sleep released him, he must struggle to breathe this air, heavy
with the smells of unwashed bodies, of vile smoke, and of the
uncovered night-pot in the anteroom, must watch with scared
greedy eyes the haggard branded faces, the ragged grimy figures,

and, even when he lay with closed lids, must listen to the oaths, the guffaws, the thin clank of irons.

He awoke in the dark, shivering with cold. A drum beat the reveille at the prison gate, and the doors were being unlocked. The air was chilly and intolerably foul. The convicts stretched and yawned, sullen with sleep. They crowded around the two pails of water. Each one took the dipper, filled his mouth with water, and washed his face and hands from his mouth. There was wrangling over the single dipper. Breakfast consisted of bread and *kvass*. To get it, Dostoevsky followed the other prisoners across the yard in the gray light of dawn to a neighboring building which was at once kitchen and messroom. While the others were mustered out to work beyond the walls, he was sent to the smithy to have his fetters changed. The first three days a convict was allowed to rest from the fatigues of the journey, and so he went back to the barracks. He got there near mess hour, when some of the prisoners were already returning from work.

In all his comings and goings he was conscious of hostile eyes furtively watching him, this newcomer, this "gentleman." But there were a few convicts who, smelling money on the "gentleman"—he had indeed succeeded in smuggling in a few rubles in the binding of his New Testament—made up to him, showing him how to wear the fetters, procuring a box with a lock on it for his clothes, helping him to get a teapot of his own, as many of the prisoners managed to do. After mess, when he had gagged over the cockroaches in the cabbage soup, he was able to comfort himself and Durov with a pot of tea. The two of them were sitting quietly over their cups when a convict, a slouching hulk of a man, furious with drink, lumbered into the messroom followed by an entertainer in the shape of a little fellow with a fiddle, also a convict. At once the giant, Gazin by name, began taunting the two tea drinkers, for whom the prison fare was not good enough. Dostoevsky and his companion thought best to ignore the bully and this enraged him further. He snatched up the first weapon that came to hand—a huge, heavy tray. The rest did not move a finger to defend the newcomers. For a breathless second it seemed as though the two of them would have their heads bashed in. A sudden shout from the passage: "Gazin, your vodka's stolen!" diverted his attention at the crucial instant and saved them. That evening after dusk Dostoevsky walked beside the stockade, and with a sick heart pondered the day behind him and the years ahead, until the drum summoned him back to his second night in the barracks.

The prison population was a very mixed crowd in which practically every type of criminal and every section of the immense country was represented. With the exception of Dostoevsky and Durov and a few Poles, who were also political offenders, all were common criminals. "The devil must have worn out three pairs of boots before he brought us all here," the men would say of themselves. It is not strange that crime became a major interest with Dostoevsky or that in each of his major novels a murder is either attempted or committed.

The convicts were herded in two decrepit log houses, long since pronounced unfit for human habitation. The ward to which Dostoevsky was assigned held about thirty men. Here they lived "all in a heap," as he put it. The roof leaked and the walls were drafty. The wooden floor was rotten through and through and slippery with filth, though a convict was delegated to scrub it. As for the men, they got baths only on the eve of high holidays, and the dirty, steamy, crowded bathhouse made Dostoevsky think Hell must be something like that. The inmates stank "like swine," as he later wrote to Mikhail, adding: "They say they can't help being swinish, for they're 'living human beings.'" In winter the tiny windows were always dimmed with thick frost, and the place was so cold that the water in the pails froze. The convicts did their laundry indoors and the room was flooded with slops. The stove, for which only six logs were allotted at a time, gave off not so much heat as poisonous fumes, which at best produced a sick headache. The warm months were even more difficult to bear. The work day was longer and harder, and the nights were agony, what with the stifling air and the sleeping platform alive with fleas, lice, bedbugs, and cockroaches that murdered sleep.

The prison was located in a fortress and so subject to a stricter discipline than the Siberian civil penitentiaries attached to mines and mills. The inmates were always under guard, always in irons. When Dostoevsky and Durov had completed more than half of their term, the commandant of the fortress petitioned his superior for permission to relieve the politicals of leg irons. The Czar refused the request. The authorities had been notified that it was the Emperor's will that both political prisoners should be shown no lenience, but be treated as convicts "in the full sense of the word." Major Krivtzov, "Eight Eyes" as the prisoners nicknamed the bespectacled warden, needed no such injunction. He behaved as if all the convicts without exception were his personal enemies. Moreover, he was given to arbitrary tyranny. He would have a man flogged for sleeping on his right side because, he said, Christ slept on His left and so everyone should do likewise.

Dostoevsky was allowed to do clerical work in the prison office, but only for a while. Several people in the town who could have been of help were disposed in his favor, but could do practically nothing in a community crawling with sycophants and self-appointed spies. Some cadets on guard duty—they had been transferred to Siberia for a misdemeanor—went out of their way to lighten his lot, but he seemed to resent their kindnesses. It was as though he took a bitter pleasure in his misery. He seems to have been afflicted with a morbid sense of guilt. If this was indeed the case, the catastrophe that befell him must to some degree have lightened that sense of guilt and assuaged his craving for suffering.

Life in prison was life still. It asserted itself in this bleak place like grass thrusting its way between slabs of granite. The brutal severity of the regimen was to some degree mitigated by incredible laxity. The convicts were not permitted to do any work for themselves or to earn money. Nevertheless, as soon as the doors were locked for the night the barracks would turn into a humming workshop. Many pursued a craft, some engaged in buying and selling and in financial transactions of sorts, and there were those who hired themselves out to their mates as entertainers, lookout men, factotums. All managed to earn something and were able to secure certain amenities. Some ate other than prison food. Cards, tobacco, vodka were strictly forbidden, yet gambling, smoking, and drinking thrived, and the more enterprising even got themselves women by bribing the guards. Money was precious as a symbol of freedom, the dream even of "lifers." Yet they used it in the most spendthrift fashion, fearing that it would be snatched from them before they could enjoy it, and also in order to secure the respect of their fellows by a splurge. Of course, all infringements of discipline were committed at the peril of reprisals. Eight Eyes would descend like the wolf on the fold, goods and money would be confiscated, and the offenders flogged.

Only Christmas and Easter were days of leisure, and on these occasions relaxation of discipline was, if not sanctioned, at least connived at. New Year's Eve, 1852, was marked by a unique event: the convicts, under Dostoevsky's direction, staged a comedy, a farce, and a musical pantomime. The spectacle was attended not only by the inmates but also by the prison officials and other "noble and highborn persons," for whose benefit a playbill was posted. There were no theatricals in the city and the show was a huge success. It is said that Krivtzov tried to break up the performance but was prevented.

# ( III )

Forced labor was the least harassing feature of Dostoevsky's situation. Work, though compulsory, was in itself a purposeful and to an extent satisfying activity. True, occasionally it had to be carried on in the open, where one was exposed to rain or bitter cold. But generally the conditions of labor were tolerable. Having no trade, Dostoevsky was described in the prison register as a "common laborer, can read and write." When he was with a gang, his fellows, out of spiteful contempt for the "gentleman," would try to prevent him from taking part in the common task, such as the wrecking of an old barge. What irked him was the thought that the prisoners, who could not possibly believe in the readiness of a *barin* (gentleman) to get calluses on his hands, were mistaking his zeal for an attempt to make up to them and were thus justified in despising him. But he insisted on his right to work, and he won out. He baked and pounded alabaster, turned a lathe in the prison workshop, carried bricks as a mason's apprentice, shoveled snow—no easy job. The rough physical labor toughened his body and saved him from too much brooding. When a task was set outside the stockade, he had the opportunity of catching a glimpse, on the shores of the Irtysh, of the prairie under the open sky, of a nomad's smoke-blackened tent. Merely to be out of sight of the fortress, with its oppressive buildings, the sentinel endlessly pacing the earthen wall, was to be strengthened against misery.

The military hospital, located outside the fortress, was also a place of refuge. More than once Dostoevsky was laid up there, with stomach trouble or pneumonia. In the wards set aside for prisoners there was filth too; there were lice; there were the eternal fetters—these were removed from the convict only when he was freed or after death—there was the tainted air of the sick-room. The days dragged on, long, dismal, monotonous, and the nights lay heavily on the sleepers and the sleepless alike. Yet there were new faces, the discipline was less severe, the food less disgusting. Some doctors were not too hard on malingerers. The prisoners were treated more like human beings and behaved more like them. All kinds and conditions of men were gathered here: local convicts, men on their way to other prisons, men who had just been sentenced, civilians and soldiers who were awaiting trial, prisoners from the disciplinary battalion. Men talked to each other more freely than they did in the barracks, and when he was not too sick, Dostoevsky hung greedily on every word. He made the most of this opportunity for learning about the life of the people, he stored up mental notes.

Sometimes toward evening a man half dead from a flogging would be brought into the ward. The attendants would at once try to remove the splinters from the victim's back, which was a mass of bleeding wounds, and then cover it with a cloth soaked in urine—this was supposed to reduce the pain and the inflamma-tion. At such moments Dostoevsky, trembling with excitement and horror, would hover about the attendants. He would beg them to save the man's life: it was not seldom that convicts died after having been treated to the sticks.

He himself had narrowly escaped a flogging, and on that oc-casion had what may have been an attack of the falling sickness. A medical certificate giving 1850 as the date of his first attack will be quoted later. Dr. Riesenkampf, who had known him in the early forties and who was later attached to the Omsk mili-tary hospital, recalled that Dostoevsky had an epileptic fit in 1851 as he watched a flogging. He had by now apparently no memory of the seizures that had occurred before his arrest. A week after his discharge he was writing to Mikhail: "My de-ranged nerves have brought on the falling sickness, but the attacks are rare."

What greatly added to his distress was the wall of hostility that encompassed him. In prison a man of the people found himself among comrades and was admitted into their confra-ternity without question. As a *barin* Dostoevsky was shut out from their company. Shortly after the end of his term he dis-patched a mammoth letter to Mikhail. As regards the attitude of his fellow convicts toward himself and Durov he wrote: "Had they been allowed, they would have eaten us alive. 'You, gentlefolk, iron beaks, you've all but pecked us to death. You used to be masters and you tortured the people, and now you're lower than the lowest. You're one of us'—that's the theme on which variations were played for four years. A hundred and fifty enemies never tired of plaguing us—it was their pleasure, diversion, occupation. . . ." This was perhaps painting the picture too black, but the reality was black enough. The chasm between the common people and the gentry was never so clearly present to Dostoevsky as in this place and at this time. His own demeanor may have contributed to the enmity that surrounded him. One of the cadets stationed in the fortress recalled that he "looked like a trapped wolf." He shunned his fellow prisoners, was always sullen, scowling, his eyes fixed on the ground. A smile rarely softened his haggard face. He answered questions curtly and only when it was unavoidable.

Doubly an outcast, he was never alone. The lack of privacy was intolerable. He was to confess to a friend that there were times during those four years when, tortured by the horror of "prison communism," he bitterly hated everyone around him. "Thieves who are stealing my life with impunity"—that was how he regarded the companions thrust upon him. On the other hand, there were moments when he felt close to his fellow convicts, when his heart went out to them. Were they not his brothers in misfortune, were they not Russians? He recorded one such occasion years later. To escape the drinking, gambling, and fighting on his first Easter in prison, he lay down on his cot, pretending sleep, and sank into childhood memories. He recalled the incident in the copse when he had been frightened by the cry of "Wolf!" and had run to the peasant Marey for protection. As he sat up, roused by the reminiscence, and looked around him, his hatred of the men dropped away. He asked himself if his branded neighbor hoarsely shouting a drunken song was not perhaps another Marey. It is doubtful, however, if at this time he cherished the belief in the unique virtues of Russia's common people which was to become a cardinal article of his credo.

Sometimes, at night when sleep would not come, his imagination led him out of the foul gloom of the barracks. Scenes enacted themselves, characters wearing their destiny like fetters worked it out before his closed eyes. It was during those vigils that he conceived the idea for a novel, his "confession," his supreme and final work. What plagued him was the fear that his passion for the theme would have evaporated before he had a chance to execute the work. Not to be able to do more than plan was an ordeal.

# ( IV )

There were other matters that occupied him during those sleep-less hours. He relived his recent past, took stock of his opinions and beliefs, subjecting them to harsh scrutiny. In the end he underwent what he called "a transformation of convictions," an ideological second birth. The radical ideas which had tempted him before his arrest he discarded as youthful aberrations. On the rare occasions when he exchanged words with the Polish politicals he spoke, much to their disgust, as a loyal subject, indeed, a chauvinist and a jingo. He praised the aristocracy, insisted on Russia's right to Poland and the other annexed lands, looked forward to the entry of Russian troops into Constanti-nople (Turkey declared war on Russia in October, 1853), and enlarged on the supremacy of his compatriots, in comparison with whom other nations were mere caricatures. He may have exaggerated his aggressive patriotism to annoy the Poles, whom he detested, but he only overstated what would become, if it was not already, his firm position.

Dostoevsky faced the fact that he was being punished for "dreams and theories" that were no longer his. Yet he continued to accept his penal servitude with a resignation that argues acquiescence in the justice of his fate. He took a perverse pleasure in one element of his situation: the humiliation to which he was subjected. He was one of the lowest, to whom it was customary to give alms. A Polish convict, upon being tendered such an offering, indignantly refused it. Not so Dostoevsky. Early in his prison days, as he was returning to the barracks one evening under guard, he passed a simple woman with her little daughter. The child whispered something to her mother, who stopped and fumbled in her pocket for a coin. The child took it and ran after Dostoevsky, saying: "Here, poor man, is a kopeck, for Christ's sake!" He treasured his first alms a long time.

The "transformation of convictions" naturally affected his

attitude toward Christianity. If it is true that he had at one time embraced Belinsky's atheism, this did not survive in the prison atmosphere. Here he formulated a credo, confided to a letter written a few days after his irons had been removed. It was addressed to the devout Mme. Fonvizina who had befriended him in Tobolsk on the threshold of hell. He began by declaring that in prison there were times when he thirsted for faith as "withered grass thirsts for water" and that his craving was slaked because "in misfortune the truth grows clear." He went on to say: "Let me tell you about myself, that I have been till now and that as long as I live I shall remain, I know, a child of this age of doubt and unbelief." Late in life he will note that his "hosanna" has been tried in a "crucible of doubts." The letter goes on: "How terribly I was tormented by that thirst, which grew all the stronger the more arguments I found against faith. And yet sometimes God grants me moments when I am wholly at peace, when I love my neighbors and am loved by them. At such moments I have composed in my heart a confession of faith in which everything is clear and holy for me. It is very simple: to believe that there is nothing [*sic*] more beautiful, more profound, more congenial, more reasonable, more manly, more perfect than Christ. And I tell myself with jealous love that not only is there nothing, but there can be nothing. Moreover, if someone proved to me that Christ is outside the truth and if it really were a *fact* that the truth is outside Christ, I would rather remain with Christ than with the truth."

Here was a variation on Tertullian's dictum: *"Certum est quia impossibile est."* A strictly private credo, ignoring the Church, could not be acceptable to an Orthodox fundamentalist. Father Bulgakov, a close student of Dostoevsky, wrote: "This antithesis between, on the one hand, Christ, who for the believer is the Way, the Truth, the Life, and, on the other hand, abstract truth, is masked blasphemy, meant to deceive simple hearts." Dostoevsky was a heretic rather than a blasphemer. The confession, unorthodox though it was, pointed to the direction his thinking would take. His plight was that he was never able to reconcile Christ with the truth or to renounce either.

A quarter of a century later, being in a reminiscential mood, Dostoevsky wrote: "We, of the Petrashevsky group, stood on the scaffold and listened to our verdicts without a trace of repentance. . . ." He somewhat mitigated this sweeping statement with the remark: "At least, most of us would have considered it dishonorable to repudiate our convictions." But immediately he returned to the inclusive first person plural: "We regarded the cause for which we were condemned, the ideas that possessed our minds, not only as not demanding repentance, but even as [offering us] something like a purifying martyrdom." One would imagine that his traumatic experience as a convict should have strengthened rather than obliterated his radicalism. Yet the opposite was the case. What, then, brought about his "transformation of convictions"?

This was not a subject on which Dostoevsky liked to enlarge. He did touch on it more than once, but left the problem unsolved. Apparently he failed to understand himself in this matter. He did state that what he called the "sobering" which changed many of his ideas was a long, painful process. Yet he denied that the hardships he had endured played any part in it. His about-face was due, he explained, to his having lived for years with the common folk "in brotherly union [*sic*] with them, sharing a common misfortune." It was easier for him, he went on, "to return to the root of the people, to come to know the national spirit, the Russian soul," because he had been nurtured in a "Russian and pious family."

The lines quoted above are from a passage in an issue of Dostoevsky's *Writer's Diary* for 1873. The religious upbringing to which he called attention may well have been in part responsible for his thirst for faith. What was more natural than for him to cry from the depths to the Christ of his childhood? His only reading as a convict was the New Testament. The phrases and parables that had been the commonplaces of his early days, the familiar stories of the miracles, must have taken on a deeper meaning for him. As for the reference to his intimate contacts with the common people, it is obvious that the years had radically changed his memories of life in prison. True, most of his fellow convicts were of peasant stock, but they were déclassé villagers who looked down on clodhoppers. They could by no means be taken as exemplars of the "Russian soul," bearers of the Russian ethos, whether as Dostoevsky conceived it at the end of his prison term or as he construed it many years later. "It is impossible," says Dmitry in *The Brothers Karamazov,* "for a convict to be without God." There is no indication that the maxim applied to the thieves, highwaymen, robbers, and murderers who were Dostoevsky's companions in misery. Being remarkable neither for piety nor for aggressive patriotism, they could scarcely have inspired him with either. In any event, the reasons he gave for his change of heart leave the matter moot.

Perhaps Dostoevsky was not exposed long enough to radical influences before his arrest for the seeds of rebellion to have struck firm root in his mind. And so, when the catastrophe came, the loyalty to Church and Throne inculcated in him in his early years reasserted itself, partly under the impact of his utter isolation from the circles in which he had recently moved. Conceivably his dread of the power for evil that he perceived in the criminals with whom he rubbed shoulders day and night inclined him to exalt discipline and authority. Yet it should be noted that whatever else Belinsky's former disciple and the frequenter of Petrashevsky's Fridays had rejected, he had not lost his concern for the underdog, his desire to be at one with the masses.

As the end of his term drew nearer, life in prison became more tolerable. This was not because of the removal of Eight Eyes, which happened at the beginning of Dostoevsky's third year, or because the prison itself shortly afterward underwent a nominal change of regime. Rather it was because habit had eased the hardships of the place. Incredibly, it had become a kind of home.

In his first Siberian letter to Mikhail, which has been quoted above, Dostoevsky depicted prison existence as one of unmitigated misery, both physical and moral. In the same letter he wrote: "However, human beings are human beings everywhere. Even in penal servitude among brigands after four years I finally discovered human beings. Believe me, there are characters, profound, strong, admirable, and what a joy it was to find gold under a coarse exterior. Some deserved respect, others were positively wonderful. . . . One convict burst into tears bidding me farewell."

Toward the last, Dostoevsky enjoyed certain unprecedented liberties. He established contacts with some friendly townspeople and was able to borrow books. He read *David Copperfield* and *The Pickwick Papers* in the hospital. One night, after the doors were locked, he actually found himself with a magazine in his hands. He drank in the words eagerly, scanned the pages hungrily for news of the world from which he had been snatched. It was his first chance at such a glimpse. The one person who might have written to him—Mikhail—sent him not a word as long as he was a convict. How utterly cut off he was! How hard it would be to get back!

In mid-February, 1854, four years after he had entered the

fortress, his fetters were knocked off by the prison blacksmith, and he walked out of the gates, a free man. Free? According to the terms of his sentence, he was now to serve as a private in Siberia, and he knew that in exchanging the convict's motley for the soldier's uniform, he was altering his appearance rather than his condition. In the meantime he enjoyed a brief respite between the two kinds of servitude. The town of Omsk he found to be dirty, dissolute, and infested with soldiery. Still, it held several good friends who did all they could for him, even to lending him money. He stayed for a short time at the home of the son-in-law of a Decembrist where he was treated like a member of the family.

He was chagrined to discover that he had been assigned to a battalion stationed in Semipalatinsk, also on the Irtysh, but hundreds of miles farther south. What could he look forward to in that hole, lost in the depths of the Kazakh wilds? To go there was to suffer yet another wrench, to be farther away from home, to be abandoned by that friendly ghost of his past which, toward the end, had visited him at Omsk.

Yet as he faced this change in his life, the curious half-acknowledged serenity that had supported him in prison turned to a kind of exultation. He was like a convalescent after a long, dangerous illness, who, having come near to tasting death, relishes living all the more. He felt that he was on the verge of the great crisis of his existence. He was ripe for the event. If fate cheated him now, everything was lost. He was satisfied with his life, he wrote to Mikhail, his mind was at rest, his future was spread out before his eyes. The only thing he dreaded was that the burden of a soldier's life under some bully of a sergeant would be too much for him.

To reassure him, friends were telling him that at Semipalatinsk he would be among simple-minded people. But experience had taught him that he had more to fear from the simple than from the sophisticated. Still, he consoled himself, he would be among human beings. He begged Mikhail for two things: books and money. "Books," he cried, "are my life, my food, my future." He must have magazines—he had had to do without them for so long—histories, ancient and modern, the Greek and Latin classics, studies in economics, the writings of the Fathers of the Church, the Koran, Kant's *Critique of Pure Reason,* and particularly Hegel's *History of Philosophy*; also a German dictionary. He will soon take up his pen again, and he must do much reading. As for money, it is as vital to a private as to a convict. If only Mikhail will keep him until he is permitted to leave Siberia and publish his work! What is spent on him will not be lost. These years have not been wasted. For one thing, he has learned to know the Russian people as few men do. He cannot write drivel now.

# 10

## FIRST LOVE

THE single road that connected Semipalatinsk with the world crossed a bare plain. Occasionally, during the journey that Dostoevsky's little party made largely on foot under guard, they would pass the nomads' black tents or encounter leisurely caravans of camels. Early in March he laid his eyes for the first time on the town's drab one-story houses, its endless fences, its unlit, unpaved streets, which at night appeared dead except for the barking of the watchdogs. As at Omsk the soldiers' barracks were located in a fortress, or rather in the ruins of one. The town—it was really an overgrown village with a population of five or six thousand—had once been a military outpost of the expanding empire, and although it was now merely the administrative center of a thoroughly subdued region, it was not sufficiently removed from the border to have lost its military air altogether.

Again he was one of a crew of wretches in uniform, again he was sleeping on a plank bed only slightly softened by a thin felt mattress that he had to share with his neighbor, again he was messing with an unsavory lot, this time scooping the cabbage soup with his wooden spoon out of a common bowl. But there was no clank of chains, no grating of keys in locks, one could breathe the air without choking and eat the food without gagging, and one was not continually followed by a guard with a gun. His companions here were, however, not so different from the people he had been thrown with in prison. Some were serfs who had been drafted into the army at the instance of their masters as punishment. There were, too, desperate characters who had sold themselves as substitutes for other men. The air was thick with threats and curses, the sound of whacks, the groans of those who had been flogged.

Among the privates there were lads in their teens, some of them Jews, who like Spartan boys had been taken from their parents in childhood to be raised as cannon-meat. One such boy, by the name of Katz, occupied the planks next to Dostoevsky's. The two became friendly, Dostoevsky playing the big brother. Katz, who did a bit of tailoring on the side, managed to provide himself with a samovar, a luxury he shared with his mate. Many years later Katz recalled him as a taciturn, unsmiling man whose few words were uttered in a soft, slow, clear voice, and who in his free moments would sit alone lost in thought or poring over his one treasured book, the New Testament. But leisure was rare, what with reviews, sentry duty, and constant drill—he had to learn over again practically everything he had been taught at the military school. He was so busy he hardly found time for sleep. All that was required of him he performed punctiliously and eagerly. One of his superiors remembered long afterward how quick he had been to salute, and how his behavior had always been marked by a deep humility. In July he was able to write to Mikhail that he was as good a soldier as the next man and that his superiors were satisfied with him. He had attained this at the cost of heavy exertions, "but," he added, "I do not complain, it's my cross, and I deserve it." He had yet another cross to bear in the shape of strange seizures which, in his opinion, "resembled epilepsy and yet were not epilepsy."

The winter brought him a godsend in the person of a young man fresh from law school who had been assigned to the post of district attorney at Semipalatinsk. He arrived from Petersburg in November, bearing with him a letter from Mikhail, another from Apollon Maikov, some linen, books, and fifty rubles. The young Baron Wrangel—he was only twenty-one—was an exception to the usual run of civil servants who found in Siberia their happy hunting grounds: alert, sensitive, sincere, bursting with good intentions and high ideals, he was the sort of person with whom Dostoevsky could feel at ease. And since he came from

Petersburg and from Mikhail, he was a piece of home. Wrangel, of course, knew the story of this morose man with the sallow, freckled face, the fair, closely cropped hair, the husky voice, who though a person of his own class stood before him in the uniform of a private. Their friendship was christened with tears. At their first meeting the young man wept with homesickness on Dostoevsky's rough shoulder, and in his turn Dostoevsky cried over the letters from home.

An intimacy soon sprang up between the young district attorney and the political exile. In writing home, the youth described his friend as a man of deep religiosity and an iron will. He loved him as a brother and respected him as though he were his father. Dostoevsky was grateful for this affection, though he could not fully reciprocate it. He would spend with Wrangel as many hours as he could, drinking numberless glasses of tea, smoking cheap, stinking Majorca tobacco in a long pipe, reading and studying. Indeed, they were planning to undertake together the translation of Hegel's *Philosophy* [*sic*] and of *Psyche* (1846) by C. G. Carus, a forerunner of Freud.

Their talk sometimes turned on politics. There was nothing in the opinions of the political exile to grate upon the respectable young district attorney. Dostoevsky never mentioned the Petrashevsky circle. He spoke as a patriot and a loyal subject of the Czar. Shortly after his arrival in Semipalatinsk he made a futile attempt to rehabilitate himself in the eyes of the authorities. Stirred up by the Crimean War, which was being fought thousands of miles away, he composed an uninspired, violently jingoistic ode, entitled "On the European Events of 1854." Therein he assured Russia's enemies that the empire would be saved by the Cross and the Throne, and prophesied that the two-headed eagle would press on toward Czargrad (the old Russian name for Constantinople). He had hoped that the ode would be brought to the Czar's attention, but it remained buried in the archives of the secret service.

In a letter to Apollon Maikov, whom he had vainly tried to interest in setting up a secret press, he wrote that what had landed him in penal servitude was "no more than an accident." He went on to picture himself as one who had always been "a true Russian," a patriot devoted to the "Russian idea," a believer, and he declared that it was the part of "great, noble" Russia, "our holy mother," to free the Slavs "morally." Furthermore, he wrote, he shared his friend's conviction that Russia

would "bring Europe and its destiny to a worthy conclusion"—
obviously assigning to his fatherland, in obscure terms, a messianic role. Even the convicts had not frightened him, he continued. He had had the happiness of discovering "magnanimity"
in a robber's soul, for he too was a Russian. He goes on to exalt
"our political idea, bequeathed by Peter the Great." In the fullness of time that monarch will become his *bête noire*.

Orthodox though Dostoevsky's views were, it argued some
courage on Wrangel's part to allow himself to be seen in the
company of this common soldier, so recently a convict. But
Wrangel went further than that. He introduced his new friend
everywhere. He even took him to the military governor's, and
after that all doors were open to him. Dostoevsky now counted
among his acquaintances the élite of the town and was "loved
and respected," as he wrote to his brother, by his superiors. Some
of the ladies, officials' wives, took an interest in this private
with a past. One of them showed him the verse she wrote. He
became a frequent visitor at the house of the battalion commander, a little pot-bellied man who was always drunk and who
was ready to give away his last shirt to the first comer. Though
Dostoevsky was often seen at the home of a Cossack officer that
was the scene of much gambling, he seems not to have yielded
to the temptation. Nor did he drink. Wrangel only once saw
him slightly under the influence of liquor. He had the sober man's
peculiar slant on a company that was almost always drunk.

For some time he had been in private lodgings, having been
permitted to live outside the barracks. He roomed with a
soldier's widow, the mother of two daughters whose youthful
and not inconsiderable charms were her chief source of income.
Her lodger, unlike the natives, could not take this kind of thing
as a matter of course. Occasionally he would be roused to remon-
strate with the woman. She would silence him by arguing that
sooner or later the girls would give themselves to a common
sergeant for two cookies or a pound of nuts, whereas if she introduced them to fine gentlemen, there was both profit and
honor. In spite of the public character of his landlady's household, he was enjoying privacy for the first time in five or six
years. When he walked from the parade ground, through the
waste of sand and briers where were scattered the wooden
houses of the Russian section of the town (so-called to distinguish
it from the Cossack and Tartar neighborhoods) and, having
opened the wicket gate, stepped behind the tall fence, past the

watchdog on its chain, entered the old log cabin, and at last found himself in the low grimy room crawling with cockroaches, he had the long-denied comfort of being at home. There he would make his meal of the cabbage soup, *kasha,* and black bread that he had brought from the barracks.

His soldierly duties were no longer so onerous. There was some leisure. He employed it to make a few kopecks by tutoring. While he taught he kept his cloak on so that his pupil should not see how threadbare his trousers were. As usual he was penniless and in debt. There was, of course, Mikhail to appeal to. Mikhail had given up literature and turned to business. During Dostoevsky's third year in prison, his youngest brother having come of age, the family estate was sold and the proceeds divided among the heirs. Mikhail used what he had received to open a cigarette factory. This change did not materially improve his fortunes, so that Dostoevsky had less to hope for from his brother than he realized. It will be remembered that he had forfeited his own share by receiving a lump sum in advance.

However much he had gained in knowledge of human nature during his prison years, when it came to other matters, he had been seriously deprived. He was now overcome by a desire to improve his mind and fill the gaps in his education. This ambition was not to last long and indeed, in a formal way, he never achieved more than a shallow culture. He enjoyed the exemption from dependence on mere learning which is the privilege of genius. Naturally, the most important thing that his leisure gave him was a resurrection of the old figments, a surrender to the new images that haunted him. The writer was reviving.

# ( II )

The sense of release that the hardships of his life as a soldier could not smother was enhanced by a friendship that had been flourishing before Wrangel arrived on the scene. It was, in fact, more than a friendship. For the first time a woman entered Dostoevsky's life. Early in 1855 he made the acquaintance of a petty official who, like most of the Siberian bureaucracy, hailed from European Russia. Alexander Isayev, an improvident, quiet, sickly fellow, drank heavily and could not keep himself in hand, in spite of the responsibility of a wife and child. He was then, as often, out of a job and the little family was in severe straits. The wife, a woman of about thirty, would have stood out even in a less crude society. Marya Dmitrievna was a fragile blonde with small, irregular, pleasant features and an eager, cultivated mind. A spirited creature with a deep sense of injury, she felt keenly the indignities of her situation, and her poor health—like Dostoevsky's mother, she was disposed to consumption—fed an irritability that could melt into a startling tenderness.

Dostoevsky was constantly at the Isayevs'. He tutored the little Pasha and spent long evenings with his parents, particularly the lonely mother. For the first time in five years he had found a woman with whom he could talk. She was kind to this exile in the uniform of a common soldier. Life had trampled on her, too. Their very quarrels—the friendship of such a pair could not always be serene—endeared her to him the more. There were nights when he left the house in a state bordering on ecstasy.

It was probably before he became absorbed in her that he had a brief intimacy with a girl to whom Marya Dmitrievna would not have bowed. All that is known of the affair is that this Liza was a striking beauty, that she sold bread in the Semipalatinsk marketplace, thus supporting her orphaned brothers and sisters, and that Dostoevsky wrote her more than a score of letters which she, though only half-literate, answered. Unfortunately, the correspondence has been lost, but it is reported that in his letters he urged her to continue taking care of the family, even if it meant sacrificing her own happiness. Such a sacrifice will occur more than once in his writings. Liza never married, though she lived to a ripe age.

As the months went by Marya Dmitrievna meant increasingly more to him. But she was the wife of his friend. His feeling for her must remain as secret as it was hopeless. Suddenly this ambiguous relationship was threatened. In May Isayev was appointed to a post at Kuznetzk, nearly five hundred miles away, and there was nothing for the family to do but to pull up stakes and go there. The money necessary for the removal was supplied by the obliging Wrangel, although nominally it came from Dostoevsky. When the time for departure arrived, he accompanied the Isayevs several miles beyond the city limits. He said good-bye to Marya Dmitrievna under a pine tree that added its pungency to the heartbreaking sweetness of the spring night, while Isayev lay in the carriage, overcome by the Veuve Cliquot with which

Wrangel had plied him. It was daybreak when Dostoevsky was in his room again, relieved to be rid of the kindly but intrusive baron. He paced the floor in misery for a long time.

Soon a letter came from Kuznetzk. He answered promptly and eagerly. What distance prevented them from saying to each other they must have confided to paper. All that has been preserved of the correspondence is his first letter, but how matters developed may be gathered from what he wrote to Wrangel when the latter was out of town, and from the baron's reminiscences. In this initial letter to Marya Dmitrievna he writes that their departure has left him orphaned. He can only compare this loneliness to what he felt when he was arrested and shut away in the fortress. Both Marya Dmitrievna and her good husband had loved him, had treated him as one of their own. Were it not for them, his spirit would have perished, but they made a human being of him again. Now that they are gone, he doesn't know what to do with himself. Even Wrangel tries him—he can't help contrasting the man with her. Does she remember Wrangel's summer cottage? The garden is the same as ever, even to the bench they sat on. He is worried about the Isayevs' circumstances. They expect an inheritance from her grandmother, but this means that they'll be burdened with the old lady and that Marya Dmitrievna will have to wash her lap dogs. They must not take her in unless she pays a thousand rubles a month for her keep and offers a written guarantee that she will die in three months. Dostoevsky concludes by embracing Isayev as a friend and a brother, and wondering if he will ever see Marya Dmitrievna again.

The letters that kept coming from Kuznetzk were upsetting. Marya Dmitrievna was ill. She was lonely. Isayev was in a bad way, as usual. Dostoevsky lived in a fever of anxiety. He was temporarily sharing the baron's summer quarters, a spacious, dilapidated house, with mushrooms growing through the rotten flooring. Externally, he led a bucolic existence, feeding the pigs and chickens or, clad in a faded pink cotton vest, working in the vegetable patch. But he was miserable. His superstitious streak got the better of him, and he visited fortunetellers. Wrangel tried to distract him, but in vain. He carried him off to visit neighboring mining towns. He took him along when he went shooting. Dostoevsky was bored by the sport and, as even under happier circumstances, rather indifferent to natural scenery, however full of dramatic surprises.

Absence had sharpened his feeling for Marya Dmitrievna.

Wrangel laid himself out to arrange a meeting of the two in a town midway between Semipalatinsk and Kuznetzk, but the lady failed to keep the rendezvous. Meanwhile events were developing rapidly. Early in August Isayev died, leaving his widow and seven-year-old son penniless in a strange town. There was not even enough for the funeral expenses and the widow was practically driven to accepting alms. The news made Dostoevsky frantic. He borrowed from Wrangel to help her. Somehow she scraped through the autumn and the following winter at Kuznetzk. The letters she was now receiving from Dostoevsky were no longer those of an affectionate friend, but of a passionate lover.

They exchanged vows. But how could they think of marriage? Aside from the fact that he was five hundred miles away from his beloved, he was still a private, relying largely for his living expenses on rare and meager remittances from Mikhail. Furthermore, the devoted Wrangel had left Siberia in December, and the friends who remained were not as dependable. The worst of it was that he couldn't be sure of her. At Kuznetzk she was surrounded by meddlesome matrons bent on arranging a match for her there. She might be forced to take shelter under her father's roof in Astrakhan. Not that this would write *finis* to Dostoevsky's hopes. He was ready to wait for her if it meant five years.

Life was hell. He suspected that she was writing less than the whole truth. Knowing his jealous nature, she was, he told himself, afraid to be frank with him. His suspicions seemed justified. In March he was overwhelmed by a letter in which she said that she had decided to speak plainly and put this question to him: suppose a man, well along in years, but of sterling character and with an assured future, say, a civil servant, were to offer her his hand, should she say yes? He must consider the matter carefully like the true friend that he was and answer her without delay. She was alone with her child at the end of nowhere, her chief support being her old father. What would become of her if he died? She ended by telling her correspondent that she loved him and that this was all a mere notion.

The mere notion threw Dostoevsky into a faint. He recalled a rumor that she had promised to marry someone in Kuznetzk, which he had carelessly dismissed. He sobbed over her letter all night. Before dawn he wrote to her. He threatened, pleaded, poured out words of tenderness. He would die if he lost her. But she must tell him the whole truth and spare him nothing.

He spent two weeks in torment. Strange that he was still alive. He did not blame her for a moment: she could not be expected to marry a private. He could not, he could not give her up. He would go mad, he would throw himself into the Irtysh. But suppose he were standing in the way of her happiness? No, she loved him, he was sure of it. She could not be happy with anyone else. She was capable of selling herself to give her child bread. His pitiful darling was so kind, so easily deceived. Curious, that he should be in the boots of the wretched hero of his *Poor Folk* —it was as if he had prophesied his own fate. Come—he had a claim upon her that could not be dismissed. At his time of life love was no light fancy. This affair had been going on for two years now, and the ten months of separation had only exasperated his passion.

He was ready to walk to Kuznetzk just to see her once more, and then let come what might. The ghost of hope restrained him from doing something desperate. He was certain that should his affairs take a favorable turn, he would be preferred to any and all of her suitors. At last a letter from her lifted the darkness from his heart. It had all been a ruse. Some time previously he had written her that during Carnival week he had attended a dance, and she got the idea that he was beginning to forget her. She became panicky. Resenting what she took to be his defection, she had written in a chilly tone. Finally, to discover where she stood, she made up the story of a suitor. Reassured by his agonized reply, she put her cards on the table. As for the rumor of her marriage, it was such a piece of gossip as commonly flourished in Siberian towns.

# ( III )

In spite of this happy conclusion to the episode, the situation remained painful in the extreme. Marya Dmitrievna was constantly ailing. He too was ill. His attacks, which generally occurred at night, were not frequent but alarming. He told Wrangel that each seizure was preceded by an "inexpressibly voluptuous feeling." For two or three days after the attack he felt broken in body and spirit. The uncertainty of their situation was maddening. She could not stay on at Kuznetzk much longer. Should she go to her father in Astrakhan? Should she tell the old man she was about to be married? To whom was she to be married? On what? Everything depended on whether or not Dostoevsky could better his position. If only he were transferred from the military to the civil service! Even in the lowest rank with the pittance of a salary. Or else, if he were allowed to take a position with a private employer. The director of the Altai mills was ready to give him a berth. He could get ahead. Siberia was the place for making money. If he had a little free cash, he could double it in a year by clever speculation. Any job would tide him over until he came into his own again by getting permission to publish.

For six years he has been fighting against hell. Has he come through all this only to fail in supporting a wife? He will soon be thirty-five. He will die if he loses her. He's not cheating her by asking her to wait. By September he will have a novel ready that will outdo *Poor Folk*. If the worst comes to the worst, he can publish anonymously and pocket the cash all the same. With time they may even put something aside. He is counting on his pen. He is a man who has something to say.

What heartened him was the knowledge that several people in Petersburg were exerting themselves on his behalf. Wrangel, before he left Semipalatinsk, had already begun prodding his influential relatives to do something for his friend. Once in the capital again the baron was besieged with desperate appeals to act promptly. And Dostoevsky had yet another cause for hope. Mention has been made of his ode on the Crimean War written in 1854. Now he penned another ultrapatriotic poem on the occasion of the birthday of the Dowager Empress, in which he lamented the passing of her august spouse (who had sentenced him to penal servitude and subsequently to years of military service in the ranks). He handed it to the commander of the Siberian Corps who happened to visit Semipalatinsk, with a request to "lay it at the feet of the Empress." Whether or not it reached her, he was promoted to the rank of noncommissioned officer by order of the new Czar, Alexander II.

Encouraged by this advancement, which occurred in November, 1855, and urged on by his need, he took a further step. On March 24, 1856, he wrote to General Eduard Todtleben, the Sebastopol hero, whom he had known in happier days and whose younger brother had been his schoolmate. He begged the general to intercede with the Emperor for a poor and ailing exile who had repented the error of his ways. Admitting that he had been

lawfully and justly punished for having intended to act against
the government, he stressed the fact that he was now suffering
for opinions that he had repudiated. No longer was he blind, no
longer did he believe in "theories and utopias," as he had done
in his youth. He wished to serve his country, but the military
career was not the one he could best pursue. Civil service would
be less uncongenial, but his most earnest wish was to be permitted to publish his writings. He had always considered the
writer's calling to be the noblest and most useful. A measure of
literary ability was his sole possession. Perhaps he, a corporal,
was rendering himself guilty of insubordination by daring to
write to an adjutant general, but he committed himself to his
superior's "noble, lofty heart," and he knew that the monarch
was "kind, merciful."

The communication was to be handed to the general by the
most devoted, the angelic, the priceless, the invaluable, the irreplaceable Wrangel. He could make it plain to Todtleben, who
would in turn be able to impress it on the Emperor, that Dostoevsky would henceforth be a loyal subject. Perhaps Maikov,
too, could put in a word for him with the general. If only the
young Todtleben could be reached! He would throw himself on
his brother's neck and implore him to save his old schoolfellow.

Simultaneously Dostoevsky gave Wrangel another commission.
He was to find out what had become of Mikhail. Had he forgotten that he had a brother? Had he given himself over to
money-grubbing altogether? Why was he letting eight months
go by without a word? An urgent request for money sent the previous December had gone unheeded. Of course, Mikhail might
be in straits, but then he must have known that, as for him, he
was in the last extremity. Now he must beg him for money again:
he encloses a letter. There may be a chance to visit Kuznetzk,
which means no small outlay. Again, he ought to insist on Marya
Dmitrievna's accepting some money from him. Only once in a
lifetime does a man need money so desperately. He cannot ask
anything of Wrangel: he is too deep in debt there already. Nor
does he want alms from Mikhail. He would rather the two of
them should go under than accept anything like that. He wants
a brother, not money. Perhaps, like relatives in novels, Mikhail
is jealous of Marya Dmitrievna. Does he forget that his brother
is a man of thirty-five, with enough good sense for ten people?
Wrangel must persuade Mikhail to come to his rescue at this

critical moment of his life. For seven years life has been gall. He is not made of stone. There is a limit to his endurance.

Todtleben showed himself to be the man Dostoevsky thought him. At any rate, according to Wrangel, the wheels had begun to turn. The exile is filled with hope and overwhelmed with gratitude, particularly to the young monarch, whom, he says, he adores. He sends Wrangel an ode of his on the coronation and the conclusion of the Crimean War, begging him to see that it reaches the Emperor. He entrusts another copy to the governor-general, who is going to Petersburg for the ceremonies and who may get him permission to publish it. He had previously started an essay on Russia, but he had given it up when he noticed that it was turning out to be a political pamphlet: certainly the government would not allow him to re-enter the literary world with such a piece, despite its patriotic tone. He had then started a paper on a safer subject: art and Christianity, which was the precipitate of ten years' meditation and which he had thought out to the last syllable while he was still in prison. He hopes to be allowed to dedicate it to Her Highness, Maria Nikolayevna, the President of the Academy of Arts, and to publish it anonymously. As a matter of fact, all these efforts to get permission to publish were really for the sake of the novel that he had under way and that was his refuge from his troubles. Neither the political nor the esthetic essay is heard of again.

And now came reassuring news of Mikhail. In a long letter he explained and justified his conduct. He had preserved silence during the four years of Fyodor's incarceration because he had failed to get permission to write, and he was afraid that secret correspondence would work his brother harm, and though he did not admit as much, since he had a large family and small courage, he yielded all too readily to the dictates of prudence. He insisted that he was as devoted as ever. But even when he was free to write, he was paralysed by the knowledge that his messages were read by strangers before they reached his brother, and so his letters were few and far between. He had not so much as said that the previous summer the family had been increased by twins, so that he was now the father of five children. As for his business, though it was expanding, it was just then going through a crisis, and so he could send no more than a hundred and fifty a year. He was fully in sympathy with his brother's matrimonial plans, but just because Fyodor was not a mere boy and because marriage involved no end of petty cares, he begged him to wait until his situation was more settled. He must have patience: many influential people had his cause at heart. Mikhail ends his letter with the assurance that he has not turned into a bloated businessman—if Emilia has put on weight, he remains lean and pale, the last of the romantics.

# ( IV )

With the approach of Dostoevsky's third summer at Semipalatinsk the outlook became distinctly brighter. There was in the offing a transfer to civil service or perhaps an army commission. Suddenly he was crushed by the knowledge that even if there should be a change for the better, it would come too late. In June he realized his dream of seeing Marya Dmitrievna. He had a ten days' leave to go to Barnaul, a neighboring town, and he risked going on to Kuznetzk. It meant a large expense and the danger of being court-martialed, but no matter. "I was there, I saw her," he wrote to Wrangel on July 14. "What a noble, what an angelic soul! She wept, she kissed my hands, but she loves another."

The other was Nikolay Vergunov, a youth of twenty-four, born in Tomsk, a country schoolteacher with a prospect of a hundred rubles a year. He was a person with little culture and less experience of life. It was plain to Dostoevsky that a union between the two was madness. He argued with her. He pointed out that she would be buried in this hole the rest of her life, with a litter of children and nothing to look forward to. She was five years the boy's senior: how long would it take before she would have to suffer her young husband's reproaches for having ruined his youth? Was it not likely that he would wish her dead? And in any case, was this half-educated little Siberian schoolmaster a fit companion for a woman who had lived, who had suffered, a woman of her refinement and cultivation?

She was not impressed by his arguments, she could not expect him to like the prospect. He knew this and it made it harder for him to speak. But there she sat, agonized by the picture he painted. He took pity on her. He began to defend her young lover. This touched her to the quick. She began in her turn to pity Dostoevsky. She became tender. Her heart turned toward him now. If he had not been devoted to her, body and soul, already, he would have fallen in love with her then; she was so animated, so full of common sense and delicious folly, so kind, so quixotic. "Her heart is chivalrous." She was the very woman to throw herself away.

She introduced Dostoevsky to his rival. The two became friendly. He reasoned with the young man and reduced him to tears. The youth seemed able to do little more than weep. After two days of mingled torture and bliss, Dostoevsky left Kuznetzk with a heart in which hope still fought despair. Toward the end the widow seemed to be swinging round to him. In parting, she asked him to write to the young man frankly and fully.

He addressed a long letter to both, repeating practically the same arguments he had advanced against the marriage by word of mouth. He made every effort to take a point of view which was completely disinterested. What was his dismay to discover that his attitude was thoroughly misunderstood! Her reply was an indignant defense of the young man, although nothing had been further from Dostoevsky's mind than to attack him. As for Vergunov, he took offense, tried to rouse Marya Dmitrievna against his rival, and generally behaved like a fool and a cad. But characteristically, without waiting for Dostoevsky's response to her first outburst, she veered abruptly round and made overtures of peace. Her later letters, however, made him feel that to be out of sight was to be out of mind. She fretted, she grieved, but the other man meant more to her. How would it all end? He did not know, but he was bent on working for her happiness, whatever it might entail for him. He was like a man who had lost his mind. This wound would never heal. If he could only tear out his heart and bury it!

What must have kept him from collapse was the fact that his soldierly duties were particularly exacting just then. Also he was busy trying to be of practical assistance to the lady. Petitions had to be written and various people approached so that her son could get a scholarship in one of the military schools. And then there was all the red tape connected with securing her pension. He trembled at the thought that she might forfeit it by remarrying before it came. Finally, he must exert himself on behalf of his rival: in addition to other commissions, he urged Wrangel to sing Vergunov's praises to the governor-general and to put in a word for the young man with another high official in the hope of getting him a promotion that would double his salary. If she did marry him, she must at least be spared certain privations.

As for himself, he was up to his ears in debt. Should his officer's commission eventuate as expected, there would be unavoidable additional expenses. Again he must ask help of Mikhail and of Wrangel. If he gained permission to publish, he would certainly repay them by the New Year. Wrangel must bear with him, for Christ's sake. He was at the end of his tether. He was in a state where a man takes to drink or drowns himself. If only he could see her, were it but for an hour.

The manifesto published on the occasion of the coronation of Alexander II in August, 1856, vaguely promised relief to political prisoners of the class to which Dostoevsky belonged. Whether because of this amnesty, or owing to the intercession of influential persons, or thanks to his patriotic poems, on October 1, Dostoevsky was promoted to the rank of *praporshchik,* the lowest commissioned officer in the army. "The Lord grant our angel monarch a long and prosperous reign!" he cried. This promotion meant the restoration of his status as a noble. It was also a step on the road to freedom. To retire from the service altogether and be permitted to write for publication—that was his heart's desire. What sort of a military man was he anyway, with his strange attacks? Every time they left him with weakened faculties and would, he feared, eventually lead to insanity.

One good thing about his new position was that leaves were more easily obtained, and so he might see her. "I am an unhappy madman," he wrote Wrangel. "Such love is a disease. I feel it." Every week he received long letters from her, bearing all the signs of deep, sincere affection. But did she love him? He did not know. Sometimes she called him "brother." Her marriage to his rival was temporarily in abeyance, apparently for financial reasons. He felt that there was no hope, but he remembered his visit and persuaded himself that then he had, after all, won her back. Hope or no hope, he must see her. She had caused his resurrection; she was the light of his life. "She is one of God's angels," he told Mikhail, "whom I met on my way, and suffering bound us together."

His salary as an officer being a mere pittance and his equipment expensive, he was now deeper in debt than ever. He assured his brother that his straits were not due to his sharing what he had with Marya Dmitrievna: she was not the sort to accept anything. As far as he was concerned, he stinted himself "like a Jew." He managed, however, to get to Kuznetzk toward the end of November.

The visit was decisive. On December 21 he wrote to Wrangel that, God willing, he would be married before Carnival. She loved him. She had loved him all along. And he hadn't a kopeck. Mikhail was not to be counted upon. His one hope was his wealthy uncle in Moscow. He would write him and, meanwhile, borrow from a newly acquired friend. If he thus ventured further into debt, it was because he had a thousand rubles' worth of manuscript. It was therefore supremely important for him to obtain permission to publish. If it should be withheld another year, he was lost. He was, of course, willing to write anonymously or under a pseudonym. In all his life he had never faced such a crisis. Wrangel must leave no stone unturned to get him that long-coveted privilege. He should also do what he could for Vergunov. The boy was taking an examination for promotion and wires must be pulled so that he would be sure to get it. He deserved this and more. Vergunov was dearer to him than a brother. He was ready to beg for him on his knees.

The following day he wrote to advise Mikhail of the important event. He told his brother that the decision was final and he was not to be argued out of it. His future wife was a woman in a thousand. If, as he hopes, "the adored being who rules us" will permit him to publish his writings, their livelihood is assured. Literature will yet hear of him. His mind is clearer and steadier, and he has laid up a rich fund of material. As for the worries and troubles that married life carries with it—well, she is dearer to him than the whole world, and he cannot abandon her, helpless and suffering as she is. If Uncle refuses to advance the necessary money, he will have to depend solely upon himself, God, and "His angel, our monarch." He knows that Mikhail's financial assistance is out of the question at this time, but he has one favor to ask of him. Will he not please send an Easter bonnet, two caps with blue ribbons, some silk material in a fashionable color for a dress—his bride is tall and has a fine figure—a mantilla, perhaps of velvet, a lace kerchief, and half a dozen fine linen handkerchiefs. There was nothing decent to be had at Semipalatinsk and what could be bought was frightfully expensive.

Until then Mikhail had been the only one he had taken into

his confidence and he had warned him to keep the love affair a
secret, since he wanted no counsels of prudence from the family.
The time had come when he must tell them. On the day that he
apprised Mikhail of the step he had decided to take, he wrote
to his sister Varya, who had a good deal of influence with the
Kumanins. He painted the situation in a rosy light, to put it
mildly. The lady was six years his junior and came of an excellent family. Her father, who held an important post, with a large
salary, at Astrakhan, was a descendant of a French nobleman
who had fled to Russia during the Revolution. She was a charming and highly educated woman, devout, sensible of her duties,
and he loved her more than his life. They were a perfect match.
They understood and respected each other and had the same
likes and dislikes. Of course, his pay as an officer would not
keep them, but she had had to manage on little before this and
she was a good housekeeper. Besides, sooner or later he would
be permitted to publish his work and so make a living by his
pen. In the meantime he would borrow the money he needed to
get married on, in the hope that Uncle would pay off this debt.
He relied on Varya to break the news to Aunt, to assure her
that he considered her his "guardian angel," and to get her blessing for him. Varya should also hand his letter to Uncle at the
right moment and, with Aunt, bring him to see this marriage in
the right light. As a political offender he was under surveillance
and would probably, and deservedly, long remain suspect. Now,
wasn't the government more likely to trust a settled married
man than an unattached bachelor without responsibilities? It was
essential for him to be in the good books of the authorities, and
marriage would be a step in that direction. Perhaps Uncle would
see the force of that argument. In any event, Dostoevsky concluded, he had made up his mind and nothing would swerve him.

If he considered his poor health an obstacle, he made no
mention of the fact. He did consult local physicians, only to be
assured that his attacks were mere "nerves" and that his marriage might improve matters. To the last, however, he was
harassed by uncertainties: Would he be able to borrow the
money? Could he get to Kuznetzk, be married, and return before the end of his leave, which was only for fifteen days? Any
one of a dozen things might interfere with the wedding. The
enterprise involved a trip of a thousand miles by carriage.

Finally, more than the six hundred rubles which he had mentioned in every letter as his minimum requirement were in his

pocket, and he could proceed to rent a flat and buy the household necessaries—all he owned was a mattress and a pillow. Alas, his officer's equipment was still to be got. Before long he realized that he would be left with nothing on his return to Semipalatinsk.

But he could wait no longer. He decided to take a chance—he had a feeling that luck was with him in all the critical moments of his life. He went to Kuznetzk and everything passed off smoothly. The wedding took place on February 6, 1857. It was a modest yet respectable affair. Nikolay Borisovich Vergunov stood sponsor for the groom. The local chief of police and his wife gave the bride away, and the officiating cleric was present at the feast.

Time was pressing, and the couple had to set out for Semipalatinsk as soon as the ceremony was over. On their way they stopped off at Barnaul. Here Dostoevsky suffered a violent seizure. The physician who was called in diagnosed the case as epilepsy, and when Dostoevsky insisted on knowing the worst, told him that in the course of such an attack he was bound to die of asphyxiation resulting from a throat spasm. The period of the new moon, he added, was particularly dangerous for him.

The news was crushing. It struck him that, had he known the truth, he would have given up the thought of marriage. Whether or not he was overestimating his own prudence, regrets were vain. What if he were to have a seizure while on duty. Strapped in the tight uniform, he was sure to choke to death. Marya Dmitrievna either had not suspected the nature of her husband's attacks or had never been present at one. In any event, she was horribly frightened and also took sick. The newlyweds arrived in Semipalatinsk in a lamentable state. Of course, things were at sixes and sevens in the flat he had rented from a postman. And to make matters worse, the brigade commander arrived and there was a parade, with all the fuss and fatigue it entailed. Their married life was beginning under ominous circumstances.

# 11

## MARKING TIME

THERE was something in Dostoevsky that fought depression. He had a blind faith in the future. It was as though his sufferings had yielded a residue of courage and optimism. The Barnaul doctor, he told himself, may have made a mistake. The bureau drawer held two hundred and fifty rubles: Uncle Kumanin had behaved handsomely, and this sum was left after Dostoevsky had paid a small part of his debts. As for his Masha, the past had left its traces on her, and she was incredibly moody and difficult, but, he wrote Mikhail a fortnight after their return to Semipalatinsk, "she never ceases to be kind and high-minded, I love her dearly, she loves me, and for the time being all goes well." After the stormy months that had preceded their union, the two tasted something like peace. Her anxiety melted away in the atmosphere of affection with which he surrounded her and her child—his judgment of the boy's character was flattering rather than perspicacious. He was happy in loving, she in being loved. They lived quietly, saw few people, and held on to the money, which nevertheless had a way of slipping through their fingers. If only he could earn his bread!

In April his rank in the gentry was restored to him, and he took this to be another token of his monarch's graciousness. Could the government withhold from him much longer per-

mission to return to European Russia and to publish his work?
He saw himself in Moscow before the year was over. It was
essential for him to go there to consult physicians. His attacks
had been more frequent and he had to take a leave of absence
to recuperate. The seizures occurred while he was on sentry
duty, as he had feared, and in his sleep. The aftereffects were
hard to bear. His condition did not remain a secret from his
relatives by marriage, and when one of his sisters-in-law sent him
a nostrum against the falling sickness, he assured her that he
would use it, for he was not opposed to "sympathetic and magnetic cures" and believed in the efficacy of folk remedies.

His whole existence centered on the expectation of leaving
Semipalatinsk. The Siberian air stifled him. There was something demoralizing in the life of this frontier settlement, overrun with petty officials as with locusts. The absence of civilized
amusements—there was but one piano in the whole town—and
of reading matter was stultifying. The men drank, gambled, and
gorged themselves. The women, of whom there were few, had
nothing with which to relieve their boredom except gossip. The
region was a godforsaken wilderness into which the dregs of
Russia had been drained.

There was one redeeming feature in the situation: his anxieties
did not prevent him from writing. He had nothing finished to
show, although as the year 1856 was drawing to a close he was
saying that he had a thousand rubles' worth of manuscript ready
for the press. Most of it existed in his imagination. During the
long oppressive nights in prison he had spun out of his head
what he conceived to be his "great and final tale." When he
was released he did not commence it, though by his own account
"everything was in readiness," because, for one thing, his involvement with Marya Dmitrievna deprived him of the necessary peace of mind, and rather than risk spoiling the material,
he decided not to touch it. Instead, he began a comedy, which
pleased him so much that in order to follow his hero's adventures
in greater detail he turned from the dramatic to the narrative
form.

As the work proceeded, not only was the form altered, but
the tone as well. In the early winter of 1857 he had on his hands
a serious novel, half of it actually written, though in a rough
state. It was going splendidly. And he had to give it up. The
thought of finishing it in a hurry made him sick. He could not
possibly complete it to his satisfaction in time to sell it before

the year was out, and by that time he would need no less a sum than six hundred and fifty rubles to pay off the debt contracted just before his marriage. His creditor, who had promised to wait indefinitely, began to dun him three months after the wedding. Besides, he would soon be without a kopeck for their daily needs. He would put his hand to something less ambitious that could be dashed off and would bring immediate returns. He decided to write a short novel, the plan of which he had formed years back, as well as a story based on a comic episode which was out of place in the long narrative that he had abandoned. What with payment for one of these projected pieces and with a loan of a thousand rubles promised by a former fellow member of the Petrashevsky circle, he could keep afloat for some months. Meanwhile, Mikhail must come to his rescue.

Mikhail did so by securing him an advance of five hundred rubles from the publisher of *Russkoe slovo* (*The Russian Word*), a review that was about to be launched in Petersburg. Of course, this was not enough to cover his debts and provide for current expenses. As the loan apparently failed to materialize, by the time the following year was under way he was again asking himself where the next ruble would come from. In his anxiety he turned to Mikhail Katkov, the publisher of another monthly, the Moscow *Russky vestnik* (*The Russian Herald*), and from him too he received an advance of five hundred rubles. He would give the comic story to *Russkoe slovo* and the novelette to *Russky vestnik*. After the lapse of all these years he was once more putting himself in bondage by selling his unwritten work, as he had repeatedly sworn not to do.

# ( II )

The story was going badly. He hinted that he was hindered by circumstances other than the arrival of a new commander. Perhaps there was trouble at home. With Pasha placed at a school in Omsk and no greater household cares than were given her by their four-room flat, his wife had little to do but brood over her situation. Rather self-important and snobbish, she seems to have decided that she had married beneath her. Nor did she keep that opinion to herself. At first her husband disregarded her allusions, but before long they began to irritate him. The uncertainties of their finances and their health did not make for conjugal harmony. Gossip had it that the situation was aggravated by her jealousy. Apparently there were scenes over a beautiful Polish girl, one time his pupil, and so wild a creature that her elderly husband, before going out, secured himself against cuckoldry by locking a bureau drawer on her long hair. The unhappiness that attended Dostoevsky's married life may have begun in those early days. Eight months after the wedding he was writing to his sister-in-law that he had a foreboding of death, not, he insisted, a hypochondriac notion, but a matter-of-fact sensation: he had experienced everything possible, and life had nothing more to offer him.

What life did offer him was a state of affairs with which he had been well acquainted before he went to prison: illness, money worries, writing against time, the feeling that, thus driven, he was botching his work, and this when he was practically making his second debut. There was yet another spoke in the wheel: on January 16, 1858, he applied for permission to retire from the army on the score of ill health, at the same time requesting the privilege of residence in Moscow. To his petition he attached the following certificate, signed by "Yermakov, physician" on December 16, 1857:

"I have examined *Praporshchik* Fyodor Mikhailovich Dostoevsky in the presence of Captain Bakhirev and ascertained that he is 35 years old and of middling physique. In 1850 he suffered his first attack of falling sickness (*epilepsia*) with these manifestations: outcry, loss of consciousness, convulsions of extremities and face, foam at the mouth, stertorous breathing, small, fast, abbreviated pulse. The attack lasted fifteen minutes. Followed, general weakness and return of consciousness. In 1853 he suffered another attack, and since then they occur at the end of every month. At present Dostoevsky complains of general weakness and a run-down condition, also of frequent facial neuralgia due to an organic ailment of the brain. Although during the past four years he has been almost constantly under treatment for epilepsy, he has had no relief, and for that reason cannot continue in His Majesty's service."

For over a twelvemonth he was kept on tenterhooks waiting to have his petition granted. Meanwhile, in February, 1858, he learned that "The Little Hero," the tale he had written in prison while waiting to be sentenced, had been published the previous year in the August- issue of *Fatherland Notes*—news from home traveled slowly. This was disconcerting, for he had wanted to rewrite the piece. Still, there was comfort in the reflection that though the story had been printed anonymously, the government was lifting the ban on his work.

It is not known when he began "Uncle's Dream," the story for *Russkoe slovo*; it was completed early in 1859, and published in the March issue of the magazine. He took his time over the work, goaded though he was. When Mikhail chided him for his tardiness, he replied with some heat that though he usually set a scene down in the first flush of inspiration as was right, afterward he spent months and years polishing it. What also kept him from getting on faster with the story was the realization that in being reintroduced to the public with "Uncle's Dream," he was not putting his best foot forward. Indeed, the story shows no evidence of the maturity that time and suffering should have brought. That he wrote in dread of the censor may account for its inoffensiveness. He was to describe it as "a trifle of dovelike gentleness and remarkable innocence." Actually it is a farcical piece, peopled with grotesque caricatures and lay figures. The chief character is Prince K., who is in the last stage of decrepitude and senility, in fact, looking as if at any moment he might fall apart. Since he is also wealthy and a bachelor, on arriving in town he becomes the object of passionate interest to the local ladies eager to marry off their nubile daughters.

There is no need to enlarge on the leading matron's unscrupulous scheme to bring about a union between the Prince and her twenty-three-year-old Liza, beautiful but dowerless. The stratagem fails; in the end Liza marries a provincial governor and her mother's social standing is restored. In the background there is the figure made familiar by Dostoevsky's early stories: the young dreamer who, through some fatal flaw in his nature, loses the woman he loves, this time in a most improbable way. The provincial setting is obviously the fruit of the author's Semipalatinsk experiences. He must have been paying off many old scores when he wrote that the provincials, because of their constant spying on each other, ought to be psychologists and specialists in human nature, but that instead they were mostly asses.

All the while he was busy off and on with the novelette intended for *Russky vestnik*: *The Village of Stepanchikovo* (known in English and hereafter referred to as *The Friend of the Family*). The manuscript was dispatched to the publisher shortly before the couple shook the dust of Semipalatinsk from their feet. Dostoevsky was not unaware that the narrative was long-drawn-out and bad in places, but, he wrote to Mikhail, "it has scenes of high comedy, such as Gogol could have signed. . . . I have put my soul in it, my flesh and blood." The novelette is superior to its predecessor. Suspense is not lacking, and the villain is memorably and amusingly characterized. The figure dominating the action is a man who for years has eaten the bread of humiliation, his dignity outraged and trampled upon. Dostoevsky places him in a position in which he is the master, pampered and adulated, and watches his antics as the absurd creature, indulging in unctuous rhetoric, gives free rein to his limitless conceit and lords it over everyone in his neighborhood. The author achieves his effect by overstatement, so that one sees his Foma Fomich as the embodiment of a monstrous self-esteem that is his overcompensation for insults previously endured. The other characters, all of whom revolve around Foma and dance to his piping, are drawn in less detail, with the exception of Colonel Rostanev, the nominal master of the house. He is a naïve soul whose boundless kindness and meekness are matched only by his reverence for learning and virtue. The tale comes to a climax when, for having slandered his betrothed, he turns Foma Fomich out of the house by flinging him violently at a glass door leading into the courtyard. Not before he has been drenched by a melodramatic thunderstorm, the villain apologizes and is reinstated. The genial tone, the happy ending of the narrative are less present to the reader than the Russian Tartuffe around whom it centers. It is possible to see some trace of the author's experience as a convict in the fact that he chose to draw a slave in power, tryrannizing over his betters, while the pure in heart is something of a gullible fool. Several more years will pass, however, before the emotions and ideas germinated in the darkness of the prison will ripen and bear fruit in his writings. It is noteworthy that neither "Uncle's Dream" nor *The Friend of the Family* bear upon a matter that was uppermost in the public mind: the impending emancipation of the serfs.

# ( III )

Dostoevsky was making final preparations for the event that had for so long been the center of his hopes—departure from Siberia. In March, 1859, he was granted permission to retire from the army. At the same time he was placed under police surveillance, from which he was not freed until shortly before his death. He was allowed to return to European Russia, though he would have to live not in Moscow, as he had wished, but in the provinces. The city he chose to reside in was Tver (now Kalinin), situated on the railway line between Moscow and Petersburg. The money at hand for the trek would take the little family only as far as Kazan. For the last time Mikhail must save him by sending a remittance *poste restante* to that city, or he would find himself stranded in a strange place.

They bought a *tarantas* in which to make the trip, with the expectation of selling it at the end of the journey. Whatever they could, they disposed of, including Marya Dmitrievna's hats, presumably because they were too outlandish to be worn at home. The great day, July 2, 1859, dawned clear and fine. The farewells were long and effusive, and there was much clinking of glasses before the late afternoon hour at which they set off.

A postilion accompanied them all the way, and they changed horses and drivers at each posting station. The weather was admirable and the road smooth. Their first stop was Omsk, that place of bleak memories. Here they picked up Pasha and went on their way. The weather continued fine, and though the road grew worse, the carriage held out bravely, nor was there any delay in getting fresh horses. Aside from two attacks during the early part of the trip, Dostoevsky kept well. The only fly in the ointment was the staggering prices they had to pay for food and other necessaries at the stations: it got so that on being told the cost of this or that article the traveler would look fearfully into the eye of the vendor to see if the man was in his right mind. Yekaterinburg (now Sverdlovsk) was the exception, and there, tempted by the cheapness of the goods displayed, they bought all manner of knickknacks to take home as presents.

One glorious afternoon toward five o'clock they came to a

forest clearing where a tall post marked the borderline between Asia and Europe. They all clambered out. His feet once more on native ground, Dostoevsky crossed himself. Before him, by the Lord's mercy, lay the promised land. It was ten years since he had stood in the snowy darkness, fronting in the opposite direction, and saying a mute good-bye to Europe and his youth. Those years had tempered and toughened him. They had robbed him of something forever and brought him strange and terrible gifts in exchange. But this was not the time for reckoning profit and loss. The vodka flask in its wicker basket came out, and everybody, not forgetting the faithful postilion and the coachman and the veteran who guarded the post, drank to the hour. Then Dostoevsky, with an unaccustomed sense of freedom, wandered off with Masha and the child to explore the woods and pick the wild strawberries that dotted this beloved earth.

When they set out again it was to travel through virgin forests so splendid that even one as indifferent to natural beauty as Dostoevsky could not but be enchanted and lifted out of his current anxieties. They seized him again when he reached the Volga and found himself in Kazan, as he had foreseen, without enough money to complete the trip. A tedious and expensive wait of ten days followed. Then the remittance came from Mikhail and they went on, catching a glimpse of the great fair at Nizhny and stopping to visit the Troitzky monastery to which as a boy he used to be taken by his mother. He was less moved by its associations than amazed by its treasures and monuments: the Byzantine chapels, the rich jewels, the old books, the needlework of czarinas, the garments of Ivan the Terrible. And then came the domes and gables of Tver, the goal of the long journey.

At Tver they were "settled on a pinpoint." They would soon be moving on to Petersburg, but how soon? The uncertainty was nerve-wracking. They were marking time. He was neither bond nor free. The promised land was proving no nearer the heart's desire than the wilderness. Indeed, Tver was the most hateful city in the world, a thousand times worse than Semipalatinsk: no interests, no life, bleak, cold, stony—a prison. He was so close to, and yet, considering the wretched postal service, so far from his friends and relatives in the two capitals. And here they had to set up housekeeping, spend their last few rubles on such essentials as a samovar, and wait. Of course, everything was very expensive, and there was no buyer for the Siberian chaise, the family's sole capital. Masha, being without a bonnet, was confined to their furnished flat, which did not improve her disposition.

At once disaster swooped. Katkov, after some hemming and hawing, turned down *The Friend of the Family* and told the author that he could get his manuscript as soon as he refunded the five hundred rubles that had been advanced to him. Far from being sunk, Dostoevsky was buoyed up by the familiar waters of calamity. His faith in the little novel was unshaken. When, therefore, at the end of August, Mikhail came to embrace the brother from whom an evil fate and long years had divided him, Dostoevsky was able to persuade him to redeem the manuscript and try to place it elsewhere. They had five days in which to renew their intimacy. It was a difficult business, but they made a start. At last there was someone to whom Dostoevsky could unburden himself, to whom he could speak freely of his plans, to whom he could retail the plots of the novels that he was revolving in his mind. When it came to the question of getting permission to live in Petersburg, they decided to do nothing until after September 8, when the Heir Apparent attained his majority and Dostoevsky might come under the amnesty that was expected on a state occasion.

Mikhail set off at once to secure the manuscript, and having obtained it, offered it to *Sovremennik*. Dostoevsky was out of sympathy with its liberal outlook, but it was an important review and he was anxious to see his name in it. His situation was desperate, but when Nekrasov, who had privately decided that Dostoevsky was played out and would not come back, offered him less than the figure he had set, he instructed Mikhail to refuse it. They must put a good face on a bad business and hold out for the right price. They must bargain, they must haggle, they must pit one editor against another. What he wants is not glory, but money. After much maneuvering and many worries, the novel was bought by his old employer, Krayevsky, at Dostoevsky's figure, and appeared in *Fatherland Notes* at the end of the year.

The sale of the manuscript saved the situation, and with a little help from Mikhail and his sisters he was able to face the future. If only he could collect his writings and publish them in book form, either on his own or through a bookseller. This would keep him going and allow him to concentrate on a big piece of work. It was October when, after some hesitation, he decided to turn his hand to writing an account of his prison days. He assured Mikhail that he would finish it in six weeks. Then he planned to settle down to his great novel. It was the work that he had conceived in prison, his "confession," the thought of which had been with him constantly. He would put his heart's blood into it. He felt that he was now ripe for it, that it would be his definitive utterance. It would be a trilogy, and would allow him to work in a story of passion, the idea for which had come to him later and which he had never used. With his incurable optimism as to his speed, he gave himself three or four months to finish the first part.

In spite of his fine intentions and his courageous mood, he could not keep his promises to himself—his situation was too difficult. His illness persisted, and what was the use of going to provincial doctors? They were either young men just out of school or old fogies who had forgotten all the medicine they had ever known. Also, he was finding a few more creases in the marriage bed. Masha was uneasy. He could not help feeling that she feared he would die here in Tver and leave her and her child in the same position in which his predecessor had left them. And there was always the oppressive uncertainty as to how soon they could leave this miserable place. The eagerly anticipated eighth of September left matters unchanged. Something had to be done.

Dostoevsky was not without friends in Tver, and though social life in the provinces was something of a nuisance, it had its uses. He was in fact received socially by the Governor himself, and this high official undertook to transmit the petition which Dostoevsky decided to address to the Emperor. It was an abject missive in which he requested permission to live in Petersburg in order to get the medical attention which would, he trusted, prevent his attacks from ending in death or insanity. He also put in a request for a scholarship for his stepson, Pavel, in a secondary school or cadet corps. In conclusion he compared the Emperor to the sun shining on the just and unjust alike, and declared himself ready to give up his life for him. He also wrote in a similar strain to General Todtleben, who had responded to his appeal on a previous occasion, and to Prince Dolgorukov, the Chief of the Gendarmerie. In fact he wrote to so many possible benefactors at once that he thereby delayed his release from the Tver captivity. In November he slipped off to Moscow for a short visit to his relatives and returned more resentful of his confinement and more fretted by the uncertainty of his lot than ever. His delivery came in the middle of December, and the Christmas Eve that marked the tenth anniversary of his departure for Siberia he was able to spend in Petersburg with Mikhail.

# 12

# RESURRECTION

LIKE birth, resurrection is traumatic. Back in the capital Dostoevsky had not only to rediscover his friends, to re-establish himself in literature, to plunge from the stagnant backwaters of Siberia into the quick current of metropolitan life, but to adjust himself to an altered world, to an age that had a complexion different from that which he had known ten years earlier.

Some suggestion of the change had reached him in his isolation. But now he had to take the full impact of the serious sixties. The Crimean campaign had had one usual effect of a disastrous foreign war in lowering the prestige of the government. The death of the iron Nicholas in the midst of defeat had brought to the throne a monarch bent on giving the country a new deal. In the forties a few earnest souls used to come together and explore roads to Utopia, and talk, under the rose, about the need for the correction of public evils. Now the government itself was pushing great reforms, chief of all the liberation of the serfs. Official corruption was denounced so volubly at every dinner table that the subject had become tedious. The press was permitted to deal with questions of policy, foreign and domestic, and forbidden topics were discussed in manuscript pamphlets. The air was astir with great expectations. This clement weather encouraged the spirit of opposition. Before long it would associate itself with the faith and works of militant socialism.

Slavophilism and Westernism continued to exist but had lost much of their actuality. What counted now was not the East-West antithesis, but the conflict between those who upheld the prerogatives of the upper classes and those who defended the interests of the peasants, between the partisans of peaceful reform and the advocates of the use of force against the established order. These extremists were apt to be designated, mostly by their detractors, as Nihilists. The term, new to Dostoevsky, was something of a misnomer, made popular by Turgenev's *Fathers and Children* (1862). It denoted a section of the younger intelligentsia of both sexes in revolt against the ancestral order. A Nihilist rejected all authority, including that of religion; he thought of himself as a hardheaded materialist guided by rational egoism and devoted to the natural sciences. He scorned whatever smacked of gentility and romanticism and was concerned for the underdog. With this went a conception of the arts that anticipated "socialist realism," an affectation of bumptious manners and careless attire. To some extent this iconoclasm was a fad. There were parlor Nihilists as there would be parlor pinks. But among the rebels there were idealistic youths who dreamed of or planned revolution.

It was not easy for the ex-convict to find his bearings in the confusion of the new era. Certainly his sympathies were not with the Nihilists. They were likely to welcome a political prisoner returning from exile, but in those ten years he had parted ways with the young man who had attended the Petrashevsky Fridays, had read Belinsky's subversive letter before a responsive gathering, and had had a hand in an attempt to set up a secret press. He was now a faithful communicant, a loyal subject.

He fell in with people of a rather conservative temper. They were his contemporaries or slightly younger, interested like himself in public affairs, and trafficking in ideas. It was not a particularly distinguished circle, composed mostly of lesser lights in the world of letters, with a scattering of members of the other professions. He found some familiars here, such as Apollon Maikov and Dr. Yanovsky. Of course, Dostoevsky took a leading place. There was something attractive about this pale, big-browed man with the military mustache and the look of a plebeian; his history—of which he said little—was unusual, his mind original, his talk simple, vehement, pregnant. He was stimulated by the presence of such new friends as the lovable and gifted critic Apollon Grigoryev and the young student of natural science and philosophy Nikolay Strakhov.

Dostoevsky was not content with being a writer of fiction. He had the urge to reshape the world, not merely in his imagination, but also in fact. Before leaving Siberia he had been nursing the notion of having a corner in some journal where he could comment on what was going on around him. In Tver the notion had crystallized into a project for founding a review with his brother. Mikhail, on his part, was anxious to go into the publishing business. Fyodor, the same man he had been a dozen years before, at least in this, was sure that the two of them together could easily make a fortune. The plan was carried out promptly. The first issue of *Vremya* (*Time*), as the monthly was called, appeared on January 1, 1861. Mikhail, the owner, was the business manager, his brother edited and determined the policy of the periodical, while Grigoryev and Strakhov became steady contributors.

The field was by no means a crowded one, but the reading public was extremely limited. *Fatherland Notes,* Dostoevsky's old market, had deteriorated. Nekrasov's *Sovremennik,* on the other hand, was flourishing under the direction of Nikolay Chernyshevsky, the leading radical, on whom the mantle of Belinsky had fallen. The Moscow *Russky vestnik* was coming to the fore. The more recent *Russkoe slovo* was soon to become the organ of an extreme Nihilist faction. There was yet another journal, *Kolokol* (*The Bell*), published abroad, smuggled into Russia, and there avidly read *sub rosa*. Alexander Herzen, its owner and editor, was the most prominent and influential of the expatriates who were beginning to cluster in Geneva, Paris, London, and there work for radical reforms and, in fact, for revolution at home.

*Vremya* was a literary magazine, but also a forum for polemics and for discussion of sundry problems, indeed, the organ of a cause. In his opening announcement the editor declared that the review would seek to bridge the abyss that the reforms of Peter the Great had opened between the educated, privileged minority and the masses. Thereafter, Dostoevsky never tired of urging the enlightened gentry to put an end to its alienation from the common people. There was no obstacle to this peaceful revolution, since, he insisted, quite forgetting his lot as a "gentleman" in prison, Russia knew no class antagonisms. For the latter proposition he was indebted to the Slavophile theory that while in the West the body politic is based on a shaky compact between conquerors and conquered, the Russian nation is essentially an expanded patriarchal family. Emphasis on Russia's distinctness was another plank in the platform of the review. "Our task," he wrote, "is to create for ourselves a new form, our own, indigenous, taken from our soil, our national spirit and national principles."

In commenting on the policy of *Vremya,* Dostoevsky attributed to his fellow countrymen a unique endowment: the instinct of panhumanism, the ability to adjust to and identify with strangers. The Russian people may thus be able, he vaticinated, to combine the separate cultures into a living synthesis and lead united mankind toward a common ideal. Vasily Kirpotin, a Soviet student of the novelist, has recently traced this curious notion to a remark by Belinsky, to the effect that because Russians have "the striking capacity of grasping and making their own everything alien to them, as a nation they may be destined to live the richest and most many-sided life." This supposition, uttered "without bragging and fanaticism," Dostoevsky changed into a tenet of chauvinistic messianism, while in the next breath crediting the Russians with freedom from self-glorification. He was to return to Russian panhumanism without making the proposition any less preposterous.

A panhuman synthesis, making room for foreign, that is, chiefly Western, cultures, was not acceptable to the Slavophiles. They too envisaged Russia's global leadership, but with Hegel they held that a nation, like an organism, can develop its potentialities only according to the laws of what makes it a unique entity. In more than one way Dostoevsky's thinking was at variance with Slavophilism. This was a backward-looking doctrine, under the spell of old Muscovy; the editor of *Vremya* had his eyes focused on the future. The Slavophiles' snobbishness irritated him. It was obvious that they were comfortable gentry with lands and mansions, and, only a short while ago, serfs. He had nothing but his pen between him and starvation. Indeed, the scorn of the literary proletarian for the privileged breaks out in his private communications. He had, however, much in common with these pietistic nationalists and before long he would find himself one of them, though not without reservations. For the time being, he held aloof.

Dostoevsky chose to cling to what he considered his own flag:

the doctrine that the country's salvation lay in the union between the intelligentsia and the people of the "soil," that is, the
simple Russian folk. This devoutly wished consummation would,
he believed, prevent the formation of a proletariat and a bourgeoisie, both of which he abominated, and would insure the empire against the disaster of revolution. The necessity of the
union was perpetually harped upon in the pages of *Vremya*, but
how it was to be achieved remained nebulous. The one practical
step advocated by the journal was the gradual spread of literacy,
regarded as a panacea. The measure, which remained a pious
wish, was opposed not only by obscurantists. Some of its enemies feared that it would increase the incidence of crime. Oddly
enough, the critics included Vladimir Dahl, a patriot of Dan-
ish stock who was a prolific writer and Russia's greatest lexi-
cographer.

Although the policy of the review was anti-Nihilist and anti-
Westernist (it attacked the Anglophile slant of *Russky vestnik*),
it was not reactionary. Indeed, the periodical was looked at
askance by the authorities. It stood for the great reforms of the
period, advocated the emancipation of women, favored the
preservation of collective land tenure. Contributions from Nekrasov and other radicals appeared in its pages, and once it took
an enlightened stand on the Jewish question. In an editorial note
appended to a translation of Victor Hugo's *Notre Dame de
Paris* Dostoevsky wrote: "The basic idea of the art of the nineteenth century is the rehabilitation of the oppressed social pariah, and perhaps toward the end of the century this idea will
be embodied in some great work as expressive of our age as the
*Divine Comedy* is of the Middle Ages."

During the winter of 1861 he figured, together with Chernyshevsky, on the program of a literary soirée which was designed
as a parade of progressives and which resulted in the deportation of one of the speakers. When, the previous fall, certain
students were jailed for protesting against the government's
attempt to restrict their liberties, *Vremya* expressed sympathy
for the rebels by sending them a huge roast beef, prepared in
Mikhail's kitchen, along with a bottle of cognac and one of red
wine.

One morning in May, 1862, Dostoevsky, like many other
people in the capital, found at his door a leaflet entitled "Young
Russia," the work of a group of students in Moscow, run off on
a secret press. "Russia," it began, "is entering the revolutionary

period of its existence." It went on to call for the total destruction of the old order by a revolution, which "must change everything down to the very roots. . . . We are not afraid of it although we know that rivers of blood will flow." Followed a detailed outline of the various elements of the new system and the announcement that Russia was destined to be "the first country to establish Socialism" and ending with the words: "Long live the Russian Social and Democratic Republic!" Several days after the appearance of this astounding manifesto a series of fires ravaged the capital and other cities. The conservative press hastened to blame the revolutionists for the conflagrations.

At first Dostoevsky gave credence to the charge. He rushed to Chernyshevsky and implored him to use his good offices with the young hotheads so as to keep them from further excesses. Chernyshevsky, who was scarcely acquainted with his visitor, was amazed by the absurd request, and fearing lest argument make the man violent, gave him every reassurance. Before long Dostoevsky changed his mind. *Vremya* tried to discredit the theory of revolutionary incendiarism and also to absolve the student body as a whole from responsibility for the "Young Russia" leaflet. The editor submitted two versions of an article on the subject, but they were not passed by the censor and the magazine barely escaped suspension.

The concessions to the liberal point of view prevalent at the time may have been made in order to secure subscribers. Was *Vremya* trying to serve both God and Mammon, as Apollon Grigoryev bluntly phrased it? Be that as it may, the review achieved a considerable financial success. In its second year it had more than four thousand subscribers and was practically a rival of *Sovremennik* and *Russky vestnik,* the two leading monthlies of the period.

# ( II )

Dostoevsky wore the editorial yoke with a will. He selected material for several departments, he revised and annotated manuscripts, he read proof, he contributed serious essays and light pieces, he engaged in controversy—polemics was the life of the magazines of the day—he wrote exhibition notices and book reviews, he had a hand in the section on current events, he composed the annual advertisement calculated to catch the subscriber. He harangued, prophesied, jeered, entertained. He was in his element. Newspapers and journals had always constituted a large part of his reading. Although he was outraged by the Nihilist idea that literature was merely a tool of social betterment, he was anything but content with an ivory tower. He was always ready to climb down and travel the dusty road of journalism. To be in the thick of things, to comment on the passing scene, to form public opinion—this was a satisfaction second only to that of his main business as a novelist.

The transition from being turned inward upon himself, in a place where the latest paper was a month old, to heading a large national review was a dizzying experience and one which fed his sense of power. No wonder, then, that he plunged into the work with a kind of frenzy. But here was this wretched unmanageable body of his. It was always on the point of playing him false. In March, 1861, when the April issue was being prepared, he was struck down by an epileptic seizure of unusual violence and lay unconscious for nearly three days. It was his fate to have to work by fits and starts.

Gradually life fell into as much of a routine as the attacks allowed. He was temporarily released from the iron vise of poverty. Shortly after returning to Petersburg he succeeded in getting a bookseller to issue a two-volume edition of his collected works, and when, the next year, *Vremya* made its appearance, there was always a little money to be had. His rooms were on a mean street in a poor, crowded neighborhood, a few blocks away from Mikhail's house, where the editorial office was located. Nearby was Strakhov's lodging. Dostoevsky usually reached the office around three o'clock, having just breakfasted on a cup of tea. At the first opportunity he had reverted to the habit of working at night and sleeping late. At Mikhail's he would generally find Strakhov and perhaps one or two others. They would look over the mail together, read the papers, discuss the news, and go for a stroll until dinnertime. Petersburg was a dreadful place—the look of it depressed, the climate killed you. But, after all, everybody who lived the life of the mind was there. Often he would drop in on Strakhov again at seven o'clock and have tea with him. There was much about this man to attract Dostoevsky: his wide culture, his knowledge of philosophy, his critical acumen. Hegel's *History of Philosophy,* sent by Mikhail to his brother in Semipalatinsk at his urgent request, had remained unread, and at the first opportunity he presented it to Strakhov. He was to admit that in philosophy he was rather *"schwach,"* even though he loved the subject. He now had a chance to discuss fundamentals with this friend, who had had the formal training that he himself had missed, and who enjoyed playing the pedagogue.

During their long hours together Strakhov observed his friend closely. He found in him "a peculiar duality": Dostoevsky was capable of giving himself up to certain thoughts and feelings, but his surrender was not complete; a part of his mind played the role of the unconcerned onlooker. It was from the deep, secret chamber of the self where the beholder was stationed, Strakhov suggested not unreasonably, that the energy came which flowed into his art. Dostoevsky was himself aware of his habit of watching his own reactions; as though in a single body there were an actor and an audience of one.

He was glad to have Strakhov by him during the fits of dejection which so often assailed him, as well as when he was recovering from an epileptic attack. Strakhov left an account of one seizure which he witnessed in 1863. It was Easter Eve, near midnight, and the two were alone at Strakhov's, deep in talk. "He [Dostoevsky] was saying something that was full of exaltation and joy. When I supported his thoughts with a remark, he turned to me with the face of one at the peak of ecstasy. He hesitated a moment as though seeking for a word, and had already opened his lips to pronounce it. I looked at him with keen attention, feeling that he was about to utter something extraordinary, that I would hear some revelation. Suddenly, a strange, long-drawn-out, meaningless moan issued from his mouth, and he sank to the floor unconscious. . . . The body was rigid with convulsions and foam appeared at the corners of the mouth." It was common for the attack to be preceded by an instant of such ecstasy as Strakhov noticed on his companion's face. "For a few moments," Dostoevsky used to say, "I experience such happiness as is impossible under ordinary conditions, and of which other people can have no notion. I feel complete harmony in myself and in the world, and this feeling is so strong and sweet that for several seconds of such bliss one would give ten years of one's life, indeed, perhaps one's whole life."

In *The Idiot* there is a detailed account of Prince Myshkin's epileptic aura. "The sensation of life, the consciousness of self,

were increased almost tenfold at these moments, which lasted no
longer than a lightning flash. His mind and his heart were flooded
with extraordinary light; all his vexations, all his doubts, all his
anxieties were laid to rest at once, as it were; they were all resolved into a lofty calm, full of serene, harmonious joy and hope,
full of reason and ultimate comprehension. But these moments,
these flashes, were only a premonition of that final second (it
was never more than a second) with which the fit began. That
second was of course unendurable." The moment is further described as giving "a feeling, unheard of and unsuspected till then,
of completeness, of proportion, of reconciliation, and of startled
devotional merging with the highest synthesis of life." Dostoevsky has his hero reflect that this moment of ecstasy, of "being
at its highest," is but part of his disease, and yet Myshkin arrives
at the paradox that this "extraordinary strengthening of the consciousness of self," however abnormal in origin and destructive in
effect, remains a real, a supreme value, and is indeed "worth the
whole of life." Dostoevsky does not mention in this passage the
depression which followed the fit and which was as acute as the
premonitory bliss. What dominated him in this black mood was
an unaccountable feeling that he was an evildoer, that he had
committed a terrible crime which had gone unpunished.


# ( III )


Dostoevsky's relations with his wife after his return from
Siberia are something of a mystery. At first they shared living
quarters—Strakhov caught a glimpse of her one day and long
remembered her delicate, pleasing features and her pallor. Later
on she stayed alone, at least part of the time, in Tver or Vladimir,
where the climate was less unfriendly to a consumptive than in
the capital. Before long she was reduced to the existence of a bed-
ridden invalid. So little is heard of her that it was as though
Dostoevsky were leading the life of a bachelor. If he did not, like
his brother Mikhail, "the last of the romantics," keep a mistress,
who bore him a son, he may well have allowed himself sexual
adventures outside the marriage bond. It is not impossible that
the lurid incident retailed in *Notes from the Underground*
derives from experiences of this period. He was moving in a

circle where, according to Strakhov, people were tolerant of "all kinds of physical excesses and abnormalities" and where, though "spiritual vileness was judged strictly and subtly, carnal vileness did not count at all." Such an attitude toward sins spiritual and carnal was peculiarly congenial to Dostoevsky. The evidence, which is incomplete, of his own indulgence in a sexual abnormality, must be discussed elsewhere.

It is certain that his marriage had not proved a happy one. From Tver he wrote to Wrangel: "If you ask me, what shall I say? I've taken family cares upon me, and I bear the burden." He confided the nature of their private difficulties to at least one person, a woman and discreet. He had met this Alexandra Schubert, née Kulikova, during the first year of his stay in Petersburg at one of Mikhail's modest evening parties. She was a fascinating little actress who had taken his old friend Yanovsky as her second husband. She was estranged from him at this time, partly because he objected to her continuing on the boards. Dostoevsky sided with her, and she was naturally delighted to find a champion in a friend of the doctor's who was also a writer of note. Dostoevsky, for his part, relished the society of a charming woman, who was bathed in the glamor of the stage and whose grace and good humor relieved him from the tension in which he habitually lived. There was some talk of dramatizing *Netochka Nezvanova* and giving her the lead, but that came to nothing.

She was playing in Moscow when he went there for a glimpse of the old city in the spring of 1860, and it was during one of his visits that he opened his heart to her on the subject of his own domestic circumstances. When he returned to Petersburg, he wrote to her, thereby arousing Yanovsky's lively suspicions. Dostoevsky saw that the man was suffering from two kinds of jealousy: that of love and that of self-love, and said so in a letter to the actress. He also took occasion to assure her that he himself loved her too disinterestedly, too fervently, to be in love with her. Either because she had no use for his affection or because he had exaggerated its fervor, she seems to have dropped suddenly and completely out of his life. Yanovsky, too, practically disappears from the picture. As a successful administrator—he ultimately won the rank of general—he felt that it did not become him to mix with mere scribblers.

Dostoevsky was scribbling away at a great rate. In addition to his publicist writing there was his fiction. The first issue of *Vremya* carried as its chief attraction the initial installment of a full-sized novel from his pen, under the title *The Humbled and Insulted,* known in English as *The Insulted and Injured.*

This "feuilleton novel," as he called it, was far from being the masterwork that he had been planning to produce as soon as he returned from Siberia. It was an inferior performance. He had written *The Insulted and Injured* in a hurry, he said by way of excuse, because the review was in want of a novel. Yet he seems to have taken considerable time over it, and besides, some of his best work was written in haste. Much of this humorless book is derivative or half-thought-out and faulty in execution. The pages drip with syrupy sentiment, and many characters and situations are the dusty appurtenances of melodrama and the mystery tale—ranging from Sue to Hoffmann. Fourteen-year-old Nellie and her unhappy mother have stepped out of the pages of Dickens. The child is the first of Dostoevsky's characters to be shown in an epileptic fit. She and her mother figure in a subsidiary plot. The main fable deals unconvincingly with love in a fashion not often exploited in melodrama. Vanya (Ivan Petrovich), the narrator and protagonist, loves Natasha, an impecunious girl given to moralizing at length, who is in love with Alyosha, a contemptible fellow; he includes in his affections both Natasha and Katya, a beautiful young millionairess. Vanya is at pains to promote Natasha's union with Alyosha, she being glad that her flame makes her suffer ("Everything is purified by suffering" is one of her maxims), and anticipating the pleasure of tormenting him. Furthermore, each of the two girls is prepared to surrender Alyosha to the other.

The novel is undisguisedly autobiographical. Ivan Petrovich is an ailing penniless man of letters whose debut is a replica of Dostoevsky's experience and whose role is not unlike that of the hero of "White Nights" and that of the novelist when he all but assisted his future wife into marriage with another suitor. One recognizes Dostoevsky's hand in the passages on Prince Valkovsky, Alyosha's father, the chief villain of the tale, whom Ivan Petrovich likens to a huge spider. An immoralist, rumored to have indulged in secret loathsome debauchery, he is the first of the demonic characters who inhabit Dostoevsky's major fictions. He confesses that at one time he had wanted to be "a benefactor of mankind" and had founded "a philanthropic society" (a hint at the Petrashevsky circle?), but he now delights voluptuously in excoriating what he calls "Schillerism": starry-eyed idealism.

It is clear that the author is on the side of the angels. Yet he allows virtue to be its own, and only, reward. The insulted and injured go unavenged, while the pure-hearted Ivan Petrovich is doomed to die destitute and alone, the unconscionable Alyosha gets Katya, and the unspeakable Prince, favored by fortune, is left in secure possession of his ill-gotten gains and is about to marry a young heiress. If the story has any point, it lies in the contrast between the love that "seeketh not itself to please" and the lust of the man who knows no law but that of his own appetites. It is of interest to compare the finale with that of *The Friend of the Family,* in which goodness triumphs, rejoicing all hearts.

# (IV)

Though Dostoevsky had the unhappiness of knowing that his first ambitious effort since his return to literature was a mediocre piece of work, he had reason to feel that it was merely a misstep. He was certain that he would yet find a way to say what he must say. For the present he had another iron in the fire: a book on convict life. He had begun jotting down reminiscences of his years at hard labor shortly after his release. He is said to have started writing them even before his irons were struck off. He had brought back from Siberia a notebook containing scraps of prison argot and barracks talk that he had put down on the spot. It was during the miserable weeks in Tver that the work had assumed definite shape in his head. He called it *Notes from the Dead House* (known in English and hereafter referred to as *The House of the Dead*—Constance Garnett's translation of the title). It would be a gripping thing, he wrote to Mikhail on October 9, 1859, and full of stuff new to literature. He expected to have it ready by December 1. Actually it was serialized in *Vremya* during 1861–62. Baron Medem, the chief Petersburg censor, questioned the wisdom of publishing Chapter II on the ground that it pictured penal servitude as not harsh enough to deter crime, but in the end he relented.

In spite of the thin pretense of being a landed gentleman's memoirs dealing with the ten years of hard labor that he had served for killing his wife, *The House of the Dead* is virtually a record of Dostoevsky's experiences as a convict. He did not, however, as he had planned to do, make the book impersonal. His private reactions to what he endured are by no means excluded.

It stands apart from the body of his work. In substance it is a documentary, rich, of course, in psychological insights. Turgenev wrote of this masterly thing that the bath-house scene is "simply Dantesque," and Herzen likened the characters to the figures in Michelangelo's frescoes. A keen, candid observer, the narrator, while sketching in the physical environment and even devoting a warm, unsentimental chapter to the prison animals, focuses his attention on his fellow convicts. At first they are shown as sullen, touchy, envious bullies, slandering each other, stealing from each other, prizing money no less than freedom. As professional criminologists have told us, those not depraved before being sentenced became so in the penitentiary. None appears to repent his crimes, some of these horrible in the extreme and committed in cold blood. Though the brutish regime is mitigated by official laxity, the prison is described as "hell, outer darkness." The narrator's attitude toward the other inmates is not one of loathing or even repugnance. He has no fear of them, he studies them, he tries to understand them. What results is a cross beween a series of portraits and a set of case histories by a perceptive layman. They offer glimpses of life chiefly in Russia's lower depths. This applies particularly to a transcript of a conversation between two convicts about the hideous murder committed by one of them—a story that reads not as if it had been overheard, but as if it had been invented by an older, more embittered Dostoevsky.

The few political offenders, including the author, form a group apart. Among the common criminals, certain figures stand out. Several monsters stalk the pages. Such is the local informer. Another is the prison Hercules, who is rumored to take pleasure in cutting the throats of little children. Dostoevsky solaced himself with the company of a young Caucasian Tartar whose place on the sleeping platform was beside his own. The youth had been sentenced to hard labor because, out of respect due to his elder brothers, he accompanied four of them on a bloody robbery which resulted in the capture of the band. To have known this Tartar, always considerate, scrupulous, full of the intelligence of the heart, was, he declared, the best memory of his life. There were others with whom he became friendly. One was an Old Believer, a gentle soul who accepted his punishment for having had a hand in burning an Orthodox church as "martyrdom for the old faith." Again there was a fearless fellow of latent, if violent, passions, capable of vigorous action (a soldier, he had stabbed his commanding officer). There was, too, a notorious robber and cutthroat, a man of unlimited will power, an example of the triumph of the spirit over the flesh.

As the narrator painfully, gradually resigns himself to convict life without fully adjusting himself to it, he decides that his misery may have made him too harsh in judging most of his fellows and that he may have painted too bleak a picture of prison existence. He ventures to say, paradoxically, that the convicts were "perhaps by no means much worse than the people beyond the prison walls." To know a man's inner being is all but impossible. After observing someone for years you may conclude that he is a brute, but a moment comes when you find in him such compassion, such an understanding heart, that you are astounded. No such revealing moments are recorded in *The House of the Dead*. Nor does it support the amazing observation with which the work closes, namely, that the inmates of "the dead house" were "perhaps the most gifted, the strongest of our people."

Dostoevsky's reflections bear not only on crime, but also on punishment, chiefly the corporal punishment inflicted on the convicts for any misdemeanor. The book contains a substantial excursus on the science, the art, the psychology of the *palach* (torturer, executioner), that is, the supervisor or executor of the flogging or the bastinado. In these pages on sadists and sadism the narrator drops a remark to the effect that "the characteristics of a *palach* in embryo are in nearly every man of today." He does not maintain, however, that one is born a sadist. The embryo will develop only under certain social conditions, such as one man's limitless power over the body and mind of another. The narrator inveighs against corporal punishment—so did Belinski —a "plague," a threat to both the individual and society. The years that he lived with transgressors had taught him that a criminal, however brutalized, corrupted, crushed, had the potentialities for goodness and the basic needs of a human being: the assertion of selfhood and at least the illusion of freedom. That he ought to be treated humanely is the lesson of the book. Tolstoy, who was generally out of sympathy with Dostoevsky, called *The House of the Dead* an "edifying" work, placing it at the head and front of his confrère's performance.

1. *Dostoevsky's parents.*
*From pastel drawings made in Moscow, 1823*

Θ. М. Достоевскій. 1847

2. *Dostoevsky, age twenty-six. From a drawing by
K. A. Trutovsky, a former fellow student*

3. *V. G. Belinsky. From lithograph of a drawing by A. K. Astafyev, 1881*

4. *Maria Isayeva, Dostoevsky's first wife.*
*From a painting made probably before their marriage*

5. *Dostoevsky, age thirty-seven.*
*Photograph taken in Semipalatinsk*

6. *Polina Suslova. Photograph taken in middle age*

# 13

## A PASSIONATE INTERLUDE

IN the last century Western Europe exercised the same fascination over the Russian mind that to some extent it still does over the American. Dostoevsky had no memory of the time when he had not dreamed of visiting that part of the world, particularly Italy. If only he had a chance to tread Europe's fabulous soil while there was some vigor and heat and poetry in him! Finally in the summer of 1862 the wish was realized. He had completed *The House of the Dead,* which was running serially in *Vremya,* and moreover he had sold the right to its publication in book form for the substantial sum of twenty-five hundred rubles. *The Insulted and Injured* too appeared as a book. The magazine was doing well enough for him to leave it in Mikhail's hands with only a few qualms for thus shirking his responsibility. He found reasons, not really adequate, for leaving his wife behind.

He set out with high expectations. As the train crossed the frontier at Eydtkunnen his heart leapt. But when, after a two days' tiring, largely sleepless trip, he reached Berlin, he found that the city looked and smelled just like Petersburg. Without tarrying in the German capital for more than a day and a night, he traveled by way of Dresden and Cologne to Paris. The weather was nasty. There wasn't a soul he knew in the town. In the several weeks that he spent there he formed a most unflattering opinion of the Parisian bourgeoisie with whom he equated all the French. "Honestly, they are a people who make you sick," he wrote to Strakhov. "No ideals, no convictions, not even reflections." He crossed the Channel for a brief visit to London, where he did some sightseeing and called on Alexander Herzen. The celebrated émigré described his visitor as "a naïve, somewhat unclear individual but very likeable. Believes with enthusiasm in the Russian people."

Back on the Continent, Dostoevsky traveled to Switzerland by way of the Rhineland. In Geneva he met Strakhov and the two went on to Florence, spending a leisurely week there. They walked into the Uffizi and, despite Strakhov's protests, promptly walked out again. Except for the Madonna della Sedia, Dostoevsky was bored by the canvases. The other monuments of the city meant no more to him. He was interested above all in the new faces that he saw about him, the private conflicts that he could read into them. He had no eyes for landscape and cared little for the sights of the town except as a backdrop for the human drama. They spent the days walking the streets where the crowd was thickest, and in the evening they would sit over a glass of the local red wine and talk. They saw Milan, but not Naples or Rome, and though they visited Venice, Dostoevsky seems to have forgone the chance to "caress a young Venetian girl in a gondola," as he had playfully anticipated in a letter to Strakhov when he was planning the trip. Instead, they recrossed the Alps, and Dostoevsky's ten weeks' stay abroad was over.

Once home again he took up his life where he had dropped it. He had reason to be heartened by the turn that affairs were taking. He had brought back with him material for some travel sketches. His *House of the Dead* was having a great vogue. The review was forging bravely ahead. If it held its own for another year or two, they would be able to pay off all the debts that they had incurred in connection with it, and *Vremya* would become a profitable enterprise. True, his editorial duties left small leisure for the kind of writing that he most wanted to do. Nevertheless the November issue of the magazine carried a substantial narrative over his signature: "A Nasty Incident."

It is a vitriolic satire on the lip service to enlightened liberalism which was fashionable in high places during the sixties, "the epoch of reforms." A civil servant with the rank of General and the reputation of being an "arrant liberal" opines that one should treat one's subordinates humanely, no matter how low their rank. Such behavior, he argues, is indeed the cornerstone of the reforms, for then people of all ranks will "morally embrace" and all problems will be solved "amicably, thoroughly." To demonstrate that he is humane, he appears uninvited at the wedding of a minor clerk in his department. The man's salary is ten rubles a month and his circumstances are wretched in the extreme. The bridegroom is frightened, and some of the guests take a shockingly hostile attitude toward the eminent intruder. His Excellency, who does not hold his liquor well, has too much to drink and behaves accordingly. This is the climax of a chain of disasters, each more mortifying to the wedding party than the last. Things are at such a pass that the General must be put to bed, and only the bridal bed is available. The groom's kindly old mother acts as his Excellency's nurse. As for the bridal pair, a featherbed spread on chairs is their improvised couch, which goes to pieces under them, landing them on the floor with a crash and rousing the household.

It takes his Excellency more than a week to recover from his adventure, and he returns to the office apprehensive of what his reception will be. No notice is taken of the untoward events. But shortly afterward one of his subordinates tells him that the groom is applying for a transfer to another department and requests the General's approval. This is freely granted, and his Excellency adds, with supreme condescension, that he does not wish any harm to the man (of whose wedding night he had made such a hell), adding, "I am prepared to forget everything that happened—everything." Structurally this is perhaps one of the best of Dostoevsky's shorter fictions, and in every respect, especially with regard to its acerb humor, it is handled with great skill.

He also wrote for *Vremya* a rambling account of his trip, which he called "Winter Notes on Summer Impressions." They exude a virulent venom against the West. Germany and its people get only a few stings. Unless you are used to Germans, the traveler observes, in large numbers they are hard to bear. In Berlin he dislikes even the lindens. There are no more repulsive women, he declares, than the Dresden type. In Cologne the proximity of the famous eau de Cologne shop to the Cathedral annoys him. He concedes, however, that the Rhineland itself is delightful. Switzerland and Italy are passed over in silence. The main target of "Winter Notes" is the Parisian bourgeoisie, which he identifies with the French people. The principles of the great Revolution are mouthed while disregarded in fact. Instead of liberty, equality, and fraternity, there is ubiquitous hypocrisy that crooks the knee to honor and virtue; corruption that has penetrated Church and State, manners and morals, and made a mockery of popular sovereignty; the triumph of an exploiting, predatory spirit, dominated by the rule of each-man-for-himself.

Externally, the tourist observes, London is quite different from the French capital. It is on a grander scale. The streets are more crowded, the traffic heavier. He even finds striking beauties among the Englishwomen. The parks are magnificent, the slums distressing. Sharply contrasting aspects of London are in close contact. There is no attempt, as there is in Paris, to hide the sores of the city. One Saturday night the author loses his way in a workers' neighborhood and is horrified by what he sees: gas flares shining on the gloomy faces of men and women sodden with drink and on the urchins running about among them. In the Haymarket he watches the prostitutes in and around the splendid cafés, sees girls barely in their teens soliciting and mothers bringing mere children for the trade.

The indigent are jostling one another in the darkness into which their brothers have carelessly thrust them. The ministers of religion are plump, dignified gentlemen who preach to the rich. They send missionaries to convert the African heathen and ignore the destitute savages at home who mistreat small children and habitually beat their wives, Dostoevsky confidently declares, with pokers. The World Exposition, which opened on May 1, awes and horrifies him. He senses something apocalyptic about the vast agglomeration of men united in worshiping Baal, an unclean spirit, arrogant and blind. Is it for this victory of soulless materialism, he asks, that men had worked and suffered over the centuries?

The author concludes that both Paris and London equally epitomize Western civilization. Ruled by acquisitiveness and a divisive individualism, it has not been able to solve the problem of how to contrive a system free from manmade miseries. The beneficiaries of the bourgeois order regard it as the acme of progress and therefore beyond improvement. Desperately clinging to the status quo, they are troubled at heart and fear to look into the future. In the West the bourgeois order has assumed its final form—the finality of death. The whole framework of this petrified society, Dostoevsky prophesies, is doomed to come down with a crash, as did Babylon.

Some of his invective is directed against his compatriots, but it is confined to the educated gentry. He upbraids them for their ignorance, their smugness, their tendency to overreach themselves, and he has harsh words for the behavior of Russian tourists abroad. Aping everything foreign and despising indigenous ways are repugnant to him, and, of course, expatriates are the object of his loathing. He derives gratification from the thought that a handful of his privileged and cultivated countrymen, while owing much to the West, remain essentially Russian. Is there some curious chemical reaction, he asks, between the human spirit and the soil in which it is rooted? What heartens him most is the conviction that the untutored Russian masses are immune to the bourgeois infection. They are endowed with the *natural* ability to live together in true brotherhood. The implication is that the people owe this endowment to their Christian faith and that the building of the good society is in their power.

Dostoevsky had gone abroad with the reverence for Western Europe that was common to Russian intellectuals, but he carried in his baggage a complete set of prejudices against the more recent phases of Western civilization. The ten weeks that he spent *in partibus infidelium* served only to intensify his intolerance and hostility. At the same time his own belief in his compatriots' moral superiority and high destiny was strengthened. Those convictions became tenets of his credo and he clung to them to the end.

# ( II )

The year 1863 began darkly with the Polish insurrection. After some hesitation the general public allowed itself to be overwhelmed by a wave of belligerent patriotism. Dostoevsky was not an exception. There was no place in Slavdom, he decided, for Poland, with its Catholicism and other elements of Western civilization. Strakhov was invited to write an article for the magazine. The editor liked the piece, the censor passed it, and it appeared duly in the April issue. And then the blow fell: a notice in *The Moscow Bulletins* accused *Vremya* of having printed a masked defense of the Polish cause. Strakhov's style was so abstruse that it was possible to put such an interpretation on his words, although nothing was further from his mind than to give aid and comfort to Russia's hereditary enemy. The press raised hue and cry against the ill-starred article. It was soon the talk of the town, and the matter came to the Emperor's ears. "All Moscow is indignant about it," he observed one morning to the Minister of the Interior. The latter promptly responded that the review had been suppressed. The diplomatic lie sealed *Vremya*'s fate. According to the official statement, the punitive action against the magazine was taken because of the "outrageous" article about Polish affairs and the "harmful policy" of the publication.

Here was a piece of ill luck. The magazine was the innocent victim of a misunderstanding. Its suppression was hard on all those connected with it and was a disaster for Mikhail. Shortly before the crash he had sold his cigarette factory, which had been steadily going downhill. Now he had debts amounting to twenty thousand rubles and nothing to fall back upon. For Dostoevsky it was the old story of disappointment, defeat, endless anxiety. His wife was ill and he was again short of money. The sums that had come to him during the past year or two he had somehow been unable to hold on to, and for the present he had no prospects. Yet in the midst of it all he found himself preparing to go abroad once more. He borrowed the money from The Society for Needy Authors. How could he take such a step at such a time? He had his reasons.

There was his health. The falling sickness was getting worse. His memory was failing rapidly, and the depression that followed each attack was so severe that he feared he would ultimately be driven mad. The Petersburg doctors gave him such contradictory advice that he felt he must seek counsel elsewhere —from Ramberg in Berlin and Trousseau in Paris. His seizures occurred at least once a month and sometimes twice in one week. There was another motive for his journey than the need for consulting physicians, though it is doubtful if it was a conscious one at the outset. The gaming tables of the German watering places offered him the chance of mending the family fortunes by a rapid stroke of luck. The gambler in him had long been waiting his chance, and now he leapt at it. He reached Berlin about the middle of August, and from there went straight to Wiesbaden, one of the four towns where roulette flourished under the aegis of the law.

Here he succumbed to the fever that was to ravage him for years. Watching the men and women at the tables, he discovered the secret of winning. It was very simple. Fate was in his grip. He worked out a system. The thing was to follow it faithfully and keep cool whatever turn luck took. He had two difficulties: he couldn't stick to his system, he couldn't keep cool. He applied his system, won over ten thousand francs, and locked them up, determined to leave town the next morning without looking into the casino again. The next morning he was back at the tables. He failed to follow his system, lost most of his winnings, returned again in the evening, followed his system, won three thousand francs, and was able to leave Wiesbaden the next day with five thousand francs in winnings.

If, in spite of the fact that he believed in his system and that he had money in his pocket to back his belief, he left the place for Paris after four days, it was because he was obeying another, stronger pull. He was off to keep his rendezvous with Polina.

Dostoevsky may have come to know Apollinariya Prokofyevna Suslova—Polina or Polya to her friends—the second year after his return to Petersburg. She contributed a story to the September issue of *Vremya* for 1861, and her literary ambitions may have brought them together. She was then an extremely attractive girl of twenty-one. He soon began to visit the house, where he met her younger sister, Nadezhda. Both sisters, though of peasant stock, were well educated and exemplified the "emancipated woman" who had emerged in the early sixties, that era of feminism. They belonged to the Nihilist generation which at once repelled and fascinated him. As a matter of fact, in 1862 Nadezhda belonged to an underground revolutionary group that went by the name of "Land and Liberty." She was entrusted with keeping the seal of that ephemeral organization. Whether Dostoevsky knew of it or not, he was very friendly with her. On one occasion he wrote to her: "At every painful moment I would come to you to rest my soul, and lately to you alone. I love you as a cherished sister."

There was nothing brotherly about his feelings for the elder girl. Nadezhda, the first Russian member of her sex to become a physician, was of the rigoristic, puritanic type. Polina, under the composed, matter-of-fact exterior that was the fashion, concealed an emotional instability that was to work havoc with her life. Hers was a fiery nature, intransigent, impatient of restraint, avid of experience, and with a streak of cruelty.

They were friends. They were lovers. It is said that she took the initiative in declaring herself. Both by nature and conviction she was careless, in fact scornful, of the proprieties and she had no inhibitions regarding physical intimacy. It was her first affair and she took it seriously. Yet the celebrity may have meant more to her than the man. He—at forty—was thrilled to find this girl half his age in love with him, but he failed to live up to her idea of what a man in such a relationship should be. Either because he showed a disconcerting lack of loverly abandon or because she felt humiliated by not coming first with him, indeed by being sometimes treated as a convenience, she repeatedly wanted to break with him. Many years later she was able to tell her husband that she had not been able to forgive Dostoevsky his unwillingness to divorce his wife on her account. As a matter of fact, to protect Marya Dmitrievna's peace of mind, he went to great lengths to hide his liaison from her, and he succeeded.

In the spring of 1863 Polina went to Paris, as so many of her compatriots did, to breathe the free air of the West, to study, to live. Perhaps at moments the trip seemed to her to be in the nature of a flight from her entanglement. Nevertheless, it was understood that Dostoevsky would join her in Paris and that together they would go to Italy. His unfaithfulness to Marya Dmitrievna was no secret from his brother or from his sister-in-law, who apparently did not condemn him.

Urgent business kept him in Petersburg until mid-August, but he wrote to Polina that he would be in Paris shortly. In the meantime she had become deeply inolved in a passionate affair with a Spaniard, a medical student or a young doctor. Of this change of heart she had failed to inform Dostoevsky, and his letter disturbed her deeply. She feared his coming, while half desiring it. She pitied him and yet with unacknowledged malice anticipated the pain that she would cause him. To avoid a distressing explanation face to face, she decided to make an avowal in a note and send it to him when he reached Paris.

After leaving Wiesbaden with the money won at roulette, Dostoevsky landed in Paris on August 26th and immediately sent word to Polina, announcing his arrival and giving his address. She received the note the next day and forthwith dispatched the following letter: "You are coming a bit late. Just a short time ago I dreamed of traveling with you in Italy, I even started studying Italian—then in a few days everything changed. You once told me that I would be slow to surrender my heart. I surrendered it at the first call, without a struggle, without assurance, almost without hope of being loved. . . . Do not imagine that I am reproaching myself. I only want to say that you did not know me, that indeed I myself did not know myself. Good-bye, my dear!"

Before her letter had time to reach him, he came straight to the pension where she was staying, barely recovered from the fatigues of his journey and from the slight attack that he had had en route. What then passed between them is retailed in her diary.

She was taken aback: "I thought you wouldn't come, after my letter."

"What letter?"

"Telling you not to come."

"Why?"

"Because you are too late."

His head sank: "Polya," he said, after a short pause. "I must know everything. Let's go where we can be alone. Tell me everything or it will kill me."

They left the parlor of the pension and got into a cab. They did not look at each other. He clung to her hand, now and then squeezing it convulsively. "Don't, don't," she tried to soothe him. "I am here." He did not open his lips except to shout to the driver in a voice of despair: *"Vite, vite!"*

When they were alone in his room he fell at her feet, and clasping her knees burst out crying: "I have lost you. I knew it."

As soon as he could master himself, he began to question her. The other man, is he young, handsome, clever? She was reluctant to answer these queries. Is she his mistress? She protested: it wasn't right to ask such questions.

"I don't know," said he, "what's right and what's wrong."

She volunteered the information that she was deeply in love with the man. As Dostoevsky kept on probing, she admitted that the Spaniard did not love her and that she was unhappy. He clutched his head. She was bound to turn to another. He had known it. She had fallen in love with him by mistake, because her heart was roomy. He was somewhat relieved to learn that Salvador was a commonplace young man, without any distinction, without literary interests. The conversation turned to other matters. He was happy, he assured her, to know that there was a human being like her in the world. They must remain friends and write to each other. They had planned to travel in Italy as lovers. Why not let him take her there anyhow? They would be as brother and sister.

Oh, yes, she believed he was able to maintain such a relationship! He would have his novel to occupy him. She spoke thus perhaps because she was somewhat piqued by the rapidity with which he had accepted the new state of affairs. He demurred: didn't she know how hard it would be for him to get over this? When they separated, she promised to come to see him the next day. She felt better after having spoken to him. He understood her.

All this occurred Wednesday evening. The following day she called on him and they talked at length. Next morning she received a note from a friend of Salvador's telling her that he had typhus and could not be seen. She immediately wrote to the man, begging him to keep informing her about the patient's condition. Not to let her see him, she added, was barbarous. She also wrote to Salvador, saying that he was sure to recover, "else it would be an injustice." She was in a state of utter despair, having decided that he was "on the brink of the grave." Dostoevsky, to whom she turned, heartened her by saying that in the air of Paris and with the available doctors typhus was not dangerous.

On Saturday she accidentally ran into her supposedly stricken beloved. He looked pale but otherwise was his old self. He made a lame attempt to explain what had happened, but it was clear to Polina that the typhus story was his invention. Left alone, she locked herself in her room and gave way to hysteria, shouting that she would kill him. She quieted down but spent a sleepless night, unable to decide if she should kill him or herself. Early Sunday morning Dostoevsky was roused from sleep by a knock at his door. It was Polina, red-eyed and white-faced, come to ask him to call on her at the pension as soon as possible. Then she left. She dared not stay away from her room, for she hoped against hope that her faithless lover would yet come to make amends.

He did not, and indeed ignored her ever afterward. Dostoevsky was there promptly. She unbosomed herself to him, saying that she had not seen Salvador since the previous Sunday, that he had failed to keep an appointment with her and to answer her letter, and she detailed the typhus fraud. He listened to her story, sympathized, dismissed the whole affair as an ugly incident: the young man had needed a woman, so he had briefly taken advantage of a pretty girl who was at hand; and he advised Polina to give up all thought of vengeance. Their conversation is recorded in her diary. "I wouldn't like to kill him," she said, "but I wish I could torture him for a long time." "Don't," Dostoevsky replied, "it isn't worth while; on such creatures one uses insect powder. It is foolish to ruin your life on his account." She agreed, yet she was still madly in love with the Spaniard, and her wish for revenge continued "to smolder," as she put it.

She wrote to Salvador that she had no desire to pursue him, that he need not be afraid of her and hide from her. This was, however, subject to one condition: he must accept the small sum that he had once spent on her and that she enclosed with the letter. Otherwise she would be angry with him and become dangerous, for she was an uncivilized type, in fact, a complete barbarian. Dostoevsky, on being consulted, remarked that this was, of course, an unconscious pretext on her part for getting in touch with Salvador, but he did not object to her mailing the letter. She never heard from the Spaniard, but two or three months later the money was returned to her by his brother.

Dostoevsky now found himself in a situation all too much like that which had preceded his marriage. Again he was the displaced lover comforting the woman he had lost to a younger man. Polina continued to confide in him fully and lean on his advice. Consumed with the fury of a woman scorned, she seemed to have no thought for him. Would she or would she not join him in his trip south? She did not keep him long in suspense. She had the courage to tear herself away from Paris and the cruelty to let him take her to Italy. He was glad to leave this magnificent, abominable city, where the only things one didn't tire of were the fruit and the wine; but the whole adventure was madness. He was going off on an ambiguous, expensive journey as though he were free of worry about either health or money, as though there were no brother in desperate straits, no sick wife, no troublesome stepson to consider.

# ( III )

The trip thrilled and exhausted him with the fever of balked sensuality. Having just emerged from a passionate affair and plainly still burning with the agony of it, Polina was doubly desirable. If he had gone out of his way to contrive a situation abounding, for a man of his make-up, both in subtle torment and in that perverse pleasure which he was able to suck out of pain, he could not have done better. She had consented to become his traveling companion, as originally planned: might he not yet succeed in persuading her to become his mistress once more? Her behavior was not such as to make him despair, but on the other hand she said nothing to give him hope.

They were both unhappy, but they pretended to each other and themselves that they were off on a lark, and his tension and anxiety expressed itself in an exaggerated gaiety. They traveled via Germany and when, on September 5, they reached Baden-Baden, they engaged two connecting rooms. They had tea in her room—it was about ten o'clock in the evening—and then, feeling tired, she slipped out of her shoes, lay down, dressed, on the bed, and asked him to pull his chair closer. She took his hand and held it in hers. He said he liked sitting that way. She told him she had been harsh with him in Paris and had seemed to be thinking only of herself, but she had been thinking of him, too. Did she guess what was going on within him? Suddenly he got up, stumbled over her shoes, and sat down again. He explained that he had wanted to close the window, but, no, he confessed that what he had really wanted was to kiss her foot. She was embarrassed, almost frightened, and tucked her feet in, but invited him to stay on. He stared at her till she hid her face in the pillow. Finally she dismissed him, saying that she wanted to go to sleep. He lingered on, then kissed her good night, all too warmly, and went out with a smile, but returned, ostensibly to close the window, and advised her to get undressed. She said she would do so as soon as he left. He did not close his door until, under a flimsy pretext, he had come back once more.

The next day he apologized profusely for his unbrotherly behavior, saying that he had been drunk, but she passed the matter over in a manner that left him as uncertain as ever where he stood. Did he have a gambler's chance of winning her? His attention during their Baden stay was divided between this and the gaming tables. Perhaps, under the circumstances, his gambling was in the nature of a substitute for another form of excitement. He spoke of his gambling fever as a "damned revolt of the passions."

He made no progress with the lady, and he lost practically everything at roulette. In his first quarter of an hour at the Baden tables he won six hundred francs; his Wiesbaden "system" was working. But he could not stick to it, and disaster followed. How could be keep away from the tables? He needed money for

Mikhail, for his wife, for his literary future, and for the immediate expenses of the trip. Hadn't he gone abroad for no other purpose, as he wrote to Mikhail, than "to save you all"? Far from playing the savior, he was reduced to begging for help. He had to write to Mikhail to remit what he had sent him from the Wiesbaden winnings for safekeeping, and to his wife to return part of the money he had sent her. The thought that this might cause her inconvenience, ill and needy as she was, only added to his torments: after a fashion, he loved her. Meanwhile, in the hope of recovering something, he took as many as he dared of his last francs, won a considerable sum with them, staked it all on one throw, and lost the whole. There was nothing for it but to leave Baden-Baden at once. At Geneva he pawned his watch and Polina her ring. This enabled them to go on to Turin, where the remittances from home were to reach him. He lived in daily terror that the hotel bill would be presented and he would not be able to meet it—the scandal of the situation would be terrible. As soon as the money reached them they made for Rome, and from there went on to Naples. There they ran into the Herzens, whom Dostoevsky perplexed by introducing Polina vaguely as a relative, while flaunting his intimacy with her.

She took pleasure in provoking him, but now and then repented her cruelty. There was a day in Turin when she was affectionate toward him. He responded so eagerly that she redoubled her tenderness and ended by crying on his breast. He did not know what to make of her. Sometimes her resistance seemed mere coyness. In allowing certain intimacies without yielding to him, was she leaning toward surrender or was she denying his manhood? Was she making him the scapegoat for her Spaniard, or was she avenging herself on him for his own sins against her in the past? Was it just heartless coquetry? When, one day, he told her that she must not keep a man cooling his heels too long or he would bolt, she smiled. Was she still thinking of "the Peninsula," as he called her Salvador? She denied this, but only with her lips.

There must have been moments when his passion for her was mixed with intense hatred. Occasionally he would allow himself to taunt her. One night in Rome he did so with a peculiarly offensive gaiety. He did not try to keep it up. He was having a bad time of it, he confessed. Everything presented itself as an onerous duty, a tiresome lesson to be learned. At least he was trying to divert her. She was touched and threw her arms around his neck.

But he was not deceived and told her sadly that she was on her way to Spain. Abruptly he began to joke again, and when he left her—it was one in the morning and she was in bed undressed—observed that it was humiliating to have to leave her thus: "Russians," he concluded with a military flourish, "never retreat." And he retired. There may have been occasions when he did not retire.

Polina, being subject to the literary itch, used this phase of her relations with Dostoevsky as material for a story. It is the kind of fiction that is only a very thinly veiled transcript of truth. The hero who plays Dostoevsky's part in this narrative relieves the ennui of the lady in the case by relating to her his adventures with a prostitute. When this form of entertainment disgusts her, he ventures that such low pleasures serve only to heighten the transports of exalted love. So closely does the story follow the record of the affair in her diary that although this incident does not figure there, it is highly improbable that she invented it. If the conversation did indeed take place, he may have talked as much to vex as to amuse.

Toward the end Polina's story moves rapidly. The heroine discovers more things to dislike in her companion, their relations become intolerable, and she drowns herself. Actually, the end of the lady's trip with Dostoevsky was less dramatic. From Naples they retraced their steps to Turin, where he must have received money from Russia—he had written Strakhov that when he reached Turin again he would be flat. There they parted peacefully enough, she going back to Paris, he making his way home. They had been together a little less than two months. He stopped in Homburg sufficiently long to lose everything he had at the gaming tables, and having exhausted all other resources, was forced to appeal to Polina. She raised a small sum to send him, even pawning her watch, rather relieved that she could thus pay off some of the money he had spent on her. She could not bear to feel obligated to this man whom she had once idolized, but whom she was now beginning to hate.

# 14

## ENDS AND BEGINNINGS

IT was October before Dostoevsky was home again. He found that Marya Dmitrievna, who was staying in Vladimir, had grown much worse. She could not brave a Petersburg winter, so he took her to Moscow and stayed there with her. It must have been clear to him that her end was coming, and pity, which had played no small part in drawing him to her at first, kept him beside her at the last. His own health was deplorable: either he had not profited by the advice of the European physicians or, in the stress of his affair with Polina, he had not consulted them at all. The change of air and scene had wrought an improvement, but it was short-lived. And then, although it was understood that Mikhail would be allowed to resume the magazine under another title, permission was slow in coming and the uncertainty was harassing. The sole comfort was a legacy of three thousand rubles from Uncle Kumanin which Dostoevsky received in November and which meant a temporary surcease from money worries.

Finally the authorities relented and in 1864 *Epokha* (*Epoch*), the new monthly (at first it was planned to call it *Pravda* [*Truth*]) materialized. It was started under unfavorable auspices. To begin with, the permit came so tardily that the double January–February number appeared only late in March, when the subscription season was over. Even the established reviews were doing poorly, the reading public being in an apathetic mood. The first issue was not without distinction, containing as it did a story by Turgenev and the initial installment of a remarkable contribution by Dostoevsky, *Notes from the Underground*. But the make-up of the magazine was shabby and the contents of the subsequent numbers singularly flat. Mikhail had little cash to invest in the enterprise and, as he was far from well, could not bring to the business the energy and shrewdness it demanded. To top it all, Dostoevsky, who was expected to edit *Epokha,* could not be of much help, since he was absent from Petersburg most of the time and absorbed in his private affairs.

Masha, like his mother and like several creatures of his imagination, was the victim of consumption. She was virtually wasting away, now lamenting her end, now making wild plans for years she was never to see. Her irritability grew extreme and at times her mind was unsettled. She had a mania for winding up clocks until the springs broke. She would imagine that the sick-room was full of devils—the doctor had to chase them out of the window with his handkerchief. For days, for weeks, for months, Dostoevsky had no respite from this misery.

His one refuge was the house of his sister Vera, the only member of the family in Moscow whom he cared to see. Nothing could have been in sharper contrast to the sick chamber than this happy household, bubbling with the activities of eight children, the youngest an infant in arms, the eldest, Sonia, a girl of eighteen. Dostoevsky grew quite fond of his brother-in-law, the excellent Dr. Ivanov (who was treating Masha), admired the little ones, and made a favorite of Sonia.

But for all the comfort that Vera and her family afforded him, he felt that his burden was more than he could bear. He kept having attacks and, in addition, was again suffering from piles. What with his debts and the expenses of his wife's illness, the legacy was soon spent, and when the spring thaws came, he had to go on wearing his winter overcoat for want of the price of seasonable apparel. By nightfall his nerves were in tatters, and he would sit down to his desk stale and sick. He had all kinds of tempting ideas for articles, but he couldn't manage to write one of them. And the thought that he was useless to the magazine at this critical time—the first issues were decisive—tormented him. At least he was able to go on somehow with that queer, savage story, *Notes from the Underground*. It was slow work at best, and it was bound to suffer a dismal interruption. He was laboring over the brutal details of the story to the sounds his wife made in the next room over the business of dying. He wrote to Mikhail that he had never been in a worse state. The Tver lodgings, the barracks, forced labor, the cell in the fortress— these were shadows: only his present hell was real.

Before he went abroad Dostoevsky had installed a tutor in his Petersburg rooms to take charge of his stepson, and the two were still living there. Pasha, who was now in his teens, showed signs of being a bad egg. Toward the end Dostoevsky sent for him, but the impossible boy was no consolation to his mother. In fact, she showed him the door, saying she would summon him when she felt that she was dying. When that event seemed imminent, Dostoevsky wrote Mikhail to get the boy a black suit, cheap, and ship him to Moscow for the funeral.

Finally the fretting and the coughing were over, and even the solemn bustle of the death chamber hushed. It was the evening of April 15. The following day Dostoevsky snatched time from the unfinished *Notes from the Underground* and found composure of spirit to make a long entry in the small brown leather note-book in which he recorded expenses and jotted down passing thoughts.

"Masha lies on the table," * he wrote. Will he ever see her again? To love another as oneself, according to Christ's com-mandment, is impossible. The ego is in the way. But after the appearance of Christ as the ideal of man in the flesh, it became clear that when the individual reaches the highest point of his development, he finds that the noblest use he can make of his personality is to surrender it to all and sundry completely and selflessly. This can occur only when man's nature is transcended and he finds himself in a timeless, but otherwise unimaginable, paradise. Surely he will be so different from the old Adam that he may not even bear the name of man. These creatures will neither marry nor be given in marriage, but live like the angels of God. The family, with its exclusive tie between man and woman, must be discarded in the name of the ultimate ideal. Each, while preserving his identity—for in my Father's house are many mansions—will merge with all in a divine synthesis.

Toward the end of the note Dostoevsky's thoughts were more closely connected with his dead wife. "On earth," he wrote, "man strives toward an ideal that is contrary to his nature. When people fail to fulfill the law of that striving—as I and

* Before placing the body in the coffin it was customary to lay it on a table.

Masha failed—they call this state sin and suffer accordingly. The suffering is balanced by the paradisal delight of fulfilling the law, *i.e.,* sacrificing one's ego." He concluded with an outburst against the teachings of mechanistic materialism, that unripe fruit of paltry knowledge, that principle of stagnation and death, as opposed to the teaching of true philosophy, which means God and life eternal.

These were jottings, made on the impulse of the moment, presumably for no eye but his own, to satisfy some inner need for self-clarification. He had once asserted that if the choice must be made, he would stand with Christ rather than with truth. It is not surprising to find him now standing with Christ against human nature, but he oversteps the bounds of orthodoxy when he insists that the Christian ideal can be realized only when man shall be man no longer, but shall have become as the angels of heaven. What could this mean but that he was bidding Utopia farewell, and further, that in setting up Christ as the pattern for humankind, he was setting before himself an ideal that he knew to be poles removed from his own native impulses? The family must ultimately be transcended. He had married; nay, more, he had committed adultery. He might do both again. He looked forward to a state in which man should live free from the lusts of the flesh. He knew himself hopelessly driven by them.

He was writing in the detached strain of a fuzzy-minded Christian philosopher, meditating on things earthly and paradisal, rather than in the tone of a bereaved husband with the death-rattle still in his ears. That at such a time he should reflect on the limitations of earthly love points to the tragic flaw in the relation to which death had put a period. If he felt remorse for sin, it was that against Christ rather than that against his late wife. If he spoke of heaven, he seems not to have been deeply concerned with meeting Masha there. It was as if he had long since accustomed himself to the idea of being without her. As far as possible he had provided for her physical needs and cared for her son, yet she seems to have faded out of the picture long before her end. He had behaved like an unattached man even in the Petersburg days when they were living together. She bore him no children. Hard words were frequently exchanged—it is said that in her rages she did not hesitate to throw up to him the fact that he had been a jailbird. He seems not to have kept their incompatibility a secret from his intimates, though only one revealing reference to the subject has been preserved. It occurs in a letter to Wrangel. Nearly a year after his wife's death Dostoevsky was writing to the man who had witnessed his frantic wooing: "Oh, my friend, she loved me boundlessly. I, too, loved her without measure, but we did not live happily together. I shall tell you everything when we see each other. Now I shall only say that in spite of the fact that we were positively unhappy together (because of her strange, suspicious, and morbidly fantastic character), we couldn't stop loving each other. In fact, the more unhappy we were, the stronger our attachment grew."

One imagines their life together to have been a succession of stormy quarrels and equally stormy reconciliations. This marriage appears to have been presided over by a passion that now took the aspect of love and now that of hatred. Such a relationship is all the more plausible since we find Dostoevsky's imagination playing perpetually and illuminatingly upon the ambivalence of emotion. Moreover, this love that feeds upon mutual unhappiness fits into the picture of a man who had a curious faculty for finding pleasure in painful experiences. That he could love his wife sincerely while at the same time being passionately attached to another is intelligible enough. He had, as he had said of Polina Suslova, and as could be said of many of his characters, "a wide heart."

The character of Dostoevsky's first wife was assailed by his daughter Liubov (Aimée), the child of his second marriage. In her life of her father she makes out her mother's predecessor to have been a deceitful, dissolute woman who on the very eve of her wedding spent the night with a lover, and not only made a cuckold of Dostoevsky afterward, with the same insignificant youth, but taunted her husband with it later. This story, like so much else in the book, is untrustworthy. It is barely possible, however, that here the biographer was embroidering, in her prejudiced and sensational manner, upon fact. Perhaps Marya resembled her husband in this—that she was capable of continuing to love the one to whom she was unfaithful. In any event, his daughter's malevolent words are contradicted by his own remark in the letter to Wrangel quoted above: "She was the most honest, the most noble-minded and generous-hearted woman that I have ever known in my life." Nearly ten years after her death, when he was married a second time, and happily, he described her to a new-found friend, in whom he discovered a resemblance to her, as "a woman with the loftiest, most rapturous soul . . . an idealist in the fullest sense of the word, yes,

and at the same time as pure and simple-hearted as a child."
This must be the last word on the subject.


# ( II )

Losing no time, the widower returned to Petersburg and to his
editorial work. He was back in his old apartment with Pasha—
he had sworn to his wife on her deathbed that he would never
abandon the boy. His first disagreeable duty was to evict the
tutor who, it transpired, had maltreated and starved his pupil,
had debauched the fifteen-year-old boy by bringing women from
the street into the flat, and ended by carrying off a pair of his
employer's sheets.

A little older, a little lonelier, Dostoevsky resumed his former
way of life. His immediate task was to complete *Notes from the
Underground*. This he did, and the final installment appeared in
the April issue of the magazine which came off the press in June.
The financial situation was not as acute as usual. Before leaving
Moscow, he had sent his brother explicit instructions as to the
proper means of squeezing some money out of their godmother,
and thanks to his strategy, Mikhail had secured ten thousand
rubles from Aunt Kumanina. Furthermore, he had borrowed six
thousand rubles from Dr. Ivanov. The sum was sufficient to
allow Mikhail to set up a printing establishment as a prop for
the review. There were heavy odds against them, but it looked
as though, if they worked hard, they might yet put *Epokha* on
its legs.

And then Fate struck again. Mikhail, who had been ill for
nearly two years, took to his bed. On July 10, a little less than
three months after burying his wife, Dostoevsky stood beside the
lifeless body of his brother.

"I loved my brother infinitely," he wrote to Wrangel; and to
Andrey, a fortnight after the blow had fallen: "He loved me
more than anyone in the world, more than his wife and children,
whom he adored." Dostoevsky was using the hyperbole of bereavement. In his grief he forgot that during his four years of
prison Mikhail had let prudence get the better of affection and
sent him not a single word, and that there had been a sad scarcity
of both letters and remittances during his years as a soldier.

There had been occasions when he had grave doubts of Mikhail's devotion. But no matter. Mikhail had shared his earliest memories. They had grown up together in the same house. For years they had attended the same school. They had lived together. They had worked together. With Mikhail gone, to whom could he confide his anxieties and disillusionments, his hopes and ambitions? Death had never trod so close to him. He had lost a part of himself.

But grieving was a luxury for which he had no leisure. Mikhail's estate consisted of three hundred rubles, which went to cover the funeral expenses. In spite of the money sunk in it, the liabilities of the magazine, in the shape of debts that Mikhail had incurred to run it, far exceeded its assets, so that the family was left without visible means of support. The widow and her children, all of them minors, gathered around Uncle Fyodor, their sole hope, and wept. He shouldered the responsibility.

Two courses were open to him. He could abandon the review to its creditors, take the widow and the four orphans—one of the children had died that year of scarlet fever—into his own household, and slave at his pen to support them all, his stepson, and himself, not to mention his dead brother's mistress and her child. This would leave the blot of bankruptcy on Mikhail's memory—an intolerable thought. Although he was himself an incurable borrower, indebtedness always impressed him with a sense of more than merely legal obligation and seemed to him somehow to involve the very personality of the debtor. The other possibility was to continue with the magazine, in the hope of ultimately paying its debts and turning it over to the family as soon as it was a profitable enterprise. After taking counsel with himself and with all concerned, he chose the second course—to his sorrow.

The deceased had been able to run the review partly on credit. Dostoevsky needed cash. Perhaps Andrey would lend him something, at ten-per-cent interest. But the little brother was not a prey to generous impulses. There was yet another hope: Aunt Kumanina. He had never yet asked anything of her. He would not be asking for himself now—it was to save Mikhail's stricken family that he would swallow his pride. When, a few months previously, he had advised his brother how to get around the difficult old lady, he had mapped out a detailed plan of action: there must be no preliminary skirmishing, but a bold attack, thus: "You have a fortune, ten thousand rubles will not ruin you. If you do not come to the rescue, your godson and nephew and his helpless babes will be lost! You have one foot in the grave—how will you appear before Christ and before your late sister?" One must work on her conscience, on her piety, on her family feeling; she would be torn between fear for her money and the dread of taking a sin on her soul; she would wave her hands, she would cluck, she would groan; she would yield. The strategy had worked once, and he may have used it this time. As he sat in the drawing room of the sprawling Moscow house that he had known since childhood, confronting the quaking, whimsical old woman, was he pierced by the injustice of it all—that he, with his health broken, his work still to do, a mounting load of responsibilities on his shoulders, should be at the mercy of this foolish, useless relic, squatting on her moneybags?

Whatever he may have done or thought, he returned to Petersburg with ten thousand rubles from good old Aunt Kumanina. The sum, like the similar amount Mikhail had received from her, was in the nature of a loan, which was never repaid and which was reckoned as his share of his inheritance from her. With this he could make a start. After some casting about, he found a figurehead to act as nominal editor, since as an ex-convict he could not serve in that capacity, and so set *Epokha* on its way again. Legally he had no share in the enterprise, the review being the property of Mikhail's heirs.

Permission to publish *Epokha* had been granted to Mikhail on condition that the orientation of the review would be "irreproachable." As the helmsman of *Vremya* Dostoevsky had steered a middle course between the liberals and the conservatives, the Westernists and the Slavophiles, in the hope of bringing together the irreconcilable trends that those groups represented. Inevitably, the journal fell between two stools and, as has been stated, it was coldly eyed by the authorities. Nevertheless, Dostoevsky announced that *Epokha* would follow the same path that its predecessor had taken. Actually, it failed to do so. It took a sharp turn to the right and ceased to be the organ of a separate group. "The Soil" continued to be its pseudo-democratic shibboleth, but only lip service was paid it.

An editorial in the last issue for 1864 declared triumphantly: "The Slavophiles have prevailed!" It came from the pen of Strakhov. He prized Slavophilism, which admittedly stemmed from German metaphysics, as an antidote to the spread of French socialism. Dostoevsky's commitment to the Slavophile position was still shaky, but this scarcely affected the policy of the magazine. It supported the autocratic regime at home, with its centralized bureaucracy, and upheld reaction abroad. "Russia," the reader was bluntly told, "can no more imagine living without a Czar than a man can live without a head. Russians want and hope for protection and salvation from God and the Czar." The journal was an apologist for belligerent patriotism, not without an anti-Semitic slant. As the panacea for all of the country's ills it proposed loving-kindness. *Vremya* had sometimes criticized the rightist *Russky vestnik* and had disagreed with the "doctrinaires," as the Slavophiles were termed. The polemical invective of *Epokha* was directed against the journals of radical opinion, *Russkoe slovo* and especially *Sovremennik*. The latter, which, like *Vremya,* had been suspended for eight months, resumed publication and was as aggressive as ever, although it had lost the captaincy of Chernyshevsky, who was by now serving his term as a convict in Siberia. The incipient revolutionary ripples of the early sixties had subsided, but the ferment remained at work.

In journalistic pieces *Epokha* continued to give battle to the Nihilists as "a duty, a service to truth." Dostoevsky was not content to oppose their advocacy (in Aesopian language) of the use of force for political and social ends, their fanatical adherence to utilitarianism and "rational egoism" (what Charles S. Peirce called "intelligent greed") as the basis of morality, their materialistic and simplistic concept of human nature, their cult of science. He also had much to say against his adversaries' aesthetics. In this field he was confused and given to self-contradiction. He would argue for and against the same thesis, simultaneously uphold opposed viewpoints. Not seldom his shots went wide of the mark. He lumped together, on the one hand, the followers of Chernyshevsky, for whom literature was "the textbook of life" which was socially useful, indeed, essential, and, on the other hand, the disciples of Pisarev, the moving spirit of *Russkoe slovo,* which declared war on all art as a luxury that the country could ill afford, and which would have the literati use their skill in popularizing science. He misjudged the "theoreticians," as he liked to call the *Sovremennik* group, in other ways. Dostoevsky's own view of literature, as it emerges from these desultory discussions, is that of an art true to life, but not enslaved by cramping adherence to barren fact or preconceived bias, a medium needing the air of freedom, hospitable to invention, fantasy, poetry, indeed, akin to music. This, he wrote to Turgenev at the end of 1863, is "a language expressing things that total consciousness, not *reason,* has yet to grasp." He will continue to hold the conception of literature expressed here, amplifying it in ways to which his major novels testify.

# ( III )

All during the autumn and winter he was in a continuous fever. He haggled with the printer, he ran to the censor, he placated subscribers, he begged for contributions, he edited manuscripts, he read proof, he borrowed money, he paid some of the bills, he borrowed more money. By the end of 1864 he had all but succeeded in making up for the delay of the earlier issues. He did it by bringing out two numbers every month, but he had to sacrifice the quality of his material. He had high editorial standards, but he had to print what he could get, which wasn't very good. One of his best contributors, Grigoryev, had died shortly after Mikhail did. The turn of the year brought no change in the magazine's fortunes. The subscribers numbered only thirteen hundred, as contrasted with *Vremya*'s four thousand. He slaved twelve, thirteen, nineteen hours a day, but he could work only intermittently. He made promises. He couldn't keep them. He tore his hair over his mistakes. He committed them again. He worked furiously, but all he produced was confusion. He brought out one issue. He brought out another. The cash box was empty. Not a kopeck with which to pay the paper manufacturer, the printer, the contributors. He made a few feeble efforts to save the magazine and then surrendered. *Epokha* was done for.

Dostoevsky's work on it had been chiefly editorial. In all he contributed to the magazine a grotesque skit, "Crocodile," in which contemporaries saw a malicious jab at Chernyshevsky, and *Notes from the Underground*. The word translates the Russian for the space under the floor of a hut, usually the habitat of mice, hence the protagonist's references to himself as a mouse. He is shown at the start as a recently retired minor official, an educated man, forty years old. He is a solitary idler, dependent on a tiny legacy and living in a dismal room on the outskirts of the capital, "the most abstract and contrived city on earth." The first of the two parts of the *Notes* is the exacerbated, painfully discursive monologue of the denizen of the underground, who is never named. The second part is a narrative of extraordinary power and inwardness, reaching its climax with an account of an unforgettable episode in the undergroundling's early manhood. Here is an example of the reversed chronology favored by Dostoevsky, to which Proust called attention. Throughout, one is in a confessional, listening to a person tell the whole truth about himself in all its loathsomeness, watching him strip himself morally naked. Here is frankness previously seldom matched in literature.

It is in the second part that the circumstances under which the eventual denizen of the underground grew up are indicated. A homeless orphan, reluctantly provided for by distant relatives, he was thrust into school without a thought about the matter. His years there were "penal servitude." Looking savagely at everyone around him, he hated his fellows from the first and they repaid him in the same coin. He also despised them, regarding these boys as vulgar, hopelessly stupid, and monstrously depraved. To escape from their gibes, he succeeded in making his way to the top. Their jeering stopped but not their enmity. He was reduced to a proud isolation that was increasingly hard for him to bear. His sole chum became someone for him to tyrannize over, and so the friendship did not last.

Entering the civil service, he failed to win promotion and remained a minor official. He despised his work, prizing it only as an opportunity to be disagreeable to petitioners; as for his colleagues, he never even looked in their direction. His ill-kept, filthy lodging he described as "my private residence, my shell, my sheath, in which I hid from all mankind." In short, the underground. He became a troglodytic dreamer like certain characters in the early stories. But while those were anemic, gentle souls, he was full of gall and venom. Furthermore, he mocked his reveries. This, although they made up for the meanness, the gloom, the inanity of his days and allowed him to go on squatting in the filth undisturbed. After a stretch of daydreaming, in which he posed as the doughty hero serving the cause of "the beautiful and the sublime," he would plunge all the more greedily into petty, furtive, shameful debauchery. He alternated between a sense of his shortcomings and a conviction of his superiority to everyone else. A touchiness like that of a hunchback exposed him to constant fear of humiliation, yet he courted it, finding it a source of perverse pleasure.

He reveals his tormented and depraved self when he emerges from his cave and attempts to enter real life. In a moment of abysmal loneliness he forces himself on a group of his former schoolmates who are arranging a farewell dinner for a comrade of theirs, an army officer by the name of Zverkov, who is about to leave for a post in a distant province. The undergroundling abominates the guest of honor, he has had no traffic with these men, and they make it clear that he is not wanted. Things go from bad to worse. His companions wipe the floor with him, but he sticks to them, all the while cursing himself for having insisted on joining them. He tells himself that as long as he lives he will remember the dinner as his most painful experience. At the end, in a fever, he apologizes to them all and asks for their friendship. With stinging rudeness Zverkov repudiates his apology. Not throwing him a word, they then decide to go off to a brothel. He first manages to borrow money from one of them and, after some delay, leaves for the same house. En route he indulges in a fantasy about slapping Zverkov's face. But when he arrives at the house, he finds that the men have separated and that there is no trace of Zverkov.

Waking in the small hours, he is assailed by misery and spite. He had not previously said a word to his bedfellow, and now he questions this Liza, a young girl with something good-natured and "strangely grave" in her look. He proceeds to paint the frightful picture of the future that awaits her. For some time his rhetoric appears to be unsuccessful, because she masks her feelings with irony. He renews his efforts and she finally breaks down, torn by the violence of a despair that she vainly seeks to hide. Panic-stricken by the effect of his eloquence, he leaves in a hurry, but not before giving her his address and asking her to come to see him.

As the following day wears on, a vague unease, as if he were haunted by a crime he had committed, starts to gnaw at him. He tells himself, less than convincingly, that he had spoken to Liza sincerely the previous night—he had wanted to arouse "an honorable feeling" in her. For the next few days he alternates between daydreams in which she eventually becomes his adoring wife, and fear of what will happen should she appear in his shabby quarters, a fear giving way at times to savage hatred of her. Sure enough, one evening Liza turns up, surprising him in the midst of a humiliating scene with his servant, who is marvelously portrayed. He withdraws into a malicious silence. Liza breaks it by bringing out that she wants to leave *that* house. Her faltering words make his heart ache with pity for her, but this feeling is crushed by uncontrollable spite. He blurts out the truth about their night together at the brothel, a truth so hideous that he had hitherto concealed it from himself. Nothing was further from his mind, he says, than the wish to redeem her. He had simply been making game of her. That evening, he explains, he had suffered an intolerable insult, and as he failed to get at the offender, he had avenged it on her. He goes on to declare that he doesn't care what becomes of her or of anyone, and in the next breath calls himself the most despicable worm on earth. Then he asks her why she doesn't go.

Disregarding his last words, Liza is overcome by the thought of how painful it was for him to revile himself before her. She rises and shyly holds out her hands to him. Then suddenly and less than credibly, she throws her arms around his neck, bursting into tears. And so does he, as he responds to her embrace. Even before his sobs give over, he is stabbed by the thought that the tables have been turned and that she is the heroine of the situation, while he has become the low, pitiable creature that she had been that night. This intensifies his ill-will toward her. Hating her, he also abruptly desires her. For an instant she is amazed, frightened; then she embraces him "ardently, rapturously." He commits the final atrocity, deliberately turning her gesture of love into the prelude to the act of lust that is the routine of her trade, and presses the outrage home by cramming money into her hand as he shows her the door.

This last cruelty, he knows, came from the top of his head, not from his heart. When he finds on the table the crushed bill he had given her, he dresses in haste and rushes out of the house to look for her. But he reflects that shortly after their reconciliation he is sure to start hating and torturing Liza again. Is it not better for her to live with that brutal insult? It will uplift and purify her by hatred, perhaps by forgiveness. And so he returns home. He is never to see her again or learn what becomes of her.

In telling his story the underground man clings to the fiction that he is writing it down without thought of readers, in the hope that this would free him from an unbearably oppressive memory and possibly be an atonement. Before he makes his confession he delivers himself of the monologue, some of it directed against imaginary opponents, which has already been mentioned as forming Part One of the *Notes*. This outpouring greatly modifies the portrait of the undergroundling as a young man presented in Part Two.

Having declared that he cannot rightly claim any human characteristic ("I have not known how to become either spiteful or kind, a scoundrel or an honest man, a hero or an insect."), he offhandedly ascribes to himself a variety of all too human traits, some of them morbid. He dwells especially on what he terms his excessive "consciousness," by which he appears to mean an over-developed intellect, a proneness to tireless reflection. In contradistinction to the natural man, instinctual, possessed of strong nerves, practical-minded, who does the world's work, the man of the underground is an intellectual, a creature issued from a retort, doomed to inertia. For no sooner does he decide to act— for instance, to avenge an insult—than he is assailed by doubts and questions, arguments pro and con, and his resolution withers, "sicklied o'er with the pale cast of thought," leaving behind rankling malice.

In one other respect the quasi-Hamlet differs from the generality of mankind. They accept the laws of nature, the authority of science, the axioms of mathematics, and carry on their activities within the limits of the possible. He, on the contrary, is disgusted with "the whole legal system of nature," and is offended by such propositions as two times two makes four. He is aware that he sounds irrational, but "rational" is a word that "sticks in one's throat." Reason, he argues, knows only what it has learned, and some things it will never learn; it is only a fraction of man's total capacity for life, say, one twentieth.

His attack on rationalism goes hand in hand with the exaltation of freedom of the will. All we know of history with certainty, he points out, is that it has little to do with reason. He defines man as at bottom an irrational and perverse creature. Man can deliberately act against his own interest; he loves well-being, but also suffering, not only building, but destruction, chaos; he is interested in breaking a path, but not in the final goal, for life is incompatible with finality. Furthermore, what man wants is to act as he chooses, following his own sweet foolish impulse, regardless of the consequences. This is man's chief advantage, his *summum bonum*. There is an idea abroad that since he is within the order of nature, human behavior is subject to the natural laws discovered by science. Doesn't it follow, the under-groundling asks, that freedom of the will is an illusion beyond the shadow of a doubt, that man is a marionette, a "piano key"? What if science reaches a point where the feelings, the thoughts, the actions of a given individual can be calculated thirty years in advance? The undergroundling does not deny such a monstrous eventuality. In his horror at the prospect his own reason totters. Many people, he supposes, would then lose the desire to exercise the act of volition and would sink into torpor. He would not be surprised, however, if one day a gentleman of retrograde and sardonic appearance were to rise and say: "Hadn't we better smash all this reasonableness to smithereens and live once more at our own foolish will?" Others will go mad on purpose in order to prove that they are human beings, not "piano keys."

The undergroundling is depicted as a spiteful, perverse, de-praved human being, incapable of devotion or love. The impli-cation is that he is an intellectual of the type Dostoevsky ab-horred, a man divorced from the "soil," cut off from the sources of life. No effort is spared to show him in all his shame. Yet his tirade is in substance an extravagant sequel to the polemics against Nihilism that were going on in the pages of *Vremya* and *Epokha*. He speaks vehemently for the humane values, such as free will and self-definition, that are threatened by positivism, with its mechanistic philosophy. In fact, this wretched creature, while not a self-portrait of the novelist, is incongruously his mouthpiece, except when the monologist announces that he stands for his whim and for having it guaranteed him. It has been seen that at the very time when Dostoevsky was writing the *Notes* he set down an entry in his notebook declaring *inter alia* that the ultimate use one can make of one's ego is to surrender it completely in loving-kindness, according to Christ's injunction. In the author's view unbridled self-will, that extreme manifes-tation of egocentric individualism, is odious to the Russian.

Toward the end of his monologue the speaker intimates that he too cherishes an ideal. If he spat at "the beautiful and the sublime," it was not because he upheld the ugly and the de-grading. He had reviled the Crystal Palace that figures in Chernyshevsky's novel as the mansion housing people under the blessings of socialism. Now he admits that he is not really so fond of sticking out his tongue at things. On the contrary, he would have his tongue cut out if this were to enable men to erect an edifice at which he would not want to jeer—one not to be found among the palaces "you" (socialists) have dreamed up. If he goes on to shout hurrah for the underground, he forthwith reverses his position, confessing that he thirsts for something other than the underground—"damn the underground!"

What he wants in its place remains undisclosed. A clue to it is found in the letter that the author wrote to Mikhail immediately after the publication of the first part of the *Notes*. Of the tenth chapter, "the principal one, in which the central idea is set forth," he has this to say: "It would have been better not to print it at all than to have it appear in its present shape, self-contradictory and with phrases out of context. Oh, these censors, these swine, where I scoffed at everything and sometimes *simulated* blasphemy—that they passed, but where I deduced from all that the necessity of faith and Christ—that they cut. What is the matter with these censors? Are they in a conspiracy against the government, eh?" Unfortunately, the passages expunged from the text have not been preserved. Nor were they restored in later editions of the story. It would seem that Dostoevsky's youthful Utopianism had not lost its attraction for him, but now it rested on a religious foundation.

*Notes from the Underground* concludes with what suggests a variation on a theme familiar to readers of Dostoevsky's journals: the saving power of "the soil." The typical educated Russian, the undergroundling intimates, has been wholly estranged from real life, even from his "*own* body and blood"; he is ashamed of what he is and tries to be "some sort of generalized man." He breaks off these reflections to address his compatriots thus: "For my part, I have merely carried to the extreme what you have not dared to carry even halfway, and what's more, you have mistaken your cowardice for good sense, and found consolation in that, deceiving yourselves. So that perhaps, after all, I am more alive than you." As Ronald Hingley puts it in his pointed book on the novelist, "The paradoxical anti-hero, as he describes himself, leaves the pages of *Notes from the Underground* as its hero."

A decade later the novelist jotted down a complacent entry in his notebook. The gist of it is that he takes pride in having been the first to disclose the tragic side of the typical Russian that the underground man is. He is painfully aware of his baseness, indulges in self-punishment, yet is convinced that no one is better than himself. "The underground, the underground, the poet of the underground!" the note ends. "Feuilleton writers harp on it as if it were something humiliating for me. Fools, this is my glory, for it is the truth."

The *Notes* is the most arresting of Dostoevsky's shorter fictions. At one point the monologist indirectly refers to himself as "the intelligent man of our unhappy nineteenth century." The anguished tone of the writing, the morbid contradictory impulses that lacerate the protagonist, the belittling of the intellect in the name of the total human being, the attack on utilitarian ethics, the anarchic overtones in the defense of freedom, the rejection of determinism, of the claims of scientific materialism and progress—all this, and the very word for the lodging from which, through a crack, the central figure observes the world, have resonance for the intelligent man of the incomparably more unhappy twentieth century.

*Notes from the Underground* marks the end of Dostoevsky's preoccupation with dreamers and troglodytes. It also introduces themes and concerns on which the novelist will enlarge in the massive works of fiction that are to follow.

# 15

## LUCKLESS SUITOR

LIFE had snapped in two. He was left alone. He had nobody, nothing, to live for. Masha was gone, Mikhail was gone. The magazine was bankrupt. Existence was a dismal, inane bustling in a vacuum. To establish new contacts, to form new ties— the very thought was an abomination. He felt sterile, he was empty of everything but despair. As he looked back to the past he saw only its warm, familiar, homely aspects, the comradeship it had held, the love, the rewarding work. The future was a blank in which the sole certainties were loneliness, epilepsy with its threat of madness or sudden death, old age.

Shortly after Mikhail's death Dostoevsky expressed these sentiments to Andrey. He reiterated them to Wrangel months later, after the review had gone under. He said the same thing to Polina Suslova's sister. And yet—it was absurd!—at the same time he had the paradoxical feeling that life was just beginning for him. He had, he said as much in earnest as in jest, the nine lives of a cat. There were in him reserves of vitality larger than he guessed. They had not failed him in previous crises; they did not fail him now. He had neither rebelled against nor been crushed by imprisonment and hard labor. Now Fate was punishing him again, and again disaster gave him a curious sense of release and renewal. His feeling that life was beginning for him had a far sounder foundation than his feeling of having come to the barren end of it. He was indeed on the threshold of a period in which he was to discover the satisfaction of married happiness and fatherhood, and in which he was to reach his full stature as a writer.

As a matter of fact, there was not as wide a gulf between his past and his present as he sometimes imagined. There were bridges across the chasm. He had told Wrangel that the two who died were the only ones he had ever loved and that he could not love again, nor did he want to. At the same time he was writing to Polina's sister that he still loved Polina. Furthermore, he was occupied less with this desperate old attachment than with more recent ones. Unthinkable as new ties seemed, the need for them asserted itself, and that in the months which immediately followed the funerals. Of one bizarre relation which engaged Dostoevsky at this time little is known beyond what is revealed in a bundle of letters dating from December, 1864, and January, 1865, and signed "Marfa Brown."

Her Anglo-Saxon surname notwithstanding, the woman was a native Russian of the lower middle class whose maiden name was Panina. Dostoevsky had come to know her through a certain Gorsky, who contributed stories of life in the slums to both *Vremya* and *Epokha*. At the time she was living with this man, a wretched drunkard, having been passed on to him by another literary hack with whom she had sunk to the depths of destitution. Her youth and such looks as she may once have possessed had vanished. Dostoevsky took an interest in this wreck of a woman and, as she was familiar with English and possibly with other Western languages, he offered her work as a translator. She fell ill and was admitted to a hospital. He may already have known something of her past, but it was through the somewhat incoherent letters which she wrote him from her sickbed and those which she asked him to read before transmitting to her lover, that he learned some of the details of her history.

Her easy virtue consorted with a roving disposition. By her own account, she was "a pauper and a universal vagrant," and she lived for the moment: "I have always been of the opinion that life is made for impressions. . . ." For logic she had no use. Her early career is a blank. She had been in Russia for two years. Before that she had been roaming Western Europe. One of her letters contains an extraordinary account of her wanderings, ending with her marriage in England to a sailor from

Baltimore, who seems to have given her his surname, if nothing else. How much was fact and how much fantasy in this story? Whatever the answer, she refused to make literary capital of her adventures, though Gorsky kept insisting that she do so.

Had it not been for him, she might sooner have left the hospital to which her checkered career had brought her. Gorsky, penniless, homeless, jealous as a cat, feared that on leaving the infirmary she would take up with any man who could give her a place to lay her head, and so he would come drunk and storming to the ward and make a scene, demanding that she stay on by malingering. Dostoevsky, from whom she seems to have hidden nothing, also came to see her there, gave her money, gave her sympathy. At one time he advised her to stay with Gorsky. Again, in the teeth of the man's jealousy, he suggested that she come direct from the hospital to his own flat. Did the lost creature attract him as a woman, as she had so many other men? In her last letter to him, which is formal in tone, if not in content, she thanked him for all his kindnesses, saying: "In any event, whether or not I shall succeed in satisfying you physically, and whether there will be that spiritual harmony between us upon which the continuation of our acquaintance will depend, believe me that I shall always remain thankful to you for having honored me, for at least a moment or for some time, with your friendship and favor." She was happy, she went on, to have met, after all her sufferings, a man like Dostoevsky, "possessing such serenity of spirit, tolerance, common sense, and candor. . . ." She concluded: "It is all the same to me whether our relationship lasts a long time or not, but I swear to you that far beyond any material advantage, I prize the fact that you have not scorned the fallen part of my nature, that you raised me above the level on which I stand in my own estimation." With this letter Marfa Brown retreats into the obscurity whence she came.

So little is known about this strange incident, about the character of the woman and the nature of her relations with Dostoevsky, that it is impossible to speak with any certainty of the part she played in his life and the imprint she left on his work. Perhaps some memory of her helped him to delineate those of his women who have left the path of conventional virtue without degrading themselves.

# ( II )

Possibly the enigmatic Marfa faded out of the picture because Dostoevsky's attention was diverted by the appearance of a girl who had everything that she lacked—youth, beauty, health, spirit, and who, moreover, came of a distinguished and well-to-do land-owning family. If Marfa, in her pitiableness, bore some faint resemblance to his poor wife, the newcomer was like a younger and lovelier Polina. Like Polina, she had swum into his ken as a contributor to his review. Soon after Mikhail's death forced him to take over *Epokha* he received two manuscripts from a novice who used a masculine pseudonym and whose real name was Anna Korvin-Krukovskaya. One was a romantic short story, the other a novelette about a young man's futile quest for a morally ideal way of life, first in a monastic retreat and then in a mundane setting. Robert Belknap, an American scholar, has pointed out that the novelette contributed, perhaps through subconscious memory, to the shaping of the image of Myshkin in *The Idiot* and of Alyosha in *The Brothers Karamazov*. Dostoevsky found these efforts not without merit, wrote to her encouragingly, and printed and paid for both tales.

On February 28, 1865, she informed him that she had arrived in the capital, and invited him to call on her at the home of her grandfather, with whom her family was staying. When he reached the mansion on Vasilyevsky Ostrov and was admitted to the drawing room, he discovered that his contributor was a Lorelei of a girl with golden hair and green eyes, in her early twenties. They were not alone. Her mother and her little sister, a sharp child of fourteen, sat with them during the entire visit, and two elderly aunts kept peering in at odd moments, staring at him as though he were a wild beast. Disconcerted by all these supernumeraries, the pretty bluestocking maintained a stubborn silence. The mother exerted all her social gifts to relieve the situation—in vain. Dostoevsky, no less vexed than his young hostess, answered questions rudely in monosyllables, kept plucking nervously at his thin blond beard and biting his mustache. He looked old and ill, as always when he was not at ease. After half an hour of this misery, he got up, bowed awkwardly, and shaking hands with no one, made his exit. Anna burst into hysterical tears. To have anticipated for months this first encounter with the great writer who had set her on the road to fame and to be thus spied on, babied, and thwarted! It was intolerable! The mother joined her tears to the daughter's, and everyone was wretched.

For the young authoress, Dostoevsky's visit was more momentous than he could have guessed. Aside from anything else, it put a seal on her declaration of independence from her family. Their attitude was such that she had had to keep her literary venture secret from them. When one of his letters, enclosing a remittance, had come by accident into her father's hands, there had been a terrible scene. General Korvin-Krukovsky was a gentleman of the old school who looked forward to seeing his lovely daughter shine at court balls and who had a particular horror of lady authors. "You begin by selling your writings," he shouted at Anna, "and you will end by selling yourself." Nevertheless, the culprit was allowed to read her story to the domestic circle. The General was so moved by it that he relented to the extent of granting Anna permission to meet Dostoevsky on the family's next visit to the capital. Of course, her mother must be present when the journalist and ex-convict came to call.

A few days after Dostoevsky's first unhappy visit he called again. He had to. He had fallen in love with his fair contributor at sight. This time he found the two sisters alone, and, freed from constraint, both he and Anna were different persons: he, youthful, amiable, brilliant; she, eager, interested, gay. The ice once broken, he kept on coming to the house, rather too frequently. And yet he was made to feel at home, even by the mother. Except when there were other visitors, he was quite at his best, thrilling his sympathetic listeners with monologues delivered in his broken, passionate whisper. Showing no reserve before the two sheltered young girls, one of them in her early teens, he outlined to them the plots of his projected novels, mentioning the rape of a ten-year-old girl and describing episodes from his own life, such as his first epileptic attack. The mother must have become genuinely fond of him to continue putting up with him.

Although he was so much of a social liability, she had the rashness to invite him to an evening party at which she was entertaining all her most fashionable acquaintances. He came, in an ill-fitting dress suit, and proceeded to embarrass his hostess in every way. He would respond to an introduction by mumbling unintelligibly and turning his back on the guest. The worst of it was that he monopolized Anna, holding her hand, whispering in her ear, repelling every intrusion upon their privacy, and when her mother finally succeeded in separating them almost by main force, he sat sulking in his corner and glaring at the company. The particular object of his angry regard was a handsome young colonel, a cousin of Anna's, who was quietly but firmly courting her. Dostoevsky decided that the family was bent on marrying her off to this wealthy fop with the epaulets and the shapely legs, and the only time during the whole evening that he opened his mouth, it was to utter a broad hint about mothers who were eager to find rich husbands for their daughters.

That evening was the beginning of the end of Anna's infatuation with the great man. He found himself at a disadvantage: a middle-aged man in love with a young vixen. Feeling that he was losing her, he came more frequently, he exacted accounts of how and with whom she spent her time in his absence. She was out, she was dancing, she was with her cousin—and this while he had been struggling with chaos in the *Epokha* office. He fairly invited her to tease him, which she did with the cruelty of youth. One way in which she taunted him was to flaunt the radical ideas she had recently acquired. He scolded her for a little Nihilist. They argued. They quarreled. He left, saying that he would never see her again. He returned the next day.

Anna's little sister, Sonia, was generally on the scene, drinking everything in and watching her sister's suitor with worshiping eyes. She was rather pleased to see them quarrel. The cooler Anna grew, the more serious became Sonia's transports. Dostoevsky fell into the habit of holding her up as a model to the frivolous Anna. He praised her earnestness, her looks, her manners. A warm word from him about her playing set her to securing a good teacher at once and to spending hours at the piano every day. She was at particular pains to learn the *Sonate Pathétique* because he had once said that it stirred up in him a whole world of forgotten emotions. He was ordinarily deaf to music, but in the right mood he could be shaken by Beethoven as well as by a barrel-organ tune.

One night, toward the end of their stay in Petersburg, Dostoevsky came to the house to find the two girls alone. The hour, the impending departure, the unexpected privacy, all wrought them up. Sonia was not long in sitting down at the piano and starting her *Sonate Pathétique*. Ignoring her sister, she played for an audience of one, trying to wake in him that "world of lost emotions." She did not look up from the keys until she lifted her hands from the last chord, to discover that she was alone. With a heavy heart she wandered from one room to the next and, lifting a portière, saw Dostoevsky sitting on a sofe beside Anna, holding her hand, his face pale and distraught, and heard him telling her in a shaken whisper how passionately he loved her. Sonia rushed off to her own room to hide her shame and sorrow, dreading nothing more than that she would be summoned—she knew they had heard her—and that she would have to face those two. For the first time she became aware of the nature of her feelings for Dostoevsky. The pages from her diary that described those moments might have come from one of his novels. She got into bed and lay there sobbing. As the hours passed and no one called her, her dread changed to indignation at such neglect. She hated them both. No one could have understood her emotions more fully than the man who had roused them. But he was not concerned with Sonia just then. Anna had refused him.

As she confided to her little sister the following night, she could give this genius her respect, her admiration, even her affection, but she could not marry him. With astonishing insight she realized that he needed a wife who would have no life of her own, but would devote herself wholly and cheerfully to his needs. She was not that sort; even now she was constantly irritated by not being herself in his presence. The prospect of being "sucked into" him, and lost, terrified her. In rejecting her suitor she must have told him these hard truths. He came only once more, to make his farewells.

The episode in which the two sisters figured so romantically is set down in Sonia's reminiscences, written many years later. She adds that some six months after their departure from the capital Dostoevsky wrote to Anna that he had fallen in love with "a wonderful girl," who had agreed to marry him. The betrothal occurred in November, 1866. It has therefore been generally assumed that the memoirist committed an error, speaking of six months instead of a year and six months. A suggestion has recently been made that the novelist proposed to Anna, not in the spring of 1865, but in the winter of 1865–66, when the Korvin-Krukovskys were again on a visit to the capital. It is certain that in 1865 and 1866 the two kept up a desultory correspondence and that he expressed a desire to visit the family on their estate.

According to her successor in his affections, Dostoevsky was actually betrothed to Anna and they parted because of the incompatibility of their views, but he loved her enough to wish her a mate who would share her crooked opinions. She did indeed marry a socialist, and a Frenchman to boot. They were both active in the Paris Commune, and a secretary of the Russian embassy in the French capital described her as a Megaera. After the fall of the Commune she saved her husband from the guillotine by arranging his escape from France. Eventually they settled in Russia. There Dostoevsky, then a married man, met her again and the two families became friendly. He also saw a good deal of her sister. She had married a certain Kovalevsky, whose name her mathematical genius made internationally famous.

# (III)

He was a bankrupt lover. He was a bankrupt publisher. He had sunk his legacy from Aunt Kumanina in *Epokha,* and the failure of the review left him not only penniless but, since he had taken over Mikhail's obligations, saddled with debts amounting to thirteen thousand rubles or perhaps it was fifteen thousand—he was hazy on the subject. "Oh, my friend," he wrote to Wrangel, "I would gladly serve another four-year term of hard labor, if that would enable me to pay my debts and again feel free."

And what would become of the widow and the orphans? There was his work to fall back upon, but he was in an awkward position with regard to marketing it. He had perforce to offer it to editors of reviews that had been decried in the pages of *Vremya* and *Epokha.* His first step was to obtain a loan of fifteen hundred rubles from the Fund for Needy Authors. He had indicated in his application that he was threatened with debtors' prison, where in his present state of health he could not write. He then turned to his old employer, Krayevsky, and asked an advance on the novel, *The Drunkards,* to be delivered in the autumn, but met with a refusal.

Suddenly immediate payment was demanded on some of his overdue notes. On June 5th he received a notice to the effect that his household goods would be seized to obtain payment of two debts amounting to five hundred and ninety-nine rubles. Debtors' prison loomed all too close. Matters went so far that he was visited by a police officer. He got into talk with the man and was soon listening interestedly to all manner of details about the work of the police. The bits of information supplied by this casual acquaintance were stored away and eventually put to good use in the writing of *Crime and Punishment*. The officer did not have to discharge the unpleasant duty of carrying him off to jail. At the psychological moment Stellovsky, a Barabbas of a publisher, came forward with a shameful contract that Dostoevsky promptly signed. It allowed Stellovsky to bring out an edition of all of Dostoevsky's previous work, and further provided that he should receive an unpublished novel on or before November 1, 1866. Failure to deliver this manuscript on time gave the publisher the right to issue, without payment to the author, everything he would write within the next nine years. In consideration of all this, Dostoevsky received three thousand rubles. Two-thirds of the sum went toward the payment of the protested notes. He did not then know that the money actually reverted to Stellovsky: the IOUs on which immediate payment was demanded were in possession of this shark, who had quietly bought them up for a song. At the end of July, with a small residue in his pocket, hardly enough to live on for any length of time, Dostoevsky went abroad.

He had long ago decided to spend three months in every year out of Russia. He was lonely abroad and the alien surroundings disgusted him, yet, oddly enough, he felt better and worked better away from home. This time he had some hope of seeing Polina Suslova again. The previous year she had written him that they might meet at Spa and upbraided him for writing a cynical story quite out of character, by which she meant *Notes from the Underground*. But Mikhail's death had kept him at home. Europe offered also the lure of the gaming tables, and there may have been the added urge to escape the scene of his present embarrassments.

As though he were ever able to escape! He fell from the frying pan into the fire. The trip was a disastrous one. True, there was a letup in his attacks, but at the beginning of the journey he caught a chill and the fever clung to him relentlessly. From Berlin he went to Wiesbaden, where he found Polina.

One can only surmise what happened between the two during the few days they spent together. At the time when *Epokha* was still a going concern an acquaintance had jokingly suggested to her that she marry Dostoevsky and turn the review into a radical organ. She would not hear of it: "What kind of Iphigenia am I?" she wrote in her diary, with more self-knowledge than classical learning. She told herself that she hated Dostoevsky— he had caused her needless suffering, he had killed her faith in men. In the angry letters that she had sent him she accused him of sadism, coarseness, cynicism. His answers have not been preserved but in a letter to her sister, dated April 19, 1865, he denied Polina's accusations. She had been offended, he wrote, because he had at long last dared to talk back. "Her egoism and *amour-propre* are colossal," he added. "She demands *everything* from people, never forgives anyone a single imperfection, and exempts herself from the slightest obligation to others. . . . There isn't any humanity in her relations with me. She knows that I still love her. Why, then, does she torture me!" The Wiesbaden meeting apparently did not improve Dostoevsky's standing with her. She continued to treat him contemptuously and pitilessly. Yet she did not put an end to their relationship, and when she left for Paris they parted amicably.

As before, she brought him bad luck at the tables. At the end of five days he had lost everything, was reduced to pawning his watch, and owed money at the hotel. He was still sick and was worried about Polina, who had left with so little cash that he feared she might be stranded at Cologne, and starving. He certainly was. Nothing but tea was set before him; the servants did not answer the bell, didn't clean his shoes, were altogether wanting in respect for him. He kept as quiet as possible, so as not to get up an appetite.

Knowing that Turgenev was in Baden, he appealed to him for a loan. And he disliked the man, all the more intensely since he had once been in love with him. One of the first books he had read on coming out of prison was *A Sportsman's Sketches* and it had filled him with delight. When Turgenev's *Fathers and Children* appeared, the same year as *The House of the Dead,* Dostoevsky wrote an enthusiastic letter to the author, and was assured that he was one of the two men who understood the novel. As an editor he had had some friendly interchanges with Turgenev and, indeed, had coaxed a story, "Phantoms," out of the literary lion for the first issue of *Epokha*. In discussing this piece with Mikhail privately, Dostoevsky had said that it was "fairly decent," but that there was "much trash in it, something nasty, sickly, senile, impotent, and so without faith—in a word, the whole Turgenev with all his convictions." Yet here he was, making a clean breast of his shameful predicament to this objectionable creature and even saying that it was morally easier to turn to him because he was more understanding than others. Turgenev did indeed send half the amount requested—a debt which was not to be repaid for eleven years—but this was only a drop in the bucket.

Dostoevsky also turned for help to Herzen, who was then in Geneva, and even to Polina, saying that if she had reached Paris and could raise some cash, she should send him one hundred and fifty gulden forthwith. Herzen was silent. Herzen was dismissing him as a disorderly wretch who didn't deserve help—was that it? To think of this socialist upholding middle-class morality! He was forgotten by God and man. And this intolerable idleness, this waste, this uncertainty! He hated the town and its last inhabitant. He had struck bottom. For three days he had gone without dinner, but what was worse than hunger was the meanness of the servants in refusing him a candle in the evening if he had so much as an end left from the night before.

At last there was a kind letter from Herzen, but no money. Again he appealed to Polina. Another fortnight passed, and his situation was unchanged. Then he confessed everything to Wrangel and begged for money with which to pay off his debts and go to Paris. There was no reply and he wrote again. He was threatened with arrest; there was no question of Paris now, he must go home. But on what? He was in utter despair. At least he was idle no longer. He was working day and night on a story, a new version of the piece refused by Krayevsky. He had a thousand rubles' worth of manuscript and would surely be able to repay his friend within a month.

And then, a hundred thalers! Wrangel was to be counted on. But the hotel-keeper got most of it and Dostoevsky was just where he had been before. Finally, the local Russian priest came to his aid, giving security for him on what he owed the hotel-keeper, and advancing him the fare home. On the way he stopped off at Copenhagen to see Wrangel. About October 15 he was back in Petersburg.

The very first night home he had a violent attack. He had hardly recovered from it when he was struck down by one that was even worse. Within six weeks he had four seizures. The one bright spot in the gloom that enveloped him was the fact that

Katkov accepted the novel he was busy with, and sent him the advance he had requested. But what was three hundred rubles when he had just added two more creditors, in the persons of Wrangel and the Wiesbaden priest, to his long list, when he had not only himself to support, but his stepson Pasha as well, and Vasya, Mikhail's bastard, when he had his sick brother Kolya to help, and when Mikhail's widow and her children were hanging on his neck like so many millstones! Emilia made it plain that she considered him obliged to support them. Hadn't her poor husband kept sending him remittances when he was in Siberia? Hadn't he founded a journal to give him a place to print what other reviews rejected? And hadn't he, Dostoevsky, in the end wrecked the enterprise that should have supported them all?

Before the week was out the money was gone, partly into the widow's pocket, and he had to borrow another hundred to live on. Where should he turn next? If he could only get a government pension for Mikhail's family, or if he could revive the magazine! But he dared not think of any new venture until he had brought his name before the public again by finishing his novel.

He had not been home long when Polina arrived in town. As indicated above, he had written her sister in the spring that he still loved her, if against his better judgment. Now, in the midst of these desolate, harassing days, he threw his better judgment to the winds. Perhaps they could still make something of life together. He pursued her as before. They quarreled as before. While abroad she had been moving in radical circles, and intellectually they were further apart than ever. Knowing his weak spot, she poked fun at religion. He reminded her ungallantly of her previous complaisance: "You cannot forgive me the fact that you once gave yourself to me, and so you take revenge on me." On November 2, 1865, she made this entry in her diary: "He (Dostoevsky) has long been offering me his hand and heart, but he only makes me angry by it." Some three months later she left Petersburg. The break was now final.

# 16

# A RUSSIAN TRAGEDY

AS noted, shortly before Dostoevsky went abroad he had
vainly tried to get an advance on a novel about the drink evil.
At the time the excessive consumption of vodka with all its deplorable consequences, such as prostitution, was much in the
public mind. Thus the narrative would have a bearing on a current social problem, a consideration that never ceased to count
with the quondam disciple of Belinsky. The plot underwent a
radical change during the author's Wiesbaden captivity. Alcoholism receded into the background, becoming a subsidiary theme
in what was to be *Crime and Punishment,* a project that had occupied him for some weeks. After having been turned down by
three publications, it was accepted by *Russky vestnik.*

Dostoevsky wrote to the editor that he had been at work on
the novel for two months and that he expected to finish it in a
fortnight. But he soon realized that unexpectedly he had a long
novel on his hands. The story grew not only in volume but in
depth. His feeling was that he was at work on "the best thing"
that he had ever written. He made preliminary notes for it,
which, with later jottings, were eventually published in the
original and in translation. Moreover, he started more than one
draft of the book. The right form for it he had difficulty choosing. He attempted to offer the reader the protagonist's reminis-

cences in the first person. He tried a combination of a third-person narrative and the criminal's diary. Finding these unacceptable, by late November he burned them, an act of exceptional courage for a man in his circumstances. The method that he now adopted was that used in the final version: a story related by the omniscient and omnipresent author.

Through all the vexations that met him on his return home Dostoevsky kept steadily at *Crime and Punishment*. He was not going to spoil it. By the end of December he had only a small part of the text ready. Nevertheless, Katkov was rash enough to begin publishing the novel in the January number of the monthly for 1866. Thereafter, for a whole year, the author raced against time to furnish copy for successive issues. Luckily for him, they were always late in coming out.

It was a bitter and lonely winter. His sole companion in the disorderly rooms was Pasha. The novelist lived like a hermit, saw no one, went nowhere. No sooner did the epileptic attacks abate than he was laid up with piles—nothing new, but more virulent than ever. The worst part of it was that his ailment made writing impossible, so that when he recovered, he had to sweat to make up for lost time. And then the seizures commenced again. He had fits of irritability that exceeded all bounds. There were constant money worries. He pawned his clothes. He sold his books. He borrowed right and left. He lived in the shadow of debtors' prison, horrified by the thought that it would wreck his novel. The more he paid his creditors, the uglier they got. He was killing himself for Mikhail's family, and the children didn't even bow to him. He was so wretched that as he looked back to the period before his brother's death it seemed a time of peace and plenty.

And yet, after enumerating all his troubles in a letter to a friend, he concluded: "But do not imagine that I am altogether miserable. No, there have been many happy moments. Life and hope have not ended for me yet." Although his seizures meant intermittent traffic with death, his mind was turned toward life. He seemed to be quickened and energized by punishment. To Strakhov he had the jaunty appearance of an eligible on the lookout for a wife.

Indeed, the sad state of his health and of his finances notwithstanding, the thought of marriage was always there. He had been refused by Anna and by Polina. He was not discouraged. In the early spring he went to Moscow to get an advance from

Katkov. This time he stayed with his sister Vera and was in the unaccustomed position of being a member of a large jolly family. On Easter Eve the whole household went to church for the midnight service, but he remained at home in the company of a young thing, a friend of his twenty-year-old niece, Sonia. The girl made up for what she lacked in looks by her gaiety and vivaciousness. When the family returned in the small hours, she laughingly confided to Sonia that her uncle had actually proposed to her and that, in turning him down, she had teased him with Pushkin's verse about "an old man's heart the years had petrified."

His sister Vera, seeing the matter in a sober light, sought to engineer a match more suitable to his age and circumstances. The lady she fixed upon was her own sister-in-law, Yelena Pavlovna Ivanova. True, Mme. Ivanova was not free, but her husband, Dr. Ivanov's brother, had been ill for years and his death was hourly expected. Dostoevsky lent himself to Vera's plans for him so far as to ask the prospective widow some months later whether, if she had her freedom, she would marry him. She would not say yes or no, so that he felt himself nowise bound.

He had intended to go to Germany in the spring and finish his novel there in peace, but this proving impossible, he spent the summer with the Ivanovs in the country just outside of Moscow. He occupied a room in an empty cottage, but he went there only to work and sleep, taking his meals with his sister's family. It was delightful to be with them all again, particularly Sonia. The more he saw of her, the more he loved her. He admired her restraint, her clear intelligence, her probity and native dignity. He especially prized her freedom from a bad trait that he attributed to himself: proneness to compromise.

The Ivanov house was overflowing with young people, the children, already numbering nine, and their friends, so that there would not seldom be twenty at the dinner table. In this holiday atmosphere Dostoevsky relaxed and soon found himself taking part in the moonlight walks, the games, the charades, the practical jokes, the amateur theatricals, with the best of them. There was a good deal of music, mostly Chopin, which Dostoevsky rather disliked, finding it "consumptive." He was more careful of his appearance than usual, his shirt well starched, his blue jacket and gray trousers neatly pressed. He had long since given up shaving his chin soldier-fashion, and the thinness of his beard touched his vanity, a fact that his young companions were not

slow to discover. They teased him about it, admitting among
themselves that he looked younger than his forty-five years.

"When I write something," he had once said, "I think of it
while I dine, while I sleep, while I am engaged in conversation."
For all his immersion in his work, he could turn from the writing
of *Crime and Punishment* to the composing of a piece of nonsense
verse on a young physician who was a gullible fool. He was apt,
nevertheless, to leave his young friends abruptly and go to his
desk, and the servant who was sent to sleep near him, so that
he would not be alone during a seizure, came back one day
refusing to spend another night with the master: why, he had a
murder on his mind, he walked the floor all night talking about it
aloud to himself.

Autumn found Dostoevsky again in Petersburg, busy with the
last part of *Crime and Punishment*. It was not until Christmas,
however, that he turned in the final installment, but since the
monthly was late, as usual, he was still able to see the concluding
chapters appear in the December issue.

# ( II )

"A psychological account of a crime," thus Dostoevsky defined
the novel in the letter of mid-September, 1865, in which he offered
the work to Katkov, assuring him that it was in line with the
magazine's conservative position. By and large the plot remained as it was outlined in that letter, of which only a draft has
been preserved. Raskolnikov, a destitute student, expelled from
the university for failure to pay tuition, kills and robs an ogrish
old pawnbroker (and then murders her simple-minded, pious
stepsister, to eliminate a witness to the crime). He leaves no clues
behind, so that he is beyond the reach of the law. In the end an
inner compulsion brings him to confess.

There are two sides to Raskolnikov's nature—his very name
connotes schism (*raskol* means "split," especially separation from
the official Church). A high-minded, idealistic youth, he is obedient to generous impulses and his instinctive reaction to human
misery is eagerness to alleviate it. His beggarly appearance notwithstanding, he remarkably gives the impression of a prepossess-

ing, attractive, fastidious young man. On the other hand, he says that he has a vicious heart. It is not only that in addition to being inordinately proud, arrogant, and vain he is capable of callousness and cruelty. He has flashes of what Coleridge called "motiveless malignity." There are moments when the tones of his voice betray the murderer. He calls to mind the dreamers and recluses whom Dostoevsky used to conjure up in his early manhood and the inhabitants of the underground who had haunted his imagination more recently, but the resemblance is superficial. For them reverie was an escape from reality or a substitute for it, and they were unable to act. He dreams of a means of changing reality. The turbulence within him must sooner or later precipitate an explosive deed. It is thus that Dostoevsky takes the great stride from pathos to tragedy.

At the opening of the narrative Raskolnikov, morbidly withdrawn, "like a tortoise in its shell," spends his days brooding in his closetlike attic or dragging himself through the slums of the capital. The sights he sees there exacerbate the thin-skinned young man's sense of the injustice of life, the depravity of men. Himself on the verge of starvation, he is plagued by the knowledge that he is the only hope of his mother, who lives on a tiny pension, and of his sister, who is in pitiable circumstances. He receives a long letter from his mother explaining their situation in detail and wavering sadly between the desire for his happiness at any price to themselves and a shrinking from the cost. It has a shattering effect upon him. While he is reading those pages his cheeks are wet with tears, but when he has finished reading, his pale face is distorted by a grim, spiteful smile. In his desperation he fastens on the idea of doing away with and robbing a nasty old pawnbroker, whose life must soon end in any case. With her money he will be able to re-enter the university, make something of himself, save his mother from penury and his sister from a loveless marriage or worse, and eventually do good in a larger way. Convinced that because he was planning the murder for "a noble object" it was "not a crime," he believes that he will carry it out with no failure of either will or reasoning power, such as affects one who knows himself a criminal. As a matter of fact, he does lose his self-control. If he leaves no telltale traces behind, it is pure luck.

The deed once done, he is seized by emotions that he had not counted on. He is pursued by the Furies. Anguish, sometimes yielding to panic, alternates with periods of merciful sleep or

torpor. Worst of all, he feels himself cut off from mankind "as
with scissors." It is as if he had suffered an irrevocable excom-
munication from his fellow men. At the same time he conceives a
loathing for them, hating even his mother and sister. His return
to the place of the murder, his circling around the police inspector
"like a moth around a candle," point to an unconscious impulse to
confess. Yet he is also heartened by the belief that the authorities
have no conclusive evidence against him. He loses his assurance
after a mysterious stranger confronts him in the street with:
"You are the killer," and disappears. He must have botched the
job after all, he tells himself.

The burden of this thought and his terrible isolation—he made
it more terrible by breaking with his family—becomes unbearable. He must share it with some living soul. His choice falls
upon Sonia, the prostitute. She is the image of chastity and an
exemplar of simple faith, humility, self-immolation. She has
gone on the streets to feed her father's second wife and her
children, whom the man's drinking has reduced to destitution.
Raskolnikov is irresistibly drawn to her. He feels a similarity in
their fates, and that not merely because both are outcasts. Between them there is an abyss and a kinship. She had sacrificed
herself; he had sacrificed others, but, he sometimes believed, with
a noble end in view, and further, he had also victimized himself
in the process.

It is to Sonia that he admits the truth. During his confession he
makes an effort, in travail of soul, to arrive, by candid, vigorous
self-probing, at an understanding of what had moved him to the
act. Yes, he tells the trembling girl, the end he envisaged justified
the dreadful means. But what nonsense! He might have plodded,
starved, gotten on somehow. But he would not. He lay in his
dusty den, like a spider, and sulked, brooded. Perhaps he was sick,
a little mad. He nonplusses the girl with a question that had long
been tormenting him: What would Napoleon have done if he
could not have entered upon his phenomenal career without killing and robbing a useless old hag? One day it had dawned on
him that Napoleon would have strangled her without a qualm.
So he emulated the great man. But, of course, that's nonsense,
too.

The monologue continues. Lying in the dark, he says, and
endlessly arguing with himself, he seized upon a theory that
seemed to him as original as it was sound. The common run of
men are born to obey the law and are content to do so. There are

others, the extraordinary kind, men of firm and often noble purpose, to whom everything is permitted, who even shed blood with a clear conscience. In fine, his crime was not an act of altruism. He killed to find out, and quickly, if he was one of the strong and the daring. It was an experimental crime. Yet the very fact that he had to test himself was proof enough that he was not one of them. Furthermore, with a part of his mind he had known this all along, and that, indeed, he would be admitting as much to himself after the murder. Had he swung the axe merely to escape debating with himself about it any longer?

In spite of his uncompromising intelligence and his habit of introspection, Raskolnikov can offer only a variety of rationalizations in explaining his crime. Early in the writing of the novel the author had recognized that ambiguity in accounting for the murder would work confusion in the story. He made a note to the effect that he must explain it "either this way or that way." His failure to do so is a tribute to his understanding of the complexity and evasiveness of motives.

Appalled by Raskolnikov's confession, Sonia urges him to go at once to a crossroads, kiss the earth he has defiled, and publicly declare himself a murderer. He will expiate his crime by suffering, she tells him, and God will restore him to life. He refuses. There is no direct evidence against him. (He had learned that the stranger who had accosted him on the street was merely a police plant.) He is not ready to give himself up.

Several days of "cold, leaden misery" follow. Intermittently his mind is clouded. Suicide beckons to him. After bidding his mother farewell, the superman manqué decides to surrender, but does not know why he will do so. Never before has he believed more firmly that his crime was no crime, but an act for which "forty of his sins" should be forgiven. He had walked "not on his own legs" into the pawnbroker's flat with a concealed axe and had carried out the killing "as though the hem of his coat were caught in the wheels of a machine and been drawn into it." In this respect Raskolnikov answers to the description of a type of transgressor called "the neurotic criminal" in a study by two noted psychoanalysts. He gives himself up, too, as if driven to do so. Kneeling in a public place, he kisses the dirty earth and then goes to the police station to confess, but leaves without doing so. Directly afterward, meeting Sonia's despairing look, he returns to the station and declares his guilt.

Raskolnikov goes to Siberia unrepentant. What gnaws at him

is that he has failed the test. No, he is not one of the "extraordinary" men. He does not admit to himself that his "theory"
is bankrupt. It is only at the end of his first year as a convict that
he shows signs of a change of heart. This is due in part to Sonia's
devotion to him—she has gone into exile in order to be near him.
Her love is at last reciprocated. The novelist leaves Raskolnikov
on the threshold of spiritual regeneration.

# ( III )

Dostoevsky's chief purpose in *Crime and Punishment* was to show
that Raskolnikov's theory is not only invalid ethically but also
fails to reckon with human nature or to make for a more equi-
table social system. The young man had set down his theory in an
article months before the murder, and he expatiates on it at some
length for the benefit of the police inspector. It is obviously a
variant of the superman motif that Nietzsche was to formulate.
When Dostoevsky was working on the novel, the phenomenon of
Napoleon, who is for Raskolnikov an exemplar of the type, was
being discussed in the Russian press. This was owing to the appearance of *Histoire de Jules César* by Napoleon III, published
in 1865–66 and translated into Russian. The work indirectly
pays tribute to the author's celebrated uncle. Dostoevsky must
have read a review of the book which quoted a passage from the
preface, to the effect that exceptional men should not be expected
to abide by the morality binding on ordinary people.

This proposition, with its sanction of violence and its justification of evil means by noble ends, was, Dostoevsky wrongheadedly
believed, a natural product of Nihilism. He had inveighed against
it in his publicist ephemera, as also in *Notes from the Underground*. He was attacking it again in *Crime and Punishment*.
It was, he held, a danger to the moral fiber of the nation. In a
sense, it was to medicine the times that Dostoevsky was writing
his book.

Raskolnikov's crime was intended to illustrate the extremes
to which Nihilism may lead. Yet he was not representative of
militant youth. His theory was incompatible with the revolutionary action for which Chernyshevsky supplied the ideology,
and which was in support of a broad-based cause. In fact,

Raskolnikov never moved in radical circles. "All radicals are socialists," Dostoevsky was writing to Katkov late in April, 1866. Socialism holds no attraction for Raskolnikov. He does not protest when Razumikhin, his close friend, delivers a blistering tirade against that doctrine, declaring that it denies the living soul and smells of death.

Raskolnikov does, however, have two chief lineaments of a Nihilist. For one thing, he is not a believer. Had he been one, he could not have developed his theory. When Sonia reads him the Gospel passage about Lazarus, he horrifies her by saying: "Perhaps there is no God at all." (This is in direct contradiction to his telling the police inspector that he believes in God and in the literal raising of Lazarus. Either he was trying to mislead the guardian of the law or the statement points to his Dostoevskian ambivalence.) After hearing his confession, Sonia tells him: "You turned away from God and God has smitten you and given you over to the Devil." He responds with a skeptical smile.

To Dostoevsky, exclusive reliance on the intellect was an equally heinous sin of the Nihilists. Raskolnikov was emphatically guilty of it. "Here are bookish dreams, sir, a heart unhinged by theories," thus the astute police inspector puts a finger on the influences that made a murderer of this decent young man. When the novel was still in embryo, the author, in accounting to Katkov for the murder, singled out "the influence of certain 'unfinished' ideas that are in the air."

In the epilogue to the novel Raskolnikov has a delirious dream, wherein a mysterious microbe infects mankind with intellectual arrogance to the point of insanity. The nightmare is a vision of the world falling apart because reason alone cannot hold it together. Significantly, Raskolnikov has this dream when he is at last on the verge of repentance. It is as if an understanding of his own folly were struggling to reach his consciousness. Had he not himself been possessed by this disease of overweening intellection? The beginning of his regeneration is indicated thus: "Life took the place of dialectics."

Dostoevsky tries to make clear that Raskolnikov's redemption, and that of his generation, will come through faith. For the novelist this, not reason, was the precondition of virtue. Such is the basic lesson of *Crime and Punishment*. Man cannot be good, indeed, cannot live, without God. This cry will reverberate throughout the body of Dostoevsky's fiction. Another lesson of the novel is one not borne out by his experience among the convicts: that the criminal craves punishment. A corollory to this is his belief that suffering leads to atonement and so ensures the salvation of the transgressor. The exaltation of suffering, which goes along with his scorn for the comfort-loving, is recurrent in his work. It will be recalled that in his first novel, *The Insulted and Injured,* a character is introduced who announces that suffering purifies everything. Since, according to Dostoevsky's credo, every Christian is guilty of all the sins and all the crimes committed by his fellows, he should accept, nay, seek, suffering as penance and the instrument of redemption. In middle life he will announce that "the main and most fundamental spiritual need of the Russian people is the need of suffering, constant and unquenchable suffering, everywhere and in everything." The idea that suffering, felt as undeserved, may issue in bitterness and vengefulness, disregarded by the religionist, was recognized by the novelist.

In order to respond to the impact of *Crime and Punishment* one need not share the author's beliefs and prejudices. It owes its extraordinary effectiveness to the body and pressure of the story. Tightly packed, taut with controlled suspense, abounding in psychological subtleties, it moves at great speed (the action, except for the epilogue, is limited to fourteen days). The reader is scarcely aware of this and might be made uncomfortable if he were. There are some pathetic scenes and others lurid with melodrama. The long arm of coincidence is overactive: when two characters have to be brought together, one of them bumps into the other in a crowded street; when the plot requires it, one person overhears another confessing a dreadful secret under the most improbable circumstances. The reader tends to ignore such flaws, yielding to the power of a work that has the urgency, the tension, the seriousness of high drama, without abandoning the large privileges of the novel.

A few days before the appearance of the first installment of *Crime and Punishment* the newspapers carried the story of a Moscow student who had committed a murder remarkably like the one depicted in the novel. Dostoevsky was quite proud of this mark of his astuteness. Here was proof that Raskolnikov's crime was no mere figment of the writer's fantasy but rather the symptom of a disease that was ravaging a rootless generation. Young men perpetrated monstrous deeds. When only a small part of the novel had been printed, on the afternoon of April 4, 1866, a member of a student circle fired at the Czar. Dostoevsky, rushing to tell Maikov the shocking news, confronted his friend pale and trembling, hardly able to express his horror at this attempt on the father of the Russian people, to whom every subject owed filial love. Everywhere he saw signs of moral chaos.

The background of the action is sketched in deftly and with a concern for countless precise details, such as the seven hundred thirty paces between the gate of the house where the murderer lives and the tenement in which the pawnbroker has a flat; the glass of "yellow" water handed Raskolnikov at the police station (in the sixties of the last century drinking water in the capital was not filtered). The atmosphere of gloom and desolation is made heavier by the settings: a coffinlike den that "cramps the soul and the mind"; a dismal hotel room with a filthy bed and wallpaper so dusty that its pattern is indistinguishable; the stinking pothouses of the red-light district; a dirty basement tavern with sticky tables. The pawnbroker's flat, too, because of a spotlessness favored by "evil-minded old widows" contributes to the effect.

The novel has two subplots. One has to do with the afflictions of the Marmeladov family, a theme stemming from the project that was supplanted by *Crime and Punishment*. Alcoholism has made a derelict of the father, formerly an official of the lowest rank. The family is dependent chiefly on the earnings of the daughter, Sonia, the prostitute. Early in the story Marmeladov unburdens himself to Raskolnikov as the two sit over their glasses in a tavern. These pages are alive with pathos and pity and attest to Dostoevsky's ability to lacerate the heart. The drunkard exemplifies the Russian soul (as the novelist conceived it): "I drink," he tells his companion, "because I want to suffer doubly." His perversity has its comic aspect. When, after a long spree, he comes home and his wife drags him into the room by the hair, he exclaims: "This too delights me." She behaves like a mentally deranged woman. The feast that she arranges in commemoration of her husband is a remarkable mixture of the pathetic and the bizarre. However extravagant the Marmeladovs may be, they remain credible. Not so Sonia. She is one of the Dostoevskian characters of whom Philip Toynbee wrote: they "leave the ground so far below them that we can no longer accept their reality in any of the senses of that ambiguous word."

Half a dozen characters are involved in the second subplot. Central to it is Raskolnikov's sister, Dunya, beautiful, highhearted, free of prejudice. In her readiness to accept a loveless marriage for the sake of her mother and brother she somewhat resembles Sonia, and in fact, the two become close. Razumikhin, a hearty, jovial fellow, as good as bread, to a degree relieves the gloom that hangs over the story. Although in important respects quite different from Dostoevsky, as has been seen he speaks for the author on ideological matters. He falls in love with Dunya at first sight and eventually marries her. There is every prospect that their union will be an admirable one. Some comedy is supplied by a minor character, a young man in the civil service who is at once a dunderhead and a decent sort. Having swallowed some Nihilist principles, he innocently reduces them to absurdity. He declares that he regards Sonia's occupation as a protest against the existing order, and rejoices when he looks at her. Again, he announces that he is ready to clean cesspools, a task nobler than the activity of some Raphael or Pushkin because it is socially useful. If he ever contracts a marriage, he says, he will provide his wife with a lover, should she be slow about taking one, in order to earn her respect for his broadmindedness.

A leading role in the second subplot is assigned to Svidrigailov. In the last part of the novel his thwarted attempt to rape Dunya all but eclipses Raskolnikov's situation. A Nihilist in the literal sense of the word, a projection of Raskolnikov's lower self, afflicted with *taedium vitae,* he is a demonic as well as a melodramatic figure out of Gothic fiction. Rumors of perverse sexuality and of casually committed murders attach to him. The nightmarish episode of his suicide, preceded by a pedophilic dream, is among the great scenes in imaginative literature. Before his exit he gives unexpected evidence of a generous humanity. He provides for the Marmeladov orphans, and with startling prevision of Sonia following Raskolnikov to Siberia, forces a considerable sum of money upon her. It is not this *âme damnée* who is the wholly repulsive character in the story but Luzhin, Dunya's rejected suitor. The acquisitive man, self-seeking, cold-hearted, mean-spirited, not stopping at base behavior, he is everything that Dostoevsky loathed, what he meant when he occasionally spat out the word "bourgeois."

Compared to later novels, *Crime and Punishment* has the advantage of a relatively simple structure. The secondary plots are tributary to the main one—the drama of Raskolnikov. His story affects the reader almost as if it were an actual experience, related by a man laboring under the compulsion to relive it in all its poignancy. Every movement of the murderer's body and mind, every detail in the interplay between his physical sensations and his psychic states, the thrusting and parrying in the duel between him and the detective—all that is set down with complete authority. One feels, thinks, dreams, with Raskolnikov. Vicariously the reader commits the crime and endures the punishment. Freud suggests that to Dostoevsky the criminal was virtually a savior, who by his act freed his fellows from obeying the murderous urge common to all of us.

Dostoevsky is obviously on the side of the angels, championing the ethics that holds every human being inviolate. Yet he presents with considerable persuasiveness Raskolnikov's "theory." The novelist plays the devil's advocate too ably not to have had some lurking sympathy with the devil's viewpoint. In a note for the book the detective's remark that the moral law is binding upon all is countered by Raskolnikov thus: "Well, but suppose conscience doesn't accuse me—I seize authority, I get either money or power—not for evil. I bring happiness. Well, and because of a miserable fence, to stand and look over it, to envy, to hate and yet to stand still. That's base!" On the margin Dostoevsky scribbled: "Devil take it! He's partly right!" A decade after the appearance of *Crime and Punishment* the author received a letter from a bank clerk arrested for embezzlement. Paid a pittance and unsure of his position, the man wrote, he had stolen exactly three per cent of the bank's annual profit, to help his family and "many other insulted and injured, without doing any substantial harm to anybody." He must have acted under the influence of Raskolnikov's logic and, like Raskolnikov, he remained impenitent. In his reply the novelist said that he fully agreed with his correspondent's view of the matter, but did not quite like his lack of compunction. "There is something higher," he concluded, "than the arguments of reason and the force of circumstance—before that everyone must bow."

If Dostoevsky's sympathy with the murderer goes beyond an author's identification with his characters, it may have been because Raskolnikov is one of those who know no limits, whether in good or evil. Dostoevsky was repelled by the Laodicean, middle-of-the-road temperament. The inwardness with which the criminal's torment after the murder is made present to the reader probably owes much to the sense of guilt which was the deep undercurrent of Dostoevsky's emotional life. If unconsciously he craved punishment, he must have been satisfied in no small measure by recording Raskolnikov's experience so unflinchingly.

# 17

## A LITTLE DIAMOND

THE long months devoted to the writing of *Crime and Punishment* held for Dostoevsky, in addition to the usual burden of money worries, ill health, loneliness, yet another cause for vexation: the novel he had contracted to deliver to the robber Stellovsky. It will be recalled that it was due November 1, 1866. He pleaded for an extension of time; he begged Stellovsky to take a promissory note instead of the manuscript, but the man was adamant. How could Dostoevsky wrench himself away from the work which was then wholly absorbing him? Yet there was something attractive about performing the impossible. He would write two novels at once: to one he would give his mornings, to the other his nights. Was there ever a writer who worked like that? The mere idea would kill Turgenev.

Not that Dostoevsky acted on this notion. By July he had no more than a plan for the tale, and the wretched business was spoiling his waking hours and harrowing his dreams. October 1st came and went, and not a line had been written. A little group of his friends suggested that he farm out the novel among them. But he wouldn't consider it. He did, however, fall in with the extraordinary suggestion that he hire a stenographer and dictate the story. He began dictating the evening of October 4 and in twenty-six days the novel was completed and Dostoevsky's part of the contract fulfilled.

He originally called the story *Roulettenburg,* but at the instance of the publisher changed the title to *The Gambler.* It is probable that he did some work on it before those hectic October weeks. Certainly he had had the subject in mind for a long time, perhaps ever since he had first haunted the tables. In September, 1863, while he was traveling with Polina, he wrote down on little scraps of paper a sketch for a story about a Russian living abroad who wandered from one gambling resort to another, completely possessed by a mania for roulette. He hoped to repeat his success with *The House of the Dead* by a description of another kind of hell that he also knew intimately. The hero is a cultivated person, but, as Dostoevsky put it, "half-baked in every way, a man who has lost his faith, but dares not disbelieve, a man rebelling against the authorities, yet fearing them. He comforts himself by saying that he *has nothing to do* in Russia and he excoriates those who summon our expatriates back home. . . ." The novelist also saw the story as an opportunity to set forth his observations on his countrymen abroad—a topic then widely discussed in the press. This tale of a gambler was the subject he seized upon when, three years later, he found himself in need of a theme that could be worked up quickly and at no great length.

The rather limited space at his disposal did not prevent him from saddling himself with a fairly complicated plot and a number of characters. The setting afforded him a welcome chance to spill his venom upon the French, polished and hollow, and the Germans, grasping and dull. His mouthpiece is his protagonist, Alexey Ivanovich, a young man employed as a tutor by a Russian family living in "Roulettenburg." Probably because he wrote in such haste, this central character is not sufficiently elaborated, while the *femme fatale* who is the heroine of the story remains something of an enigma, her behavior subject to various interpretations. At least one of the secondary characters, notably the wealthy old *babushka* upon whose death the family's prospects wholly depend, is superbly drawn.

Greed and lust dominate these pages. The leading theme is the tutor's passion for his employer's stepdaughter, significantly named Polina, who is involved with two suitors, a rich English industrialist and a titled French bounder, her lover at the time. The tutor's is an exasperated, sadomasochistic feeling compounded of love and hate. He sees the erotic relationship and the sensual pleasure it involves as dependent on the slavery and abasement of one partner and the complete domination of the other. Dostoevsky will keep coming back to this emotion, the *odi et amo* of Catullus, in his later writings, and perhaps present it more subtly but never in firmer outline.

Just as the gaming tables figured in his curious journey with Polina Suslova, so here too Dostoevsky links gambling with sex, intimating, as it were, a hidden connection between the two. This link has been examined by psychoanalysts, Freud among them. In the story, Polina's French suitor and lover, casting her off, outrages her by an indirect gift of fifty thousand francs. She had always shown the tutor contempt and sometimes hatred, and had appeared not to prize her limitless power over him. Now she goes to his hotel room, resolved to give herself to him. Does she hope to wipe out the affront to her pride by thus proving to herself that she is not to be bought? Here as throughout her behavior leaves room for speculation. She lets the tutor read the Frenchman's insulting letter, and in a frenzy he leaves her in his room and rushes off to the tables, ecstatic with absolute self-confidence. He will win fifty thousand francs and Polina can throw them in the face of the despicable Frenchman. He returns in an hour with four times that sum. While he was making his phenomenal kill, the woman for whose sake he was playing was obliterated from his mind by the excitement of the game. Memories of that excitement, flooding in upon him after his return to her, momentarily make him forget her presence. Nevertheless the two spend the night together.

Morning brings a revulsion of feeling on her part. She demands the fifty thousand francs as her pay, flings them in his face and leaves him. One thinks of the scene in which the protagonist of *Notes from the Underground* turns on the prostitute when he realizes that their relative positions have been reversed. Having lost Polina, the tutor squanders his fortune with a *cocotte* in Paris and returns to the tables as if blindly seeking to recapture the great moment when he had brought both chance and the inaccessible lady to their knees. He becomes utterly and hopelessly a slave to roulette. Not even the knowledge that Polina loved him all along and still loves him after a lapse of two years can save him from his obsession. That knowledge, which is disclosed at the end of the tale, comes as a surprise to the reader as well as to the tutor. The theory has been advanced by an American critic, D. Savage, that the idea of the novel is the connection between the protagonist's failure as a lover and his fatal shortcomings as a spiritual being, one lost between belief and disbelief, a man suffering from "metaphysical impotence"; but if Dostoevsky intended to bring this home to his public, he failed to do so.

When his stenographer expressed her scorn for the gambler, the author took his part, saying: "Many of the young man's feelings and impressions have been my own." Indeed, his own experiences, especially his affair with Polina Suslova, are plainly reflected in *The Gambler*. He was to know more of the gambler's hell in the years to come. In this respect the story was not a farewell to the past, but rather an anticipation of the future.

# ( II )

Dostoevsky scarcely saw the girl who walked into his study that October morning at exactly 11:30, the time he had set, to take dictation on *The Gambler*. He talked of this and that, unable to get down to work, and finally declared that he could dictate nothing then and that she must came back in the evening. He was glad, he added, that the stenographer was a woman: a man would have been sure to go off on a spree sooner or later. In the evening he continued to put off the unfamiliar business of dictating, but managed to get the novel started and arranged for her to return the next day.

She was late. He was in a panic. He had forgotten her name and had failed to take down her address. He knew he had been difficult. Perhaps she would not show up at all. But she did, full of apologies for the extra half hour she had taken to make a handsome copy of what he had dictated, and for the next several weeks the efficient, imperturbable creature, looking graver in her neat mourning, appeared regularly and punctually.

It had taken some courage for her to return. She had been so elated over this first job of hers, more especially since her employer was to be the celebrated author whose name had often been on her late father's lips, and who was the object of her girlish adoration. And her first impression had been so painful, so dismal. His flat was shabby and gloomy, and he himself looked worn-out, ill, and queer, with his odd eyes, the pupil of the right one dilated with atropine (he had injured it during an attack). And he behaved strangely. He was nervous, irritable, abrupt. He kept forgetting her name. He smoked continuously and repeatedly offered her cigarettes, though she had said she thought the habit unwomanly. Almost directly on seeing her he had told her that he was an epileptic and had had a fit only recently. In the evening he showed an even greater lack of reserve, describing to this stranger, among other things, his sensations as he stood on the scaffold on Semyonov Square waiting to be executed. When she left him at the end of that first day, her disappointment and bewilderment were tinged with pity for a man obviously lonely and miserable.

As the days went by, Dostoevsky found dictation less of a strain. Decidedly the little stenographer suited him. She showed herself not merely self-effacing and methodical, but heartily interested in the work. His friends offered advice, reproached him for having entered into this arrangement with the accursed Stellovsky, commiserated with him in his predicament. Anna Grigoryevna Snitkina—he did learn her name at last—was helping him out of it. The pile of manuscript was growing daily. She kept assuring him that they would finish the thing in time and it actually looked as though she were right. He came to take comfort in his contacts with this demure, dependable, cheerful girl. If she was plain, she had—it eventually dawned on him—pretty gray eyes, a firm chin, and a pleasant smile. If her judgments were naïve and shallow, she took the book seriously. Fictive characters were real to her. Indeed, her first love had been the hero of his *Insulted and Injured*. When she confessed this to Dostoevsky, he said that he had only the vaguest recollection of what that novel was about and promised to reread it.

While they sipped tea or munched pears out of a paper bag, he would unburden himself to this sympathetic listener. He complained about his money troubles—she had seen for herself the table set with wooden spoons when the silver was at the pawnbroker's—he reminisced, he told her about his luckless affair with Anna Korvin-Krukovskaya, he showed her his late wife's photograph, a sad one, taken the year before she died. But Polina Suslova was not mentioned. His happy moments? He had none to tell her about, and yet . . . he still hoped for happiness. In time he made a habit of recounting to her where he had been and what he had done while they were apart. On one occasion he told her that there were three ways open to him: to settle in Constantinople or Jerusalem, to go abroad and give himself up to roulette, or else to get married. What should he do? Would any woman have him? Of course, the girl answered, and marriage was the step for him to take.

Gradually he learned some things about her—she had lost her awe, and spoke to him as to an uncle. She was only twenty. Her father, a civil servant with a taste for literature, the theater, and old china, had died in the spring, leaving in modest but comfortable circumstances a family consisting of her mother, who was of Swedish or Finnish descent, herself, a married sister, and a brother, now a student at an agricultural college. A sensible young woman, competent in money matters, she had taken up shorthand not so much because she needed to earn her living as because, like many a young miss in the sixties, she wanted to be independent. She was a girl of the period also in her objection to having her hand kissed and being helped out of a cab, but her unconventionality stopped there. She neither bobbed her hair nor affected spectacles; she was a filial daughter and a devout Christian. She had two suitors, she told Dostoevsky, but intended to accept neither—she would wait until she could marry for love.

He caught himself thinking of her ever so often. As their sessions drew to an end the idea that he would no longer see her regularly filled him with regret, and it was plain that the prospect of parting distressed her. She had received his confidences with such a friendly, even a motherly, air. She had taken his occasional brusqueness with perfect good nature. She was eager to come and so sorry to leave. A man did not have to be a novelist to see how it was with her. Perhaps that way some makeshift happiness awaited him.

It was his forty-fifth birthday, October 30, when she brought him the clean copy of the last installment. The sight of her, looking taller and more graceful than usual in a long lilac silk dress that she had put on in honor of the occasion, brought a flush to his cheeks. His pleasure in the visit was, however, abruptly checked by the entrance of Emilia Fyodorovna, who, either out of arrogance or because of an intuitive grasp of the danger to herself in the situation, chose to snub the little stenographer. He was mortified and, finding that he could not persuade the girl to remain, saw her to the door and pressed her to name the day when he might call at her home.

He came, as appointed, four evenings later, met her good mother, to whom he tried to be attentive, and found Anna Grigoryevna herself more responsive than ever. He told them

that within a week he was going to start work on the last part of
*Crime and Punishment,* and in that connection he would want her
services again. Three days later—it was Sunday—he paid a
second call, this time uninvited. Before he left she promised to
come on Tuesday to arrange for the dictation.

On Monday night Dostoevsky had a dream. He was rummag-
ing among the papers in an old rosewood box, given to him in
his Siberian days, in which he kept manuscripts, letters, and
objects that had a sentimental value for him, when he noticed
something twinkling and vanishing among them. The thing caught
his attention and he went after it. It proved to be a small,
sparkling diamond. When he awoke, he could not recall what he
had done with it, but he felt that the dream was of good omen.
Wasn't he at last going to come upon a tiny brilliant that would
light his days? He was still under the spell of his dream when
Anna Grigoryevna came in, a little tardily, from the bright frosty
street, and he told her about it at once. On her remarking that
dreams went by contraries, his mood dropped. But with her usual
tact, she tried to cheer him up and began asking him what he had
been doing since she had seen him last.

He had been busy, he said, with the plot of a new novel. The
end, which hinged upon the psychology of a young girl, somehow
eluded him, and she must help him with it. He went on to outline
a story which even her modest intelligence easily discerned to be
a disguised version of his autobiography. It had to do with an
artist, unsuccessful, ill, lonely, burdened with debts and responsibilities, who had fallen in love with a girl less than half his age.
So as not to call her the heroine, he called her Anna, "a lovely
name," he observed, although on a previous occasion he had said
that he disliked it, having found all Annas dry, reserved creatures.
This Anna was gentle, sensible, and cheerful—not a beauty but
not bad-looking either. The oftener the artist saw her, the more
convinced he grew that she would make his happiness. But would
it not be a terrible sacrifice on her part, and would she not soon
repent her step? Did Anna Grigoryevna think it psychologically
possible that such a girl could return the love of such a man? Of
course it was possible, she asserted hotly. If the young woman
loves the man, she will be happy and never repent. He bade her,
in a voice that shook, put herself in the girl's place and him in
the hero's, and imagine that he had asked her to be his wife:
What would she say?

"I should answer that I loved you and would love you all my life."

# ( III )

Anna's mother made no objection to the match. The groom's relatives, however, behaved quite differently. When Pasha heard the news—they were able to keep the engagement secret only a week—he came to his stepfather's study and made a scene. He was astonished and outraged, he stormed, not to have been consulted in a matter which touched him so nearly. He reminded Dostoevsky that he was too old a man to think of beginning life over again, and besides he had other duties and responsibilities. Nor did Emilia Fyodorovna and the other relatives conceal their disapproval. Indeed, they went so far as to try and frighten the young fiancée out of the marriage by malicious gibes and hints. And there were some among Dostoevsky's friends who, for disinterested reasons, warned him against this rash step. But his determination remained unshaken.

Not that the twenty-five years' difference between him and his betrothed failed to weigh upon him. He even teased himself, and her, too, by impersonating the would-be-youthful senile ruin of a man from his story "Uncle's Dream." Anna did her best to quiet him on this score, promising him to age quickly, and trying, by her dress and demeanor, to appear older than her years. As for him, he acted the part of the conventional fiancé, calling on her every night, bringing her sweets from Ballet, taking her, on one extravagant occasion, to the theater. Yet he had his misgivings, tinged, doubtless, with self-contemplative irony.

What with the distraction incident to his matrimonial project, Dostoevsky let *Crime and Punishment* ride. At the end of November it suddenly dawned on him that the installment of the novel for the month's issue of *Russky vestnik* was still unwritten. As the magazine regularly appeared a month late, the delay was not fatal. With characteristic firmness Anna, who from the first regarded herself as his helpmeet in every sense of the word, took matters in hand. He must lock himself in every day from two to five and work, and when he came to her in the evening, dictate the final version. In this fashion the last part and the epilogue were completed in reasonably good time. That part includes the scene between Svidrigailov and Raskolnikov, in which the middle-aged roué gloats over his coming marriage to a sixteen-year-old girl, whereupon the young man observes: "The fact is this monstrous difference in age and development excites your sensuality! Will you really make such a marriage?" One wonders what Dostoevsky felt as he dictated this passage to his prospective young bride.

Christmas he spent with his sister Vera and her family in Moscow. The great news had not reached them yet. He confided it first to his favorite, Sonia, who rejoiced at it. Then he told Vera and the others. The sister-in-law to whom she had hoped eventually to marry him off was there, apparently no nearer to widowhood than before and more unhappy than ever, but holding nothing against Dostoevsky, which rather relieved him. Among the giggling girls was the vivacious young thing who had rejected him the previous Easter. The house was full as usual, everybody wished him well, and on New Year's Eve at midnight the head of the family raised his champagne glass in a toast to the newly affianced pair. But in spite of the good will and general gaiety, there were often times when he was the victim of unaccountable gloom—the familiar oppressive feeling like the consciousness of having committed a crime.

The purpose of his Moscow visit was to see his publisher. He wanted Katkov to give him a substantial advance on his next novel. Indeed, without it, they would have to postpone the wedding. On January 2, 1867, he was able to write his "priceless and eternal friend, Anya" the good news that Katkov had proved obliging: he had advanced one thousand rubles, promising another thousand within two months, so that nothing stood in the way of their union.

As soon as he got home, however, the money began to melt away so rapidly that only by placing part of it in Anna's hands for safekeeping could he be sure of the wedding expenses. Preparations for the event were begun at once. Anna was if anything the more eager of the two: she could scarcely wait for the time when she would be entitled to take such care of him as she felt he needed. Once they were married his fur coat would not be pawned in midwinter to help his relatives-in-law, as had happened during the courtship. With her dowry she assembled a trousseau that he insisted on seeing as it came from the dressmaker's. With the same money she furnished the new home—

they rented a five-room flat in the neighborhood of his old apartment, which he turned over to Emilia Fyodorovna and her family. On the fifteenth of February, the very month of his first wedding, Dostoevsky went through the marriage ceremony for the second time.

The marriage was solemnized in the Trinity (Izmailovsky) Cathedral at seven o'clock in the evening. They could not afford a wedding trip, but Dostoevsky invited the company to the new apartment, where champagne flowed freely until midnight struck the signal for the guests to leave the couple alone.

Whether or not Dostoevsky remembered the violent attack that had followed quickly upon his first wedding day, he must have wondered nervously how soon his young bride would see him in a fit for the first time. They were married about a week when he had a sudden severe attack during an evening they were spending at her sister's house. His first wife, on a similar occasion, had been terribly frightened. Anna was made of different stuff. Her sister went into hysterics, and the rest of the household devoted itself to her. But the bride kept her presence of mind. She held his head on her knees all through the convulsions and did not break down even when he had a second and worse seizure an hour after recovering from the first one. The ordeal of that night, with no one to help while he lay screaming with pain or muttering like a man out of his mind, tried Anna and found her not wanting. Even in the evil mood that followed the fit he must have recognized that he had married a woman whose strength was equal to her devotion. Before he had ever proposed to her, he had asked her whether, if he married again, he should choose a kind or a clever woman. For himself, he thought it should be a kind one, so that she might love and pity him. He could not hide from himself that, at bottom, this was his reason for marrying Anna. The time was over now for the storms of passion that had marked his relations with Polina Suslova. He was seeking a safe haven. With this girl, who respected him as she would her father, and pitied him as she would her child, he would find it. It was not a step to be particularly proud of, but there it was.

# ( IV )

The first few weeks of married life were a period of relative peace, in spite of the alarming frequency of his attacks. The public that not so long ago had relished Turgenev's *Fathers and Children,* and was even now being regaled with the first part of Tolstoy's *War and Peace,* was going mad over *Crime and Punishment.* The novel had brought the magazine five hundred new subscribers and was immediately published in book form. Dostoevsky had not yet embarked on any fresh venture, and meanwhile he was free to savor his new life and discover what leisure was like. Now he had a companion on his walks. On one of them he led Anna into the deserted courtyard he had described in *Crime and Punishment*—he had found the place, he told her, in looking for a convenient spot to answer a call of nature—and showed her, off in a corner, the stone under which Raskolnikov had buried his loot.

He was glad to see that Pasha was attentive to his young stepmother; indeed, it looked as though her presence had a refining influence upon the boy. Emilia Fyodorovna was giving Anna the advice of an experienced housewife. The nieces and nephews who used to pay him stiff, infrequent visits were now running in at all hours and often staying for meals. This was just the companionship Anna needed. True, with all the entertaining, expenses were mounting. Besides, the constant stream of guests was rather tiresome and quite put a stop to those long intimate hours he had enjoyed with Anna before they were married.

One night he returned home from a visit to the Maikovs and found the house dark and Anna in bed, crying. But why? What had happened? Between sobs the story came out. She couldn't stand it any longer. She had done her best, but it was useless. Life in his house was no longer endurable for her. Emilia Fyodorovna kept loading her with admonitions and drawing invidious comparisons between her and Pasha's late mother. But it was chiefly Pasha who was making things impossible for her. He was continually heaping insults on her. He made fun of her housekeeping in front of guests, when it was he himself who, out of sheer spite, had emptied the cream jug before his father's breakfast, made off with the matches, sent the maid on a wild-goose chase, so that she didn't have time to dust the study. That very morning he had told her that his father had made a mistake in marrying her, that she was a poor housekeeper, that she spent too much of the family's money, that his father's attacks were getting worse all on her account. And wasn't Pasha setting her husband against her? Fyodor scarcely talked to her any more. Indeed, when were they together, with this crowd of silly young people filling the house? He couldn't have cared, this master psychologist, this seer into the human heart, if he hadn't noticed what they were doing to her!

Dostoevsky listened to this outburst in amazement. It had never entered his head that things were at such a pass. He assured Anna that he loved her as deeply as ever, but the more he comforted her, the more freely her tears flowed. When she was finally quiet again, he told her that he had been thinking of going to Moscow. Now he would surely do so and take her with him. He would persuade Katkov to give him an additional advance and they would go abroad on the money. Hadn't that been one of their dreams?

Two days later he was introducing his bride to his sister Vera and her family. He noticed that the young people, with the possible exception of Sonia, received Anna somewhat coldly. The truth was they were cross with her for having upset their plans for marrying off this favorite uncle to their favorite aunt, Yelena Pavlovna, as soon as she should become a widow. The ice was broken, amusingly enough, by the very girl who had rejected Dostoevsky's suit the previous spring. Before the Moscow visit was over Anna was on good terms with the whole household, and if he had ever doubted the strength of his affection for her, he now proved it by finding himself an excessively jealous husband. They left the city, feeling that the week they had spent there had been their real honeymoon and carrying with them a thousand rubles from Katkov. The trip abroad seemed assured.

Of course, both Pasha and Emilia Fyodorovna set their faces against such an extravagance. What would they live on while the couple were making a summer's jaunt? Besides, there were the creditors. The seven thousand rubles he had received for the separate edition of *Crime and Punishment* had gone into their pockets. But this only whetted their appetite. Again they were threatening to attach the household effects and put Dostoevsky in debtors' prison. It occurred to him that this last might not be so bad. It might even give him the stuff for another *House of the Dead* and bring in four or five thousand rubles. But, of course, even if there were not Anna to consider, he might not be able to write in the stuffy cell during the hot summer months. Europe offered itself as a refuge. He needed a trip abroad for his health: he was in a state of intolerable nervous tension. And yet the more he thought of it, the more he felt that under the circumstances the journey was out of the question. Emilia's notion of their taking a house in the country together, with her to spare Anna the trouble of housekeeping, was not so bad. They would stay home; Anna would adjust herself; everything would be all right.

Two days after they came home—he had already decided to abandon the trip—Anna took a walk with him. At her suggestion, they stepped into a chapel to say a prayer before the icon of the Virgin. And then, after some little hesitation, she drew for him a fresh picture of her situation. They must have at least a month or two of peace together, she pleaded. Their married life was at stake. If she was to be constantly at the mercy of Pasha and Emilia Fyodorovna, a separation was inevitable. They must go abroad to save their happiness. Didn't he see it? She broke into tears on the street. If she had but a taste of undisturbed comradeship with him, their union would grow strong enough to withstand strains and shocks. Money? There was the new furniture, the piano, the silver, her jewelry, and some securities of hers, too. If they pawned it all, there would be enough for the trip and something for Pasha and Emilia Fyodorovna to live on as well. She had spoken to her mother, who had approved the plan. Her tears were her strongest argument. Before Dostoevsky had done comforting her, he agreed to her scheme. They went at once to apply for a passport. Here was a woman of action. Three days later, on April 14, at five o'clock in the afternoon, they entrained for Berlin.

# 18

## THE GAMBLER

AFTER a day or two in Berlin, where Dostoevsky enjoyed a Russian bath and bought some clothes for himself without giving any thought to Anna's wardrobe, the couple settled in Dresden in a furnished flat of three rooms. Why Dresden? It didn't really matter to him where he was. At any rate, now they were completely alone: there was no one to interfere with their privacy, no one to sow dissension between them. Yet it was scarcely an idyllic existence. Even when he did not have one of his frequent attacks, he would be likely to wake up in an ugly mood. There were days when nothing pleased him; he grumbled at the food, at the landscape, at the layout of the streets. The Germans annoyed him intensely. The attractions of the city—the open-air concerts, the galleries—gave him only shallow satisfaction. They had practically nowhere else to go except to the post office, where they were always being disappointed, and the library, where there were a few musty Russian books.

The pair quarreled perpetually: over her soiled gloves, over the sunset, over the right way to handle an umbrella, over the brewing of a cup of tea. He scolded her for stopping too often on their walks, for not keeping in step with him, for everything. He would scream at her; she would tremble with rage. In his

presence she did not cry, because he could not stand tears, and
that made it harder for her. He had always thought, he said,
that a wife was her husband's natural enemy. But they made up.
Their fallings-out were of the kind that all the more endears.
There were, too, many moments of jollity and intimate companionship, particularly in the small hours of the morning when,
after a night's work, he would wake her to say a lingering good-
night.

The precarious conjugal peace was sometimes shaken by gusts
of jealousy. Anna had reason to be anxious. Her husband's affair
with Polina Suslova had not remained a secret from her, and
in Dresden she discovered that he was keeping up a correspondence with the woman. Finding a letter from Polina in his desk,
she read it with the unscrupulousness characteristic of her where
her affections were concerned, and the effect was shattering. "I
felt cold, I trembled, and even cried," she wrote in her diary.
"I was afraid that his old attachment would revive, and that
his love for me would vanish. Lord, do not send me such misery."

She would have been even more enraged had she seen the
answer that he penned almost as soon as they were settled.
Polina knew nothing of his marriage, and Dostoevsky was
under the necessity of breaking the news to her. He did so in
a manner that was slightly apologetic. When he had finished
dictating *The Gambler,* he wrote, he noticed that his stenographer, "a young and rather attractive girl . . . had fallen sincerely in love" with him, and for his part, he "liked her more
and more." His brother's death had left him depressed and
lonely, and so he had proposed to her. In spite of the frightful
difference in their years, he was increasingly convinced that she
would be happy: "She has a heart and is capable of love." Then
he broke off abruptly to discuss his financial situation, but closed
on a personal note, addressing Polina in the words he had used
in writing to his fiancée from Moscow, as his "eternal friend."
He knew that it was difficult for her to be happy: "Oh, darling,
it is not to a cheap, *necessary* happiness that I invite you. I
respect you, and always did, for your exacting nature, but how
well I know that your heart cannot help demanding much from
life, and people seem to you either infinitely dazzling or else
utter scoundrels and vulgarians."

Cheap happiness, a makeshift, a compromise—was that what
he had achieved? Polina would have lifted him to the heights
and cast him down into the depths. Anna, the kind one, seemed

capable of giving him the tenderness, the comfort, the protection that were necessary to a man broken by years of suffering—but that was all. This must have been one of those moments when a vague shame, a slight rebellion crossed his contentment.

Polina's reply to Dostoevsky's letter arriving ten days later, in his absence, Anna did not scruple to open it, read it, and seal it up. She had the bitter satisfaction of seeing how he received it. He took a long time over the first page and, as he went on reading, his face flushed and his hands trembled. She pretended to think the letter came from his niece and asked for news, but he said briefly that it was not from Sonia and smiled forlornly. He was absent-minded the rest of the evening and could hardly grasp anything his wife said to him. The next morning he reread the letter, pacing up and down the room as though looking for something he had lost, and for days afterward he was out of temper.

Anna had, however, nothing further to fear from her husband's former mistress. Late in May there was another letter from Polina, apparently the last one. She is known to have opened a village school the following year, but the authorities closed it on the grounds that she bobbed her hair, wore blue glasses, and never went to church. In a police report dated 1868, she was accused of having "close relations with persons abroad hostile to the Government." Later she again tried her hand at literary work, translating a biography of Benjamin Franklin— she had long been interested in America—and for a while she attended the first university courses for women in Russia. In middle life she married a student many years her junior. An ardent admirer of Dostoevsky, this Vasily Rozanov in time wrote commentaries on the novelist and composed miscellaneous works in a mystical and retrograde vein. Six years later Polina left him, having fallen in love with a young man who spurned her, whereupon she denounced him to the police as a revolutionary. Perhaps she had already undergone the change of heart which eventually landed her in the camp of black reaction. According to another report, she drove a foster child to suicide. In *The Insulted and Injured* Rozanov found a description of a woman that, he declared, fitted Polina perfectly: Prince Valkovsky's sketch of an ostensibly cold and unapproachable beauty who secretly savored a depravity so monstrous that she could have given lessons to the Marquis de Sade. Rozanov also likened her to Catherine de' Medici, saying that Polina would have been capable of lending a hand in the St. Bartholomew's Day Massacre. Her father spoke of her in less literary terms as a she-devil.

These characterizations help to support the impression that she contributed something to the creation of those wayward, passionate women who figure in Dostoevsky's major novels. It seems, also, that the lacerations these two inflicted upon each other helped to shape the novelist's conception of "the great constringent relation" between the sexes. His daughter, an unreliable witness, recounts how one day in the late seventies a veiled woman clad in black came to see the novelist, refusing to give her name, and in answer to his query as to her reason for coming, simply threw back her veil and looked at him. Dostoevsky stared at her without a flicker of recognition, and only after she had swept out of the room in mute pride it flashed upon him that this woman whom he had failed to recognize was Polina. Perhaps it was by stepping out of his life that she made a place for herself in his fictions.

# ( II )

The couple had scarcely been a week in Dresden when Dostoevsky began to get restless. He was idle, he was bored, he was getting fat! He stood it another week and then he succumbed to the old fever, taking the train for Homburg and the tables. He had to spend several hours at the Leipzig station, and as he paced the huge waiting room full of smoke and the smell of beer he asked himself how he could have left his young, innocent, patient angel alone and friendless in a strange town, while he was going . . . where? On what fool's errand? It was sheer madness. The reason that offered itself readily was the money he hoped to win, the money he needed to live on, the money with which he must pay off his creditors. On previous trips abroad he had offered a similar excuse for his gambling. But the author of *The Gambler* must have understood that it was not hope of gain alone that was sending him to the tables. At the moment he was not in urgent need, though his funds were low. He may well have been driven by the desire to challenge Fate, by the craving for risk, and for the anguish, the humiliation that such an experience held for him. Freud suggested that the gambling mania offered him "opportunities for self-punishment," thereby unburdening his conscience.

He intended to stay away no more than four days. They stretched out into ten. He still firmly believed in his "system": if you keep cool and calculate your moves, you are bound to win. The trouble was that he couldn't keep cool for more than half an hour at a time, and yet he did not leave the tables for longer than it took to smoke a cigarette. Gambling was never meant for a nervous man like himself. And so in the end he always lost. Oh, it was vile, sordid, contemptible! But he needed the excitement, though his nerves were ragged with it. On the whole his health was excellent and there was no thought of an attack.

Every day he poured out his hopes and fears to Anna in a letter full of self-reproach and extravagant assurances of his love for her. God had given her to him that he might expiate his enormous sins by guarding and preserving this young soul in all its purity, and now perhaps he was injuring it irreparably. But she must continue to love him. Only now that he was away from her did he realize how much he loved her; they were becoming truly one. When he was with her, he hid his tenderness under sullenness and irritability, but that was his wretched character. Would she ever forgive him all the torture he had caused her? And how could she ever respect him again? He had appealed to her for the fare home and had immediately gambled it away. She must send him another remittance, but she mustn't dream of coming to fetch him. Such want of confidence would kill him.

As soon as he received the money, he went back to her, having wasted the staggering sum of three hundred and fifty rubles and left his wat h in the hands of a Homburg pawnbroker.

Anna received him without a word of reproach, and they settled into a placid, if somewhat dismal, routine. They looked in at the post office, they went to the library, they roamed through the museums, they stopped for a cup of coffee and an ice or for a try at the shooting gallery. After dinner they strolled in the gardens and listened to the orchestra; in the evening he read or tried to work: he was then busy setting down his reminiscences of Belinsky, but with little success. Meanwhile she was assiduously filling her notebooks with mysterious hooks and dashes. What could she be writing there? She refused to tell him. She had promised her mother, from whom she was absent for the first time and for whom she was frightfully homesick, to write down every detail of her life abroad. And so she was doing this, as she did everything, dutifully, patiently, with an unmitigated interest in trifles and a total lack of discrimination. She recorded the changes in the weather and in Fyodor's moods, his quarrels with waiters, librarians, and post office clerks— German words, which ordinarily failed him, came in a flood when he was furious. She retailed his frequent absurd quarrels with her, their reconciliations, and the exchanges of loverly nonsense that lightened their dull existence and made her supremely happy. She listed everything each of them had to eat and drink and never omitted to mention the exact cost of everything they bought and some things they didn't buy, and how the price compared with the price of the same items at home.

One night early in June she had something important to tell him: she suspected that she was pregnant. They both rejoiced when the suspicion became a certainty. If it were a girl, they would call her Sonia, for the heroine of *Crime and Punishment* and for his favorite niece; they rather hoped for a boy—then there would be no need for a dowry, and in that case they would of course call him Mikhail. Now there was something pleasant to tease her about, and a new source of worry. It looked as though they would have to stay abroad much longer than they had originally intended, a good deal to Anna's relief, since however homesick for her mother she might be, she dreaded the return to Petersburg, where she would again be at the mercy of her relatives-in-law.

But what would they live on? And what would become of Pasha and Emilia Fyodorovna and her children? The money they had taken with them was rapidly melting away, and there was not a word from Katkov, to whom Dostoevsky had written for an additional five hundred rubles just after the Homburg disaster. Moreover, toward the end of their Dresden stay he had a most alarming experience. In the state of irritability which always followed one of his seizures he had a tiff with a clerk at the Russian Consulate, and in the midst of it he had a hallucination: Mikhail suddenly appeared, head and shoulders, in the doorway. Was he going mad? As he looked back upon the weeks just before he left Russia, it seemed to him that he had then been in a state verging on insanity. Now, at least, his attacks were less frequent.

Homburg had cured him completely of his gambling fever, Dostoevsky thought. He had really benefitted by the adventure.

The lesson was cheap at the price. But the day after writing this to Anna he made up his mind that his great mistake had been in not taking her with him: then he would have been mentally at ease and able to take advantage of his system. Back in Dresden this idea grew upon him: the thing for them to do at the first opportunity was to go together to some gambling resort for an extended stay. Anna let herself be persuaded. It did not matter where they lived, provided he was with her, and besides she might conceivably exercise a restraining influence upon him.

In spite of the boredom, the sense of waste, the anxiety that these Dresden days held, they effected what the two had hoped of them: they cemented the union. Dostoevsky's cruel nerves gave his young wife moments of childish panic and despair, and at times she was ready to throw herself out of the window, but when, late in June, the money from Katkov arrived and they were leaving the city, Anna wrote in her diary: "Good-bye now, Dresden. . . . How happy we have been here together; I don't really count our little differences one bit, as I know Fyodor loves me, and the cause of it all is nothing but his irritable, volcanic nature; even for that do I love him beyond all words."

# ( III )

As soon as they had the fare the couple took the train for Baden. True, when he had been in this gambler's paradise with Polina he had had a run of bad luck, but going with Anna, it would be a different story.

They arrived in Baden on July 4, and for the seven miserable weeks that they remained in the town their existence revolved around the gaming tables. He would work spasmodically at his article on Belinsky, which was still far from finished, and without putting anything on paper he was brooding in the night hours over a project that he hoped to make a bigger thing than *Crime and Punishment*. But he was not free to give himself to these occupations. He was a man possessed. It was an illness, a mania. He cursed the game, he cursed his luck, he called himself a weakling and a scoundrel. But as long as there was anything at stake, he was in a fever until he got to the gambling rooms.

At first, gains and losses alternated, but the former were always modest until, on the twelfth day, he won heavily. It was a
stormy evening and by the lightning flashes the couple counted
out a fortune of three thousand francs. The next day luck turned
against him, and thereafter smiled on him intermittently and
briefly. He continued to hope, in vain, that he would repeat his
coup. When he did win, there was a feast: fruit, berries, wine,
pastries. More frequently he lost. Two fairly large remittances
from Anna's mother were promptly gambled away, and gradually her brooch, her earrings, her lilac dress, her fur coat, her
lace scarf, a pair of his trousers, his old hat, their wedding rings
found their way into the pawnbroker's shop, only to be redeemed
with his winnings and pawned again. He had to slink out of the
house with his bundle concealed from the landlady's eye, cool
his heels in dingy rooms, waiting for some shady trafficker in
second-hand goods, receive such characters in his own lodging,
run from one moneylender to another, and when he finally got
his man, there was disgusting begging and haggling.

As if there were not enough to make their heads ache, they
were roused early every morning by the thumping boots of the
smith's apprentices in the attic overhead and kept awake by the
hammer and bellows belowstairs. It was to this wretched lodging
that Dostoevsky would return from the casino, so often empty-
handed, to face the girl whom he had married less than six
months previously and who was now carrying his child. He
shouted that he was to blame, he cried that he hated her, he
threw himself at her feet, he beat his head with his fists, he
sobbed—and he went back. The thing was stronger than he. How
would he take care of Pasha and the others? How would he ever
pay off his debts? He screamed, he wrung his hands. He would
go mad or shoot himself! And what if Katkov should suddenly
die? He was full of whims. He worked himself into a frenzy
over trifles. There was constant wrangling, no less bitter for
being absurd. He was ruled by superstitious fancies. He blamed
his losses on a Pole who stood next to him at the tables, on a
Russian woman who chattered too much, on an Englishman who
reeked of eau de Cologne, on Anna who had refused to take a
walk with him. She continued the patient Griselda: she bore with
his ugly temper, his unjust reproaches; she soothed him; she
hid her own tears from him; though she tried to shield him
from himself, she let him have his way.

She had her moments of inward rebellion at his egotism, his

lack of kindness and appreciation of all she was doing for him. She could bear to trudge to the pawnbroker's for him, to wash his shirts, to nurse him during his seizure, even to watch him as he stood at the tables, his face flushed, his eyes bloodshot as though he were drunk, but she was enraged at the thought that he was more concerned about Mikhail's widow and orphans than about his own wife and their unborn child. She told herself that all their sufferings were for the sake of strangers and that she herself meant nothing to him. But these were only transient moods. A tender word from him, a gesture of affection would dissipate them.

The very miseries of their situation drew the two together as prosperity and pleasure could not have done. When he would come in sad-faced and then dazzle her with the gold he had won —he had a habit of showing a woebegone face in good fortune, as though to propitiate jealous Fate—there would be flowers and wine and delicacies, and life would have a sparkle. But even when his sorry looks were unfeigned, when their things were in pawn, the rent unpaid, the coffee and candles got on credit, the news from home devastating, the future frightening—even then they would turn to one another with a smile or a kiss, and feel that where all else tottered, their affection was secure. So many entries in her journal conclude on a confession of complete conjugal bliss. At the end of one of their most dismal days, when they were wondering how they would go on at all, she wrote in her diary: "It seemed to me that all this trouble was a kind of atonement for the tremendous happiness that had come my way in marrying Fyodor." Was she repeating something that her husband had suggested to her in one of their midnight talks? Was it thus that he accounted to himself for his pathological and ruinous passion?

# ( IV )

The pair were the more dependent upon each other because they lived in complete isolation, too poor and too absorbed in their predicament to be aware of the glittering life of the resort, let alone take part in it. But even if they avoided the promenade by daylight because Anna had nothing to wear (and the couple

had certainly not come to drink the waters in the company of
pampered fashionables), Dostoevsky could not help chancing
upon Russian acquaintances among the cosmopolitan crowd at
the casino. The very first Sunday he ran into Goncharov, already
the renowned author of *Oblomov*. A solid citizen and a state
councillor, Goncharov was at first somewhat abashed at being
caught gambling, but seeing Dostoevsky's matter-of-fact acceptance of the situation, he admitted that he was playing and the
two drifted into talk. Among other things, Goncharov said that
Turgenev, who was then a resident of Baden, had noticed Dostoevsky at the casino the previous day but, knowing that gam-
blers dislike being interrupted at play, had not accosted him.

What a nuisance! He still owed Turgenev the money he had
borrowed when he was stranded in Wiesbaden two years earlier,
and now he would have to go and call on him or the man would
think he was being avoided. He knew how it would be: Turgenev
would pretend to embrace him, but only offer his cheek to be
kissed. He had the manners of a fop, of an aristocratic trifler.
His latest novel, *Smoke,* with its paean to Western civilization,
was enough to turn the stomach of any Russian. And to think
that this man, with his ample income, was paid at a higher rate
than he, with all his responsibilities and burdens, could hope for!

It was Wednesday morning before Dostoevsky forced himself
to call on Turgenev—a duty all the more disagreeable since he
was not in a position to pay his debt. The visit lasted an hour or
so. Straight from the quiet house on Schillerstrasse he went to
the casino. He won a considerable sum of money and after a
sumptuous dinner returned to the gambling rooms, but luck
turned against him, and though he went back to the tables three
times the same afternoon, he always lost. He became so irritable
that, there being nothing else to complain of, he worked himself
into a rage because it took so long to get dark. It was in this
angry mood that he told Anna, over their evening tea, about his
visit to Turgenev. The man was embittered by the failure of
*Smoke* and kept returning to the sore subject, but he, Dostoevsky, had said nothing about it. He had, however, advised
Turgenev to get himself a telescope and train it on Russia, otherwise he could not hope to understand what was going on there.
He had also told Turgenev frankly that he was not the realist
he thought himself. Before taking leave, he could not help vent-
ing his animosity against the Germans, saying that they were
stupid and often deceitful. Although this had offended his host,

who declared that he had become a German himself, the two managed to part with a show of friendliness.

The following morning Turgenev, who wished to save appearances, returned Dostoevsky's call, but at an hour when he knew he would not be received. When, later, they ran into each other at the casino, neither bowed.

Nearly two months later Dostoevsky gave a fuller account of his visit to Turgenev in a letter to Maikov. The conversation, he wrote, had first centered on *Smoke,* and Turgenev had been shameless enough to say that the main point of the novel was that mankind would lose nothing if Russia were to sink through the ground. And of course he was an atheist: he had said so flatly. Good God! Religion gives us the incomparable beauty, the serene ideal of Christ, while all these Turgenevs, Herzens, Chernyshevskys—the whole Belinsky progeny—present nothing but a spectacle of emptiness, vanity, and abominable self-love! Turgenev pretended to love Russia, but he hated and made a mock of everything original there. Among other things, he had said that the Russians "must crawl before the Germans," that civilization was the one common and inevitable road, and that any attempt on the part of Russia to go its own gait was "swinishness and folly." He was going to put all these ideas in a pamphlet he was writing against the Slavophiles. It was at this point that Dostoevsky had mentioned the telescope. Here was a home thrust and it annoyed Turgenev accordingly. The rest of the account agrees with Dostoevsky's report to his wife.

The story of the quarrel was soon common gossip in literary circles. A copy of the passage relating to it in the letter to Maikov was sent anonymously, in all probability by Strakhov, to the editor of *Russky arkhiv* (*Russian Archives*), a historical review, with the request to preserve the document for posterity. Before the year was over, Turgenev learned of it, and believing that Dostoevsky had been responsible for this step, hastened to write a letter of protest to the editor, Bartenev. He said that he could not possibly have expressed his intimate convictions in the presence of his visitor, for the simple reason that he thought the man "not wholly in possession of his mental faculties, an opinion shared by many other persons." Dostoevsky, he went on, "sat with me no more than an hour, and retired after having relieved his heart by ferociously abusing the Germans, myself, and my latest book. I had neither the time nor the desire to argue with him. I repeat, I treated him as I would a sick man.

The arguments which he expected from me must have presented themselves to his deranged imagination. . . ." A few years later, writing to a friend about the affair, Turgenev said: "He [Dostoevsky] came to me . . . not to pay the money he had borrowed of me, but to upbraid me for *Smoke* which, according to his notion, should be burned by the hand of the executioner. I listened to his philippic in silence, and what do I learn? That I expressed within his hearing criminal opinions, which he hastened to communicate to Bartenev. . . . It would have been simple calumny, if Dostoevsky weren't crazy—which I don't doubt in the least. Perhaps he hallucinated."

It is not probable that Turgenev listened to Dostoevsky "in silence," but it is more than probable that Dostoevsky, in his wrought-up state, distorted and exaggerated whatever his host may have said. Just at that time he was locking the door for good and all on those aberrations of his youth that he identified with the name of Belinsky. Turgenev, appearing to him as the spiritual son of the dead heresiarch, drew down upon his own head all the lightnings Dostoevsky intended for Belinsky. More than likely he attributed to Turgenev not the opinions that he heard but those that he expected to hear from that quarter.

# ( V )

By August the fortunes of the couple were at low ebb and Anna's patience almost gone. A remittance from her mother relieved them slightly. With part of this sum in his pocket, Dostoevsky went to redeem Anna's ring, brooch, and earrings, but before he reached the pawnbroker's he found himself at the casino, where he gambled the money away. He came home in a desperate state, sobbing, and calling himself a worthless scoundrel. This was the last drop. They would leave this accursed place the next day. No longer able to trust him, Anna accompanied him to the pawnbroker's to redeem her trinkets. The following morning—it was August 23—he was again at the tables, having pawned his ring, and lost the twenty francs that he had got for it. As before, he came home agonizing, calling himself a blackguard and entreating Anna's forgiveness on his knees. Instead of scolding him, she gave him twenty francs with which to redeem the ring. An hour before the train left, he managed to gamble away a few more thalers. That day Anna closed the entry in her diary thus: "I will forbid my children ever to come here, so much have I endured in this place."

They had planned to go either to Paris or Italy, but this being too expensive, they went to Geneva instead, so that Dostoevsky was again following the route he had previously taken with Polina. On their way they stopped at Basel, where they did some sightseeing. At the museum he stood in fascinated horror before Holbein's "The Dead Christ." Anna, in her oversensitive condition, found the picture so distressing, not at all "aesthetic," as she put it in her diary, that she went into another hall. When she rejoined her husband after a quarter of an hour he was still standing before the canvas, with that seemingly frightened expression on his face which frequently betokened an approaching attack. To have a closer look at the picture, he climbed on a chair, and she was afraid that he would have to pay a fine, "for here," she explained, "there is a fine for everything." She led him away and seated him on a bench, expecting a fit from minute to minute, but he gradually quieted down, and as he left the museum he insisted that he would return to look at the picture again.

The impression that the canvas made upon him he transcribed in the bitter testament ("An Essential Explanation") of the consumptive Ippolit in *The Idiot.* If the transcription is a faithful one, as is likely, this realistic picture of the corpse of Jesus came as a challenge to his faith, a dark echo of his doubt. "When you look at this picture, nature appears to you as an immense, merciless, dumb beast, or more correctly, much more correctly, speaking, though it sounds strange, in the form of a huge machine of the most modern construction which, dull and insensate, has senselessly clutched, crushed, and swallowed up a great and priceless Being, a Being worth all of nature and its laws, worth the whole earth, which was created perhaps solely for the sake of the advent of that Being! This picture expresses and involuntarily suggests to one the conception of a dark, insolent, unreasoning and eternal Power to which everything is subject." How could men see this corpse and believe? "These people surrounding the dead man . . . must have experienced terrible anguish and consternation on that evening, which had at once crushed all their hopes, and almost their beliefs. They must have parted in the most awful terror, though each one carried away within him a mighty thought that could never be wrested from him." One imagines Dostoevsky looking at this dead body and paraphrasing Scripture: Blessed are they that have seen, and yet have believed.

The couple's circumstances when they arrived in Geneva were dismal. They had only a few francs left and nothing to expect but a paltry fifty rubles from home. So, the earrings went back to the pawnshop. It was terrible for Dostoevsky to think of the straits Pasha and the others must be in. If only he hadn't burdened himself with all those debts! He must throw himself on his friends again. He begged Maikov to lend him a small sum, turning part of it over to Pasha. Maikov's response allowed them to keep their heads above water for a while. To add to his troubles, his attacks became more frequent; horrible as those seven weeks at Baden had been, he had suffered only two seizures there. At Geneva there was hardly a week without an attack, and for days thereafter he lay exhausted and depressed. Sometimes he was beset by the fear of imminent death, and he would ask Anna if he was really alive. How, under such conditions, could he work? And yet only work could save them.

The setting of his days was changed, but it was no less foreign. If the people around him were not Germans, he found them just as alien, repellent, chilling. Russia was further away than ever. And return was indefinitely postponed. He was like a fish out of water. True, there were some Russians in Geneva, but they were professional revolutionists, expatriates, and so there was no question of commerce with them. They only helped to make him feel that he was a castaway, living on an uninhabited island. Oh, for Russian faces, Russian speech, Russian interests! He longed for them, he needed them for his writing.

His writing? He had nothing black on white to show for the summer. He had carried no manuscript with him to Geneva. All he had was an idea for a novel. It would be a big thing. "I love it terribly," he was writing to Maikov a few days after his arrival in Switzerland, "and I shall be writing it with delight and anguish." Months earlier Katkov had told him that he wanted to start printing a novel of his in January, 1868. But he must first be quit of the essay on Belinsky. He had been working at it on and off all summer, and now at last, before September was half over, he completed it. It had been a ticklish job. He couldn't face squarely the issues involved in any discussion of Belinsky and still hope that his article would pass the censor.

He felt like a man walking on eggs. He wrote, he tore up, he rewrote, and finally produced a piece that was neither here nor there, much to his disgust. As the manuscript was never published and has been lost, irretrievably it appears, one can only guess at what he actually said. It must have been a farewell to the short-lived radicalism of his youth, a renewed attack on socialism and unfaith.

Just about the time that he was putting the finishing touches to this ill-starred essay, the International League for Peace and Freedom was holding a congress in Geneva in the hope of averting an impending Franco-Prussian conflict. The shades of opinion represented ranged from a pallid liberalism to communism and the most violent anarchism. As Dostoevsky was not among the crowd that packed the huge Palais Electoral at the first session, the afternoon of September 9, he did not hear the wild applause that greeted alike the address delivered by the representative of the Workers' International and the more sentimental eloquence of Garibaldi. He went with Anna to get a glimpse of the proceedings the next day. One of the first speakers at that session protested against Garibaldi's declaration of the previous day that the congress should adopt "the religion of God," even though what he meant was the religion of reason. Far from creating a new religion, the orator argued, reason should destroy those that exist. Churches, no less than barracks, must be razed to the ground. This sentiment elicited loud applause, in which Garibaldi himself joined.

Then a shaggy, unkempt, toothless giant, wearing a nondescript gray cloak with a red flannel shirt showing from under it, made the steps of the rostrum creak under his elephantine tread. It was the veteran revolutionist and apostle of anarchism, Bakunin. Garibaldi, who was the chairman, stepped toward him and they embraced. Bakunin's program was simple and bold. The Russian Empire must go. All the monarchies of Europe must go. The false principle of nationalism must go. Peace and freedom would come only through a spontaneous federation of communes. A United States of Europe must rise upon the ruins of the existing empires. May Russian arms suffer every defeat, may the power that rests upon them suffer every humiliation—this was his wish as a liberty-loving Russian.

Other speakers followed. So here they were in the flesh, these European socialists, these prophets of the new order, who except for Bakunin had been only disembodied names to Dostoevsky until now. It is not certain that he heard Bakunin's speech, but the whole thing turned his stomach.

After two more days of speechifying, the congress disbanded. If he did not attend all the sessions, he must have followed the reports of them in the papers. The departure of Garibaldi, before the opening of the third session, removed a restraining influence, and during the final days the socialist faction and its opponents were at it tooth and nail. To Dostoevsky the congress was one continuous squabble, a Babel, a bedlam. What was there to hold these saviors of mankind together? They wanted to achieve peace by fire and sword; they wanted to get men to share their possessions fraternally—by decree. Naturally, they would abolish Christianity. And to think that these wretches were stirring up the unhappy workers! Thus he set down his impressions of the congress in letters home. The moments of enthusiasm, of glorious accord, the noble gestures, the universal reverence for the Italian hero and the exalted principles he stood for—all this went unnoticed. All Dostoevsky could see was that these members of the League for Peace and Freedom were dangerous fools who did not understand that peace could not be legislated and that the only safeguard of freedom was religious faith.

# 19

## THE PURE FOOL

AT last he was able to take his novel in hand. It was mid-September and high time to get to work. Aside from the old debts, there were all those thousands of rubles he had taken from Katkov. And the people at home had to be provided for. He would share his last shirt with Pasha, the poor dear boy. As for themselves, soon there would be the additional expenses of Anna's confinement and, please God, another mouth to feed. The novel was his only hope. And it stubbornly refused to take shape. Images, ideas, situations were churning in his head, but the characters somehow kept slipping away from him, and in consequence the plot was always shifting.

His point of departure was the character of "the idiot," a member of a landed family brought to ruin by the father. The only thing that the youth has in common with the hero of the novel in its final version is the sobriquet given him by his mother, who has an aversion to him. He presents himself to the novelist's imagination in a variety of forms, some repellent. An important role is played by a character partly modeled on a fifteen-year-old girl who figured in a sensational trial that was going on at home when Dostoevsky was at work on the novel. She had been so cruelly treated by her parents that she tried to commit suicide and repeatedly set fire to the house. It is curious that when the author was joyfully anticipating the arrival of his own firstborn, he should have been haunted by the thought of a child suffering from the unnatural enmity of her parents.

He made one draft after another, changing the plot, shifting the emphasis, introducing new characters, summoning up half-formed shapes of men and women. It was already November and he had apparently still done little of the actual writing of the text. On the seventeenth of the month he abandoned the manuscript on which everything depended and his darling Anna for the little watering place of Saxon-les-Bains, the only resort in Switzerland offering the attractions of Baden-Baden, Homburg, and Wiesbaden. This was not his first visit to the town. He had been there weeks previously and come home with empty pockets, having left his wedding ring in pawn. Now, against every persuasion of reason, he was going there again.

Anna had offered no resistance: she knew that opposition would only fan the flame. She stayed behind in their dingy furnished room and waited for tidings of disaster. They came in a letter, dated the day after he left and announcing that he had lost everything, that his overcoat was in pawn and so again was his wedding ring, and that he was forced to stay in the accursed hotel until she sent him a remittance. Never, never again would he go near the tables! Never again would he steal her money "like a low, dirty thief." The time will come when he will be worthy of her. She must love him as he loved her, "infinitely, eternally." She must not grieve over the loss—he will tackle the work with love and hope, and it will be sure to pay off. As soon as he gets back to Geneva he will borrow three hundred francs from a compatriot there and ask Katkov to double their allowance (the publisher had agreed to send him a hundred rubles a month). He would yet make her happy. A new life was beginning. The novel, the novel would save them! "Oh, why, why did I leave you?"

Back at his desk, he attacked his work with fresh energy. For two weeks he labored steadily, so that by December 4 he had several chapters ready for the printer. And then he discarded everything he had written. The first installment of the novel was due for the January, 1868, issue of the magazine. He had taken an advance of no less than forty-five hundred rubles and had not one page to deliver. In panic he began to plan anew. His head was a mill, grinding out on the average six different variants every day. That he did not go mad was a marvel to him.

The room was like an icehouse—these brainless Swiss in the midst of forests did not know how to heat their houses, he wrote. He sat at his desk in his overcoat—he had somehow, perhaps with money from Katkov, managed to redeem it. And in addition there was the racking thought that Pasha, to whom he had not been able to send a kopeck, might be starving.

On December 18 he resumed the actual writing of *The Idiot*. He made use of certain characters and situations from the earlier version, but he was really at work on a new novel. The central figure is now antipodal to Raskolnikov, to the man of the underground, to the Nihilists, to the heroes of western literature. On January 5 by dint of half killing himself he was able to dispatch the first installment in time for the January issue, which, luckily for him, was late as usual. But it was a bad business. Here he had sent off the first seven chapters of the novel, but he had only the foggiest notion of how the action would develop. Furthermore, even the central figures had not matured in his mind. Two or three of them were fairly present to him, but the Idiot, the chief character, the one upon whom the whole significance of the novel depended, was far from clear. To have dispatched the first chapters under these circumstances was staking everything on the next turn of the wheel. It was a good thing Katkov did not know this: he had told him a deliberate lie to the effect that much of the novel was written in the rough and he only had to polish it off. The one comfort was that the first part was more or less in the nature of an introduction and allowed him a free hand later on. Would it whet the appetite of his audience as he intended it to? Anna liked it but, as he wrote to Maikov, she was no judge of his business.

The new year brought word that Dr. Ivanov, the husband of his sister Vera and the father of their ten children, had suddenly died. Dostoevsky immediately dispatched a tender letter to the bereaved family. He told the widow for Christ's sake not to despair, thus honoring the memory of the deceased. "You do believe in a future life, Verochka, don't you?" he wrote, "as you all do; none of you is infected with rotten and stupid atheism. . . . A future life is a necessity, not only a solace."

Ivanov had left his family virtually destitute, and this concerned Dostoevsky nearly: he had gone surety for Mikhail when the latter had borrowed five or six thousand rubles from the doctor, which had never been repaid. He assured Vera that although the pledge was informal, he held it to be his "most sacred duty" to repay the sum as soon as possible. This added considerably to his indebtedness, but there were more immediate matters to worry about: how to make ends meet from day to day while he was trying to get on with the novel. He was missing Anna's help, now that she was no longer able to take dictation or to copy for any stretch of time. She spent long hours sewing baby things. Meanwhile he kept steadily at work, and by the end of February he was able to send off another installment, the last nine chapters of Part One. Writing to Maikov on March 1, he said that he liked the finale of the second installment, but that the rest of Part One seemed to him "rather dull." He would be satisfied, he added, if the public would find these chapters "not too boring." He changes the subject to exocriate the Westernists. The best of them, such as Belinsky, he declares, are "inveterate and conscious enemies of their fatherland." They are not aware that within a century the whole world will be regenerated by Russian thought, which is inseparable from the Orthodox faith—such is his "passionate conviction." To fulfill that high mission, Russian supremacy over all Slavdom must be "established and universially recognized." And to think that those miserable radicals preach the breaking-up of Russia into a federation! "Oh, the dung beetles!"

# ( II )

At the end of February the weather, which until then had been excellent, changed abruptly and it stormed every day. This further irritated his nerves. He had two seizures in rapid succession. That was the price, he thought, of the tumultuous scene with which the second installment closed. On March 3 he went to bed at seven P.M. in a befogged state. Some time during the night he felt Anna's hand on his shoulder and heard her say: "I think it's beginning: I am in pain." "My poor darling," he murmured drowsily, "how I pity you!" The next thing he knew it was daylight. Anna was suffering severely. It happened that the landlady and the servant had left them alone in the house, and Anna had not renewed her attempt to rouse him for fear that he might have another attack. She had spent the whole night in an agony of pain and dread, listening to the wind and the rain beating against the window, and comforting herself as best she could with prayer, while her husband slept heavily beside her.

Fully awake now, Dostoevsky rushed for the midwife. For thirty-three hours Anna was in labor and was only delivered at dawn on March 5. The baby was a girl, large, healthy, and in her father's eyes pretty. The terror of those endless hours, and then the sense of having participated in a mystery, having witnessed a miracle, were unforgettable. Dostoevsky set down the experience years later in a passage of *The Devils*. "There were two and now there's a third human being," says the husband, "a new spirit, finished and complete, unlike the handiwork of man; a new thought and a new love . . . it's positively frightening. . . . And there's nothing grander in the world."

He doted on little Sonia. He couldn't tear himself away from the baby, rocking it, crooning to it, helping with its bath, and pinning it into its swaddling clothes. She looked remarkably like him, he found, even to the wrinkles on her little forehead, and as she lay in her crib he could have sworn she was composing a novel. He communicated the great news to his family, although he had no illusions as to how they would take it. His sister Vera would be the only one to share his joy. To the others the baby's arrival was something of a disaster. Indeed, Maikov urged him to make his will without delay, for if anything happened to him, the Petersburg relatives were capable of trying to snatch the inheritance from his widow and orphan.

It was all very well to talk about wills and bequests, but just now all that he had to leave his family was debts. The baby's coming had only piled them up higher. She was not two weeks old when everything they could possibly raise money on was in the pawnshop. His attacks were getting worse, and what if the baby or her mother took sick? He had asked Katkov for a further advance, so there was still hope. But even that well might conceivably dry up. What then? And to crown it all, the excitement, the distractions, and the sleepless nights had prevented him from touching the novel!

Katkov's kindness knew no limits. He granted the advance, so that Dostoevsky could ease his conscience by helping Pasha and Emilia Fyodorovna once more. He had been excused from contributing to the March issue, but here it was April and not a line written. He acquainted the invaluable Maikov with his desperate situation in a long letter, dated the second of the month. Among other topics he touched on European politics. The outlook, he feels, is ugly. Louis Napoleon has expanded his armed forces, Turkey "hangs by a hair," Austria's position is "all too abnormal," the proletarian problem has been aggravated. It will all come to a bad end, and perhaps soon, he prophesies; and Russia must prepare for it without delay: build strategic railroads and supply herself with the new rifles. The situation at home is far from satisfactory, to judge by what he reads in the press, but then there is the people's love for the Czar, on which the country's strength is based and which is, indeed, Russia's unwritten constitution. As for himself, his stay abroad has made him "a complete monarchist"—as though he had been anything else for nearly a score of years. He concludes by begging his correspondent to tell him what is being said about *The Idiot.*

He had given the good Katkov his solemn promise to send copy in on time for the April issue. He was under the most pressing obligation. He must not lose a moment. He must work as he had never worked before. He kissed Anna and the baby, and with a portion of the advance in his pocket, boarded the train for Saxon-les-Bains and the tables.

Within a few hours of his arrival he was writing to Anna for money with which to redeem his ring and pay his fare back. He had taken the bread out of the mouth of his wife and baby. His baby? What kind of a father was he, anyhow? He didn't deserve to have a child. He was doomed to torment those whom he loved most. He had done an abominable, an inexcusable thing. But it had taught him a lesson. And it was not without a good side. Perhaps the Lord in His infinite mercy had led him to the tables again in order to save him, "dissolute, low, petty gambler" that he was. For the disaster had left him with an amazing idea which was bound to prove the salvation of them all. It had come to him as he was walking in the park at night after he had gambled away the last franc; it was just as in Wiesbaden when, in the same desperate state, he had been at work on *Crime and Punishment* and at the same time had conceived the extraordinary notion of offering the novel to Katkov.

Here was his remarkable plan: he would write to Katkov to help them move to Vevey! This is what he would say: Mikhail Nikiforovich, you have been my Providence; you made my marriage possible; you've been my support through all these months; now you must do one more thing; Geneva doesn't agree with us; Vevey, on the contrary, is rural, quiet, cheap; my attacks will cease in that wonderful climate, which will also benefit my wife and baby, and, with all of us well, my novel will march; by autumn at the latest you shall have it complete, and your generosity will be fully repaid; only now do send me the three hundred rubles we need for the removal. He outlined this plan in a letter to Anna from Saxon-les-Bains, adding that in the autumn they would return to Russia via Italy, which he must show her. If only she knew how full of hope and confidence he was now.

He was no sooner back in Geneva than his elation gave way to despondency. He worked doggedly, indeed he forced himself to write directly after a severe attack, in a state that he described to Maikov as "resembling insanity." But the thing refused to shape itself properly, and in the end he had only two ragged chapters to send off. Geneva seemed windier and gloomier than ever, and the one thing that made life bearable was the baby. Even his joy in her was embittered when he thought of the future.

In the middle of May his mother-in-law joined them. Her coming heartened Anna, made both of them feel less forlorn, and was a blessing for the baby. It was part of the daily routine for it to take its nap in the Jardin Anglais. One afternoon a treacherous *bise* blew up and the child began to cough. The cold developed into pneumonia. For a week the doctor came every day and assured them that the baby would recover. Nevertheless, Dostoevsky, uneasy and unable to do any work, hung over the crib constantly. The morning of May 24 the doctor told them that the baby was much better. At the usual time Dostoevsky left the house for the café to look through the Russian papers. Two hours later little Sonia was dead.

The light, the warmth went out of the world. He thought he could not bear the pain of it. A small creature, scarcely three months old, hardly human yet, one would think, strange that she counted so heavily with him! They would have to bury with her so many hopes, so many dreams. She had already begun to smile, to recognize him, to quiet her crying when he came close. She had been a person, a separate spirit. And where was she now? There was no comfort for him anywhere. Some three months previously, writing to his sister Vera on her husband's death, he had spoken of other worlds than this, of resurrection. There was no echo of such solace in the words in which he announced his sad news to Maikov. He begged his friend to keep it from the family for a while. They were capable of being pleased at the baby's death, and this thought was intolerable.

From the first he had disliked Geneva, finding it a grim, gusty place, thick with Calvinists and drunks. Now he had good reason to hate it. These vile winds, that stupid doctor, the careless nurse—they had taken his Sonia from him. And where else would one find neighbors who would knock at the door and ask a bereaved mother not to sob because it annoyed them?

On a warm cloudy day that suited their heavy mood Dostoevsky went with Anna to pay a farewell visit to the little grave, and from the cemetery they went straight to the steamer that was to take them across the lake to Vevey. Yes, they were indeed going there, but under what heartbreaking circumstances! As they glided over the quiet waters mirroring the enchanted landscape, all the cruelties that life had shown him, from his mother's death, through prison and exile, his plaguing illness, the harassments of his first marriage, the vexations of his literary career, his gambling passion, his unhappy loves, down to this last desolating grief, rose up to crush him.

That summer among the cool beauties of Vevey was the bleakest the pair were ever to know. They avoided the streets so as not to see other people's children. There was nothing to distract Anna from her sorrow, and night after night she gave herself up to the luxury of tears. But she was sustained by the hope of being a mother again—this was her constant prayer. As for Dostoevsky, he wanted Sonia. If another child came, he asked himself, where would he find love for it in his heart? Time only sharpened his anguish. He could not forget how the baby's eyes had followed him on that last day when he went off to read the newspapers. That memory was a wound that would not heal.

By contrast with his mood, the serene charm of the town was painful. Where was the demi-Eden he had imagined Vevey to be? Why, it was worse than Geneva. True, the scenery was incomparable, and the place was free of the *bise* that had robbed him of Sonia. But the air he discovered to be enervating in the extreme, as did Anna, as did her mother, who, having come to help care for the baby, now found her occupation gone. The natives here were just the same dishonest, mean, filthy imbeciles they were elsewhere—indeed, he asserted, the Kirghiz in their *yurtas* were cleaner in their habits than the Swiss. A vile place, this republic, bourgeois to its rotten core! Like all Europe. No, for true high-mindedness, simplicity, and understanding, you must go to the Russian masses. For them, he had written to Katkov, Christianity means faith in goodness, not in bourgeois comfort.

Dostoevsky had thought that at Vevey he would feel better and work better. He was mistaken. His health was worse. During May, the month of little Sonia's fatal illness, he had succeeded in writing but a paltry two chapters, and in the summer months that followed he managed to squeeze out of himself only driblets. He noted with horror that his powers were failing. He could no longer work at his old speed. The last installment of the second part did not appear until the July issue. If only he could break the evil spell and make something good of the rest of the novel, he might yet revive, otherwise he was lost. To add to his distress, he could not get a Russian paper to read. And, after a long painful silence, a letter from Pasha saying that he had lost his job sent his stepfather further into debt for his sake.

Dostoevsky lived for letters from home, especially Maikov's, and he began to suspect, justifiably, that his mail was being tampered with. Certainly the letters he wrote were read by the police—its long hand reached even to Geneva, where the Russian priest was in the secret service. And to think that he, Fyodor Dostoevsky, a nationalist, a patriot, a man adoring his sovereign, a man who was with the government to the point of "playing traitor," so he said, to his "former convictions," was held suspect. It was almost enough to turn him from his allegiance.

They had stayed over a year in hateful Switzerland, and another winter in this "Lapland" was unthinkable. Both of them were literally sick of it. By September they were in Milan—their money would not take them farther south. The journey refreshed him; the Lombard peasants reminded him of muzhiks. The climate of Milan agreed with him, and the sights, particularly for Anna, were diverting. But living was more expensive; it rained a great deal; and again there was not a Russian face, not a Russian book or newspaper. They were bored, they were gloomy, they had not left their grief behind them at Vevey. And his prospects were as uncertain as before. How could they return home? And how could he live away from it? The novel kept to its slow pace. It was already November, and he still had the whole of the fourth and last part to write. Indeed, this was to be the crown of the work, that portion for the sake of which he now believed that he had written the whole. If only he could have had the chance to revise it all before publishing any of it! Now that he was on the last lap the conviction grew upon him that he had never touched a richer subject than this of *The Idiot,* and that, Heaven help him, he had come near botching it. At any rate, he could not rush the last part so as to publish it before the year was out. In order to avoid carrying it over into the January number for the following year, Katkov would have to issue the remaining chapters separately as a supplement, and Dostoevsky, to make up for the expense and inconvenience, would waive payment for that part. And how he needed the money!

This unusual arrangement was actually carried out. The last chapter is dated January 17, 1869. Toward the end he was delayed by two severe attacks coming in swift succession. He finished the novel in deep anguish of soul.

# ( III )

Shortly after Dostoevsky finished *The Idiot* he observed that much of it was a failure, but some passages had turned out well. "I stand up not for the novel," he said, "but for my idea." What he meant by his "idea" is clear from the letter that he addressed to Maikov a few days after he had sent off the first installment to *Russky vestnik*. He had intended above all, he wrote, to portray "a wholly beautiful human being." The idea had long haunted him, but he was still unsure of the plot and even the central character was blurred in his mind. Circumstances had forced him to pluck an unripe fruit.

He was aware, he said in a letter addressed a little later to his niece, Sonia, to whom he was dedicating the novel, that the task he had set himself—that of fashioning an image of moral perfection—involved great, perhaps insuperable, difficulties. Jesus was the only embodiment of that ideal the world has known, but can a novelist, he asked, presume to give substance to it in an age of confusion and unbelief? Nevertheless, the likeness on the icon was undoubtedly present to the author of *The Idiot* while he was planning the book. In the preliminary notes for it the protagonist is called "Prince Christ" three times. Traces of this conception remain in the finished work. Prince Myshkin's large blue eyes, hollow cheeks, thin blond beard, suggest the revered face as usually limned. He turns the other cheek, avoids judging people, befriends a woman who is an outcast, suffers little children to come to him. But the resemblance to the Galilean is by no means emphasized and, as the story unfolds, is all but obliterated.

In the letter to his niece the novelist reflected that sucessful attempts to portray moral excellence had been made before. There was, for example, Don Quixote. But we sympathize with "the most masterfully drawn admirable character in Christian literature" because he is also a figure of comedy. The predicament that Dostoevsky faced was how to save his book from insipidity by making his paragon believably human. He never forgot that he must hold the interest of his public, especially since the novel reached it piecemeal at long intervals. He solved his problem by making his hero an "idiot," the incompletely cured victim of an obscure nervous ailment from which he had suffered since childhood. It had left Prince Myshkin bodily and, to a limited degree, mentally unfit.

Like the author, Myshkin is afflicted with the "sacred disease." Naturally, the passages on his epilepsy owe their authentic quality to the fact that here Dostoevsky must have leaned on his own experience. This applies particularly to the twilight world in which the Prince moves when he is on the brink of an attack. The sickness is presented as threatening mental decay, but also as a source of mystic ecstasy. Just before the onset of a seizure the epileptic knows a lightninglike moment of exaltation so intense that it shatters consciousness and so precious in retrospect that life seems not too high a price to pay for it. Thus the "idiot" is set apart from his fellows both because of his ailment and by virtue of his experience of "higher being." He is akin to Ivanushka the Simpleton of the folk tales, or rather the *"yurodivyi"* (a weak-minded man, believed by the folk to be divinely inspired), the Russian equivalent of the Germanic *"reiner Tor"* (pure fool). Dostoevsky is working a native vein here.

As the novel opens, the young nobleman, who has spent several years in a Swiss sanatorium, is returning to Petersburg, without any visible means of support and practically no connections. Before his first day in the capital is over, he finds himself involved with half a dozen people whom he has just met. Among them are the Yepanchin family, to one member of which he is akin; the crude Rogozhin, heir to a fortune; the dazzling demonic beauty, Nastasya Filippovna, whom he is out to win. The subsequent entanglements form the substance of the massive tale. It is the work of a prodigal writer, given to extravagance. Subplots ramify and a multitude of men and women throng pages not wanting in surprise and mystery. The narrative moves through a series of climaxes to the foreshadowed tragedy with which it ends. The action halts for lengthy digressions, and there are comic interludes, especially when General Ivolgin, a quasi-Dickensian character, appears on the scene.

More than once, with no great regard for appropriateness, the characters voice Dostoevsky's convictions and obsessions. The novelist uses as one of his mouthpieces the devious toady, Lebedev, a pathological liar and an enthusiastic exegete of the Apocalypse—a triumph of the art of the grotesque. It is even more startling to hear Dostoevsky's beliefs from the mouth of the Prince. At a reception given by the Yepanchins to introduce him to their circle (the highborn guests are touched in with an acid pen) the usually tongue-tied simpleton delivers a remarkable tirade. During his few months in his native land he has acquired "a passionate faith in the Russian soul." At the party he bursts into a "wild" attack on the Church of Rome as anti-Christian, the mother of atheism and socialism. To these Western plagues Russia must oppose the true Christian ideal which she alone has preserved and which the other nations have never known, and he prophesies that eventually mankind will be saved by "the Russian God and Christ." This is a piece of ventriloquism. The voice is the voice of Myshkin, but the doctrine is the doctrine of Dostoevsky, the anti-Catholic thesis being its latest accretion. Clearly nothing could be more incongruous with the Prince's character than the role of an ardent champion of Russian messianic chauvinism.

While *The Idiot* can be regarded as a thriller centering on such concerns as who will marry whom, will there be a marriage or a murder, the unique personality of Myshkin is the paramount feature of the book. It is his figure that dominates the manifold that the novel is and makes for its chief interest as well as its coherence and depth. Throughout, the elements of the young man's character are in sharp contrast to the greed, lust, vanity, meanness, envy, the sheer perversity of those whose lives are caught up with his. From the first he is seen to be innocent, frank, utterly devoid of self-interest, as ready to unbosom himself to a servant as to a high dignitary. His other amiable traits soon become evident. His dealings with people are marked by considerateness and compassion. At one point the Prince reflects that "Compassion is the principal and perhaps the only law of mankind's being." A limitless tolerance for the failings of others goes hand in hand with a sense of his own inadequacy. He confesses to having "double thoughts," in which a high motive is coupled with a base one. The fact that he invariably acts upon the former does not mitigate his feeling of unworthiness. There is something odd about his responses. He lacks the proper gesture, the sense of measure. Unfortunately for everyone concerned, he has only the feeblest awareness of reality. His behavior arouses condescending smiles or laughter (in which he joins). People begin by suspecting him of being a schemer or an imbecile; many end by falling under the spell he exercises. His chief trait is meekness. One cannot imagine him chasing the money-changers out of the temple. He is poles removed from Don Quixote, who haunted Dostoevsky while the novel was in the process of gestation. The hidalgo fights, if only against windmills; the Prince is apt to remain a passive, if pained, bystander.

# ( IV )

Early in the story the Prince becomes heir to a fortune. Characteristically, he does little with it. And this in spite of his telling Rogozhin, "There is much to do in our Russian world." The inheritance attracts the attention of the local Nihilists. Here Dostoevsky displays his anti-Nihilism, using the domineering, delightful Mme. Yepanchin as his mouthpiece. Four members of the group, an unsavory lot, call on the Prince; one of them, supported by the rest, lays claim to part of the inheritance, believing himself to be an illegitimate son of the Prince's quondam benefactor. The novelist's economy in portraiture is shown in his description of the claimant's face as expressing nothing but "innocent impudence" and "complete infatuation with his own rights." Although it is at once made clear to Myshkin that the claim is groundless, to the disgust of the Yepanchins and others present, he offers the young man a gift of ten thousand rubles. In the end the claimant realizes that he has no case and accepts nothing. Before long the Nihilists become Myshkin's friends, all except Ippolit, a refractory, malicious teen-ager who is in the last stages of consumption and knows it. Toward the end of the scene he falls to sobbing and screams that he hates the whole eminent company but chiefly the Prince, that "treacly little soul."

Unlike his comrades, Ippolit plays a large, if secondary, part

in the novel. On the night of Myshkin's birthday celebration, in
the small hours, Ippolit reads his testament aloud to a mixed
gathering. The testament is a prolix medley, not without moving
passages, such as that voicing the rebellion of this dying boy
against the senseless cruelty of the natural order. He has resolved
to shoot himself when he has finished reading and the sun has
risen. The act will mark his revolt against that cruelty, against
the humiliation, the mockery that it involves. The pistol fails to
go off: he has neglected to load it properly. Just before he makes
the attempt he embraces Myshkin, saying that he wants to bid
farewell to "a Human Being." Yet the Prince proves unable to
offer anything like comfort to Ippolit as he faces death. When the
boy asks how he shall make the most virtuous end, Myshkin
answers: "Pass by us and forgive us our happiness." Ippolit
guffaws.

The agony of facing death is a theme that recurs in the novel,
here in the case of Ippolit, earlier as the experience of the condemned the moment before execution, again, in terms shocking to
the religious sentiment, in a description of Holbein's painting
of the dead Christ (which, it will be remembered, had such a
terrible fascination for Dostoevsky when he saw it in Basel).
Nature is here represented as Christ's victorious enemy. In none
of these passages is there a hint of the consolations of the Christian faith. Dostoevsky had never needed faith more desperately
than during the bleak months when, in a strange and hated land,
harassed by all his usual anxieties, and, worse, bereft of his firstborn, he was composing this work. It is as though the doubts
that were crowding the author's heart were confided to the book.

If Myshkin is shown to be ineffectual in helping Ippolit to make
a Christian end, his relationship with the two women who play
a dominant part in the book, a relationship which largely shapes
the plot, is maleficent. Nastasya Fillipovna had been carefully
brought up for his pleasure by Totzky, a wealthy sensualist who
made her his mistress when she was a mere girl. This passionate
woman, capable of savage cruelty, to herself as well as to others,
is tormented by an implacable sense of her degradation. It impels
her now and again to take delight in behaving like "the abandoned creature" that she is far from being. Is she loath to bury
her past because that would mean to forgive the unforgivable
offense she had suffered? Or is she reveling in her shame as the
obverse of her intense self-love? The author leaves the reader to
decide for himself. Of her two suitors, one has been bribed by

Totzky to marry her so as to enable him to take a wife, one of the Yepanchin girls, who is in a social class above his own. The other, Rogozhin, is possessed by a violent lust that in the end is compounded with a murderous hatred.

Myshkin first sees Nastasya the very evening of his arrival in the capital, at the stormy gathering in her home. He is moved to rapture by her beauty, but this response gives way to pity for a woman whom he perceives to be a badly, perhaps fatally, injured and deeply suffering human being. To save her from her suitors and herself, he forthwith offers her marriage. She rejects him because, having fallen in love with him at first sight and responding to a complete humanity which she had never known before, she does not want to inflict herself upon him. She promptly goes off with Rogozhin on a wild spree. Nevertheless he sees in the Prince a dangerous if baffling rival. In vain Myshkin goes out of his way to persuade Rogozhin that he feels only pity for Nastasya. At one point Rogozhin offers to withdraw; a few hours later he is about to kill Myshkin, but is prevented when the Prince has an epileptic fit. On closer contact Myshkin comes to believe Nastasya deranged, and pities her the more. Rogozhin, tormented by her, beats her up. Yet in spite of their being poles apart, the two men are linked by a strange affinity. From the first they are attracted to each other. In one of the early drafts of the work they figure as brothers. In the novel they exchange the crosses they wear next to the skin, in token of spiritual kinship. It seems to be more than the attraction of opposites.

Almost as important as Nastasya in relation to Myshkin is Aglaya. In every respect save beauty she is strikingly different from Totzky's former mistress. Myshkin's first interest in this delightfully virginal, self-willed girl develops into a strong attachment, which yet does not become a normal passion, carnal and exclusive. If he proposed to Nastasya out of pity, he looks forward happily to marriage with Aglaya, though all he wants is her companionship. As for her, while fully aware of Myshkin's failings, she recognizes and delights in his immense superiority to the men around her. Everyone, she says, has two minds, a "principal" one and a lesser one. If the Prince's lesser mind is defective, she finds his "principal" one surpassingly fine.

Both women love him in an earthy, possessive way. It is in defiance of her feelings that Nastasya, believing Aglaya alone could make Myshkin happy, begs her to marry him. She does this in what amounts to love letters to the girl, adding that she herself will marry Rogozhin. Aglaya, recognizing that Nastasya is jealous of her, and, as she tells Myshkin, loves not her but him, asserts that Nastasya will marry Rogozhin, but the day after their wedding will kill herself. As for Myshkin, he sees no reason why he should not love the two women at the same time after his own fashion. On first meeting the Prince, the bribed suitor of Nastasya asks him if he would marry a woman like her (it will be recalled that he did propose to her the same day). Yet his answer is: "I cannot marry anyone. I am ill." This is not the only broad hint that the Prince is sexless. Indeed, Mme. Yepanchin's suspicion of it helps to make her anxious about Aglaya's possible marriage to him, an event which she fears is inevitable.

What follows is climactic. Outraged by Nastasya's letters, Aglaya confronts her in the presence of Myshkin and Rogozhin. The two women exchange accusations of jealousy and stinging insults. These drive Nastasya to test her power over the Prince. Turning to Aglaya and pointing at him, she cries out: "If he doesn't at once come over to me, take me, and leave you, then you can have him, I don't want him! . . . Take your treasure, and get out!" Myshkin, overwhelmed, hesitates momentarily, per- haps not grasping the necessity of choice; Aglaya, taking this to mean that he has given her up, runs out. He is on the point of following her, when Nastasya clutches him and detains him by fainting in his arms.

In the succeeding days Myshkin for the most part stays by the side of Nastasya, but also, in a state of inexpressible anguish, seeks in vain to see Aglaya. At the same time, absent-mindedly as it were, he prepares to go through the ceremony of leading Nastasya, whom he fears as well as pities, to the altar. At the last moment the bride deserts the "babe," as she calls the Prince —she had done this on a previous occasion—and goes off with Rogozhin.

The day after that on which his wedding was to have taken place Myshkin spends many hours looking frantically and vainly for Nastasya and Rogozhin. In the evening the latter accosts the Prince on the street and takes him to his own dismal home. As they walk toward it he tells Myshkin, in response to his question, that Nastasya is there. What the Prince had foretold when he knew no more of her than what her photograph showed him has come to pass. The final scene, one of the great passages in fiction, lends *The Idiot* a symmetry unusual in Dostoevsky's work.

The novel opens with Myshkin seated beside Rogozhin in a railway carriage talking about Nastasya. It ends with the two men side by side on the floor next to the alcove where the body of the murdered woman lies. People finally coming in find the murderer delirious and the Prince, though tenderly stroking Rogozhin's face, unconscious of everyone and everything else. He enters the novel a young man, just emerged from the shadow of mental illness; he leaves it, his mind deranged beyond recovery.

This example of the Christian virtues has brought destruction on, or failed to avert it from, those with whom he was most intimately involved. Although the evil seething around him cannot submerge the radiance of his personality, he is the center of calamitous events. For all his powers of intuition, which nearly amount to second sight, he did not recognize that the pity he felt for Nastasya would only confirm her conviction that she was beyond redemption. He realized that Rogozhin was a tigerish character, and indeed foresaw how he would act if baited, but did not prevent the tragic dénouement. Aglaya, who believes herself repudiated by Myshkin, marries a bogus count, a Pole to boot, and in embracing Catholicism sinks as low as Dostoevsky could conceive. There is no satisfactory explanation for his having dealt so scurvily with this attractive girl, who has suffered enough to deserve a better fate, considering his view of the redemptive value of suffering.

*The Idiot* embraces the quietist variety of Christian ethics, but fails to show that it is valid. The novel implies that goodness alone, unsupported by a sense of fact, unguided by a discriminating intelligence, will not enable a man to surmount the difficulties presented by an imperfect world, and may indeed prove a curse. This, however, does not appear to have been the intention of the novelist, who was rather inclined to hold that it is a mistake to weigh the Christian ideal on the pragmatist's scale.

The tumultuous, bewildering, profoundly ambiguous book is not the modern *Imitatio Christi* that the author had hoped against hope it might be. But if it disappointed in some ways both Dostoevsky and his readers, it has attracted successive generations of these for a century. It exhibits, as might be expected, extraordinary understanding of the more delicate nuances of motives, an astounding grasp of character, not excluding some of the lesser figures, and as a foil for melodrama and awkward dialectics it offers passages quick with excitement, with anguish, with high comedy. Above all, the image of Myshkin, however pathetic and occasionally ridiculous, leaves an impression of warmth and radiance. It is as benign as the memory of a good dream, but enduring.

# 20

## THE SECOND EXILE ENDS

So often the completion of a piece of work left Dostoevsky with a sense of failure. He felt acutely how far his imagination outstripped his craftmanship. *The Idiot* was a case in point. The novel didn't express a fraction of what he had wanted to say, but there was no helping it now. How was his public reacting to it? What were the critics writing? In his isolation he could not know. As a matter of fact, they were content to say little about a book that puzzled and discomfited them. The most ominous thing was that the publishers were in no hurry to bid for the rights to a separate edition.

The one good thing the new year brought them was the discovery that Anna was again pregnant. But how would they meet the expenses of her confinement, and what would they live on in the meantime? He was still in debt to Katkov, and he had no other source to look to for money. Besides, after all the many months of labor entailed by *The Idiot* he needed a fallow period. And Emilia Fyodorovna was asking for a regular allowance, instead of casual remittances. That ancient enemy of his couldn't get it out of her head that he was obliged to support her and her family.

By the time he had sent off the last part of the novel, they had been settled in Florence for two months. He had pleasant mem-

ories of his visit there with Strakhov, and it proved a more congenial place than Milan, not so much because of the chance of
seeing again his beloved "Madonna della Sedia" as because of
the Russian books and papers. The Florentine winter was mild:
in February roses were blooming in the Boboli Gardens. On
sunny days he wrote to his niece Sonia, Florence was "almost
paradise." But the damp, warm air was enervating and he held
it accountable for his frequent attacks. Soon he would be facing
the second anniversary of his European exile. This was worse
than hard labor in Siberia. There had been no such sunlight, no
miraculous works of art at Omsk, but there, in the Asiatic wilderness, he had been at home, among his own people. He was not
afraid that he would become assimilated like Turgenev: he hated
foreigners. But living abroad, he felt that he was losing the little
talent that he possessed. Maikov was the only one who could
keep him in touch with affairs at home and to whom he was able
to open his heart. But this friend had not written in months. They
were forsaken by God and man. He simply must return to Russia. There he was certain of making a living. He had a great
idea: a yearbook, a reference work that was sure to be a huge
financial success and that would not interfere with his writing
fiction.

By March things had come to such a pass that the couple had
pawned their underwear, and if they had not been able to
borrow a small sum from a stranger, they might have perished.
Again Katkov saved the situation. The remittance as usual was
insufficient, and Dostoevsky soon found himself appealing for
more money as an advance on a novel which *Russky vestnik*
could start running in 1870. He had yet another project. Strakhov
had become the editor of a newly launched magazine, *Zarya*
(*Dawn*), and Dostoevsky promised him a short narrative, which
could be tossed off without much effort and would not conflict
with his larger work. He liked the idea of contributing to a
periodical that, from the first, struck a clearly nationalistic, conservative chord. The advance, he thought, would permit them to
leave Florence for a place where they would at least be familiar
with the language, possibly Germany.

Early in April he was heartened by a letter from Maikov.
His response was a lengthy communication, in which he outlined
his circumstances and gave his friend several "ticklish" commissions having to do with monetary matters. He also urged the
poet to write a sequence of ballads forming an epic of Russian

history against the background of that of the West, and concluding with a vision of Russia's glorious future, alongside Europe with its "faded, mutilated, brutalized" civilization. It would be, he raved, "a new word," an achievement of national import, at once instructive and edifying, a captivating masterpiece for children and adults alike to learn by heart. Apparently he had in mind a work that would do for Russia what *The Iliad* had done for Greece and *The Aeneid* for Rome.

It was spring now and the city was getting hot. But the publisher of *Zarya* was dilatory and they were forced to stay on and on. July came and they were still stranded there. In Switzerland Dostoevsky had known the rigors of cold, now he was tasting the torments of heat. He could only compare Florence to a Russian steambath. The three of them, for Anna's mother had remained with them, were crowded into one small room. The windows looked out on the stone arcades of a marketplace that at midday was like an oven. At night they were kept awake by people making merry in the streets, and with dawn came the babble of market women and the braying of asses to keep them from sleep. Work was out of the question. As he watched the tourists parade the blazing streets—the city seemed to him much more crowded than when he had been there with Strakhov seven years previously—he marveled that those who had the price of the fare in their pockets stayed in this hell. Torn between boredom and irritation, he looked at everything with the eyes of a caged beast. What was this flower of cities but a prison? And a foul prison, too: twice he had the horrible experience of catching a tarantula in their room.

Katkov came to the rescue once more and the three were finally enabled to flee Italy. To break the journey, they stopped off in Bologna, in Venice, where Anna lost her fan, a mishap that made her cry like a child, and in Vienna, which he preferred to Paris. They had hoped to settle in Prague, where there would be a chance for him to get in contact with the Slav world, but lodgings proved too expensive, and so, early in August, they found themselves in Dresden again, almost precisely two years after having left it (he was entered in the police records as "a retired Russian lieutenant and *rentier*").

Away from Florence, Dostoevsky discovered that he had been unjust to it. Why, the heat had actually benefited him. Here in Dresden his epilepsy was worse, and he suffered from fever. It was already September, and he had not done a stitch of work either on the piece for *Zarya* or on the novel for *Russky vestnik*. Furthermore, Anna's second pregnancy was a difficult one: she was ill, nervous, and terrified of dying in childbed. When he thought that they would have to expose the second baby to the Western methods of child rearing that had killed the first, he was in despair. No, no, they must go back to Russia, for the child's sake, for their own future, for his work, his work! Better debtors' prison at home than this empty freedom abroad.

# ( II )

On September 26 the child was born—a big, healthy, pretty baby. When he was registering his daughter's birth, he amazed the clerk by being unable to remember the mother's maiden name. It was plain that he was losing his memory. In announcing to Maikov the good news of the little Liubov's arrival, he confided that there were less than ten thalers in the house and that neither the doctor nor the midwife had been paid. He dared not appeal to Katkov again, and so he turned to the publisher of *Zarya*. He could not let himself think what a refusal would mean. He would have to sell his overcoat, his suit, his underwear. Pasha and Emilia Fyodorovna would suffer too—mentally he had already set aside part of the money for them.

There was yet another humiliation for him to swallow at this time. They were scarcely settled in Dresden when a letter from Maikov brought word of a rumor that Aunt Kumanina had died, leaving a bequest of forty thousand rubles to a monastery. The exciting side of the news, as retailed by Maikov, was that, in the opinion of the executor, the will could be successfully contested, since it had been made when the old lady was of unsound mind. This would mean ten thousand rubles for Dostoevsky and an equal sum for Mikhail's family. Maikov advised immediate action. Dostoevsky wrote at once to the executor for further information. He also sent the news to Sonia, saying that he considered her his conscience and asking what she thought it would be right for him to do in the matter.

In due time he received a letter from Sonia telling him pointblank that she disapproved of this move. Further, there came a letter from his brother Andrey, the aunt's guardian, declaring that the old lady had no such fortune to bequeath, that there was no such clause in her will, and that, although she was quite off her head, she was otherwise hale and hearty. He said further that the annulment of the will would undoubtedly benefit all the Dostoevskys, but it was not to be thought of. Andrey's words, too, implied that his brother was an unscrupulous schemer. Apparently all the relatives had been apprised of the affair and the wildest rumors concerning him were in circulation. A pretty kettle of fish! Here he was painted as a monster of greed and selfishness, ready to snatch the bread out of the mouths of orphans, when he had been weighing so carefully the ethics of the step! True, he had told Maikov that if he did decide that it was right to act, he stood ready to bring suit on his own account as well as on that of the others—certainly he needed money sorely enough. But what had been his first thought? Mikhail's orphans. He had sacrificed the share of the inheritance he had received earlier to save the review for Mikhail's family. To pay their debts he had robbed his own wife and child. And what thanks, he asked himself privately, did he get for it? To be despised as their slave and hated as the author of their ruin. And so Sonia was looking down on him, too. This was a pleasant thought to brood on.

A series of misunderstandings, as well as carelessness on the part of the publisher of *Zarya,* delayed some six weeks the arrival of the money Dostoevsky had asked for. In the meantime they were starving. Anna, who was nursing the baby, had to pawn her last warm skirt, with the snow already on the ground, and in order to get two thalers to send an urgent telegram to the publisher, he had to raise money on his trousers. He could not bring himself to disclose the shameful details of their situation. But worse than all these humiliations at the hands of strangers was the affront to his dignity from a man who knew who he was. The swine of a publisher was treating him like a flunkey. His heart was swollen with indignation. And after this, he wrote to Maikov, "people demand of me art, pure poetry, without strain, without poison, and point to Turgenev, to Goncharov! Let them look at the conditions under which I work."

He did work in spite of everything, and when the worst period of stress was over, life fell more or less into the old lines. He rose at one o'clock, managed to do a little writing in the afternoon, went for a stroll through the gardens to the post office, which he so often left with empty hands, came home to dinner—there was one most of the time—and then took another walk

to the library, where he devoured three Russian papers down to
the last word. Not seldom the reading left him with the unhappy impression that things at home were not as they should
be. But he consoled himself with the thought that at this distance he was bound to misjudge the situation.

From half past ten at night to five in the morning he was
at his desk. He cursed this vile tale he was writing—he had conceived a hatred for it from the beginning and described work on
it as "drudgery"—but he kept at it. Early in December it was
finished, months late and five times as long as he had originally
intended it to be. At least he had the comfort of being able to
revise the manuscript as a whole. He had to wait for additional
money from the publisher before he could send it off: he wasn't
able to pay the postage.

Dostoevsky regarded *The Eternal Husband* as a diversion
from his more serious literary pursuits. Indeed, the story, or
rather short novel, travels light. *The Eternal Cuckold* would
have been a more appropriate title for it. A provincial official
named Trusotzky discovers after his wife's death that she had
had a series of lovers, one of whom, Velchaninov, had fathered
Liza, the little girl he has brought up fondly as his only child.
The widower is presented as a uxorious, henpecked husband,
born to be deceived. The lover is the typical gay deceiver caught,
however, in a moment of physical and spiritual distress that ill
befits the character of a Don Juan. Interest centers upon the
husband. His habitual self-restraint gone, he arrives in Petersburg with the child, ostensibly on business, but actually on an
errand of vengeance against Velchaninov directly, and indirectly
by tormenting his child. He tracks down Velchaninov and there
ensues a psychological duel between the two men which forms the
substance of the narrative. All the moves that they execute in
obedience to their ambiguous impulses make an absorbing spectacle. These passages are written with great subtlety, penetration,
dramatic power, and display an astonishing grasp of the role of
the subconscious in human behavior. The chapter that exhibits
this understanding most fully is called "Analysis." Toward the
end of the story, Liza having conveniently died, the cuckold takes
Velchaninov to visit the family of the fifteen-year-old girl to
whom he is tentatively engaged. He wants to parade his clever
companion before them; further, he is eager to test the conduct
of his intended fiancée in the presence of a brilliant man of the
world. And perhaps unconsciously he is tempted to put himself

again in the shameful position in which he had been placed years previously by the same Velchaninov. In fact, the epilogue concludes with a scene suggesting that the cuckold, now married to a beautiful young woman, is again in the situation that he was born to occupy.

It is possible to see a reflection of certain of the author's personal experiences in the story. The family on whom the two men call is largely patterned on the Ivanov household, with its jolly crowd of young people who made the summer of 1866 so pleasant for Dostoevsky. It has been intimated that the story is anchored in his relations with his first wife. One need not, however, assume such a basis for this anatomy of cuckoldry. His interest in every form of humiliation was sufficient to draw him to such a subject, and he needed but the shadow of an actual experience to release his imagination.

# ( III )

The year and a half that remained of this second exile saw no relief from the miseries of want, worry, ill health, isolation. As before, he took refuge in his work, upon which he spent all the intensity of which his nature was capable.

A new idea had begun to haunt him while he was still busy with the final chapters of *The Idiot*. In fact, he had been thinking about it for a year or so. It was a project for a colossal novel on atheism. The pivotal figure was to be a staid, comfortable office-holder who, at the age of forty-five, suddenly loses his faith. This affects him deeply. In his quest for God he mingles with all manner of people, searching the hearts and exploring the minds of Nihilists, atheists, Slavophiles, Westernists, priests, hermits. He is trapped by a Jesuit, but escapes and joins a body of sectarians. In the end he recovers his faith and establishes it on the Russian Christ. Here, Dostoevsky felt, he would express all of himself, say his final word. If only he could write this book, he would be content to die. If he did not write it, it would torture him to death. But he was not ready for it yet; he must first read a whole library of religious and antireligious works. And in any case, it wasn't the sort of thing that he could write abroad.

In the fallow months that followed the completion of *The*

*Idiot* his mind kept returning to this mighty theme. Several characters took shape in his head, among them an ardent Catholic, modeled somewhat on Loyola's right-hand man, St. Francis Xavier, the Apostle to the Indies. All that Dostoevsky had done until now he dismissed as "trash and introduction" compared to the titanic "parable of atheism" that he was planning. He would give the rest of his life to it. As he brooded over the thing it altered, so that by the time he had finished *The Eternal Husband* he saw the novel still as a work on a tremendous scale and concerned with the problem, which was his lifelong torment, of the existence of God, but he had conceived a new plot. He started working on it in December, 1869. *The Life of a Great Sinner* was the title that he chose for the narrative, which would be his "last novel." It would trace the hero's fortunes from his unhappy childhood through years of transgression and crime to his final regeneration. Dostoevsky first touched upon this theme of redemption in the last pages of *Crime and Punishment*; it colored faintly his original drafts for *The Idiot*. Now that he was seeing it more clearly, he decided to make it the cornerstone of a vast work. This would be a cycle of five novels which, though having the same protagonist, could be published separately. Some details are known only about the first two.

The first would deal with the hero's early years. The illegitimate son of a landowner of gentle birth, the motherless boy is entrusted to the care of strangers. They are a corrupt and dissolute couple, who disgust him. The child withdraws into himself. From the start he instinctively feels that he is destined for great things. Books help him to escape into a dream world. The sensitive, refractory boy has as companion a crippled little girl. He is in the habit of beating her, yet he confides to her his most private thoughts. Already the question of the existence of God frets him. "I am God," he tells her, and forces her to worship him. Later, together with the little cripple, he goes to live with his father and stepmother. Accused by her of a theft that he had not committed and whipped by his father, he repudiates him and takes refuge in the servants' quarters. The stepmother has a lover and the boy witnesses their lovemaking. The father knows that his bastard knows that he is a cuckold. Then the boy watches his father being done to death by his own serfs ("Alas, poor ghost!"). Boarding schools: Souchard's, Chermak's (Dostoevsky's old schools). Further humiliations and injustices. The boy despises adults and seeks deliberately to earn their disapproval. He tests himself, and tries to purge himself of fear and strengthen his will. He resolves to become rich in order to gain power and also the right to scorn people. But is power worth having? At moments "the pure ideal of the free man flashes before him." He runs away from school and becomes involved in a murder. Back in Moscow he falls in with a schoolmate, a lad of French parentage and corrupt to the marrow. The two plunge into debauchery. With this companion he steals the jewels set in an icon frame. In court he declares himself an atheist and is committed to a monastery for correction.

The second novel was to be *The Monastery*. Here the routine of monastic life was to be carefully set forth. What a chance to show the strength and beauty of the Russian spirit! All manner of men inhabit monasteries and visit them. There will be an opportunity to introduce monks of militant piety, characters modeled on Belinsky, on Chaadayev, the extreme Westernist, perhaps on Pushkin. But the center of the stage is to be occupied by a saintly old churchman living in retirement and the delinquent boy, "a wolf cub and a Nihilist." An affection grows up between the two, though sometimes the lad torments his aged friend. The latter preaches meekness and extols "the living life," but with little effect. Indeed, the boy's unbelief becomes "organized" in the monastery. He leaves it unregenerate. Still clinging to his dream of wealth as a source of power, he is certain that he is destined to become the greatest of men, and he treats everyone with disdain. What he has learned from his saintly mentor is that in order to conquer the world he must first conquer himself.

The hero has a long, arduous road to travel before he achieves salvation. He yields to the temptations of the intellect as well as to those of the flesh. He commits monstrous crimes and performs highminded deeds. Moved by overweening pride, which alternates with abject humility, he becomes a wandering monk, thus offering the author an opportunity to present a panorama of Russian life.

So much can be gathered, with some difficulty, from the few rough jottings for *The Life of a Great Sinner* extant and from a letter to Maikov. It is also evident that Dostoevsky had a definite idea as to the style that he would use. He would give up his dramatic effects and write with the quiet simplicity that marks the nameless lives of saints that had cast their serene light over his own boyhood. In fact, it was to be just such an edifying story, every incident in it, however vile, carrying some hint of the grace to come, the final victory of the spirit.

Significantly enough, while the outline offers a vigorous sketch of the sinner, the redeemed soul is left blurred and unreal: no acceptable psychological clue to the hero's reformation is given. Whatever Dostoevsky said or felt to the contrary, he was not now, nor was he ever to be, sufficiently at peace to undertake this tranquil and pious tale. Certainly the epic tone was not in accord with the exigencies of his temperament either as a man or a writer. *The Life of a Great Sinner* went unwritten. It remained, however, a source that fed all his subsequent work. Traces of it are present even in the novel of a totally different tenor to which he now turned.

# ( IV )

Dostoevsky was an assiduous reader of the dailies, believing that they held much of interest to the perceptive novelist. It was from the papers over which he habitually pored in the Dresden public library that he learned a staggering piece of news. On November 25, 1869, the body of a young man, with bricks tied to his feet and his head pierced by a bullet, was found in a pond on the grounds of the Moscow Agricultural Academy. The youth was identified as Ivan Ivanov, a student in the school, and the police established the fact that he had belonged to a revolutionary cell. The assassination had been initiated by the moving spirit of the group, one Sergey Nechayev, a disciple of Bakunin, and had been perpetrated with the aid of four other members of the cell. The organization went by the name of The People's Vengeance and its objective was a popular uprising preceded by acts of terror. It happened that Anna's brother, a student at the Agricultural Academy, was visiting Dresden at this time. He had known the victim and was able to give his brother-in-law some details about the event. Murder had an unusual fascination for Dostoevsky, and this one interested him particularly. It was just as he had predicted—Nihilism was bound to result in wanton killing. Here was the very stuff for a book against the rebels. With his eagerness to treat matters of current concern, it is not surprising that he seized upon the murder of Ivanov as crucial to his next novel. Here, avoiding the indirection of the two previous ones, he would expose the danger with which society was threatened by militant Nihilism, regardless of whether or not he met the requirements of fiction. The book was not *The Life of a Great Sinner,* which he had laid aside, but was to be *The Devils.* Thus, like Dreiser's *An American Tragedy,* it is based on an actual occurrence. It is first mentioned in a letter dated February 24, 1870. Dostoevsky felt that he had struck a rich vein, and he was working it with pleasure. He would not try to make it anything more than a pamphlet, by which he meant a vehicle for his most cherished ideas. Once and for all he would pour out his wrath upon the traitors to the Russian people and the Russian God, and let literature go hang.

The new year, 1870, had found the couple without resources, and with many of their belongings in pawn. How would they manage until autumn? They had to keep postponing the baby's baptism because there was no money to pay for the ceremony. At least there was one great expectation: Pasha, yes, the impossible Pasha, armed with power of attorney, was trying to arrange for a separate edition of *The Idiot.* It would mean a thousand rubles! January passed, February . . . had he embezzled the money? Had he lent it to a boon companion? Was he speculating with it on the stock exchange? The oaf who at twenty did not know the multiplication table was always full of wild schemes and crazy ambitions. In desperation Dostoevsky offered a novel to *Zarya,* asking for a sizeable advance. It would be the first part of *The Life of a Great Sinner.* He would do his best with it, even if he had to write it abroad.

By March it transpired that Pasha's negotiations had come to nothing. And Kashpirev, the publisher of *Zarya,* was silent. And the baby was teething. And Maikov had admitted in a letter that *The Eternal Husband* struck him as somewhat forced. So it was plain, then, that he was losing his grip! Life was closing in on him. "I am positively in Mr. Micawber's terrible state," he wrote to Maikov early in April. "Not a kopeck. And there will be no money until autumn." It appears that he was overly pessimistic. As a matter of fact, Kashpirev came across with five hundred rubles. At the end of the month, with part of them in his pocket, he was off to Homburg and the tables, where he lost as usual.

This time Anna's distress was increased by the fact that she had to conceal the nature of his trip both from her mother, who was still with them, and from her brother. In addition to the five hundred rubles, the publisher had promised to remit a hundred monthly. The first remittance having failed to arrive on time, the wolf was soon again at the door, and to make matters worse, the baby took sick. Dostoevsky managed, however, to work away at the novel for Katkov, but his heart was no longer in it. There was some fatal flaw in the thing. He was sorry he had begun it. He would much rather have busied himself with something else. And would *Russky vestnik* print his drivel? If only he could get back to Russia!

Summer brought with it a series of violent attacks, the like of which he had not had for a long time. For a month work was out of the question. When he was able to get back to his desk, he suddenly perceived what was wrong with the novel. And then in a flash he saw a new plot with a new hero. After a fortnight of agonizing indecision he made up his mind: he put aside the entire pile of sheets—over two thousand rubles' worth of copy— and began the whole thing afresh. It was a truly heroic decision. As August had already set in, it was obvious that he would not get through with the novel by Christmas, as he had hoped. In fact, there was no telling when he would finish it. And what of the novel he had promised to *Zarya,* and on which he had taken such a large advance? Well, those people would have to wait or else have their money refunded, whenever he could scrape it together. What was much worse, he had managed to disappoint Katkov, and that after he had solemnly promised to hand in copy in time for publication during the year. Would not the long-suffering man at last tire of his procrastinations and throw him over? In any event, there was to be another winter of exile.

Another winter, besides, of pinching and worrying, and trembling over every thaler. Oh, if he could have an assured livelihood for two or three years, like Turgenev or Tolstoy, he could write a thing about which people would be talking a century hence. His new project was so fine, so rich in meaning, that he was awed by it himself. But he knew he was going to ruin it in his haste and turn out a half-baked product. He had the vision and the fire, but where was leisure and peace in which to shape his stupendous imaginings? Meanwhile, he worked away fiercely. He kept changing the plot and recasting what he had written. It was a task like Penelope's. He piled up such a mountain of notes that he could no longer find his way among them. It was only on October 19 that he was able to send off the first chapters. They appeared in the issue of *Russky vestnik* for January, 1871, as the first installment of *The Devils*. He confided to Sonia that he had rewritten it at least twenty times. When the second installment was printed in February, he was in a state of panic, "trembling like a frightened mouse," as he wrote to Maikov.

Do what he might, the work would not satisfy him. How could he accomplish anything when the hunger for Russia was tearing at his vitals? It terrified him to see what homesickness was doing to Anna. She missed the good black bread, the deep drifts, the creak of the sledges gliding over the hard-packed snow, the booming of the bells, so different from the thin chimes of Western churches. What was worse, she was fretting over affairs at home—the family real estate, a share of which was to come to her, was, she knew, badly mismanaged in her mother's absence. Besides, in Petersburg she might add a bit to their income by doing a little stenography in her spare time. The baby, though amiable and possessed of a healthy appetite, was a drain on her energies, since she nursed it herself and lacked the domestic help that was so easy to secure at home. Dostoevsky was sure that if they were only in Russia, her apathy and exhaustion would vanish.

Communications from home reached him seldom and generally in a roundabout way. The most amazing piece of news was that Pasha was about to be married. It was hard to believe it. What changes these four years must have wrought in the boy! Pasha, steadily employed, settling down, and with a nice girl, too! Dostoevsky was filled with pity and fear when he thought how young the two of them were, how unprepared for their venture, how little he could do in a material way to help them. In reply to what he called Pasha's "romance in several parts," announcing the news, he wrote his stepson a long, tender, if somewhat sententious letter. He warned the young man of the seriousness of the step he contemplated, of the necessity for mutual respect; spoke of the influence of a good woman as a man's "second and final education"; urged him to continue his studies, so as to be worthy of that gifted, cultivated, and lovable man, his father, whom physically he so much resembled.

The bleakness of the winter was increased by the war, which had been raging since July. If the siege of Paris added to the excitement of living, high prices and straitened credits made hardships for everybody, not least for a poverty-stricken foreigner. In the early months of the war Dostoevsky, who was not a pacifist either by nature or conviction, was inclined to look at it with a hopeful eye. Perhaps it would prove a healthy stimulant and, among other things, rescue science from the morass of materialism. Disaster might rouse even the French to new life. Perhaps Russia would begin to see through the Germans and abandon its traditional Germanophile policy. His sympathies were vaguely with the French, not because he liked them more than he did the Germans, but because he hated them a little less. As the war dragged on, month after month, he was increasingly irritated by the jingoism of the people among whom he was living. He heard, so he wrote home, a white-haired savant shout: *"Paris muss bombardiert sein!"* So that was the fine fruit of Western learning. The Prussians owed their victory to their schoolmasters. What an obscene thought! The schoolmasters had raised a generation worthy of Attila.

Sometimes the small shopkeepers with whom he dealt would show him letters their sons had written from the front. It wasn't those sick, hungry lads under fire who were shouting for blood. No, it was the professors, the banner-bearers of culture, who clamored for the triumph of brute force! Who says "young Germany"? On the contrary, a dead people. And France, too, would go to the dogs unless a strict ruler were somehow put into power there. At heart Dostoevsky cried: a plague on both their houses! The future lay with Russia. She must prepare for the inevitable conflict over the Balkan Slavs. She must build strategic roads, fortresses, add at least a million rifles to her equipment, take thought for taxes and military service. (His military education had not been wholly lost on him.) Russia's strength was her spiritual unity. But she must become fully conscious of her high mission, must bring back the true Orthodox faith to a blind world that has denied Christ. The whole of Russian history was an epic of Orthodoxy. True, the present age with the decay of the nobility and the general disintegration that followed the freeing of the serfs was a sad passage. But look ahead two hundred years. Russia would yet spread the gospel of love, though she had to beat her ploughshares into swords to do it. He clung to his convictions with more passion than consistency.

Meanwhile he was struggling like a madman with that savage satire, *The Devils.* He wasn't sure where it would take him, but it was a mighty, exhilarating effort in an otherwise dreary existence. Dresden was as alien to him as when they had first come there. They had made some acquaintances among the many Russians settled in the city. The expatriates only made him feel how far he was from home. It was horrible to find that the children in some families did not know their native tongue. Contacts with the Russian colony were only an annoyance to him. When one compatriot called twice to discuss the state of Russian literature with him he refused to see her. Confound Russian literature! He was killing himself to get his copy out on time for *Russky vestnik.*

# ( V )

This exile must be brought to an end! He had been telling Maikov and others that he had fled abroad to save his health, to escape his creditors. The real reason why Anna had snatched him away from his Petersburg circle had somehow been obliterated from his mind. But now he was willing to face the worst at home rather than endure another year abroad. He had figured that they would need at least seven thousand rubles to return to Russia. Next he set the sum at three thousand, then at two thousand. Now he decided that one thousand must suffice. It might mean debtors' prison, but was that worse than Dresden? He would brave the consequences of the step. There was one circumstance which raised his hopes of securing this sum: it would come from a new edition of *Crime and Punishment,* issued by Stellovsky at the end of 1870. But it soon became clear that the money would not be forthcoming without a lawsuit.

A few weeks before Easter he dreamed that he was talking to Aunt Kumanina in her drawing room when he noticed that the pendulum of the clock had stopped swinging. He went over and pushed it, but after two or three strokes it stopped again. Dostoevsky took his dreams seriously. He recounted this one to an acquaintance, who suggested that he inquire about the old lady, and indeed he soon learned that she had died. As he had long since received his share of the inheritance, this event was of no immediate consequence to him.

Again it was Katkov who saved him. He sent a remittance at Easter and promised the necessary thousand by June. But would the money come in time? Anna was expecting to be confined again in July or August, so that the slightest delay would force them to remain in Dresden and inflict another year of exile upon them. They rejoiced over the baby's coming. This time it must be a boy. They joked happily about the future of "Mr. N.N." But the fear of another year abroad left Dostoevsky too worried to work and he was ill himself. Spring brought on a series of attacks, which were followed by long periods of intolerable spiritual anguish, as was always the case when the seizures came after a long interval. He took one hundred and twenty thalers and went to Wiesbaden.

All fell out as usual: he lost everything and had to beg Anna to send him the fare that would take him home. He swore to himself that he would not risk that money. The day it arrived there was fear in his heart. The previous night he had dreamed of his father, seeing him in the same terrifying guise in which he had appeared on two previous occasions, each time boding calamity. Furthermore, shortly before that he had dreamed that Anna's hair had turned white.

With the fare in his pocket, he wandered into the casino just to watch the play. Ten times running he guessed the outcome correctly. After that, could he hold back? How fine it would be if he could bring home even a small sum! And for a whole year he had been wanting to redeem Anna's earrings. At nine-thirty he left the rooms half crazed: the last pfennig was gone.

He found himself running to the Russian priest: To clear his soul? To confess? He hardly knew. It was dark, the streets were strange, he lost his way. Was this the Russian church? No, it was a synagogue. He was brought up short, went home, and wrote to Anna. He must have another thirty thalers. By what shall he swear that he will not take them to the tables? He has deceived her once. She has the right to despise him. But she must believe him now. He is not utterly mad. Now he will work, work for her, for Liubochka, for "Mr. N.N." One thing is certain: a new life is dawning for them all. A miracle has been vouchsafed him. The abominable fantasy that has tormented him for ten years has been swept away. It had fastened itself upon him, kept him from thinking of his work for nights on end —now he is blessedly free of it, and forever. In the past only half of him had belonged to Anna. The other half had been given to that accursed passion. Now he is wholly hers. Of course, things would not be easy at once. There would again be trips to the pawnshop, but not many. He would write to Katkov. Soon they would be back home and make a fresh beginning.

His only worry was Anna. How would she raise the money again for the fare back, and how would she explain matters to her mother? He made up a story for her to tell the old lady: he had had an attack, soiled the mattress, and in his embarrassment paid for a new one. In his last letter he warned her that as he could not afford meals on the way, he would come home hungry. Would she not have at least a bite ready for him? And, out of Christian charity, also a package of cigarettes?

Anna could not have taken seriously his vows to renounce the tables—she had heard such protestations too often. But this time, as events were to prove, he spoke truly. The mad dream had inexplicably lost its power over him. He never gambled again. Nor did he furnish any clue as to how he found release from his obsession.

When he returned to Dresden, it was hard to resume work. There was the fearful uncertainty as to whether Katkov would send the money in time for them to make the great removal. And along with their private unrest there was the public disturbance of those May weeks. He had foreseen a conflict in France between town and country, and now civil war had indeed broken out, but it was between the Commune of Paris led by communists, socialists, and that crew, on the one hand, and the rest of France, on the other.

Writing to Strakhov two days after the slaughter of the Communards was over and Marshal MacMahon had declared law and order restored, Dostoevsky reflected on the lesson of the Commune. Its failure, he felt, was rooted in the very nature of socialism. Those men had to fail. Not reason, but Christ is the secure foundation for society. The downfall of the West is the direct consequence of the fact that under the tutelage of the Roman Catholic Church He has been forsaken. If Belinsky (how the ghost haunted him!) and his ilk had lived to see the burning of Paris by the Communards, they would have said: "No, that is not what we dreamed of, no, this is a deviation; no, let us wait, light will come, progress will reign, and mankind will rebuild its life on rational principles and be happy!" He would have gone further: he would have blamed the failure of the Commune on nationalism, on its being a *French* Commune. "Foaming at the mouth," he put himself out to make Russia "a *vacant* nation capable of heading a universal cause."

In his, Dostoevsky's, presence Belinsky had cursed Christ in unprintable words. And this stinking little insect did not wonder with whom he would replace Christ. Certainly not with himself and others of his kind, all filled with spite, impatience, irritation, vileness, petty self-love above all. Even as a critic he lacked the true flair.

The venom sputtered from Dostoevsky's pen as he poured himself out to Strakhov. He was like a man wrestling with a demon, like Luther flinging his inkpot at the Devil's head. But this devil was no black fiend with horns and a tail—it was a slender, pale, consumptive little man with big eyes, it was his old mentor, or was it another small, pallid, fervent person—young Fyodor Dostoevsky? He wrote wildly, savagely, with hatred, impatience, irritation, perhaps with self-hate above all.

But now he could forget the Communards and the Catholics, the vapid French and the abominable Germans. They were going home! The money had arrived from Katkov in time. They paid their debts, redeemed their belongings, burnt many of his papers for fear of being held up at the frontier—he was aware that the chief of the Russian secret service had instructed the frontier police to subject his baggage to a thorough search.

On July 8, 1871, they arrived in St. Petersburg. It was a clear, warm day. As they drove past the Trinity Cathedral, where they had been married, they murmured a prayer, and the baby, imitating her parents, made the sign of the cross. In the four years that they had been away, the city had scarcely changed. And what had those years done to him? They had visited him with poverty, isolation, sickness, death, but he saw now that through it all he had lived deeply and intensely. His faith had been tried in those fires. He believed. Or at least he wanted desperately to believe, without apologies or qualifications, in the simple wholehearted fashion of the peasant who worships the miracle-working icon. The future was full of uncertainties. He was practically beginning life again, and that at fifty. Between him and destitution stood sixty rubles and the contents of two trunks. But no matter. He had something to say. A word that clamored for utterance. He had been confirmed in his abomination of the West, his devotion to Russia. If only he had time, if only he had peace in which to shape it!

# 21

# A TORTUOUS TRACT

THE first days at home were hectic. To the fatigues of the journey were added the troubles incidental to settling in a furnished flat. Anna was helpless. The baby needed constant attention. And, of course, there was the descent of friends and relatives. It was pleasant to find that Emilia Fyodorovna was now in reasonably comfortable circumstances, with both her boys earning money. The widow appeared to have come to realize that her brother-in-law had a family of his own to care for. Pasha, on the other hand, though now a married man, still seemed to expect help from his stepfather.

Just a week after their arrival Anna presented her husband with a son, whom they named Fyodor after him. Chaos reigned in the two dingy rooms, which were crowded with the *accouchée,* the infant, the baby, an incompetent domestic, and the harassed father, when he wasn't out running errands. Under these conditions how could he think of work? Especially since he was in momentary expectation of an attack brought on by excitement and lack of sleep.

Gradually matters righted themselves. Katkov was as always a very present help in time of trouble. They were able to rent a small flat on Serpukhovskaya Street and to furnish it on the installment plan. Anna had to buy practically everything: her ·

pots and pans, which had been left with a friend, were gone;
her china and glass, including some precious heirlooms, which
had been deposited with her sister, had been broken by a careless maid; their winter things, left in pawn, had been forfeited
by Mikhail's quondam mistress; Pasha had disposed of the
library, and of the other objects entrusted to his care returned
only two icons minus their silver mountings. He had, after all,
not changed much. He was now proposing that he and his wife
should live with them. He was told to shift for himself. The young
bride, who had known when to snatch her husband away from
his demanding relatives, had learned in the bitter years abroad
how to hold her own against them. Her friends found her aged
and reproached her for her dowdiness. She was indifferent. If
she looked older than her years and was not attractive to other
men, so much the better: it would save Fyodor a jealous pang.
And saving him, guarding him, was her one care.

What she had now chiefly to protect him against was the creditors. As soon as his return became known, they swooped down
upon him. They cursed, they wept, they threatened to attach the
furniture, they talked about debtors' prison. Dostoevsky would
come from an interview with them tearing his hair and on the
verge of an attack. Then Anna took matters in hand and faced
unaided the swarm of boorish retired officers, tearful widows,
and insolent shyster lawyers who had bought up the promissory
notes and were now coming to collect. She explained coolly that
they could not attach the furniture because, being bought on the
installment plan, it still belonged to the shopkeeper, that all the
family possessions were in her name, and that if they chose to
send Dostoevsky to debtors' prison, he would go, and they would
have the pleasure of paying his keep until his time was out, as
was customary.

The creditors gave in and exchanged the promissory notes for
agreements involving payment in installments. Anna was counting on money from real estate which she had inherited earlier,
but of which she was only now to come into possession. Here
was another cruel disappointment. Through the carelessness and
dishonesty of those who had been managing the property for
her, it proved a dead loss. She succeeded in getting stenographic
work, as she had hoped all along, but it was out of town and
she was forced to give it up for the sake of her husband's peace
of mind: he was of too jealous a disposition to tolerate it. He
was perhaps excusing himself when he wrote in *The Brothers*

*Karamazov* that "there are men of noble hearts" among the jealous. As a result all that they had to depend on for their living and the payment of the debts were his literary labors and her managerial skill.

Dostoevsky took more than one flying trip to Moscow to see Katkov, and spent New Year's Eve at his sister Vera's as he had five years previously. How sad and shabby everything was there now! He tried not to dine there in order to avoid adding to the household expenses of the orphaned family. There were his own worries, too, and plenty of indignities, but he was in his element again, at home, among his own, no longer living on print and memories as he had been doing all these years. And at last there were likeminded people with whom he could discuss the ideas about which he felt so strongly. There were Maikov and Strakhov, and he made a few new contacts now. He fell in with Nikolay Danilevsky, whom he had not seen since the days of the Petrashevsky circle. The man had written a remarkable book, *Russia and Europe,* which had stirred Dostoevsky deeply when he read it in Florence. Here was someone who saw eye to eye with him in the matter of the superior genius and high destiny of the Russian people.

As the season wore on Dostoevsky even ventured to give a dinner or two. He regularly attended Prince Meshchersky's Wednesdays at which, among the most distinguished guests he met, was a lean, cool-eyed, scholarly-looking man, Senator Pobedonostzev. The eminent jurist, formerly tutor to the Crown Prince, was to acquire sinister fame as the power behind the Throne when his quondam pupil became Emperor. The fact that this learned dignitary had recently translated *Imitation of Christ* must have made him all the more interesting to Dostoevsky. Indeed, the two were soon on a friendly footing, in spite of a fundamental difference in their natures—Pobedonostzev was a stern, hard, utterly consistent reactionary, "the Russian Torquemada," as he was called by Vicomte de Vogüé of the staff of the French Embassy in St. Petersburg. The Senator, like Dostoevsky, was hostile to the political institutions of the West and to the rationalist spirit informing them. Although the gentry had a place in his scheme of things, he too pinned his faith to the instinctive virtues of the peasantry, which he regarded as the bulwark of the Orthodox Church and the autocratic State. Back of it all was a distrust of human nature, which Dostoevsky shared to a greater extent than he realized.

That first winter brought an impressive proof of the novelist's growing fame. The Moscow Maecenas, Tretyakov, commissioned the already renowned Vasily Perov to paint Dostoevsky's portrait for his private gallery. Before taking up his
brushes, the painter visited the flat on Serpukhovskaya Street
every day for a week. Dostoevsky talked to him freely and by
the time he sat down to pose he was quite at his ease. When
the painting was completed, Anna, who had been present during
the sittings, saw on the canvas not the jealous husband, or the
anxious paterfamilias, or the plagued debtor, or the mad gambler who had made her life more miserable than she was ever
willing to admit. She saw the man whom she would surprise in
his study, so absorbed in his own thoughts that he would afterward deny that she had entered the room. Whatever the merits
of Perov's portrait as a work of art, he produced an authentic
and satisfying image of the novelist: the broad shoulders are
slightly bowed; there is coarse strength in the hands, in spite of
the narrow wrists and long fingers; the face, framed in thinning
hair and a soft straggling beard, is waxen, big-browed, sensitive;
the temples are hollowed, and there are lines of suffering under
the somber, smoldering, inquisitorial eyes—the eyes of a man
bent inward upon himself.

If the winter had its satisfactions and interests, with the turn
of the season fortune turned too. The family gave up their flat
and rented a little house for the summer at Staraya Russa, a
town some hundred and fifty miles away, among the lakes of
the Novgorod province, which, what with the mineral waters
and the bathing, was something of a health resort, and cheap.
They went all this distance not so much for the sake of the
unweaned infant, who might have taken a prize at a baby show,
but for Liuba, who at two and a half was frail and thin, and
whom her father loved "more than anything else in the world."
The day after their arrival they discovered an alarming bump
on her wrist—she had sprained it before they came away. The
local doctor said it was no sprain but a fracture, and the bones
had not grown together properly. There was nothing for it but
to return at once to Petersburg for an operation, leaving the
infant behind to get along as best he could on cow's milk. The
operation went off successfully, and Dostoevsky returned alone
to his two treasures at Staraya Russa: the baby and the manuscript of *The Devils*. During the fortnight that Anna had to stay
in the hospital, watching Liuba every moment to see that she

did not break the cast, she learned that her only sister had died abroad and she had to witness the scene when the news was broken to her mother.

Fretting over how Anna and little Liuba were faring, Dostoevsky was dreadfully unhappy. Staraya Russa was a dirty hole. The people, he wrote to his wife, were "terribly queer, stupid and coarse" (no better than the Germans or the Swiss?). The heavy rains had turned the town into a sea of mud. There was nothing to read. Work was impossible. Life was so boring that if it weren't for the baby he would go mad. He almost regretted the absence of attacks: they would at least be a distraction. The night after he wrote this to Anna he had a violent seizure. He kept on having bad dreams: surely they must be in for a run of ill luck.

Indeed, no sooner did Anna come back to Staraya Russa than she was taken sick and was so sure that she was dying that she said her last farewells to her family. But she recovered, and during the rest of the summer the fates were kind, so that Dostoevsky could keep steadily at his work. Dissatisfied with what he had done on the third (and last) part of the novel, which had occupied him since the beginning of the year, he rewrote it completely. It was only finished in the autumn, and appeared in the issues of *Russky vestnik* for November and December, 1872, after an interval of nearly a year.

# ( II )

When Dostoevsky was back in Petersburg, the trial of the Nechayev group was in progress—immediately after the arrests began Nechayev himself had absconded, and remained in hiding abroad—and the court proceedings were fully reported in the press. Those columns were so much meat for the novelist. They threw ample light on Nechayev's personality and activities.

The son of a seamstress and a house-painter, he was a non-matriculated student. In September, 1869, he had arrived in Petersburg after a stay of several months in Geneva, the foreign base of the Russian underground, such as it was. He bore credentials signed by Bakunin to the effect that he was an agent of the Russian Section of the World Revolutionary Alliance, a figment of the anarchist's imagination. His luggage contained a few incendiary leaflets and a copy of *The Catechism of the Revolutionist,* a pamphlet printed in cipher, presumably Bakunin's work. Quotations from this material appeared in the newspapers. The *Catechism* opens: "The revolutionist is a doomed man. He has no interests, affairs, feelings, attachments of his own, no property, not even a name. . . . He has no regard for the laws, conventions, morals of civilized society. He lives in it solely to destroy this vile order." It is further affirmed that "Whatever promotes the triumph of the revolution is moral. . . ." Lenin will restate this proposition thus: "Morality is what helps destroy the old capitalist society and unite all workers around the proletariat that is building the new society of communists." The aim of the organization is "the liberation and well-being of the masses, that is, the common laborers." Some of the pillars of the established order are to be temporarily spared, so that "by their brutal conduct they may drive the masses to inevitable rebellion." The revolutionist's business is "frightening, complete, ubiquitous, pitiless destruction."

Guided by the *Cathechism,* Nechayev engaged in bringing into existence the imaginary body of which he was the emissary. His plan was to set up cells of five members, who were required to obey orders blindly and spy on one another, and whom he regarded as expendable. The first Russian professional revolutionist, he was a fanatically dedicated, fearless, wholly unscrupulous activist. He pretended to represent a mysterious Central Committee, hedged about with the utmost secrecy and controlling a powerful far-flung hierarchical network of cells. Actually there were perhaps a dozen such cells, and the Central Committee existed only on paper. What did exist was a seal showing an axe as the emblem of the society and bearing the legend: "The Committee of the People's Vengeance, February 19, 1870." This, the ninth anniversary of the emancipation of the serfs, was the date set for the popular uprising.

Ivanov, a refractory youth who was a member of the first cell, had antagonized Nechayev, especially by questioning the existence of the Committee. He may have been suspected of intending treachery. Nechayev's chief motive for executing him is believed to have been the wish to cement the union of the cell members by community of blood-guilt. For some years a few hotheads had been demanding that the enemies of the people be killed. Ironically enough, their first victim was one of their own minute number. The arrests that followed the murder crushed The People's Vengeance.

The reader who turned from his newspaper, in the summer of 1871, to the installments of *The Devils* could not help recognizing in the fictive conspirators a resemblance to the defendants in the sensational trial. In drawing the ringleader, the author undoubtedly used Nechayev as his model. Having left Geneva, young Verkhovensky arrives in the provincial city where the action takes place. He is shown constantly on the go, tirelessly plotting. To undermine the foundations of society, to poison the very springs of Russian life, are the aims of Verkhovensky and his comrades.

The city harbors a small circle, reported to be "a hotbed of libertinism, free-thinking, and godlessness." From this group Verkhovensky recruits five men, the first cell of the prospective secret society that he pretends is already in existence. They are a mixed lot. One is Liputin, a minor official with the reputation of an atheist, a usurer on the side, a domestic tyrant, and an ardent Fourierist. Another is a post office clerk, "the little Yid," Lyamshin, who will eventually inform against his comrades and has other characteristics of the anti-Semitic stereotype of the Jew. The bloody task that these men are to carry out is for the time being unrevealed. Meanwhile they distribute subversive leaflets and otherwise help to throw the town into a turmoil.

By playing the gentleman and parading his social charm, Verkhovensky himself gains entrée to the beau-monde, thereby enlarging the area of his operations. Forthwith he establishes himself as an habitué of the Governor's mansion. The Governor is a pathetic blockhead whom the young man entangles in his net and uses to advance his schemes. Verkhovensky readily makes himself a favorite of the Governor's lady, Yulia Mikhailovna, an early example of the parlor pink. She has set her heart on arranging a grandiose festival for the benefit of the needy governesses of the province. Of course, Verkhovensky plays a leading part in preparing the program and his satellites exert themselves to turn the affair into a scandal.

If the guardians of law and order are shown to be so inept that unwittingly they offer aid and comfort to the enemy, sarcasm and indignation are also meted out to a family of industrial magnates and to members of the upper strata of the landed nobility. The clergy, too, come in for criticism. Almost the only truly religious person in the novel is the crippled servant, Maria.

She has a mystical sense of union with God and His world. This poor creature ends by becoming demented, while continuing to be close to a clairvoyante. Obviously, while *The Devils* is a counter-revolutionary tract, it is scarcely the work of a spokesman for the beneficiaries of the established order. His professions of loyalty to it notwithstanding, his fictions point to disorder and corruption behind the social façade, suggesting upheaval and impermanence.

An anti-Nihilist novel, one of a dozen such by Dostoevsky's lesser contemporaries, this *roman à thèse* is dominated by an anti-liberal, and therefore anti-Westernist, bias. The criticism, directed from the right, is well aimed at some of the failings of the middle-of-the-road position. (Calling *The Devils* a book of current interest, James Baldwin not long ago recommended it to a Northern liberal.)

It was Dostoevsky's firm and enduring conviction that the Nihilists were descendants, according to the spirit, of the liberals of the thirties, who were too deeply concerned for mankind to care either for their country or their God. He abominated them as much as, perhaps more than, he did their progeny. A specimen of the breed is Pyotr Verkhovensky's father, according to the flesh. Ironically enough, he had laid eyes on his son only twice before he appears on the scene as a grown man. Verkhovensky *père* is delineated as a self-important poseur, who pretends to be a public figure under a cloud because of his dangerous views, but is merely the chicken-hearted, slothful hanger-on of the wealthy, domineering widow of General Stavrogin. The bond between them makes for a remarkable novel within the novel. Theirs is one of those ambivalent relationships to which Dostoevsky attached such importance in his conception of the psyche, and of which he was a matchless portrayer. The many pages devoted to the pair offer two of Dostoevsky's finest character studies.

Liberalism is further excoriated in the person of Karmazinov, a literary celebrity on a visit to the city. This finical, disingenuous peacock courts the Nihilists, partly to ingratiate himself with the young, but also to find out when the upheaval is due, in order to have time to sell his lands and escape to his beloved Karlsruhe. The contemporary reader had no difficulty in recognizing Karmazinov as a malicious caricature of Turgenev, drawn with a pen dipped in poisonous spittle.

# ( III )

The narrative is in large part a bystander's chronicle of events, made in ignorance of what is going on behind the scenes, which contributes to the murkiness of the atmosphere. The chronicler generally shares the viewpoint of the author. More than Dostoevsky's other major fictions dealt with so far, *The Devils* is bewilderingly complex. It is as rich in melodrama as any Gothic thriller. There is no less blood spilt than in an Elizabethan drama, what with a duel, two suicides, six murders, one of them a lynching, and arson to boot. Some of the intrigues, matrimonial as well as political, are jerrybuilt, and the whole is enveloped in an aura of mingled suspense and mystery, the surprising and the ominous.

The characters vary greatly, alike in their social backgrounds and in their personalities. Weird eccentrics who go to extremes intellectually and emotionally are presented with such vigor that they assume credibility. Like every good novelist, Dostoevsky was able to identify himself with the most diverse sorts of men and women. Rebels in particular fascinated him as much as they repelled him. The fact is more in evidence here than in any of his other novels. This is at once a work of political fiction and a novel of felt ideas. They bear on the ethical, metaphysical, basically religious matters with which the author was deeply concerned. The two disparate subjects are closely interwoven. The account of the revolutionary conspiracy captained by Verkhovensky is linked with the story of that attractive, demoniac, enigmatic character, Nikolay Stavrogin. He may be regarded as the chief protagonist of *The Devils*. "Stavrogin is everything" reads a preliminary jotting for the story.

The only child of Varvara Petrovna, during his most malleable years he was the pupil and admirer of the elder Verkhovensky. The young man is cloaked in mystery. The rumor is that, as an officer of the most exclusive Guard regiment, he engaged in riotous living with shocking viciousness, and flung himself into debauchery so perverse that he could have taught the Marquis de Sade a thing or two. Then he withdrew from the fashionable society of the capital to associate with riffraff, wallow in mud, essay crime, simply to escape from the vacuity of his life. During this period the brilliant young aristocrat entered into a secret marriage with the servant girl, Maria, crippled and feebleminded, who was covertly in love with him. He gave no satisfactory explanation of this inconceivable marriage, which was never consummated. Did it titillate him to outrage peoples' sense of the fitness of things? Was it a sadomasochistic experiment? A monstrous practical joke? After a short stay at home, where he at first behaved like a gentleman and then like a nasty lunatic, Stavrogin left for foreign parts, remaining abroad three years.

His diverse occupations there, like those in the capital, are carried on offstage, as it were. While in Paris, he engages the affections of two girls: the beautiful heiress, Liza, in whom Mme. Stavrogina sees a most desirable match for her Nikolay, and her attractive foster daughter, Darya, the child of her deceased footman. Stavrogin would like to make a conquest of Liza, with whom he is not in love. As for Darya, he looks down on this gentle, self-effacing soul, who hopes only for a chance to serve him. Nevertheless, he makes her his confidante. Varvara Petrovna, suspecting that her son is seriously involved with Darya, decides to marry off the girl to the elder Verkhovensky, telling herself that this will be best for all concerned. She assures Darya that her future husband will love her because he ought to. The girl consents to the marriage, and so does Mme. Stavrogina's pensioner. But then he conceives the idea that he is being used to cover the consequences of an affair between his bride-to-be and his former pupil. He writes to his son, begging him to come and save him from the disgrace. The very day young Verkhovensky appears on the scene he maliciously lets Varvara Petrovna know about the letter. Infuriated, she sends the father packing, only to relent later and agree to raise his pension, on condition that he make a speech at the charity fête.

Stavrogin arrives in town the same day as Verkhovensky. The former despises the latter and cares nothing about the revolution. Nevertheless, in Geneva, with time on his hands, he had rendered some services to the cause, and was considered a fellow traveler.

At that time he had seen much of Alexey Kirillov, an engineering student. Though indifferent to public matters and also deeply religious, he was a member of the secret society. The question of the existence of God had "tormented" him, he said, all his life. (This echoes Dostoevsky's confession in a letter to Maikov, dated April 6, 1870.) When Kirillov's talks with Stavrogin turned to religion, the latter firmly maintained that God did not and could not exist. To one familiar with Nihilist thinking, the proposition can hardly have been new. Stavrogin lent it fresh vigor, and he may also have planted in his friend's mind the seed of ultimate rebellion, what the sophisticated theologian Father Sergey Bulgakov was to call "anti-theism." All through history, Kirillov asserted, man had been inventing God to protect himself from the horror of extinction. But, he, Kirillov, would destroy the very idea of deity. Yet without this idea, existence is unthinkable and unbearable for him. The void must be filled: if there is no God, he, Kirillov, is God. This is not the megalomania of a child or a Caligula. Man-god does not claim the powers of the deity whom he has supplanted. The sole attribute of his godhead is self-will, absolute freedom. This is a terrible freedom, for his only way of manifesting it is by voluntarily surrendering his life.

Accordingly, Kirillov decides to kill himself. By another mammoth non sequitur, he reaches the conclusion that his self-crucifixion, parodying Christ's, will be an object lesson, teaching his fellow men how to achieve divinity. Will this depopulate the planet? No, Kirillov declares that all humanity will enter into glory and undergo a physical transformation. For man in his present state—here as elsewhere Dostoevsky was anticipating Nietzsche—is a creature to be transcended. Stavrogin was to describe his former disciple justly as a great-souled man who was out of his mind. With all respect to the late French philosopher, it must be said that when Albert Camus termed Kirillov's suicide logical and pedagogical, he was having an adventure in the absurd.

Kirillov did not conceal his resolution from his comrades. They seized upon the idea that should the organization be responsible for a crime, and the police look for the culprit, this crackpot of theirs could serve the cause by taking his own life, leaving a note in which he would assume the blame. He accepted the proposal. His one condition was that he kill himself on Russian soil. He departed for the provincial town which was the scene of most of the action, and there held himself in readiness.

Stavrogin also influenced another intense, serious young man. This Ivan Shatov, Darya's brother, had been expelled from the university for participating in disturbances there. A born follower, he sat at the feet of Stavrogin and took his solemn dicta for gospel. It is in the limited fanatical mind of the disciple that some of the cardinal articles of Dostoevsky's credo, including, of course, the idea of Russian messianism, find permanent lodgment. It was a passing fancy with Stavrogin; it is the rock of faith for his dull follower. This uncouth plebeian is possessed of complete integrity, ferocious earnestness, and a strong will to believe, but he is a man who, like Kirillov, is "swallowed by an idea." For a short period he was nevertheless a member of a secret society, but soon resigned from it. The comrades insisted that he render one last service by taking a printing press to Russia and keeping it in a safe place until called for. Reluctantly, he agreed.

As Shatov and Kirillov were on friendly terms, they learned that while Stavrogin was "sowing the seeds of God and the Fatherland" in the heart of one of them, he was simultaneously encouraging the other to deny and, in spite of denial, revolt against God. As Stavrogin affirmed later, he was lying to neither of them. In diversely indoctrinating these two men, was he arguing with himself? "In trying to persuade you," he told Shatov, "I was perhaps more concerned with myself than with you." In any case, so powerful is the spell that he casts on both that Kirillov long reveres him and he remains on the pedestal set up for him in Shatov's mind.

# ( IV )

On his return from abroad Stavrogin contributes to the action proper of the novel. It proceeds at breakneck speed. Events crowd the few days allotted to the narrative. Coincidences assist the climaxes, which are apt to end in catastrophe.

Some of Verkhovensky's feverish activities in furtherance of the conspiracy have been mentioned. As for Stavrogin, he behaves, unexpectedly, like a decent human being, but at bottom he is apathetic. Unexpectedly, too, he discloses his marriage to the half-witted crippled servant. One evening he calls on Kirillov to ask him to act as his second in a duel that had been forced upon him. Incidentally, he does not shoot, saying that he had shed enough blood. He finds Kirillov blithely playing ball with an eighteen-month-old baby. Kirillov declares that there is no death and reaffirms his decision to commit suicide. Stavrogin takes this with a smile, but neither mocks him nor attempts to dissuade him from his purpose.

That same night Stavrogin visits Shatov, to warn him that his life is in danger and that Verkhovensky's aim is to have him done away with. Shatov is too scornful of the plotters to take the matter seriously. In the long dialogue that follows he recapitulates what his visitor had taught him back in Geneva, turning it into an arch-chauvinistic pietist doctrine, bordering on that later professed by the Black Hundreds. When Stavrogin puts the blunt question to his disciple: "Do you believe in God?" he receives the frantic answer: "I believe in Russia. . . . I believe in her Orthodoxy. . . . I believe in the body of Christ. . . . I believe that the Second Coming will take place in Russia. . . . I believe. . . ." Stavrogin insists: "And in God? In God?" Shatov can only stammer: "I . . . I will believe in God." Is this an indirect acknowledgment of the infirmity of Dostoevsky's own faith and his terrible need of that faith?

Stavrogin admits that he is an atheist, but Shatov cannot tear him out of his heart. He still sees him as potentially the standard-bearer of "the Russian idea." Rising against his idol, Shatov calls him to account with regard to his monstrous marriage and the rumor that he had "decoyed and corrupted children." At the close of the dialogue the rebellious disciple urges his false teacher, just as Sonia urged Raskolnikov, to kiss the earth that he has defiled, water it with tears, and ask forgiveness. A clarifying commentary on this admonition may be gathered from the words of that pitiful sybil, Stavrogin's "wife," to the effect that Mother Earth is really the same as the Mother of God, and that from the tears with which men water the earth springs joy.

When he leaves, Stavrogin makes his way to the quarters on the outskirts of the city where his wife lives with her brother. He offers to take her away with him. But the poor creature is now completely demented. She does not recognize her husband, her "prince," and chases him out with a curse.

Shortly afterward Stavrogin consents to grace the clandestine meeting called by Verkhovensky. It is attended by "the flower of the reddest liberalism of the town," along with the Five, as well as the reluctant Shatov and Kirillov. After some footless discussion, the floor is given to Shigalyov, who announces his unfinished plan for the society of the future. Mankind is to be divided into two parts: say, one tenth, a dictatorial elite, enjoys freedom and limitless power over the others, who become a contented, submissive herd. A voice is raised in protest, but Shigalyov insists that this alone is the way to bring about paradise on earth. There is laughter. Verkhovensky, who has been contemptuously trimming his nails, now remarks that he has not come for idle talk, but on serious business. Actually, his purpose is to compromise Shatov. He manages to do so by making him appear a probable informer. Stavrogin's suspicions are confirmed.

The meeting over, Verkhovensky has a long talk with Stavrogin. The former has conceived a scheme for having Stavrogin's wife and her brother murdered by Fedka, the local thug, a believing Christian (this escaped convict is sketched in with matchless skill). Verkhovensky knows that Maria's brother, an agent of the secret society, had written to the Governor offering to disclose the details of the conspiracy for a consideration. Thus Verkhovensky would dispatch an informer and put Stavrogin in his debt, while implicating him in the crime: he is to supply the necessary money. Verkhovensky represents the plan as one for merely shipping the pair out of the city.

Stavrogin is not hoodwinked. He refuses to make the cash available and will have nothing further to do with the man. But Verkhovensky pleads with him stubbornly. In the belief that Stavrogin lusts for Liza, he offers to act as pander. And he agrees to spare Shatov. With an enthusiasm bordering on frenzy he talks of the revolution that the two of them could make together. Stavrogin wants to be left out of it: let him make use of Shigalyov instead. At the meeting Verkhovensky had dismissed Shigalyov's plan as rubbish; now he calls him a genius, like Fourier, "only bolder, stronger." But the man's plan, he adds, is an ideal, a matter for the future. Attention must be centered on the impending overturn. This is Verkhovensky's obsession. The sober, shrewd conspirator holds forth on that subject like a semimadman, as Stavrogin puts it. Confidently he details the ways in which people are speeding the disintegration of the country that prepares the ground for the upheaval. He is content to play second fiddle to the leader of the revolution. That role he assigns to Stavrogin, as an aristocrat possessed of "a magnificent, despotic will, such as men idolize," and with "an extraordinary aptitude for crime." Verkhovensky, like Shatov, is not quite ready to recognize that his idol has feet of clay.

For all his preoccupation with trying to win over Stavrogin, Verkhovensky has other fish to fry. For one thing, he has to assure the collapse of the charity fête. It consists of a literary matinée, followed by a bal masqué. The conspirators assisted by the riffraff of the town, shrewdly manage to turn it into a scandal, with vulgarity and hooliganism rampant. The whole performance, which gives the author the opportunity to display his gift for comedy and grotesquery, has an ominous aura. The elder Verkhovensky contributes to the fiasco with the speech that he had promised Varvara Petrovna to make. He throws down the gauntlet to the fashionable Nihilist ideas, declaring that Shakespeare and Raphael are "higher" than chemistry. Reduced to hysteria by an avalanche of indignant and scurrilous outcries, he raises his arms, curses the audience, and departs, leaving bedlam behind.

The ball, a wretched affair, is interrupted by a vast conflagration, which is the work of several locked-out factory hands, instigated by the conspirators, and the fête ends disastrously. Verkhovensky has engineered the murder of Maria and her brother that he had been planning. Contrary to his expectation, the house where their dead bodies and that of a servant were lying escapes the flames. Verkhovensky, having also persuaded Liza of Stavrogin's passion for her, gets her to his quarters just before the opening of the ball. They spend the night together. The next morning there is a vehement exchange between them which only beclouds the situation in a manner not foreign to the author. When, a little later, they hear of Maria's murder, Liza demands to know if he is implicated. He admits that he is morally responsible, since he took no steps to prevent it, whereupon she leaves, and makes her way to the house where the murders were committed. There she finds a mob, which lynches her as "Stavrogin's woman."

More blood flows.

The evening after the calamitous fête, Verkhovensky summons the members of the cell and informs them peremptorily that the time has come for the execution of Shatov. Their consent follows upon his disclosure of Kirillov's promise.

That very evening Shatov's estranged wife returns to him from abroad and the next day is delivered in his bare room of her child, begotten by Stavrogin. The reconciliation of the couple and Shatov's acceptance of the infant with awe and ecstatic joy are made present to the reader so compellingly that the incredibility of it all is erased. The conspirators, on learning of Shatov's changed circumstances, are overcome by doubt as to

whether he will now play the informer. Verkhovensky is adamant. Shatov, in his exalted state, is utterly without suspicion.
The assassination is carried out in a manner closely approxi-
mating that of the murder of Ivanov by the Nechayev group.
The pathos of the situation is heightened by the fact that the
crime is perpetrated a few hours after the victim has had his
first delighted glimpse of the baby. Dostoevsky spoils the unforgettable passage by piling Pelion on Ossa in the way of
melodrama. Panic-stricken by Shatov's absence, the newly delivered woman, in spite of her condition and the evil weather,
wanders through the streets looking for him, with the infant in
her arms. As a result, the two die within a few days of each other.

Verkhovensky wastes no time in finding Kirillov. He fulfills
his vow and shoots himself. The scene of the suicide has a
uniquely nightmarish quality. Of course, the act is futile. Not
even Verkhovensky profits by the would-be epoch-making event.
The police are not misled by the suicide note. Kirillov's fate is,
of course, intended as an object lesson in the death-dealing effect
of atheism. Curiously, alone Verkhovensky, the arch-Nihilist,
crosses the border and escapes scot free.

While violence was being heaped on violence, Verkhovensky
*père* was in the throes of preparing to leave the city. He had
told Varvara Petrovna that after delivering his speech he would
receive nothing further at her hands, but revering her disinterestedly would end his life as a tutor in a merchant's family or
die of hunger by the roadside. Indeed, the dawn after the fire
finds him trudging along the highroad, "in search of Russia."
Taken ill, the wanderer is lodged in a village inn, where he is
cared for by a woman who peddles the Gospels. She reads him
the passage from Luke on the devils entering into the swine—
the second epigraph of the novel. It flashes upon the dying man
that this is a parable of Russia. The country has long been
possessed by unclean spirits: his son and the like, and perhaps
himself at the head of them; but, as in the Book, they will enter
into the swine, which will cast themselves from a steep place
into the sea and be drowned. But the sick man will be healed
and sit "at the feet of Jesus . . ." and all will look at him in
amazement. Thus, the author grants the old sinner a more or
less Christian passing. What is more, Dostoevsky allows him
to voice the sanguine forecast which puts finis to the book as
political fiction. The novelist is careful to point out that Salvation will come "from on high." The Russian scene as painted

in *The Devils* offers little evidence that exorcism of Nihilist demons can be consummated without divine intervention.

In the letter accompanying the copy of the novel that he presented to the Heir Apparent, the future Alexander III, Dostoevsky wrote that his book was "almost a historical study." Nothing could be further from an adequate description of *The Devils*. The author had neither the historian's cast of mind nor the competence of a chronicler of the Russian revolutionary underground as it existed in the sixties and early seventies. The movement was then in its infancy. Drawing on his memories of the Utopian, chiefly Fourierist, dreamers with whom he had associated in his youth, on second-hand information about later clandestine activities, and on press reports of the Nechayev trial, he produced an anachronistic, distorted, venomous lampoon. Swayed by fear and fury, he painted imaginary devils he was out to exorcise. Verkhovensky, with his mania for destruction and his mad obsession about seizing power over half the world, is represented as embodying the essence of militant Nihilism in all its loathsomeness. But Nechayev, on whom, or rather, on a more odious version of whom, he is modeled, was a wholly atypical figure in the radical camp. His comrades severely condemned his views and tactics. Bakunin, who had been fascinated by this "tiger cub," turned vehemently against him. The International Workingmen's Association denounced him. One of his accomplices offered to act as a decoy, so that the man could be arrested abroad and brought to justice; another volunteered to assassinate him and go back to prison.

Not a conservative by nature, Dostoevsky kept returning compulsively to what he called Nihilism, and, with a hostility that savors of a renegade, he maliciously misrepresented both the goals and the strategies of the early radicals. Their thin ranks consisted mostly of idealistic young people with an aching social conscience. At the risk of prison or deportation to Siberia, they were shortly to engage in a peaceful campaign of carrying to the peasantry the gospel of "communism in bast shoes" under the banner of "Land and Liberty." Scarcely anyone was reading Fourier or busy drawing blueprints for the millennium. To charge the Nihilists with approving a scheme like Shigalyov's was preposterous. Only a handful favored the seizure of political power by a cabal. What figures in the novel as a revolutionary leaflet reads: "Hurry and close the churches, do away with God, break the marriage vow, abolish the rights of inheritance, get your knives." This bears little resemblance to the actual propaganda material. The revolutionists did not preach adultery or community of wives, as is hinted in *The Devils*. Moreover, the outpouring of idealism that marked the first stages of what was termed "the liberation movement" was sometimes associated with devout Christian faith.

The picture of militant Nihilists at work presented in *The Devils* is all in Dostoevsky's prejudiced mind. Yet in the light of recent Russian history the novel may be read as a blurred omen of the upheaval that occurred nearly half a century later and of its consequences. In this connection a remark of Shigalyov's has often been quoted: "Starting with complete freedom, I arrive," he admits sheepishly, having outlined his scheme for bringing about Paradise on earth, "at unlimited despotism." Verkhovensky's prediction that the coming overturn will be an outbreak "such as the world has never seen before" suggests prescience on the author's part. So, too, does the ringleader's choice of the leader of the revolution. Stavrogin, who abominates the Nihilists, declares: "All of them, because of their ineptitude, are terribly fond of accusing people of spying." Point is given to this observation by Soviet paranoid preoccupation with espionage. A peripheral figure, a convert to the revolutionary cause, throws out one of his icons, chops up another with an axe, and lights candles on a lectern before the works of Vogt, Moleschott, and Büchner which furthered the spread of materialistic and anti-religious views in the Russia of the day. It is not farfetched to credit Dostoevsky with the intuition that the new order would embrace militant atheism.

The specific prognostications set forth in his non-fictional writings are, however, severely damaging to his reputation as a seer. Yet there is a grain of truth in the declaration of Dmitry Merezhkovsky (who was to become a staunch enemy of Bolshevism) during the abortive uprising of 1905–06 that the author of *The Devils* was "the prophet of the Russian revolution." The novel found a place in the literary arsenal of the anti-Bolshevik camp and was long on the radical blacklist. Although it is included in the two post-revolutionary editions of Dostoevsky's collected works, the book has never been reprinted separately in the Soviet Union.

# ( V )

The novel has yet another finale, which is more in keeping with
its substance and which brings Stavrogin's career to a close. Some
time after the terrible events related above, he decides to settle
in Switzerland, where he had been naturalizd. He does not leave
without writing to Darya, asking her to join him. His letter
offers a self-estimate which, however illuminating, does not quite
solve the enigma of his personality. He will expatriate himself
because in Russia, as elsewhere, but in Russia especially, everything is alien to him. He has limitless strength but cannot find
anything to apply it to. Incapable of faith, he can neither affirm
nor deny. He derives pleasure equally from good and evil, but
it is a small pleasure. He warns Darya that though she is dear
to him, he can only offer her a love as petty as himself. He ought
to sweep himself off the face of the earth like a vile insect. But,
unlike Kirillov, he cannot commit suicide. It would be the last
in a long series of deceptions, for it would argue a despair he is
unable to feel. Stavrogin overcomes this scruple and hangs himself.

While the novel was still in embryo Dostoevsky imagined him
as a man with immense spiritual energy which, for lack of an
objective, made his whole life one of "storm and disorder."
Should he be drawn as a lost soul, ending as a suicide? Or perhaps at the last he would be redeemed, like "the Great Sinner,"
possibly through contact with some pious recluse, and become
"a new man." Though the novelist chose the former plan, for
all his insistence, the reader cannot quite credit Stavrogin's impotence of spirit or his complete depravity. Dostoevsky's con-
demnation of his hero is akin to Milton's judgment on Lucifer,
whom he could not help making attractive. "It is difficult not to
hate Stavrogin," Berdyayev wrote, "and it is impossible not to
love him." Stavrogin's tragedy is presented as but another symptom of the disease with which a godless generation was afflicted.
The descendant of a long line of gentlemen, because he had no
roots in the native soil, no bond with the people and their faith,
the novelist would have us believe, he was unable to take his place
among the living, was, indeed, damned.

The momentous dialogue between him and Shatov ends with
the latter advising the other man, for the good of his soul, to go

and see the retired Bishop Tikhon, who was living in a local monastery. In the novel nothing further is heard of the matter. But Dostoevsky did write the scene in which Stavrogin visits the venerable recluse. Interestingly enough, this spiritual counselor is himself a man of imperfect faith, who holds that outright atheism is "more honorable" than indifference. So, too, Coleridge had noted that "to doubt has more of faith, nay even to disbelieve—than that blank negation of all such thoughts and feelings which is the lot of the Herd of the Church and Meeting Trotters." What brought the young man to the bishop's cell was the need to confess an unspeakable, a criminal sin, the memory of which had been ceaselessly tormenting him. He handed the confession to Tikhon in the form of a printed statement.

His avowal opens with an incident involving a gentle little freckled girl in her twelfth year, Matryosha, daughter of the couple from whom, during his stay in Petersburg, he rented a room for assignation purposes. One day he tells the landlady that he cannot find his penknife. Suspecting that the child had stolen it, the woman flogs her brutally before his eyes. He finds the knife, but says nothing about it and stealthily disposes of it. Then, as he savors a perverse pleasure crossed by the sense of his baseness, he is stung by desire. At the time he had a mind to blow everything up, without any malice, just out of boredom. He had previously distracted himself by reading up on theology. Several days later he returns to the house and finds Matryosha alone. The little girl's sensuality, which he arouses, moves him to revulsion and pity, but only for a moment. He rapes the child. She is abruptly left alone, horrified, and crushed by the belief that she has committed a mortal sin.

The folowing morning he is drawn to the scene of the crime. Matryosha, panic-stricken, keeps out of sight. Obviously, she has told no one and continues to keep the secret. She is taken ill. Learning that he would find her alone one evening, unaccountably to himself he goes to the house. She gets up from her sickbed, appears on the threshold of his room, and threatens him with her little fist, her face betraying utter despair. He tries to speak to her as though nothing had happened. She moves away and disappears in a cubicle near the toilet. He remains in his room in a state of terror, haunted by a foreboding that something fatal is brewing. Finally he goes over to the cubicle and with pounding heart peers through a crack in the wall. He sees what he vaguely anticipated: she has hanged herself.

He remembered the episode, the confession goes on, with no more than vexation. There was nothing to link him to the child's suicide. His subsequent stay at home and his extensive travels abroad wiped the evil memory from his mind, until one day, waking from an afternoon nap during which he had had an enchanting dream of the Golden Age, a trick of association recalled the whole incident to him, particularly the way Matryosha, haggard and feverish, in pitiful despair had threatened him with her fist. Thereafter he knew no peace. To rid himself of the obsession, which, he feared, would drive him mad, he wrote his confession and had it printed, intending to give it wide publicity.

While shocked by Stavrogin's confession, Father Tikhon, who, like so many diverse people, is attracted by him, also recognizes that it is an act of challenge rather than of Christian penitence. His last word is the horrified prediction that the offender is on the road to another crime, in order to avoid making public acknowledgment of this one, as he had planned.

The chapter entitled "At Tikhon's" was rejected by the magazine as too unsavory. Early in 1872, while Dostoevsky was driving from one creditor to another, he kept devising versions of the confession that would not offend "the chastity of the editorial office." But none of them proved acceptable, nor did those pages appear when *The Devils* was issued in book form. The novelist must have had reasons other than the publishers' or the public's squeamishness for omitting the chapter. What they were is a matter for conjecture. Perhaps Stavrogin's attempted confession argued an active sense of right and wrong out of keeping with the picture of a man beyond redemption that Dostoevsky had painted.

# ( VI )

In the spring of 1908 the Russian papers carried accounts of the sensational trial of a certain Duloup, an instructor of French in several of the more select Petersburg schools, who was charged with raping a ten-year-old girl. In connection with the case the name of the author of *The Devils* was mentioned, with apologies, and some old gossip about him found its way into print. According to one story, the novelist, following with morbid fascination the trial of a man accused of the same offense, came to identify himself with the criminal. "There were moments," he is reported to have said, "when it seemed to me that the accused got into the dock by mistake, and that it was not he but I who had outraged the little girl, although I had never before laid my eyes on the unhappy child." As the proceedings drew to an end he found himself under compulsion to victimize the little girl in his turn, and indeed, when the trial was over, he carried out his purpose. Overcome with remorse, he opened his heart to an old friend, who advised him to do penance by confessing the crime to the man whom he hated most, and so Dostoevsky made a clean breast of it to Turgenev. The tale is supposed to have been circulated by Dostoevsky's schoolmate, that scandalmonger Grigorovich.

Another story had it that at a large gathering, the discussion turning on shameful acts committed by decent people, Dostoevsky told about a man who got into talk with a governess on the street and then seduced both her and her young charge. "That scoundrel," he is said to have blurted out, "was I." Dostoevsky's reputed pedophilic offense is said to have been frequently mentioned in literary circles during the eighties. It was alleged to have occurred before his arrest.

These rumors would not merit attention were it not that two years after the novelist's death the same damaging allegation was made by none other than Strakhov, Dostoevsky's intimate, the companion of his travels, the chief contributor to his reviews, the witness to his second wedding, the friend of the household, the man to whom Dostoevsky's widow entrusted the labor of preparing, in collaboration with Orest Miller, the official *Life and Letters* of her husband. Upon the publication of the book Strakhov sent a copy of it to an acquaintance with a note in which he remarked that the task, which had been more or less forced upon him, had been a good deal of a burden. He also sent a copy to his friend Leo Tolstoy, and followed it up with a letter, dated November 28, 1883. Herein he confessed that while working on the book he had had to combat a feeling of disgust for his subject, and closed with a resigned admission that the performance was simply another piece of eulogistic cant. After portraying his late friend as a dissolute, vicious creature, who "dearly loved himself alone," he wrote: "He was drawn to abominations, and he boasted of them. Viskovatov began telling me how he boasted that in a bathhouse he . . . a little girl brought to him by her governess."

This astounding document was not published until 1913, when

both correspondents were in their graves, and was first brought to the attention of Dostoevsky's widow a year later. The devotion she had borne her husband when he was alive had long since turned into idolatrous worship of his memory. She had once described him to Tolstoy as "the kindest, the tenderest, the most intelligent and generous man" she had ever known. Naturally Strakhov's portrait appeared to her a monstrous calumny, the work of malice and envy, perhaps the belated revenge for a slight put upon him by the dead. She says as much in her posthumously published reminiscences, where she deals with Strakhov's letter, while ignoring the other versions of the rumor. Of course she indignantly denies his charge of perversity. To satisfy such a craving, she argues, one must be a rich man, and that her Fyodor had never been. And how absurd to drag in Professor Viskovatov, a casual acquaintance who had never even been in the house! The story goes back to a variant of "Stavrogin's Confession," she suggests, pointing out that when Katkov rejected the chapter in its original form, Dostoevsky rewrote it, introducing a governess and a bathhouse, and then read it to some friends, Strakhov among them. They advised him against this version too, on the grounds that to implicate a governess in so hideous an affair would be to lay himself open to the charge of attacking the movement for the emancipation of women. And it was thanks to this piece of fiction, she concludes, that Strakhov ascribed Stavrogin's crime to Dostoevsky!

The widow is candid enough in her memoirs, but inclined to emphasize the brighter parts of the picture. Thus, she passes over in silence the murder of her father-in-law, of which she could scarcely have been ignorant. In any event, no trace of the variant of "Stavrogin's Confession" that she mentions has been discovered so far. As for the cost of gratifying the perverse desire, it could not have been great: a contemporary points out that the shameful traffic went on openly in the Petersburg "Passage," the arcade where, any night, Dostoevsky might have seen little girls as wretched as those who had wrung his heart in the Haymarket on his London visit. Further, even if Strakhov was, as Dostoevsky felt in his latter years, a fair-weather friend, capable of treachery, it is difficult to believe that he willfully twisted the facts with a view to defaming the dead man in the eyes of posterity. There are no plausible motives for his bringing falsely so grave a charge against his late companion, in a letter addressed to the master whom he venerated.

At the same time Strakhov's letter, though apparently sincere, is of doubtful value as evidence. The allegation it contains is plainly a piece of hearsay, omitting all reference to place and time, and not even completed: "Viskovatov *began* telling me. . . ." Viskovatov was a professor at the University of Dorpat who seldom came to Petersburg and whom Dostoevsky seems to have disliked. It is not even certain that he had the story at first hand. But assuming that Dostoevsky did thus unbosom himself to the man, it is still open to question whether he was confessing an act he had committed or indulging his morbid fantasy.

Strakhov's letter in itself is a psychological puzzle. Three days after Dostoevsky's funeral he had been writing to Tolstoy in quite a different tone: "In his [Dostoevsky's] presence I longed to be both wise and good, and the deep respect we felt for one another, in spite of foolish misunderstandings, was, as I see, extremely dear to me." Were these sentiments merely in the nature of a conventional wreath laid on the grave, and withering as soon? Certainly it is hard to reconcile them with the ugly effigy of the man he presented two years later. Perhaps this was as much the product of blind emotion as the widow's glorification of her late espoused saint. In spite, then, of the weight Strakhov's name lends to the charge, it must be considered not proved.

It may well be that, as the widow suggested, the ugly rumor arose simply in connection with the suppressed chapters of *The Devils,* either as they now stand or in some other form that has not come down to us. But here, too, proof is lacking. Surely there is some significance in the fact that Dostoevsky here presents so nakedly intimate a picture of this perversion, and further, that the same motif crops up in his writings with a curious persistence.

The theme is first adumbrated in a story written when he was only twenty-seven, "A Christmas Tree and a Wedding," where a middle-aged man casts guilty glances at a little girl still playing with dolls. When the novelist was courting Anna Korvin-Krukovskaya in the winter of 1865 he entertained the ladies of the family one day by relating a scene from a tale he had sketched out in his youth. He imagined, he said, a comfortably situated middle-aged man waking up one morning and plunging into pleasant reveries; suddenly in the midst of this agreeable occupation the man becomes vaguely troubled; his apparently baseless uneasiness grows; something hovers tantalizingly on the edge of his consciousness and vanishes before he can seize it; abruptly the recollection flashes upon him: years earlier, after a night of debauch, spurred on by drunken companions, he had violated a child. In *The Insulted and Injured,* little Nellie is in the clutches of a procuress and barely escapes being victimized by a middle-aged pervert. The depraved Svidrigailov in *Crime and Punishment* is said to have outraged a girl of fourteen who ended by killing herself. The night before he shoots himself, in a state between sleeping and waking he sees the familiar face of a fourteen-year-old girl who lies in her coffin: ". . . she had destroyed herself, crushed by an insult that had appalled and amazed that childish soul. . . ." The meaning of this fantasy is underscored by his subsequent nightmare. In *The Eternal Husband* the middle-aged cuckold contemplates marriage to a schoolgirl, and like Svidrigailov is represented as a man whose sensuality is aroused by innocence and immaturity. Again, in *A Raw Youth,* the same inclination is vaguely ascribed to Versilov. According to a preliminary note for the novel, he seduces his thirteen-year-old step-daughter, who eventually hangs herself. To judge by the notes for *The Brothers Karamazov,* Dostoevsky had at one time intended to make Dmitry Karamazov guilty of Stavrogin's crime.

Why did the novelist choose this particular offense as a symbol of evil? Why was he haunted by it? The morbid sexual act may have been a fantasy of his, with the incidental effect of intensifying his sense of guilt. In *The Brothers Karamazov* the prosecutor observes that epileptics are "tormented by pangs of conscience, often without cause; they exaggerate and often invent all sorts of faults and crimes." Holding that "epilepsy is apt to be associated with moral perversity," Havelock Ellis writes that Dostoevsky had "manifold perverse impulses." It is not necessary to conclude, however, he adds, that the novelist "carried morbid impulse to completed action." Wilhelm Stekel states that the epileptic fit is a substitute for a crime, "or, it may be, for a sexual act that is a crime," and suggests that in Dostoevsky's case the crime may have been child rape. The assumption that he was obsessed by a pedophilic craving, even though he did not satisfy it, would explain his preoccupation with the theme. He harped upon it for the same reason that the victim of a phobia constantly seeks to project the eventuality he fears; he kept returning to it, one surmises, for the sake of the vicarious experience and in obedience to the urge to confess.

# 22

## "THE ACCURSED YEAR"

So he had freed himself from the burden of another novel. There it was—a great, sprawling, awkward thing. It had less structural unity than its predecessors. When would he learn to master his material? When would he restrain himself from crowding the stuff of several novels into one? Perhaps never. Form, finish, craftsmanship were important, yes, but they were beyond him. He must always overreach himself, must always be stammering and stuttering with the urgency of what he had to say. At any rate, there was heat in *The Devils,* and some plain speaking. He had poured out his wrath upon the unbelievers and the rebels and taken the opportunity to settle a personal score. He had fought furiously in defense of God and country. He knew that not all his blows had struck home, but he probably did not realize that he had inadvertently shown the chinks in the armor of his own faith.

And now he must be at it again. The end of one book was but the beginning of another. His novels had something unfinished, something tentative about them. Repeatedly he was forced to return to the problems that he raised in them. The struggle to speak out all that was in him would never end. Long before he had written finis to *The Devils* new projects began to ferment in his mind. In January, 1872, when only the first two parts of that work were completed, he had paid a visit to Katkov in Moscow and outlined for him the subject of his next novel. About the same time he had confided to a friend that he was reading up in preparation for a journey to the East: Constantinople, Greece, the Holy Land. While he was still in Dresden he had been dreaming of going there and bringing back a book which would cover the expenses of the trip. It will be remembered that he had told Anna prior to their engagement that he had before him three choices: to go to Jerusalem and perhaps settle there, to live a gambler's life in Europe, to get married. Well, he had married; he had followed his gambling urge; and the East still beckoned him. There could be no thought of settling there now; he had a wife and two children on his hands. He would stay there less than a year and come back with a book. The journey could only have meant a pilgrimage to the sources of the Orthodox faith. The book could only have been a story of Christ. Some years later he was to list such a work among the things he promised himself to write before he died. He never made the pilgrimage. He never wrote the book. Nor, when *The Devils* was finished, did he turn at once to another novel. He needed a rest from the strain of fiction writing. In the meanwhile, how would they all live?

He had little to hope for from the litigation over Aunt Kumanina's estate in which he was now engaged. As related earlier, during his sojourn in Dresden, Dostoevsky, misled by false news of the old lady's death and an equally false report as to the provisions of her will, had made inquiries preliminary to claiming a share for himself and for Mikhail's family. His brother Andrey, one of the executors, informing him reproachfully of the true state of affairs, he had replied in a tone of injured innocence that he had never had any expectation of benefiting by the will, considering that he had received all that was due to him. He had repeated this to his niece Sonia, adding that in all conscience he believed that he owed Aunt's estate interest on the ten thousand rubles he had had from her. But Aunt Kumanina having actually departed this life and her will coming up for probate, he felt differently about the matter. In addition to the Dostoevskys, the will mentioned descendants of a half-sister of the deceased. If the Dostoevskys could successfully contest the will as having been drawn up when the testator was not of sound mind, the entire estate would go to them. His former protestations notwithstanding, Dostoevsky, together with his brothers and sisters, instituted proceedings to annul the will. They dealt with two lawyers, both of whom he thought incompetent and one of whom he suspected of being in collusion with the enemy, the other branch of the family. There was thus precipitated a bitter feud, which spoiled his relations with Sonia, and in which he found himself ranged not only against his distant relatives, but his own brothers and sisters, who denounced him as a robber, because if they won the suit, he would be legally entitled to a share in the estate from which the will excluded him. This, although he assured the family that he was fighting for their interests and would not claim anything beyond the expenses incurred by him in connection with the case. It was settled in favor of the Dostoevskys, but then the situation was further complicated by the fact that the youngest sister, dissatisfied with the arrangements, brought suit against the rest of the family. In February, 1874, Dostoevsky received a little over four hundred rubles, which barely covered his share of the costs. The court also granted him a portion of the tract of land which was all that was left of Aunt Kumanina's substantial estate.

Even while that unfortunate lawsuit was in progress, he was engaged with other affairs of a practical nature. He had been nursing the idea of going into the publishing business since his early youth. Now his ambitions had narrowed down to bringing out his own works. He had not been able to find a publisher either for *The Idiot* or *The Devils* after they had been serialized. With the book trade what it was in Russia, the only way to make his novels pay as they should was to issue them at his own expense. In spite of the grave warnings of friends, Anna enthusiastically embraced the idea, entered into the scheme with her characteristic energy and good sense, and rapidly became the sole factotum in the enterprise. It was decided to issue *The Devils* first. Its publication was announced in one of the newspapers on January 22, 1873. That morning Dostoevsky rose late, sulky as usual, but after two cups of piping-hot coffee he was able to ask Anna cheerfully how the book business was going. When she replied that it was going well, he remarked that she must have sold one copy, whereupon she produced three hundred rubles and a slip of paper showing that she had disposed of one hundred and fifteen copies, for cash, since nine o'clock that morning. The venture was a huge success. Within a twelvemonth they sold three thousand copies. For the next thirty-eight years Anna was to keep up the business of publishing her husband's works.

He had further money-making schemes in his head. While still abroad, he had played with the idea of compiling, on his return home, summaries of press accounts of the more notable events. He was certain that this work, brought out annually, was bound to be a huge financial success and would not prevent him from writing fiction. Liza Kalitina, in *The Devils,* plans to launch such a publication and vainly tries to secure Shatov as a co-editor. Dostoevsky had had, too, a plan for starting a newspaper. Now more than ever he needed to make some direct response to the questions that were flung at him by life in Russia. Yet these projects came to nothing for want of funds with which to start the ventures. He was therefore glad to accept the editorship of a weekly owned by his new acquaintance, Prince Meshchersky, at a salary of three thousand a year, with additional payment for whatever contributions he might make.

*Grazhdanin* (*The Citizen*), as the paper was inappropriately called, had been founded the previous year by that young aristocrat as an organ of reactionary opinion. In one of its first issues it called for an end to the liberal reforms with which the reign had opened. The Prince had the highest connections—he was on friendly terms with the Heir Apparent—and an inordinate ambition for journalistic laurels, but limited funds and a more limited mentality. He was, besides, championing a most unpopular cause. As a result, the paper, which counted among its few subscribers chiefly ecclesiastics and members of the court circle, was dragging on an inglorious existence, the butt of the press generally. It was this leaky ship, flying the colors of the aristocratic clique, that the former political prisoner, the author of humanitarian stories, the intellectual proletarian, the Christian democrat, engaged to captain.

# ( II )

Dostoevsky entered upon his duties at the end of 1872. His decision to edit *Grazhdanin* was another instance of his capacity for getting himself into wrong situations. He had been at it only a few weeks when he cursed himself for having shouldered this responsibility. He was totally unfit for a task that required steady application and businesslike regularity. Moreover, the circumstances under which he worked were extremely trying. Although he was nominally the sole responsible head of the publication, in practice the owner, who was also a prolific contributor, insisted on exercising his prerogatives and interfered at every turn. The crotchety Prince, whose wretched writings Dostoevsky had to spend hours licking into shape, neither respected his editor's opinions nor spared his feelings. There would be wrangling and procrastination through the week, and then all-night sessions in order to bring the issue out on time. And there were a thousand other minor vexations. The owner allowed only scanty funds for running the paper, and as a result the people with whom the editor had to deal were frequently careless and disagreeable. And even a patriotic publication, exempt from preliminary censorship, could not avoid trouble with the authorities. Dostoevsky had not been at his duties a month when he failed to comply with the regulation that the Czar was not to be quoted in print without permission from the Minister of the Court, and accordingly was sentenced to a small fine and forty-eight hours in jail. He served his term over a year later, relieving the tedium by rereading *Les Misérables* and listening to the keeper's admiring comment on *Crime and Punishment*. In the autumn the sale of the weekly was suspended because of an article criticizing the government's handling of the famine situation in a certain province. There were things that Dostoevsky, for all his loyalty to his sovereign, could not stomach. Later on, an article against a *bête noire* of his, the Russians of German extraction, who were favored in high places, again brought down the wrath of the authorities.

The summer was the most trying time. The family was at Staraya Russa, but he, chained to the editorial desk, had to stay in the capital. Petersburg, "the gloomiest city possible," was hot, dusty, deserted. He was alone. He missed Anna terribly, and the sight of the empty beds in the nursery hurt him. When there was a cool spell, he worried lest the children catch cold. He kept wondering if they were forgetting him. He dreamed of them: frightful nightmares in which little Fedya fell out of a fourth-story window, or in which Liuba, orphaned and in the clutches of a wicked woman, was being flogged to death with heavy rods such as were used in punishing soldiers, and, at her last gasp, was crying: "Mamochka! Mamochka!" The nightmares drove him half mad, for he believed firmly in premonition. For years his nights had been wrecked by terrifying dreams of fires, assassinations, bloody battles. He did pay flying visits to the family, but good as it was to be with them, the journey tired him and the pressure of extra work on his return exhausted him. He did not get enough sleep and was often feverish. Sometimes he had to work in the twilight state that followed an attack, and nearly fainted at the end of a long session. He did not know how he held out. Moreover, his salary and the income from the sale of *The Devils* notwithstanding, he was still making trips to the pawnbroker, and the debts were mounting.

One of the few satisfying contacts that he had during those dreary weeks was with Pobedonostzev, whom he had met the previous winter. The Senator, who had recently been honored by an appointment to the Imperial Council, went out of his way to show his interest in the editor and to give him the benefit of his advice, to the end of helping a publication which sought to stem the tide of reforms. He even contributed anonymously to its pages. Dostoevsky could not but have been flattered by these attentions from a man of such eminence.

There was yet another person who relieved his loneliness. Often that summer he worked not in his study or at the editorial offices, but in the printing house, where he would read proof, edit manuscripts, and even do some of his own writing. He was drawn there by the presence of a young woman, the proofreader. She strikingly resembled his first wife and, like more than one of the women to whom he was attracted, was touched by the liberal notions of the time. For her part, the girl did not find it easy to work with this haggard, tense, crossgrained man, who reminded her of the discharged soldiers she had often seen in her childhood. Her early experiences with him were distinctly disagreeable. He took an unmannerly pleasure in vexing her with rebukes and reproaches. And though he seemed locked within himself and perfectly controlled, he could behave like a boy in a tantrum. On one occasion he demanded that several paragraphs be inserted after the issue was ready to go to press. The make-up man pointed out that it would necessitate resetting an eight-page folio. Dostoevsky insisted that this be done without any resetting, and when the nonplussed make-up man declared that he could not do the impossible, Dostoevsky flew into a rage, shouting that as editor he needed underlings ready to do anything for him, devoted to him "like dogs," and ended by asking the proprietor of the press to discharge the make-up man.

As the weeks went by a kind of intimacy sprang up between the editor and the proofreader. There were still days when he

would come in, with the slow, dragging gait of one who had
worn irons, in a mood so black that she dared not approach him.
Sometimes he would plague her with questions about herself
and freeze if she attempted to query him in like manner. Here
was an overbearing, intolerant man, who demanded nothing less
than one's complete adherence to his way of thinking. But there
were moments when his pettiness and crustiness fell away, and he
surprised her with the face of the genius she reverenced, young,
radiant with animation, noble with spiritual power. At times he
was genial and open with her, and they would talk freely, though
there was always the risk of his snarling if the skeptic in her
peeped out. When she caught him muttering to himself and
gesticulating, she would know that he was dramatizing a scene
preparatory to writing down a bit of dialogue.

Occasionally they would sit over the ill-smelling galleys deep
into the small hours, the room in darkness except where a single
kerosene lamp shone on their work, on the pale, heated faces, and
on his lean, knotty-fingered hand crushing another cigarette butt
in the sardine-tin overflowing with ashes. At the end of one such
late session, as the exhausted proofreader was preparing to go
home, he noted her bedraggled look and was put in mind of a
story he had heard (or more probably invented), which he proceeded to relate. Some young men, walking through the streets
late at night in an exalted mood and reciting Schiller, came upon
a prostitute and were so outraged by her appearance that they
spat at her. Dostoevsky observed that, at this hour and in this
state, his companion, the honest working-girl, might be mistaken
for such a woman—truly, he wished that she were and that he
might go to court along with her and make, oh, such a speech,
against her virtuous defamers!

One night in June, having pressed her to admit that this world
was but the threshold to other worlds, he repeated after her in
an unforgettable voice: "To other worlds!" and lifted his arms
in an ecstatic gesture toward the transparent summer sky, crying
out what a glorious, what a tormenting thing it was to speak to
people of those worlds beyond this. Again, he broke off his work
to say to her, in the tone of one revealing a great and terrible
secret: "And these liberals don't even suspect that soon there
will be an end to everything . . . to all their progresses and
chatter! They don't know that the Antichrist is already born
. . . and his coming is near!" When his companion failed to
show complete acquiescence in his belief, he struck the table with

his fist and shouted with prophetic fervor: "The Antichrist is coming! Coming! And the end of the world is near at hand, nearer than people think!" It was to be nearly half a century before Dostoevsky's world came to an end.

With the return of the family from Staraya Russa in the autumn, home became a cheerful place again. There was, moreover, something of a social life for Dostoevsky. He joined the Association of Lovers of Religious Education and the Slavic Charitable Society, went to their meetings occasionally, and enlarged the circle of his acquaintances. It now included a learned, pious, and charming youth who was the son of the greatest Russian historian then living, and the brother of one of Dostoevsky's most passionate admirers. With his flowing locks, pale face, and deep eyes, this Vladimir Solovyov looked like Annibale Caracci's Christ, Dostoevsky thought, and was a reminder, too, of the companion of his youth, Shidlovsky. Indeed, Solovyov's intense spirituality, his amorousness, his fits of childlike laughter, his versemaking, his devotion to philosophy, combined to make him seem to the older man the very reincarnation of that lost friend.

As for his work, it was scarcely less of a burden than it had been during the summer. Instead of proving the relatively easy and agreeable affair he had expected, it sapped his energies and gave him nothing in return. There were not infrequent clashes with the owner of the paper. One day Prince Meshchersky sent in an article in which he recommended the establishment of cheap, attractive dormitories for students, for the purpose of preventing the spread of revolutionary propaganda among them. The dormitories, the author pointed out, would be advantageous to the students, and would enable the government to keep them under surveillance. Using his editorial authority, Dostoevsky deleted the lines about the opportunity that this arrangement would give the government to spy upon the youth. "I have the reputation of a man of letters," he wrote to the Prince, "and besides, I have children. I don't intend to ruin myself. Moreover," he concluded, in a line that he struck out, "your idea is wholly contrary to my convictions, and cuts me to the heart." One suspects that this was not the only occasion when Dostoevsky's views were at variance with those that prevailed in the *Grazhdanin* circle.

As "the accursed year"—so he described it in a letter to Anna —drew to an end, life became a nightmare. There was nothing for him to do but resign the editorship, which he did with a sigh of relief, on March 19, 1874.

# ( III )

In spite of all the attendant difficulties, Dostoevsky's journalistic activities afforded him a distinct satisfaction. The pages of *Grazhdanin* gave him an opportunity to present some of his convictions—hitherto confined to private letters—directly and unequivocally, as he could not do in his fictions. At last he had a chance to speak his mind plainly on matters that interested him. Every week or so he contributed a few pages under the general title, *A Writer's Diary,* in which he offered chatty comment on any subject that struck his fancy. These fugitive pieces, like his later work as a publicist, are of small interest in themselves, but they should be accorded a measure of attention for the light they throw upon his personality and upon his fictional writings.

The *Diary* is a prolix medley of reminiscence and anecdote, opinion and invective, observation and prophecy. He is distressed by the condition of the peasants, who, he notes, "find themselves the victims of a new slavery after having emerged from the former slavery." He is thus sharing the view of the emancipation which prevailed in radical circles. Turning to military matters, he reflects on Russia's vulnerability, observing that "every ten years, or more frequently, weaponry changes," and muses: "Perhaps in some fifteen years people will no longer fire guns, but some kind of lightning, an all-consuming stream out of a machine." He goes on to lament the fact that Russians, being backward in science, are unable to invent something of the sort and hide it away to surprise their neighbors, while within fifteen years every great Power, just to be on the safe side, will be hiding such a surprise. He could not have foreseen that within much less than a century Russia, lacking her Czar and her faith, would outstrip in technology and might all but one great Power.

Only now and then do the pages glow with life when, abandoning opinion and reportage, he notes the fancies that pass through his mind as he walks the Petersburg streets on a summer Sunday, trying to pierce the masks of the passers-by. Again, he gives free rein to his imagination and draws little sketches that might be cartoons for his canvases: a man of the people who drives his wife to suicide; a widowed workman and his little boy on a Sunday visit to a relative; a young peasant who, accepting a blasphemous challenge, is about to shoot at the Host, but has a vision of the Crucifixion, collapses in a dead faint, and spends the rest of his life in penance. Once, for want of more suitable copy, Dostoevsky offered his readers a macabre skit, in which the narrator overhears the conversation of the denizens of a cemetery. Assuming that some sort of life goes on in the grave for a short while, the dead are shown planning to spend the period of respite in unbridled debauchery, such as the restraints of life on earth had denied them. A humble tradesman is the only decent soul among these lecherous corpses.

Repeatedly the discussion revolves around the peculiar ethos of the Russian people. The features of the nation's psychology, as marked by the diarist, show a suspiciously striking resemblance to the lineaments of his own nature. The Russians, one learns, know no measure, whether sinning or repenting; they are apt to trample upon the very things they hold sacred; they are the most chaste and most foul-mouthed people; the abyss summons them and, embracing self-destruction, they leap into it; their deepest need is suffering—without it even their happiness is incomplete. In their anguish they are sustained by the love of Christ, whom they adore. Dostoevsky was speaking, of course, of the unspoiled masses. "Thirst for *pravda* (righteous truth) is also theirs. The delicate reciprocity of lying," another Russian characteristic, presumably applies to the educated classes only. Dostoevsky notes ominous signs of demoralization among the common people, but is not disturbed: secure in their Orthodox faith, they will be saved: "Light and salvation will shine forth from below." In denouncing the laxity of the new courts, he points out that the Russian masses entertain a truly Christian view of crime: it is not his environment, but his own evil will that makes the criminal, yet the community shares the moral responsibility for the crime— the guilt lies equally upon all. This may or may not have been the belief of the people, but it was that of Dostoevsky, whose self-identification with all criminals may well have been one way of acknowledging his own unappeasable sense of guilt.

He loses no opportunity to lash out at "the leaders of European progressive thought," at all these Mills, Darwins, Strausses. In the heads of their Russian followers, he laments, their ma-

terialistic theories turn into "adamantine axioms." He is willing
to concede that, while these men spurn religion, their intentions
are "humanitarian and majestic." But, he insists, give them a
chance to build a new society, and the result would be "such
darkness, such chaos, something so crude, blind, and inhuman,"
that the edifice would be cursed out of existence before it was
finished. The mind, having rejected the guidance of Christ, is
bound to go astray—"that is an axiom."

The *Writer's Diary* does not to any degree live up to its title,
although the essayist tries his hand at literary and even at art
criticism. He also comments at length on a temperance play.
When he looks backward, his attention is centered on outstanding men he had known. There is a warped passage about Herzen,
"the born expatriate," alienated from his land and its ideals. The
decidedly good-natured account of the author's few meetings with
Chernyshevsky contrasts with the biased pages about his contacts with Belinsky. An enthusiastic believer in ethical socialism,
a worshipper of reason, an atheist rejecting Christianity as "a
false and ignorant humanitarianism condemned by modern science and economic principles"—such is Dostoevsky's picture of
his former master. He offers a retrospective estimate of the
Petrashevists, too. Like the rest of them, he states, he had been
infected with "theoretical socialism" that saw things "in a pink
and paradisally moral light," and dominated minds and hearts
"in the name of some generosity." And yet, under proper conditions, he asserts, he and the others could have become the followers of that monster, Nechayev. In any event, as they stood
on the scaffold listening to their death sentence, they felt anything but repentance.

Besides the *Diary,* in the latter part of his incumbency Dostoevsky contributed reviews of foreign affairs, partly a matter of
shears and paste. He gave most of his attention to France, where
the issue between the legitimists and the republicans was then
hanging in the balance. He is not content with the role of a mere
chronicler. He seeks to go beneath the surface, reading a religious meaning into the political drama. His reflections, however,
are sometimes as unrealistic as they are unenlightened. The
journalist is apt to retire abruptly, to reappear wearing the
mantle of the prophet and uttering warnings, predictions, dark
oracles. He sees in the conflict between Church and State in
Germany the preliminary skirmish in the coming struggle between religion and socialism, "which dreams of usurping Christ's

throne." The Franco-Prussian War is to him a clash between the Catholic and Protestant civilizations, a clash bound to recur again and again. He intimates that the royalist movement in France may be really a gigantic international scheme to restore the temporal power of the Pope. Should he fail here, he will join forces with the proletarians and embrace communism, for the Catholic Church would rather see Christianity perish than surrender its secular dominion. But that "lofty soul," Henri V, the claimant to the French throne, should know that his mission is not to save the worldly power of the Church, but to give battle to Antichrist, who is even now at the gates. Only by restoring her to Christ could France be saved from the evil effects of her revolution. But can she be saved at all? Has the source of her life dried up? Perhaps, Dostoevsky hints broadly, another great nation is destined to lead Western humanity.

7. *Anna Snitkina, Dostoevsky's second wife.*
*Photograph taken in Dresden, 1871*

8. *Dostoevsky, age fifty-one.*
*From a painting by V. G. Perov*

9. *Facsimile page of manuscript draft*
*for* The Brothers Karamazov, *1880*

10. *Dostoevsky. From a sculpture by S. T. Konenkov*

11. *Caricature of K. P. Pobedonostzev, 1907*

12. *Dostoevsky in old age.*
*Pencil drawing by I. A. Charlemagne*

# 23

## THE TONGUE OF ADOLESCENCE

I T took Dostoevsky several months to wind up the red tape connected with his resignation from *Grazhdanin,* so that it was only in April, 1874, that he was again a free man. While he had been slaving away at his editorial duties, he had told himself that he would need a long rest before he could take up his own work in earnest. But he was to know no respite. He was still in harness when he set to thinking seriously about another novel. The earliest notes for it date from February. Momentarily the new work presented itself to him as a "fantastic poem-novel," with echoes of the Paris Commune, which he sketched out thus: "Future society, commune, uprising in Paris, victory, 200 million heads, terrible plagues, debauchery, destruction of art, libraries, a tortured child. Wrangling, lawlessness. Death." But his mind soon turned away from such remote scenes to others nearer home, to characters resembling Myshkin or Stavrogin, to figures out of his projected novel on atheism and *The Life of a Great Sinner.* All of this was enveloped in an atmosphere reeking with the odor of a "chemically decomposing" society, to use a phrase from a preliminary note on the novel. *Disorder* was an early candidate for its title. The images that haunted him were still fluid and an acceptable plot was yet to take shape.

But suppose Katkov had already stocked up on fiction for

the coming year. Where could he go with his novel? Before he had a chance to communicate with the editor of *Russky vestnik,* however, he received a visit from Nekrasov, of all people, Nekrasov with whom he had fallen out so many years ago, and whose path since then had diverged completely from his own. Since 1868 the man had been the publisher and editor of *Fatherland Notes,* the review in which Dostoevsky's early work had appeared, and he had succeeded in turning it into the successor to *Sovremennik,* which, like *Russkoe slovo,* had been suppressed by the authorities after Karakozov's shot. Anna, overcome with curiosity as to what had brought the distinguished visitor to their modest flat, did not hesitate to eavesdrop, and was astonished to hear the editor of the great liberal review ask her husband to give him his next novel, naming a much higher rate than the one paid by Katkov. Nekrasov was not the man to let his political opinions stand in the way of capturing an important author.

Dostoevsky replied that he was under moral obligation to offer his work to Katkov first, but should there be no place for it in *Russky vestnik,* he was ready to give it to Nekrasov's review. The higher rate was a great temptation. He then went to see Katkov, and found him willing to go as high as Nekrasov, but unable to offer an advance, inasmuch as he had just bought *Anna Karenina* for publication the following year. Regretfully Dostoevsky parted from the man who had so long been his publisher and mainstay, and agreed to turn over his novel, *A Raw Youth,* to *Fatherland Notes.*

Spring was now well under way, and with the sizeable sum he had received he was able to take the family to Staraya Russa. They were back in the same house in which they had summered the previous year. Situated on the outskirts of the town, it was more like a cottage in the country, with its flowers, its fruit trees, its vegetable garden, the detached bathhouse in which Dostoevsky could steam himself. When his little daughter grew to be a woman she still remembered the tiny rooms furnished in Empire mahogany, the mysterious mirrors, green with age, the trapdoors and winding stairs, and recognized some features of the place in the house where old Karamazov was murdered. The family liked this retreat so well that they kept returning to it season after season and, in the spring of 1877, bought it from the owner's heirs.

From Staraya Russa Dostoevsky went to Ems in June for the

cure. For some time he had been suffering from an infection of the lungs, which may have been aggravated by his spending long hours in the overheated plant where *Grazhdanin* was printed, and thence going into the cold and damp of the Petersburg winter.

Ems was romantically situated in a pleasant valley, but the prices, the prices! To be in time at the spa, he had to rise with the whole town at six o'clock, which meant that he must retire at ten, and when could be write? Surely not while the sun was blazing in the streets and his fellow lodgers were noisily going about their business. But it was not really a question of writing yet; he was only drawing up the preliminary plan, and he could make very little headway. Possibly he was no longer capable of writing. Perhaps his attacks had robbed him not only of memory, but of imagination as well. But no, it was still active enough; when he looked over his notes, he realized that his scheme was suffering not from poverty but from what Coleridge called "too-muchness": as usual he was trying to squeeze the stuff of four novels into one. But there was still time. If only he could shape a workable plot, the rest would follow easily.

But after all, he had come here not to write, but to take the waters. He did so, conscientiously and resentfully, hating everything—the crowd, offensive Germans and no less disgusting Russians, who pushed and shoved around the *Kurhaus*; the band music that always began with a dull Lutheran hymn; the climate; the food. Before he left he had come to abominate every house, every bush, and looked on everyone he met in the street as a personal enemy. When he compared this fashionable resort, frequented alike by the German Emperor and his own Czar, with the Omsk prison, he decided that as a convict he had been better off.

There was one thing to be said for Ems—his pulmonary ailment was relieved by the cure. What interfered with the treatment was two severe epileptic attacks, which were all the more discouraging since the seizures now occurred less frequently: on the average, once every six weeks. Nothing else was to be expected of such a vile hole as this.

He was horribly homesick. He worried about the children. He longed for Anna, though for one brief period, perhaps the first in his life, as he put it, he felt like a mummy. He thought about her continually—she had every virtue, he wrote to her, except that she was a little absent-minded and slovenly. He assured her that she need not fear that he would be unfaithful: he wanted her and no one else; he simply could not think of another woman; yes, there was an end to all that; habit had become too strong for him; he was a family man once and for all. She must have feared that he would succumb to temptation of another sort: What was to prevent him from rushing off to the tables? But he didn't. He stuck it out at Ems and left with his chest condition improved and with two alternate outlines for his novel. Before returning home he went to visit the little grave in the Geneva cemetery and took some cypress twigs from there to Anna. He also brought her some black silk for a gown.

He was back with the family at Staraya Russa in August. He was facing a period of strenuous work. Would his health hold out? And would they scrape along? The advance on the forth-coming novel would soon have been spent, and he could get no more out of the tight-fisted Nekrasov until he had a substantial amount of copy to show. The money that had been trickling in from the sales of *The Devils* and *The Idiot,* published early in the year, was a drop in the bucket. What worried him most of all was that Nekrasov would insist on deleting from his still un-written manuscript certain passages inconsistent with the liberal tendency of the review. In such an event, there would be nothing for him to do but withdraw his work and refund the advance, God knows how. And where would he take his book? They must economize, and speedily. At Anna's suggestion, they decided to winter at Staraya Russa, thus saving on rent and living expenses and providing him with quiet in which to work. She also looked forward to having more of him than winters at the capital gave her.

During the months that followed, the lower story of the old house on Ilyinskaya Street, where they established themselves, was the scene of domestic joys and earnest work. Of course, he was never free from the threat of an attack. He had a violent seizure on December 28, at eight o'clock in the morning, in bed. He described his state of mind on regaining consciousness thus: "Felt troubled, sad; remorse and fantastic mood. Was very irritable." He recorded in detail another fit which struck him down April 6 of the following year. It occurred half an hour after midnight and was preceded by a strong premonition. He had just rolled some cigarettes and was pacing the floor, when he dropped in the middle of the room, remaining unconscious about forty minutes. When he came to, he found himself sitting at his desk, pen in hand, and noted that he had rolled four cigarettes in an unconscious state—an instance of the automatism that usually follows the seizure. He had a headache and pain in his sides and legs, and the fear of death was so strong in him that he dared not lie down. An hour later he tried to write an account of the attack, but could scarcely marshal the words.

The seizures came at irregular intervals. When the attack was delayed, he and Anna would await it anxiously. Concealing her fears, she would try to watch her husband without his noticing it. He might drop anywhere. Once he was almost drowned in the bathtub. They would place a mattress next to the couch on which he slept, in case he should have a seizure in his sleep and roll off. When she heard the eerie cry that preceded the fit—it rang in her ears after thirty-five years—she would rush over to him and draw his head down to her breast, lest he hurt it in falling, and stuff a handkerchief into his mouth so as to prevent him from biting his tongue.

That winter at Staraya Russa, however, was a singularly peaceful one. Anna and the children kept well, and his cough was better. Never had life been so quiet, so orderly, so like the monotonous existence of a respectable burgher; never had he been so much the good family man. He would give the children sweets, romp with them, and, to distract the little girl, who was given to weeping, would get up a mazurka of an evening, in which the whole family participated. As darkness settled over the sleepy town he would tell them fairy tales or read them fables. They had, he thought, sensitive, poetic natures, and he was pleased by it, as long as they didn't take to this accursed business of writing. At bedtime he always came in to give them his blessing and say their prayers with them, preferring the little prayer of his own childhood: "All my hope I place in thee, Mother of God; shelter me under thy mantle." It was only late at night, after the children had long been asleep, and Anna, having played her customary games of patience, had been sent to bed, that the good burgher was changed into the tense writer. He worked into the small hours, the only interruption being the sound of the fire alarm—conflagrations were frequent and apt to wipe out whole blocks. He would rouse Anna when he heard the signal, and while he reconnoitered, she would dress the children and pack the manuscripts. But the scourge spared them.

In the afternoon Anna would make a fair copy of what he had written the previous night. He knew that she did not understand his business, as she had once conceded, and she sometimes admitted that what he dictated was incomprehensible to her, yet he valued her criticism as that of a candid common reader. By October he was able to inform Nekrasov that he could definitely count on having the novel the following year. Indeed, the first installment was being set up in the latter part of December. Just then it became a matter of public knowledge that *Anna Karenina* was to run the next year in *Russky vestnik,* and Dostoevsky was overcome by the fear that Nekrasov, knowing that his author's market was closed, would make him dance to his piping. He insisted to Anna that even if he had to beg in the streets, he would not sacrifice a single line where his convictions were concerned. His fears of editorial interference proved groundless, however, and the first installment of *A Raw Youth* appeared in the issue of the review for January, 1875.

Once during the winter and once again in the spring Dostoevsky went to Petersburg to see the editor, chiefly with a view to securing further advances. Nekrasov, who liked the novel, was friendly and even generous. The novelist's old cronies, Maikov and Strakhov, however, struck him as rather chilly. Were they vexed with him for having sold out to the enemy? Well, Maikov would come round in the end, but Strakhov, he wrote home, was "a dirty seminarist and nothing more." He'd played the deserter once before, after the failure of *Epokha,* and then come running back upon the success of *Crime and Punishment.* There was another fly in the ointment during Dostoevsky's winter trip to the capital: he had to listen to praise of *Anna Karenina* on all sides. He read the current installment under the bell—he was taking compressed air treatments—and found the novel nothing extraordinary—indeed, "rather dull." And to think that the Count was getting just double his own rates for this stuff!

Soon after his second visit to Petersburg Dostoevsky went to Ems again for a repetition of the cure. Once more there was a succession of dreary weeks filled with boredom, homesickness, anguished fears. He had left Anna in a delicate condition, and for some reason she thought she was going to present him with twins. He was worried about himself, he was worried about the family. He tried to find comfort by reading the Book of Job and was filled with an ecstasy that brought him close to tears. He had to work—there wasn't a line written for the August installment of the novel—he couldn't work, and besides he ought not to work: it might interfere with the cure. Still, he made an effort, producing nothing. The subscribers would simply have to wait till the following month. Once he was back home, he would get on with the book. Perhaps the novel was a failure, but no matter; his powers were still with him, he would do something yet.

Indeed, when he was back at Staraya Russa he was able to make progress with the novel in spite of the interruption caused by the birth of the baby. It was a boy, and they called him Alexey, for Saint Alexius, Man of God, whom Dostoevsky particularly revered. They stayed in the country till autumn, and on a fine Indian summer day returned to Petersburg. The trip, for a family including two small children and an infant, as well as a wagonload of household goods, was no simple matter. They had to travel part of the way by steamer, and as the harbor was too shallow for the boat, the passengers went out to board it. Stout peasant women offered their broad backs, for a consideration, to those ladies and gentlemen who were too squeamish to wade to the rowboats that took them to the steamer. Having been the first to be thus transported, Dostoevsky stood in the boat and received, one after another, the children, who were screaming with fear. In the confusion the travelers almost lost the precious chest containing the manuscript of the next installment of the novel. But they managed to reach the capital safely. There, in spite of the disturbance of settling in a new apartment, Dostoevsky succeeded in finishing the final section of the novel, which appeared in the November and December issues of the review.

# ( II )

Dostoevsky's first tale, written in his early manhood, dealt with the misfortunes of a broken-down middle-aged clerk; now, himself a middle-aged man, he was attempting, in *A Raw Youth*, to speak with the tongue of adolescence. Miraculously, he succeeded. What freshness there was in the writing, and that coming from a man past fifty, Nekrasov said to the author, on reading the first part of the novel in proof. Indeed, what one might expect Dostoevsky to have learned—sobriety in the invention and handling of his plot and his characters, economy of means, clarity of thought—is missing; but what the years might well have erased—understanding of a boy's heart, a sense of the urgent heat, of the anguish of youth—is triumphantly there.

The story is in effect a partial autobiography of the "raw youth," a member of an irregular (Dostoevsky calls it an "accidental") family. It is an account of a crucial year, the twentieth, in Arkady's life, set down with a mixture of brusqueness, tenderness, and spluttering bravado that admirably conveys the turbulent emotionalism struggling with a shamed consciousness of naïveté and inexperience. Although bearing the aristocratic surname of his mother's legal husband, actually a former house serf like herself, the boy is the son of a gentleman, and he is painfully aware of his false position. He had had a neglected childhood, and at boarding school (a thinly disguised and blackened picture of Souchard's or Chermak's) suffered untold humiliations to which he responded by further abasing himself before his tormentors. All the while he was remaking the world in his imagination and withdrawing into himself, consumed by a longing for his true father, an idealized image of whom he had built up in his heart.

He was still at school when he conceived his "Idea": he would deliberately cut himself off from all human associations and dedicate himself to the systematic accumulation of the wealth of a Rothschild, not for the sake of the power that it would bring, but for the mere consciousness of such power and for "the right to despise people," to quote a jotting. This "Idea" may be traced back to *The Life of a Great Sinner*. On the one hand, Arkady's project is a compensation for his humiliating circumstances; on the other, it offers the attractions of an ascetic discipline. After graduation he proceeds to carry out his plan, when he receives a summons from his real father, Versilov, to come to Petersburg. Without abandoning his "Idea," he sets off for the capital, drawn there by the dream of finding and at last possessing his father, and with vague notions of punishing him for his sins and avenging him on his enemies. Yet another motive impels the youth: into the lining of his coat is sewn a document which delivers into his power a young widow of high rank and great beauty between whom and Versilov there is a strong if obscure bond. In Petersburg young Arkady is certain to meet this Katerina Nikolayevna Akhmakova and to triumph over her.

Upon his arrival there develops a complicated series of events which, though presented with a concern for realistic precision, are in the main crude and tangled melodrama in the Gothic tradition. The document in Arkady's possession is desperately sought by three people: Katerina Nikolayevna, because, were it shown to the wealthy old prince, her father, she would be disinherited; Versilov's legitimate daughter (Arkady's half-sister), who wishes to marry the doddering old man for his money; Versilov himself, as a weapon in his weird combat of love-hate with the beautiful widow, of which Arkady knows nothing. The plot entails seductions, suicides, threatened duels, gambling, a legal contest over a will, with blackmailers, counterfeiters, and political conspirators enlivening the scene. Directly or indirectly, the raw youth is involved in the interplay of these desperate moves, these loves and hates.

When he catches his first glimpse of the enchanting lady, she snubs him cruelly, but he feels himself protected from her insults by his possession of the letter which puts her in his power; moreover, the hatred he thought he bore her dissolves into a tenderness for her as his potential victim. This emotion develops into a passion which has all the feverish excitement and rarefied exaltation of adolescent love.

Not for a moment does the boy cease to hunger secretly for his father. When he came to Petersburg, he did not know whether he hated or loved him, but his whole being was bound up with him, and he was continually trying to puzzle out the mystery of his character. The boy's pent-up resentment finally finds vent in an indignant outburst against Versilov, in which he bids his mother choose between this man and himself. Yet when Versilov glances at him with hatred, he rejoices, knowing that at last his father has taken serious notice of him. One generous gesture on the man's part is enough to make his son's repressed love for him find release, and, the father taking the first step toward him, the boy flings himself into his arms. He throws himself upon his newfound parent "like a starving man upon bread," idolizes him, tyrannizes over him, and yet still withholds some part of his confidence. As for Versilov, he is tender toward his son and treats him with a kind of patient wisdom, but also has his reserves.

A preliminary note for the novel reads: "All the elements of our society surrounded him [Arkady] at once." And indeed, he comes in contact with a wide variety of people, including a set of young radicals, of whom more later, and an eccentric of

Kirillov's stripe whom he—and, one feels, the author, too—deeply admires. This young man, having convinced himself that the Russians are a second-rate people with no role to play in history, commits suicide. What with one interest and another absorbing him, Arkady allows his Rothschild "Idea" to fall into abeyance. He is so sure of his devotion to it that he can permit himself to drop it temporarily without compunction. His plan, he believes, is not so much an idea, as what he calls an "idea-feeling": a theory so transfused by emotion as to be impermeable to reason and to be dislodged only by a stronger feeling.

Far from following the ascetic discipline upon which he had resolved, he plunges into a life of easy excitements, playing the dandy and gambling, all on borrowed money. He is weak in the knowledge of good and evil, and instinct is a doubtful guide. What now makes him walk on air is the sudden graciousness to him of the beautiful Katerina Nikolayevna. He cannot keep his transports to himself and makes a clean breast of his passion to his father, only to discover with horror that in this enigmatic man he has a rival! One blow follows another, until, as often happens when Dostoevsky's characters face a crisis, the curtain of illness mercifully falls between him and the consciousness of his degradation.

During his convalescence Arkady suddenly encounters his nominal father, the pious wanderer Makar Ivanovich, who is on one of his rare visits to his "family." Dostoevsky had proclaimed often enough that the Russian masses were alone the vessel of true religion. In Makar he attempted to present a concrete embodiment of the faith by which the people lived. Like the hero of *The Idiot,* he exemplifies the Christian virtues of humility, nonresistance, and a selfless love, which he has not attained through redemption from sin, which, rather, is native to him. But while Myshkin has an aristocratic background, Makar is a former house serf, a servant and the son of a servant, with the superstitions, the prejudices, and the horse sense of his class. His place in the pattern is that of a foil for the divided souls that people the novel. But he has the artificiality of a figure contrived to prop a theory. His serenity, in contrast to the mad passions of the others, fails to be impressive, because he is outside of life, not coping with its problems.

Arkady is at once drawn to the old pilgrim, who has now come to the end of his journeys. "He has something firm in life, and all the rest of us here haven't anything firm in life to stand on," cries the boy in defense of the old man, when someone, with invidious intention, calls him a tramp. The firm thing in Makar's life is an orderly view of the universe, a humble happy sense of his own place in it, and therewith a serene acceptance of life and death. It is just this dignity, a decorum religious in its basis and producing a kind of aesthetic satisfaction, what Arkady calls "seemliness," that he admires in the old man. Usually the adolescent strives to cut loose from the familiar, familial, "seemly" background; the raw youth, on the contrary, mortified since childhood by the irregularity of his position, yearns to achieve a father, a family background, a comforting sense of "seemliness."

His enthusiasm for his nominal father moves the boy to another indignant outburst against his real father, and not having fully recovered from his illness, he suffers a relapse. In his delirium he has a dream: his beautiful lady enters, abject fear in her face, and fawns upon him, in the hope of gaining the document which is in his hand; he flings it to her contemptuously and is about to leave her when Lambert, a former schoolmate turned professional blackmailer, eggs him on with a leer to demand "the ransom"; on seeing them together, the woman who had given him such exalted moments is suddenly transformed into a lewd creature; his first horror, his disgust and pity at once give way to a new feeling "strong as the whole world"; he savors the shamelessness of it as he answers the invitation of her insolent lips.

The youth perceives clearly the significance of this dream. It reveals to him that for all the urgency and sincerity of his moral yearning, there is in him a secret lust for what he feels to be depraved—that he has "the soul of a spider." The latent desires that his conscious mind dared not confront were revealed to him in his dream: ". . . in sleep the soul presented and laid bare all that was hidden in the heart. . . ." In "The Dream of a Ridiculous Man," a story written two years after this novel was completed, Dostoevsky had the narrator observe: "Dreams seem to be moved not by reason, but by desire, not by the head, but by the heart, and yet what complicated tricks my reason has played sometimes in dreams . . . ," and again: ". . . it happened as it always does in dreams when you skip over space and time, and the laws of existence and reason, and only pause upon the points for which the heart yearns." Throughout Dostoevsky's work there is scattered evidence that he had an uncanny insight into the nature of dream life.

In his previous dealings with both his father and the lady, Arkady had been strangely disingenuous—in the midst of the transports of discovering his father, at the height of the pure ecstasy aroused in him by Katerina Nikolayevna, with "music in his soul," he lies almost casually to them both about the document. It is the dream that discloses to him the dual nature of his impulses. "It has always been a mystery," he reflects, "and I have marveled a thousand times at that faculty in man (and in the Russian, I believe, more especially) of cherishing in his soul the loftiest ideal side by side with utter baseness, and all quite sincerely."

Arkady's dream is not merely revealing, it is also prophetic. He does not obey his first impulse and destroy the incriminating document; instead he listens with a thirst for shamelessness to Lambert's proposal that they use it to blackmail Katerina Nikolayevna, but with a sudden revulsion of feeling, abandons the plan. It is only when, by eavesdropping, he learns of his father's mad passion for the lady and her ambiguous attitude toward him that he makes common cause with the blackmailer, and decides to demand of her both money and an assignation in exchange for the document. He tells himself that he will show his father the sort she is, and thus save him from his infatuation; actually, he is moved by jealousy of Versilov. Again his better self prevails, and he resolves to surrender the document freely and to effect a general reconciliation, when he discovers that Lambert has stolen the letter. The final scene is as implausible as it is sensational and involves Versilov's frustrated attempt to murder the lady and kill himself. Yet Dostoevsky manages to ring down the curtain on a happy ending.

# ( III )

The novel is not confined to the adolescent's oscillations between good and evil. With his usual lack of measure, Dostoevsky brings in another motif, which runs parallel to the first and to some extent overshadows it. It is the story of the raw youth's father, Versilov. There is an air of enigma, of mystery about him, which is never completely dispelled. His son succeeds only partially in puzzling out the riddle, nor does the reader fare much better. A gentleman of intelligence and cultivation, a man of the world who has managed to run through three fortunes, he is capable of extreme quixoticism as well as of the lowest intrigues, neither consorting with his social position. He is the sort of man to whom queer gossip clings. It is rumored that at one time he had had "a fancy for unfledged girls," and again that he had had a phase of religious fervor so intense that he wore chains to mortify his flesh. He is evasive about his faith, but on one occasion describes himself as a philosophical deist. At any rate, he is far from being a Christian: he advises his son to shut his eyes and hold his nose in order to love his neighbor, since love him one must, adding: "I believe that man has been created physically incapable of loving his neighbor." (Among the notes Dostoevsky made for the novel there is this jotting, clearly belonging to the same complex of ideas: "Undoubtedly Christ could not love us such as we are. He tolerated us. He forgave us, but, of course, he despised us.") Versilov has none of the novelist's violent animus against atheists, but one hears Dostoevsky's voice when he grieves over the way they hiss God and pelt Him with mud, as also when he speaks of the forlorn lot of man, stripped of immortality and orphaned of God; too, when Versilov speaks of the eventual Second Coming, which will end with the rapturous hymn that greets "the last resurrection."

While leading a parasitic, meaningless existence, he prates of the spiritual leadership of the class to which he belongs and of his own championship of the Russian idea. The role of the nobility is connected in his mind with the mission of his country. This mission is the harmonizing and reconciling of the separate principles for which the several European nations stand. The true Russian gentleman, promenading his melancholy through the declining West, he sees himself as the only good European, worshipping every stone that tradition has hallowed, dreaming of Europe's lost Golden Age (this passage is lifted bodily from the unpublished chapters of *The Devils,* where the dream is Stavrogin's), and seeing before him its fading sunset. For some unexplained reason Versilov at one time almost committed the cardinal sin of expatriation; it would have been the act of a "crippled" soul, a "book man," a wayfarer, with no roots in his native soil (the act of a Stavrogin).

Implausibly, Versilov is made to share Dostoevsky's disgust with the materialistic solution of the social problem, "turning stones into bread," and rejects what he calls "the Geneva idea," which he aptly sums up as "virtue without Christ." Dostoevsky must have been thinking of the conference of the League for Peace and Freedom that had so outraged him when he attended its sessions in Geneva. It was a characteristic thrust at the socialists, and he allowed himself one more where Arkady, at a gathering of young hotheads in the house of one, Dergachov, repudiates their rational millennium as a thing of "barracks, common lodgings, . . . atheism, and common wives without children," and refuses to give up his "entire personality" in exchange for the "meager advantage" of their system. The group is rather closely patterned after the Dolgushin circle which, in July, 1874, while Dostoevsky was taking the cure at Ems, was being tried in Petersburg on the charge of having secretly printed and disseminated appeals inciting the masses to insurrection. For these young idealists revolution was akin to early Christianity. Whether because Dostoevsky was writing for a liberal periodical or because he was now able to recall his own youthful errors with some equanimity, the pages about the Dergachov set have none of the fury blazing from those pages of *The Devils* which deal with the evil spirits that possessed Russia.

One of the less successful of Dostoevsky's characters, Versilov is a wavering, insubstantial, incoherent image that one never quite credits. He lacks the opacity and solidity of a character existing in his own right; he suggests something transparent and fluid in which one plainly sees floating fragments of Dostoevsky's thinking. The one unmistakable feature of his make-up is his duality. He is afflicted with what Myshkin calls "double thoughts," the simultaneous presence of contradictory impulses. "I can with perfect convenience," he observes on one occasion, "experience two opposite feelings at one and the same time, and not, of course, through my own will." On another occasion he describes his state of mind thus: ". . . It is as though my mind were split in two. . . . It's just as though your double were standing beside you; you are sensible and rational yourself, but the other self, close beside you, wishes at any cost to do something perfectly senseless, and sometimes something very funny; and suddenly you notice that it is you yourself who wants to do that amusing thing, and goodness knows why; that is, you want to, as it were, against your will; though you fight against it with all your might, you do want to." He analyzes his condition thus just before he breaks in two the revered icon that Makar, the pilgrim, had bequeathed to him, an act which at once dramatizes his emotional division and represents his rebellion against his moral obligations. Similarly, Stavrogin breaks in two the crucifix that he finds on Father Tikhon's desk. Versilov's son, who resembles him in this respect, goes so far as to erect his simultaneous allegiance to good and evil into a "faculty" of the human race, and particularly of his compatriots. There is also another character, the worthless young prince, who is an example of the "roomy" heart. In fact, none of the other novels offers so thorough a study of emotional ambivalence.

In Dostoevsky's writings the theory crops up repeatedly that the Russian nature is peculiarly "broad," being able to harbor at the same time contradictory impulses. When he put forward this notion, was it because he had closely examined his countrymen or because he imagined them to be much like himself? A lady of his acquaintance complained to him that she was plagued by a duality of impulses that compelled her constantly to do things she knew she should not do and left her in a maze from which only an expert psychologist could extricate her. In his reply to her letter, Dostoevsky wrote that this was a trait common to humanity, though perhaps exaggerated in her, adding: "That is why you are akin to me, because this duality of yours is like my own to the dot, and I've had it all my life. It is a great torment, but at the same time a great delight. . . ." He knew of only one remedy: "If you believe (or strongly wish to believe), give yourself wholly to Christ. The torments of this duality will be greatly reduced, and your soul will find release. . . ." Nowhere does he indicate so definitely as in these lines, written the last year of his life, the therapeutic function of his own faith or of his will to believe. Several months later he told another correspondent that he found refuge from the torments of duality in literary work.

Versilov's personality shows itself most clearly in the history of his relations with Katerina Nikolayevna. He was deeply smitten with her on first seeing her at a German spa, while he was waiting for his son's mother, who was to join him there at his urgent request. From the first the bond between him and Katerina Nikolayevna had been one in which love and hatred, high-mindedness and baseness, were curiously commingled. When the novel opens the two are far apart, but one gathers that under his professed scorn for her the old passion still burns, while her attitude toward him is one of apparent fear. His son's raptures over her rouse the smoldering fires, and thenceforward his every move testifies to the struggle within him of conflicting emotions. Goaded by jealousy, he betrays his son's confidence and writes her an insulting letter, bidding her refrain from seducing the boy. He tries to interfere with her prospective marriage. She writes him a calm and friendly letter asking that their relations be brought to a peaceful end, and he feels miraculously released from his obsession. Almost simultaneously old Makar dies. At last Versilov can marry the raw youth's mother, that gentle creature who for so long had been his wife in fact but not in name. A new life is about to begin. He has no sooner joyfully announced his intention to his son than he turns around and offers marriage to Katerina Nikolayevna. He sends her the proposal through his legitimate daughter—he is a widower—who is herself plotting to become the lady's stepmother. Katerina Nikolayevna refuses him, but consents to see him. At the meeting he shows himself possessed by passion, while she seems to want nothing but friendship. In his despair and rage he lends his support to the blackmailer, expecting to see her humiliated. But when there is a violent confrontation between her and Lambert, Versilov, rushing from his hiding place in the next room, knocks Lambert down and attempts to kill both her and himself, but only wounds himself slightly.

The object of Versilov's passion is not much more clearly drawn and not much more comprehensible than he. She is guided by sordid considerations and yet is described as a woman of irreproachable purity. She speaks of herself as a peaceful person, liking cheerful companions, and yet as being "a little after Versilov's kind," and, indeed, he tells her that they are "possessed by the same madness." It is Arkady who discovers in her "the ideal woman," effortlessly perfect, the embodiment of what Versilov called "the living life," something which is the very opposite of the cerebral and theoretical, something so natural, so spontaneous, that one fails to notice it and so goes seeking it in impossible places all one's days. The "earthly queen," Katerina Nikolayevna, sometimes seems to be antipodal to that utterly selfless woman, Arkady's mother, who embodies the spiritual principle, so that Versilov, emotionally involved with them both, is a man torn, as it were, between heaven and earth. He gives Katerina Nikolayevna "the simple love that one feels for woman," whereas he loves the mother of his illegitimate children with a "humane and general love." She is characterized in a preliminary note as "a Russian type, one of those submissive, downtrodden creatures, hard as saints."

It has been suggested that Versilov's passion for Katerina Nikolayevna was Dostoevsky's way of symbolizing the striving of this vagrant man to re-establish his bond with his native soil. Such an interpretation is as ingenious as it is dubious. What is less debatable is the primary intention behind the book, the urge that animates it. The novel was barely begun when Dostoevsky told a friend that he had come out from the shadows of the underground and was now capable of producing a work of a serene and healing character. Certainly, *A Raw Youth,* unlike *The Idiot* and *The Devils,* essays a happy ending. The event toward which this creation appears to move is the healing of a sick spirit, the exorcism of a demon, the regeneration of a man. When the story opens the raw youth is "a bundle of all kinds of *amour-propre,"* as he describes himself, dedicated to his inhuman "Idea." The experiences of the year with which the book deals results in drawing him away from his madness; the very recording of them helps to effect the re-education of the young man. A new life is beginning for him, but, as in the case of Raskolnikov, this is merely indicated, and no attempt is made to depict it.

As for Versilov, at first he had been conceived as another Stavrogin, and he was to have had the same fate. In the end, however, the novelist decided to make him not a "cold" atheist, like that lost soul, but a "hot" one, an anguished unbeliever. Therein lies the secret of his salvation. His bullet wound healed, he begins to lead a new life—the catastrophe has been for him a spiritual catharsis. His marriage to Arkady's mother is in abeyance, but one is given to understand that he will never leave her side and that he is free of his passion for Katerina Nikolayevna. He has become wonderfully softened and sweet-natured and has received what the old pilgrim, speaking of a sinner's conversion, had once called "the gift of tears." One leaves him as he sits beside his lifelong companion, stroking her hair, kissing her hands, "with the light of perfect happiness in his face." Nothing could prove more clearly than this banal, treacly ending that Dostoevsky was incapable of portraying the shriving of a sinner.

# 24

## A WRITER'S DIARY

NOT all of *A Raw Youth* had been published, indeed, not all of it had been written, when Dostoevsky came to the desperate conclusion that the novel was "lost" and that it would be "buried with all honors under universal contempt." He was thinking chiefly of the critics, whom he had definitely alienated by *The Devils*. As a matter of fact, their hostility was somewhat mitigated because *A Raw Youth* appeared in a left-wing review. But the author himself must have been even less pleased with his work than usual. This effort, more than previous ones, gave him reason to feel that his performance lagged painfully behind his intention, and that, as Versilov puts it, the thoughts did not always ripen into words. He was never to know the sense of accomplishment, his reach always exceeding his grasp, but he was sustained by a feeling of the great potentialities within him. A few months before his death, when he was deep in *The Brothers Karamazov*, he wrote to an acquaintance: "Just imagine, at moments of inner accounting I am often painfully aware that I have expressed literally not one twentieth part of what I want, and perhaps am able, to say. What saves me is the constant hope that at some future time God will send me so much inspiration and power that I shall express myself more fully, in a word, that I shall utter everything that is locked up in my heart and my imagination."

In some ways, however, *A Raw Youth* could not but be a satisfaction to him. In no other work had he so fully objectified that sense of duality which dogged him all his life, and his straining toward a faith which would integrate his divided self and would give him spiritual health. Besides, the story of *A Raw Youth* was a partial realization of a project he had long had at heart. In Arkady's unprotected childhood, in his dream of isolation and power, in his association with a corrupt schoolmate, in his moments of tenderness and aspiration, in the influence upon him of a saintly old man (his legal father), one recognizes elements that were to have formed part of *The Life of a Great Sinner*. Yet nothing could be further from the serene piety that narrative was to breathe than the violence and sordidness which crowd with melodramatic incident the pages of this novel. Would he ever achieve sufficient inner serenity to write that edifying tale?

Meanwhile, he was not really dispirited. He was fifty-five and not in the least weary. The years had "flashed by like a dream." He knew that he had only a short time ahead of him, yet he felt, so he wrote to Andrey, as though his life "were only beginning." And here was Andrey's daughter getting married! How well he remembered the night when his father had come to wake him and Mikhail to tell them that their little brother had come into the world. His own children were growing up, and he was practically a grandfather, what with Pasha raising a large family. Dostoevsky learned to his horror that one of the babies had been relegated to a foundling asylum. Marya Dmitrievna's offspring, now a man of thirty, had not improved with the years. Unable to hold on to a job, he remained a drain on his stepfather's purse, and what with his lies, his pretenses, his general irresponsibility, an unmitigated nuisance to the end. In spite of everything, Dostoevsky continued to feel a duty toward the black sheep, and indeed, to have an obstinate affection for him. There was nothing to lessen Anna's dislike of her husband's stepson, and although little Liubov and Fyodor adored the clownish fellow, she did all she could to keep the two households apart.

Whether or not Dostoevsky agreed with his wife in this matter, he certainly wanted only the best influences in his children's lives. He felt that he must exert himself to nourish their minds in these impressionable years, to give them memories that would always sustain them. Naturally, their upbringing was a religious one. He made a point of taking Liubov, while she was a very little girl, to the midnight Easter Mass. Her reminiscences present the man who introduced child psychology into literature as a fond but unimaginative and pedantic parent, bearing some resemblance to his own father. He took the children to the opera, and finding that a comic operetta had been substituted for the serious work on the program, was about to take them away at once. Only their tearful protests restrained him, and he was annoyed to see that they enjoyed the entertainment. When they were about seven and five years old, he read them Schiller's *Robbers,* a performance that had the natural, if unintended, effect of putting them to sleep. Later on Scott and Dickens were their fare. The first book he gave his little daughter was Karamzin's *History of the Russian State,* the patriotic work that had been read aloud in the family circle in his own childhood.

The fruit of his and Anna's tender nurture was to prove disappointing. Liubov grew into a vain, hysterical, greedy spinster, whose egotism and spitefulness knew no bounds. As her father had suspected, she eventually turned to literature, but produced only a few feeble tales. She spent most of her adult life in health resorts and died, an expatriate, in 1926, a few years after having written a biography of her father that does her no credit. As for Fyodor, a sufferer from depression, allergies, and nervous disturbances, he was not without amiable traits. He appears to have been a believer but not to have shared his father's views about Orthodoxy or the Russian people, of whom he had a low opinion. A well-to-do dealer in cotton before the Revolution, he achieved something of a reputation among turfmen with his stables. He died at the age of fifty, leaving one son.

Fortunately, Dostoevsky had no second sight with regard to the future of his children. Their immediate needs were a sufficient cause for anxiety. There were still debts. What should he turn to next? Anna's publishing venture—she had by this time issued several of his novels—was bringing in money, but not enough. He decided that the best step to take would be to resume the *Writer's Diary* he had run as a department in *Grazhdanin.* But now it was to be a wholly independent enterprise, a one-man review, owned and written by himself alone. He looked upon it as a preparation for the big novel that he was projecting. When a friend wrote him deploring the fact that he had engaged on a task unworthy of his powers, he answered that a writer must not only understand his craft, but must also know, "to the last detail and with the utmost precision," the reality that he depicts, and that his work on the *Diary* was a means of keeping abreast of current problems and, particularly, of studying the younger generation. He added that at his age "one can easily lose touch with the times if one relaxes the least bit." This was, however, not his sole motive in undertaking the venture. He also had a vague notion of disseminating his views and rallying a like minded group around himself.

The unique journal made its debut in January, 1876, and thereafter appeared none too regularly every month for two years. Anna, aided by an office boy, acted as business manager and factotum, and occasionally the nursemaid or a stray relative would be pressed into service to help with the work of wrapping, addressing, and mailing.

The period that he devoted to the *Diary,* as far as Dostoevsky's private life was concerned, was unwontedly placid. The family spent the first summer at Staraya Russa as usual. Again he went to take the cure at Ems, where he wrote one desperate letter after another to his Anya, his angel, his all, his alpha and omega. He is racked by loneliness, by boredom, by "literary anguish," this time not over the next installment of a novel but the next issue of the *Diary.* And the waters do not seem to help him. Next summer he must go to Munich; there is a *Wunderfrau* there who cures the incurable; if she fails him, he can always return to Ems. He is tormented by nightmares, by fears of an attack, by anxiety over the children, and by a passionate need of his wife. Separation is becoming increasingly difficult for him. He is in love with Anna all over again and more than ever. It is a new love. He is a new man. Of course, he still has his whims and his hypochondria. How different the two of them are! He, with his simple nature—she so complex, so wide-hearted. The more he thinks about her, the more he marvels at her. She has, he writes her, a "vast intelligence," she could rule a kingdom. For himself he asks nothing better than to be ruled, indeed, enslaved, by her. If she went out more, she would have a whole string of admirers. Jealous as he was, he was prepared to suffer, if only she could have more diversion. Next winter she must certainly get herself fashionable clothes and lead something of a social life.

Next winter she stayed home, attending to her domestic duties and, in addition, managing the *Diary*. By the end of the day she was too tired to accompany her celebrated husband to the evening parties that he now began to frequent. Society was in a mood to welcome a literary lion who, for all his oddity, spoke for God and Country, and Dostoevsky, on his part, was not averse to accepting the invitations of aristocratic hostesses. When he returned home, in the small hours, Anna would be up to serve him tea and listen to his account of what had been said and what the ladies wore—he was a poor hand at this, having no eye for color and being ignorant of the vocabulary of fashion. She had her small pangs of jealousy, but feeling herself to be a mediocre, homely woman, no longer young—she was thirty—was content simply to serve and adore him. She had answered one of his passionate letters from Ems by saying that she was proud to be loved by "the most magnanimous, most noble-hearted, purest, most honest, saintliest of men." She knew she didn't deserve such love. "You are my sun," she had written, "you are up on the mountain, and I am lying below and only worship."

The summer of 1877 he did not take the family to Staraya Russa, but to his brother-in-law's estate in the South, and omitted his usual trip to Ems. He had to leave them in July, however, and go to Petersburg to see an issue of the *Diary* through the press. It was a horrible experience. Upon his arrival he had a seizure in his sleep, so that for several days he worked in a befogged state, and at night the fear of death was heavy upon him—if only he could see them once before the end! And Anya, Anya, after ten years of married life he was still madly in love with her. He missed her furiously, he prayed to her as to an icon. The days were distressing: he had to visit relatives, to settle accounts with booksellers, to run to the printer, to attend to all the worrisome details of mailing the issue, and in the intervals try to clear the house of the cockroaches that infested it. To make a bad matter worse, he did not hear from Anna. At the end of a night of insomnia he found himself pacing the floor in tears, trying to stifle his sobs so as not to be heard by the old servant, who kept screaming in her sleep.

On his way back to the country he made a long detour to visit briefly the village of Darovoye, where he had spent several of his childhood summers. He cursed this trip which was delaying his return to the family, but what could he do? He would soon be in no shape to stand the hardships of such a journey, and for the sake of his work he must refresh his remembrance of things past. "If one refused oneself these impressions, how, then, and about what would an author write?" he asked Anna in one of his unhappy letters. It was more than forty years since he had seen the place. He chatted with the peasants, went to see all the spots that stood out in his memory, and walked the road between Darovoye and Chermashnya on which his father had been murdered. The impressions of this visit did assist a work of the imagination which was vaguely shaping itself in his mind and which was soon to occupy him completely. For the present, however, he went on with the *Diary*.

# ( II )

Dostoevsky had started this enterprise with the notion of offering his readers the entries from an actual diary such as might be kept by an author keenly responsive to the passing scene. But he soon realized that this was impossible, and so had to abandon his naïve idea and content himself with something more like conventional journalism. In tone and substance the *Writer's Diary* differs little from the department under that name which he had conducted in *Grazhdanin*. By the same token, it does not concern itself to any extent with his craft or with literature in general. Having, however, more space at his disposal here, he could widen the scope of his discussion and elaborate his views more fully, with the result that he involved himself more frequently in contradictions. He skips from one topic to another as his fancy leads him, his subject matter ranging from spirit rapping to the science of fortification. As before, he indulges in polemics and in autobiographical digressions. It is curious that in this *Writer's Diary* he seldom comments on current literature, making an exception of *Anna Karenina,* which he discusses at length. He holds up the novel as proof of Tolstoy's genius, but condemns as "an act of apostasy" his disapproval of the Russo-Turkish War, "a great national cause." He commends by the way the work of Turgenev and Goncharov as fine and enduring, because the characters portrayed belong to the common people. He touches briefly on *Virgin Soil,* but does not take advantage of this opportunity to remark on the Populist movement with which Turgenev's novel deals.

It is noteworthy that in spite of Dostoevsky's eagerness to keep abreast of the times and his preoccupation with Nihilism, the *Diary* scarcely mentions the revolutionary movement which had been growing since the early seventies. The one occasion which called forth comment from him was the unprecedented event of December 6, 1876, when several hundred students and working men assembled in the Kazan Cathedral and ordered a prayer for the health of "God's slave" Nikolay, that is, Chernyshevsky, and of other martyrs to the cause of revolution. Then, emerging from the Cathedral, they raised a red flag bearing the inscription "Land and Liberty." Dostoevsky conceded that the demonstrators may have been moved by a generous impulse, but he described them scornfully as a "worked-up herd in the hands of a set of scoundrels."

The views he had set forth in his earlier attempts at journalism and which obtrude on his imaginative writings are reiterated more circumstantially in *A Writer's Diary*. Naturally, the problem of crime and punishment holds a prominent place there. He had hailed the reform of the judiciary in 1864, but in the pages of *Grazhdanin* he accused the newfangled lawyers of mendacity and the jurors of "the acquittal mania," which deprives the criminals of the benefit of suffering that they crave (to judge by *The House of the Dead,* Dostoevsky's fellow convicts manifested no such craving). Returning to the subject in the *Diary,* he holds a prominent pleader up to obloquy as typical of "the new school of cunning heads and desiccated hearts."

There is lengthy discussion of the sensational trials of the day, particularly those having to do with the brutal mistreatment of children by their unnatural parents. His attention was caught by the account of the trial of a young peasant woman who had attempted to kill her little stepdaughter, and he was struck by the fact that she was pregnant at the time. It occurred to him that the woman's condition may have been partly responsible for her act. He harped on the subject in the *Diary*. And he visited the mother in prison. That she was given a retrial and acquitted was in part due to his efforts. His behavior in this case showed him to be sensible of the physiological and psychological factors involved in crime. Yet he abominated the theory that by and large the criminal is not to be blamed for his act, that this is an effect of, a protest against, his environment, and that crime could be rooted out by abolishing poverty. No! he

cried, crime is more deeply hidden in human nature than socialists like to think.

One looks in vain for consistency in the prodigal miscellany.
The diarist will assert that the character of a nation depends
on the form of landownership, and interpret the history of
France after the Revolution, and the fortunes of the middle
class, in terms acceptable to a Marxist. At the same time he
takes the position that religion is the determining factor in human affairs and history a battle of "ideas," that is, of the faiths
by which nations live. The struggle is between Catholicism,
Protestantism, and Eastern Orthodoxy. Since Protestantism is
essentially negative and consequently negligible, the conflict resolves itself into that between the worldly dream of Rome and
the ideal of the Orthodox Church. On the other hand, the author
views the future of the Czar's dominion in a largely secular
setting. In the spring of 1876 he prophesied that within a few
years Russia would be "the strongest country in Europe." The
empire will owe its strength to its spiritual resources. Furthermore, all the other great powers will be undermined by the
disloyalty of their malcontent proletarians and beggars. On the
contrary, "our demos is satisfied," and so, Dostoevsky concludes,
"the future of Europe belongs to Russia."

He envisioned an even more grandiose role in store for his
fatherland. Both Catholicism and Orthodoxy looked to achieving the ultimate union of mankind, he had it, but by what different means! The Catholics, more Roman than Christian,
would unite men by force, relying on temporal power and thus
denying Christ. Contrarily, Eastern Orthodoxy, obedient to the
Savior's precepts, repudiates coercion. Eventually Russia, the
guardian of that faith, will unite men, not by appealing to self-
interest or force, but through love in the spirit of Christ, and
mankind will become "like a great and magnificent tree shadow-
ing the happy earth." Russia, with her "instinct for panhumanity," will achieve a synthesis of the national cultures of
Europe—which the diarist has repeatedly and somewhat glee-
fully pronounced dead or dying, though this does not prevent
him from occasionally protesting his ardent love of Western
Europe.

At least once Dostoevsky allows that the world he envisions will
include not only the Japhetic peoples but "even the seed of Shem
and Ham." On other occasions he seems to restrict it to "the

great Aryan race." An atmosphere anticipating Nazi racism dominates many pages. Every nation, Dostoevsky declares, if it is to endure, must believe that "it alone holds the salvation of the world," and that "it lives to lead the other nations toward the predestined final goal."

Throughout the *Diary* exhibits virulent animosity against the Jews—he made a point of referring to them by the derogatory term *Zhid* (Yid) rather than by the neutral *Yevrey,* and glibly repeated the charges of the Jew-baiters. Disliking these aliens, with their peculiar ways and their traditional Messianism, which was an offense to his belief in Russia's role as the savior of the nations, he identified the Jewish "idea" with the predatory, individualistic materialism of the bourgeois West. In writing to his successor as editor of *Grazhdanin,* he remarked: "Odessa, the city of the Jews, is the city of our rampant socialism. In Europe, the same situation: the Jews are terribly active in socialism, and I'm not speaking now about the Lassalles and the Karl Marxes. And understandably so: the Jews have everything to gain from every cataclysm and *coup d'état,* because they are themselves an unshakable *status in statu,* and only profit from anything that serves to undermine Gentile society." Naturally, Dostoevsky is convinced that the Jews are behind acts of revolutionary terror.

In an expansive moment, however, he disclaimed any personal feeling against his compatriots of the Jewish faith, venturing to say that the Russian masses neither hated nor despised them and would eventually accept them as brothers. He went so far as to advocate full civil rights for them, only to add in the next breath that they already had more rights than the natives, and that at the first opportunity they would invade the countryside and make the life of the peasantry worse than what it had been under the Tartar yoke. In *The Brothers Karamazov* Alyosha, an exemplar of Christian love and charity, is asked: "Is it true that the Jews steal children and cut their throats?" He answers: "I do not know." When installments of the novel began to appear, a group of Jews in Tiflis (now Tbilisi, capital of the Georgian Soviet Republic) was tried on a charge of ritual murder, and the long-lived lie was being revived in the reactionary press, including *Grazhdanin,* to which, long after he had ceased editing it, Dostoevsky went on contributing occasional feuilletons.*

---

* Not long ago Dostoevsky's anti-Semitism caused embarrassment to the Soviet authorities. The editor of the fourth, and last, volume of the novelist's letters (Moscow, 1959) wrote in his Foreword: "Our primary object was the exact repro-

An ardent supporter of the Throne, the diarist holds up to obloquy his compatriots of the privileged classes, particularly the landed gentry who squander their shrinking income on high life abroad. His sympathies are with the *narod* (the common people). Not that he is blind to their deficiencies: drunkenness, debauchery, brutality, ignorance. He is, however, "somehow blindly convinced" that this is alien to the spirit of the people and is sure to be sloughed off. Purified by centuries of suffering (a Russian monopoly?), they have preserved true Christian faith as well as high moral ideals. These have "rewarded" the masses with "genuineness, integrity, broad-mindedness." A Russian plebeian, no matter how depraved, unlike his counterpart of any other nationality, never ceases to know right from wrong, Dostoevsky holds. He asks his readers to judge the Russian common people "not by what they are but by what they would wish to be." The diarist had long been urging the educated class to respect, indeed, to pay obeisance to the *narod*. He summons the intelligentsia once more to come to the people like a prodigal son returning home, but now he sets a condition: the masses must reciprocate by accepting something of the culture that the intellectuals have acquired.

# ( III )

The Near Eastern question receives much attention. In the summer of 1876 a ripple of sympathy and admiration for the Balkan Slavs, who had risen against the Turks, ran over the country. Collections were taken up for the victims, war orphans were given refuge, Russian volunteers joined the Serbian forces. To the diarist this was "an epochmaking period." A great unifying and purifying emotion, he wrote, was sweeping over Russia. The gap between the masses and the intellectuals was closing.

---

duction of the texts." Moreover, the author of the Introduction deplored the tendency "to tone down what is false and wrong in Dostoevsky's views." Nevertheless, in nine of the letters passages were cut without a word to the reader about it. As those letters had previously been published in full, some in 1887, others in 1922 and 1926, it has been established that all the excisions contain odious remarks about Jews. (See David I. Goldstein, "Rewriting Dostoevsky's Letters," in *The American Slavic and East European Review,* April, 1961.) Oddly enough, the letter writer's expressions of other views held reprehensible by the Soviet authorities have apparently not been tampered with.

Clearly deep within the folk there was a thirst for suffering in a good cause. The people know that Russia exists solely for the purpose of championing Orthodoxy. Surely a nation capable of such a crusade is "spiritually intact."

Dostoevsky greeted the formal opening of hostilities against Turkey on April 24, 1877, with religious enthusiasm. That day, as he was on his way to the bank in a droshky with Anna, he noticed a crowd around a newsboy. They stopped to buy a paper. It contained the war manifesto. He directed the coachman to drive them to the Kazan Cathedral. Ceaseless masses were being served before the icon of Our Lady of Kazan. He disappeared in the throng within the Cathedral, and half an hour later Anna found him so absorbed in prayer that he scarcely recognized her. There could be no thought then of going to the bank. He put away the text of the manifesto among his most precious papers.

The apostle of Christian love is by no means a pacifist. In war he sees a powerful moral stimulus, a godsend. He believes this war to be a step toward the fulfillment of the high destiny of Russia. The conflict will bring all the Slavs together—the Orthodox Slavs, of course—under Russia's motherly wing, and the world will witness a true confraternity of peoples. Furthermore, as soon as the war has been won, Russia without the least delay must take possession of Constantinople, its hinterland, and the Straits. The fate of Orthodoxy depends on this annexation. Never will there be a better opportunity to carry it out. Europe is on the eve of a vast cataclysm, which will lead to an eternal union between Germany and Russia, giving the latter a free hand in the Near East. Surely as the head of Eastern Orthodoxy, she has the moral right to the ancient capital of Byzantium. This will prevent the little Balkan states from quarreling over that prize. It is wrong to suspect any less unselfish motive for this action, since Russia is innocent of designs of territorial expansion. In fact, throughout her history, writes Dostoevsky, she has been an example of "political disinterestedness." (Nearly a hundred years later, shortly after the ogrish subjugation of Czechoslovakia, this weird assertion will be echoed by the Soviet avant-garde poet Andrey Voznesensky.) The *Diary* resounds with the cry: "Constantinople must be ours, wrested by us from the Turks, and must remain ours forever." The Moslem population must not be exterminated or even deported—Dostoevsky is magnanimous— they can take to peddling soap and dressing gowns like the Volga

Tartars. He seems not to have asked himself whether Orthodoxy, fulfilling its historic mission with the aid of the sword, would be any less a denial of Christ than Catholicism.

Other momentous events will take place, the diarist vaticinates. The Pope still considers himself King of Kings, both earthly and spiritual, destined to rule a universal empire, but actually his dominion is limited to the miniature Vatican enclave. In the past he had whored it with the mighty of the earth, but finding himself abandoned by the potentates, he will turn to the common people. He will appear, a barefoot pedestrian, before the indigent multitude, and his "black army" of devoted clerics and shrewd Jesuits will persuade the people that the Church of Rome can assure the triumph of their cause. The poor will be told that since God has delegated His powers to the Pope, who is infallible, he has the right to change what he had preached before. He used to teach that all men are brothers, but now he will sanction the use of force in the interest of social justice and indeed the total expropriation of the wealthy. Easily duped, the masses, "always and everywhere upright and warm-hearted," will forthwith accept the Pope's leadership.

But no, history may take a different turn. The Russo-Turkish hostilities will become a European war. Taking advantage of the fact that Russia, Germany's "eternal ally," has her hands full in the Near East, France will be maneuvered, not without the help of the Jesuits, into attacking Germany—the Pontiff's ambitions being the greatest threat to peace. Oh, Europe will be drowned in blood! But Russia will hold aloof and ride out the storm. Should France suffer another defeat and the Pope thus lose his main support, he will turn to the leaders of the most alert and inflammatory element of the populace—the socialists—and the world will witness an alliance between the Church of Rome and the International Workingmen's Association. This will encourage the spread of godless militant socialism. The *Diary* is haunted by the sinister plotting of the Jesuits in league with the socialists. The nations of the West are ranged against one another, each threatened by a Red revolt—not that Dostoevsky regards the latter eventuality as an unmixed evil, since it promises to destroy the bourgeois civilization that he abominates. Whether Germany is victorious with or without Russia's help, the two could divide the world in half, the West going to Germany. Yet even if Bismarck reduces France to the status of Poland, he will not be able to crush the double-headed monster of Catholicism and socialism. That will be achieved by Eastern Orthodoxy and "the new word that it will utter."

As a political analyst and commentator on current events, Dostoevsky cuts a sorry figure. The tone, as in his contributions to *Grazhdanin,* is at once unsure and dogmatic. When he abandons all pretense of dealing with objective facts and engages in sweeping historico-philosophical excursions, he turns a feuilleton into an apocalypse. The tension that belongs to his fiction is felt in some of his forensic writing as well. A sense of drama, of catastrophe, of the imminence of great and dread events, haunts these pages. "The present century, it seems to me," he writes, "will end in Old Europe with something colossal, that is, with something not entirely like the upheaval which concluded the eighteenth century but with something elemental and terrible, resulting in a change of the face of the world, at least in the Western part of Old Europe." There "everything is, as it were, undermined—loaded with powder and awaiting only the first spark." On the other hand, Russia, "a mighty world apart," stands united, monolithic. (In an unguarded moment the diarist blurts out, however, that the large non-Russian contingent of the population necessitates "a strong army.") Russia will be the Messiah of the nations.

# ( IV )

Now and then the novelist peers out of the pages of the *Diary.* He builds up a situation, sketches in a group of characters, with no more to go by than a reported casual encounter on the street. At least two complete stories detach themselves from the miscellany. The first of these allows the reader to catch the author in the very act of taking hold of his subject. One sees here how an external impulse sets his imagination moving along a familiar path. In the issue for October, 1876, he quotes a newspaper notice about a poor seamstress who committed suicide by throwing herself from a window, an icon clasped in her arms; and he remarks that the thought of this gentle soul "involuntarily torments the mind." The following issue is devoted to a story,

"A Gentle Soul," which ends with a woman leaping to her death, an icon clasped in her arms.

The story, like the first part of *Notes from the underground,* is an internal monologue. The middle-aged pawnbroker, a former officer, who is the monologist here, is another denizen of the underground. He has harbored a sense of insult and injury ever since his refusal to fight a duel had resulted in his discharge from his regiment and in subsequent destitution. He had persuaded himself that his refusal was because he believed the duel unjustified—actually it was because he thought it would make him look silly. He had chosen his present occupation to revenge himself on society.

Attracted by a sixteen-year-old girl, who brought her poor trinkets to his shop, he saves her from the fat grocer who is seeking her in marriage by himself taking her as his wife. He does not quite conceal from her that he has thus put her in his debt. Though he loves her, he does not respond when she offers him affection. He cherishes the thought that while outwardly a heartless money-grubber, in reality he is a proud, noble soul. Let his young wife discover the truth by herself, she will then, he hopes, admire and adore him. Meanwhile, he perversely continues to put barriers between them by studied coldness and niggardliness. She rebels against him, turns aggressive, comes to loathe him. To mortify him, she has a rendezvous with a hopeful seducer, whom she wisely sends packing. She remains defiant, however, and is even at the point of shooting her husband, but his surprising courage when he faces her revolver paralyzes her hand and ends her revolt. He cares for her tenderly during the long illness to which she then succumbs. His deep affection for her is now combined with pity, but there are moments when her humiliation pleases him. Believing himself rehabilitated in her eyes and basking in his triumph, he persists in delaying reconciliation until she should return to him of her own accord.

Suddenly, after months of estrangement, he hears her humming —she has not done this since the early days of their marriage— and it throws him at her feet in a gust of rapture. His ecstatic response is puzzling, the more so because the servant says that his young wife is in the habit of singing when he is out. Apparently, if illogically, he interprets her cheerfulness as a sign of possible adjustment. He opens his heart to her and she promises to be a faithful wife to him. Nevertheless it is plain that she is unable to reciprocate his feelings. While he is getting passports for their projected trip abroad, to benefit her health and also to be their first honeymoon, she throws herself out of the window, with the icon that she had long ago brought him to be pawned clasped in her arms.

"Why did she die?" the bereaved man keeps asking himself. He might have found the answer in his own tragic fault: he had committed a crime against love. Possessed by a perverse pride and a thirst for domination, he had played havoc with his bride's affection and delayed too long the gift of his own. The story ends with the cry of a man who finds himself measurelessly alone.

"The Dream of a Ridiculous Man," the other story in the *Diary,* is also a first-person narrative. The hero might have stepped out of Dostoevsky's early writings. He is a solitary, inordinately proud and plagued by the knowledge that he cuts a ludicrous figure. As the years go by it suddenly dawns on him that it is all the same to him if the universe does or does not exist. Indeed, with his whole being he feels that nothing matters to him, did not matter, and will not matter. Instead of succoring him, this adds to his anguish. Furthermore, he has conceived the idea that the world has no existence outside of his consciousness. His misery becomes intolerable. He decides to commit suicide.

On the night he has chosen for the act he is accosted by a panicky little girl begging for help. He repulses her brutally: compassion has no meaning in an illusory world that will vanish in two hours. Yet there are things that do matter to him. His solipsistic obsession is dispelled. Somehow the incident has restored him to a sense of the objective reality of the world and the people in it. Instead of blowing out his brains, he falls asleep and has a dream.

He dreams that he dies and is carried through space to another planet. As he approaches it, he is pierced by a longing for the earth he had left and a jealous fear that he may forget it. "Is there torment upon this new earth?" he asks himself. "On our earth in truth we can love only with torment and through torment. . . . I want torment in order to love. I long, I thirst, this very instant, to kiss, shedding tears, alone the earth that I have left, and I don't want, I won't accept life on any other planet." Landing, he finds himself in the midst of an Eden, on an island of the blessed, where the lapping of the emerald waves, the rustle of the young leaves, the flutter of birds' wings, all seem syllables of love. The men and women who people this paradise are like our first parents before the Fall. They are radiant with beauty and serenity, innocent of pain and evil alike, and free of desires. They are without knowledge, but they possess wisdom; they have no temples, but there is a living bond between them and the universe. They are in love with each other but know neither lust nor jealousy, nothing of the cruel sensuality that is common to men on earth. They bear children, who are the children of all, since they are one family. They are spared heavy toil and illness, and death is euthanasia. Here is an elaboration of the dream of the Golden Age that Dostoevsky had given to Stavrogin and later bestowed upon Versilov—a rather jejune Eden, almost recalling the sunny Chautauqua scene from which William James longed to flee to an Armenian massacre for "an agreeable change."

The stranger tells the denizens of this blissful planet that he has had a presentiment of their blessedness, and wonders how it was that on earth he could not hate his fellow men without loving them or love them without hating them. Being "a Russian progressivist and a villainous resident of Petersburg," carrying about with him as he does the earthly contagion, the stranger corrupts this innocent world. The radiant creatures learn to lie and come to know shame. They break up into separate groups, each with a language and flag of its own. They turn malicious, while starting to talk of brotherhood and humaneness. Crime having begun to flourish, they compose codes of law, which they safeguard by setting up the guillotine. Men come forward with a scheme for bringing people together again—the hint at social-ism is too broad to be missed—"so that each, without ceasing to love himself best, at the same time might not interfere with others, and all might live together in something like a harmonious society." Wars are fought in the name of this idea.

The visitor from earth walks among these people wringing his hands and weeping, but loving them more than when they were beautiful, blameless, and ignorant of pain—yes, loving the land they have polluted more than he had loved it in its purity. Filled with remorse, he seeks crucifixion at their hands, but they laugh at him as a madman and threaten to put him away. In-tolerable grief seizes him, and he awakes.

The effect of the dream, as the narrator makes plain, is mirac-ulous. This is acceptable in a story that, like "A Gentle Soul," bears the subtitle "A Fantastic Tale." The dream has not only saved the hero from suicide, it has filled him with the limitless rapture of a man dedicated to life. He has discovered that it can be ineffably happy and beautiful even on earth—the sole requisite is to "love others as yourself." The rest of his days, he decides, will be spent preaching that simple old truth. What the story brings forward is not, however, this edifying moral. These pages unambiguously reject Utopian beatitudes in favor of the earthly, with all its evil and pain, and are, too, an emphatic reiteration of Dostoevsky's conception of the psyche as essentially ambivalent.

The two stories have the theme of suicide in common. It is a constant feature of the novels and is repeatedly dealt with in the *Diary*. Albert Camus held that suicide was "the only true philosophical problem." Dostoevsky's solution of it is simple, if not convincing. He sets forth the reasoning of "a logical suicide" as follows: Nature has endowed man with consciousness, which is mercifully hidden from the cow. As a result, he is aware of the impermanence of all things and exists in the shadow of the constant threat of "tomorrow's zero." The human predicament is thus "unnatural, unthinkable, unbearable." To anyone above the animal level, life offered on such humiliating, profoundly insulting terms is unacceptable, and since the laws of nature ("the Devil's vaudeville" Kirillov called them) are eternal, intentional self-annihilation is man's only escape—young Ippolit, in *The Idiot,* argued along the same lines.

Fearing that his more obtuse readers might mistake his argument for a justification and encouragement of suicide, the diarist returns to the subject to clarify his message. The trouble, he points out, is that his hypothetical reasoner lacks belief in the immortality of the soul, a cardinal article of religious faith. The weakening of that belief, Dostoevsky holds, accounts for the epidemic of suicides that he imagines around him. That belief alone lends meaning and purpose to life, is indeed its essence. This, he concludes, makes immortality indubitable. The loftiest idea on earth, it is the source of every good, including the love of humanity. One can offer small comfort to a man if his days are a brief and miserable interval between two oblivions. Unable to help one's neighbor, one hates him. The case of one of the suicides figuring in the *Diary,* namely, that of "A Gentle Soul," does not, alas, illustrate the author's thesis.

It was no vague, disembodied afterlife that Dostoevsky laid claim to. He made his position clear in a letter written shortly after he suspended the *Diary*. Late in 1877 he found in his mail an unsigned note accompanying an anonymous manuscript. Therein mankind is summoned to labor for the achievement of the immortality of the living and, highest obligation of all, the resurrection of ancestors resting in their graves—this to be accomplished by technological means alone. A subsequent letter disclosed the identity of Dostoevsky's correspondent (Nikolay Peterson, a former schoolteacher), as well as the fact that his previous letter was his summary of his master's views.

Dostoevsky read the manuscript to Vladimir Solovyov. Neither smiled at the mad project, and Dostoevsky wrote to Peterson to ask if by "raising the dead" his master meant the resurrection of the body, concluding that his young friend and he himself believed "in real, literal, personal resurrection, and that it would take place on earth."

Dostoevsky seems not to have learned the identity of Peterson's master. An illegitimate son of a titled aristocrat and a peasant woman, he was an obscure Moscow librarian, named Nikolay Fyodorov, known to a limited circle for his prodigious learning and complete self-effacement. Holding that any thought or feeling which contained an element of truth was a common possession, he left his manuscripts anonymous and had his letters signed by others. It was only after his death at an advanced age, in 1903, that his followers published his writings. They reveal a mind that was a grotesque cross between that of an early Christian heresiarch and that of a believer in the unlimited power of technology. Tolstoy regarded Fyodorov as a genius and even Maxim Gorky, generally level-headed, called him a remarkable thinker. It is doubtful if Dostoevsky would have subscribed to Fyodorov's philosophy had he known more about it than Peterson's digest told him. He was committed to the Orthodox dogma that resurrection lies in the gift of God.

# ( V )

D. H. Lawrence said of Dostoevsky that while "professing love, all love," his nose was "sharp with hate" and his running "shadowy and ratlike." This is an apt description of the man as revealed at his worst in the *Diary*. Rozanov, the husband of Polina Suslova and a close student of Dostoevsky's work, wrote to Strakhov that the novelist's harping on love was very suspicious. "It is as though he were blowing on his frozen fist and stamping his feet in the cold." The writing in the *Diary* is so often evasive, slippery, unctuous, snarling. On the one hand Dostoevsky exhibits a violent animosity against the peoples of the West, the Catholics, the Poles, the Jews, the socialists; on the other, he preaches reconciliation, brotherly love, universal union, in the name of Christ. His nature was too complex to fall wholly within a simple formula, yet the analysis of the epileptic make-up in medical literature seems to throw some light upon this paradoxical man.

The "epileptic character" is marked by irritability, fits of anger, a large capacity for hatred—all the earmarks of an aggressive, destructive disposition. If the epileptic's criminal impulses are inhibited, he overcompensates for them by an attitude of "clammy, saccharine kindliness and solicitude," as one psychiatrist puts it. His oppressive sense of guilt and the consequent desire for atonement express themselves in an emphatic religiosity. This is a well-recognized feature of the epileptic temperament and, as the same author suggests, gives a new meaning to the ancients' term for the falling sickness: "the sacred disease." The zealot is bent upon spreading the faith. He considers it his mission to bring peace and harmony and to root out evil. He is unaware that the source of the evil is within himself. It is probable that a psychological mechanism such as this was partly responsible for Dostoevsky's violent prejudices, for the sadistic strain in his novels, for his religiosity, and for the messianic zeal which was his and which he attributed to his people.

In Strakhov's letter to Tolstoy, which has already been quoted, he drew a portrait of Dostoevsky that is of particular interest in this connection. "I cannot," he wrote, "consider Dostoevsky either a good or a happy man (which is in substance the same thing). He was malicious, envious, dissolute, and he spent his whole life in a state of agitation which was pitiable and which would have made him ridiculous, if he had not at the same time been so malicious and so intelligent. For his own part, he considered himself, as Rousseau did, the best of men, and the happiest. . . . In Switzerland in my presence he ordered a waiter about in such a way that the man took offense and spoke up: 'But surely I am a human being, too!' " Strakhov went on to say that such scenes occurred continually because Dostoevsky could not restrain his malice and that his spiteful outbursts were marked by a womanish suddenness and obliquity; further, that he himself readily took offense, indeed rather enjoyed insults, and never fully repented his own nastiness. After remarking that Dostoevsky, "possessed of a bestial sensuality, had no taste whatever, no feeling for womanly beauty and charm," Strakhov observed: "The characters most resembling him are the hero of *Notes from the Underground,* Svidrigailov in *Crime and Punishment,* and Stavrogin in *The Devils.*"

"With such a make-up," Strakhov wrote, "he was at the same time very much inclined to a sweet sentimentality, to lofty and humane reveries, and these reveries are his particular tendency, his literary muse, his road." He could not recall, he said, "a single impulse of true kindness, a spark of genuine, cordial warmth, even a single moment of real repentance" on the part of Dostoevsky. Had he been able to do so, he could have forgiven him all his faults. "But merely putting oneself on a pedestal as a fine man, mere cerebral and literary humanitarianism—God, how disgusting it is! He was a truly unhappy and wicked man who imagined himself happy, a hero, and loved tenderly himself alone."

It is plain that in some respects this damning portrait is not true to life. Certainly Dostoevsky did not consider himself either the happiest or the noblest of men. Nor was he the monster of selfishness and perversion that Strakhov paints. The pages of this biography bear sufficient witness to the fact that, on the contrary, he was capable of true kindness—for instance, in the treatment of his stepson—of disinterested generosity, of a humility that was not merely inverted self-vaunting. Marfa Brown, that piece of human flotsam, felt ennobled by her contact with him. Strakhov distorted the likeness by oversimplifying it and exaggerating its uglier aspects. Roughly speaking, however, his interpretation of his friend's nature is in agreement with the pattern of the epileptic character. But whether or not those "lofty and humane reveries" were, in the language of the school, a reaction-formation, their suspect origin cannot invalidate their worth, since they were, as Strakhov rightly said, his "muse," and dictated some of the finest passages in his novels. It is noteworthy that it was not only the vicious Smerdyakov whom Dostoevsky made an epileptic, but also the Christlike Prince Myshkin, suggesting in a shadowy way that the epileptic in him had a share in both.

Tolstoy, saying in his reply to Strakhov that Dostoevsky was "all conflict," that he was caught in "a struggle between good and evil," came nearer than the philosopher to an understanding of the law of Dostoevsky's being and, thereby, of his art. If one remembers against him his alliance with the forces of bigotry and oppression, one must not forget that his novels affirm, though not unambiguously, the basic humane values. An unpublished entry in his notebook for 1876 reads: "Life is good. Things must be arranged so that everyone on earth could affirm this." The world of his imagination centers upon the integrity and inviolability of the individual self, and the longing for human fellowship is of the tissue of his work. These stories, these novels were composed by a man who denied the competence of science to legislate for a being whom he held to be only partly within the natural order, a man who celebrated "living life" as against everything that smacked of the cerebral and the mechanical shrinking in advance, as it were, from the triumphs of technology. He was aware of, indeed, he exaggerated, the burdens and dangers of freedom. Hence his dire predictions of what would happen if the religious sanction of morality collapsed. Yet with his "principal" mind—it will be recalled that Aglaia in *The Idiot* attributes to everyone a "principal" mind and a subordinate one —he knew that freedom is of the essence of man's humanity. The idea dominates and shapes some of his most pregnant writing.

# 25

## "THE PROPHET"

FROM the first *A Writer's Diary* found a sizeable audience
and was something of a financial success. There were months
when as many as six thousand copies were sold. Not a few people
relished the personal note and the informal manner of the journal,
even if some were irritated by the author's intellectual confusion.
In spite of his retrograde opinions, there was an eager restless-
ness about him that was apt to disarm his antagonists. He had
vaguely hoped to secure a following which might make itself felt
in public affairs, and, indeed, the expressions of sympathy that
he received from his readers made him feel that numbers of his
compatriots shared his point of view. But he succeeded chiefly
in attracting feeble souls, many of them women, who confided in
him, looked up to him as their oracle or their mentor, and heaped
his desk with pleas for suggestions as to their reading, advice
on the choice of a career, and requests for spiritual aid and comfort.

If he replied at all, it was wholeheartedly. Sometimes he forgot
whether he had answered or not—his memory was so wretched
that he could not recall the plots of his own novels. When he was
finishing *The Devils,* he had to reread the earlier parts of it,
which he no longer remembered; he had forgotten even the
names of the characters. When he reread *Crime and Punishment*

in 1878, over three fourths of it struck him as having been written by someone else. Besides, he told one correspondent, he had "a terrible, invincible, impossible aversion to writing letters. . . . If I ever go to hell, the punishment imposed on me for my sins will be to write ten letters a day." Yet as far as time and memory allowed, he was responsive, and, indeed, showed a warm interest in the problems presented to him, which, for the most part, were of a private nature.

On at least one occasion he had the opportunity to air his convictions about public matters. On April 3, 1878, a crowd of Moscow students marched behind carriages that were taking a number of Kiev students to a prison from which they were to be shipped to the provinces and there placed under police surveillance. On the way the marchers were savagely beaten up by toughs. Half a dozen young men from the university wrote to Dostoevsky, asking him to comment on the bloody affair. In his reply he allowed that never before had the young been animated by a nobler spirit, more ready to lay down their lives for what was right. It was as though they vaguely sensed that Russia was tottering on the edge of an abyss. Truly they were the country's high hope. But what would be the outcome? Not so long ago, he wrote, many youths had gone to the villages with a sincere desire to alleviate the grievous lot of the peasants, but they had no respect for the common people and the faith by which these lived. As a result, the villagers sent their well-wishers packing and rejected as absurd the remedies offered them. His advice to the group that had written him was, first, to "unlearn to despise the common people," the only healthy part of a Europeanized society, rotten to the core, having been corrupted by Western enlightenment, and, second, to start believing in God.

For the rest, he explained, he counseled, he soothed, he warned. He advised at least two young women in affairs of the heart, saying: "If you don't love him, don't marry him." He reassured and encouraged a despairing schoolgirl who had failed to pass her examinations. To a young man with literary ambitions he wrote that there was no reason why he should not, at all events temporarily, take up some practical occupation. In his own youth, he said, although he knew that he was destined to be a man of letters, not an engineer, he had been among the first at the engineering school, and for a time had practiced the profession for which he had been trained. He bade the fond mother of an eight-year-old boy teach him the Gospels, because "you can't find anything better than Christ," and enjoined her to retain a sense of measure in her love for the child, lest she spoil their relations. The role of father confessor could not have been wholly disagreeable to him, yet there were times when he realized the absurdity of his position. In such a moment he wrote to a stranger who had invited his assistance: "You believe that I am the kind of person who sustains hearts, releases souls, banishes sorrow. Many write me in this strain, but I know for a certainty that I am rather apt to instill disillusion and disgust. I am not skillful at lulling to sleep, although sometimes I have tried to do it. And, of course, what many people want is to be lulled to sleep."

In the summer of 1877 Dostoevsky was under the impression that the *Diary* was going downhill. In any case, he decided to suspend it the following year. He might later on issue a larger publication, of which it would form only a department. But now he must give it up. He was tired, he was ill, he wanted to start work on his novel.

Part of the December issue, which was the last one, he devoted to a friendly estimate of Nekrasov, who, after horrible sufferings, had recently died. The event had touched Dostoevsky more than he would have believed. The two had long been in opposite camps, but since the publication of *A Raw Youth* in Nekrasov's review their relations had been friendly, and the man's cruel illness had drawn Dostoevsky closer to him. Upon learning of his death, he spent the night poring over his poems. He was confirmed in his feeling that they were the work of a man who had sustained a deep wound in his early life, who had sinned privately against the ideals that he upheld publicly, but who had redeemed himself through suffering, a man who exemplified the moral duality and turbulence of the Russian nature—in fine, a man like a character in a Dostoevsky novel. And as he read, not only what Nekrasov had told him of his personal history, but the points at which he had touched his own life, vividly presented themselves to him, chiefly, of course, that dawn hour, now thirty-two years behind him, when Nekrasov had burst in upon him, proclaiming him a genius.

He went with Anna to the funeral—Nekrasov was buried in the section of the Volkov Cemetery reserved for men of letters, and as they stood there he begged Anna not to have him laid to rest here, among his enemies. To give the talk a lighter tone, she described in detail the magnificent funeral she would give him, provided he promised to delay the occasion as long as possible.

Years later she was to adduce as an instance of her gift of pre-cognition the fact that the ceremony, as she had then pictured it, closely resembled her husband's actual funeral.

He might occasionally think and speak of death, but he intended to hold on a good while yet. On Christmas Eve he made the following entry in his notebook:

### Memento, For Whole Life.

1. To write a Russian *Candide*.
2. To write a book about Jesus Christ.
3. To write my reminiscences.
4. To write *Commemoration of the Dead*, an epic.

(All this, in addition to the last novel, and the proposed edition of the *Diary*—that is, minimum ten years' work, and I am now fifty-six.

There is every reason to believe that by "last novel" Dostoevsky meant the work for the sake of which he was suspending the *Diary*—*The Brothers Karamazov*.

# ( II )

When Dostoevsky was in Siberia, one of his fellow convicts, Ilyinsky, a former officer born in Tobolsk, was serving a twenty-year term for parricide. Shortly after the publication of *The House of the Dead*, which contains a sketch of the criminal, the author received a communication from Tobolsk to the effect that the man had been the innocent victim of a miscarriage of justice. The murder had been perpetrated by Ilyinsky's younger brother, who, tormented by his conscience, after the innocent man had served ten years at hard labor, confessed his guilt. The murderer was arrested, tried, and condemned to hard labor in his turn, while the elder brother was set free. The matter sank into the novelist's mind. About a dozen years later he jotted down in his notebook a "drama" which in essentials is based on the Ilyinsky affair and forms in embryo the plot of *The Brothers Karamazov*. He made occasional jottings for it while he was oc-

cupied with *The Diary*. When, at the beginning of 1878, he suspended the periodical, he set to work in earnest on his novel.

In the spring his labors were interrupted by a tragic event.
Little Alyosha died suddenly of a seizure, and Dostoevsky believed that the fatal malady was epilepsy, which he had passed
on to the poor baby. Heaven could not have punished him more
terribly. This was evidently the great sorrow prophesied to him
by the fortuneteller he had consulted the previous winter. It was
not like the death of their firstborn, when they had been alone in
a strange land without other children to comfort them. But
nothing could make the loss easier. He spent the night praying
beside the crib where the little body lay, and a friend coming in
the morning found the parents so helpless with grief that she had
to attend to the details of the funeral for them.

To divert her husband, Anna persuaded him to go on the trip
he had so long wished to make to Optina Pustyn, a venerated
monastery, famous for the wisdom and loving kindness of its
elders, particularly Father Ambrose. Dostoevsky went first to
Moscow, in some trepidation, to see if Katkov would buy his
yet unwritten work. If the publisher refused, he was determined
to go on with it anyway, but what would they live on meanwhile?
Katkov, however, was agreeable and promised a sizeable advance.

From Moscow Dostoevsky went on to the monastery, in the
company of Solovyov. It was Anna who had arranged this, believing that for all his otherworldliness, the eccentric young philosopher would be able to take care of her husband in the event
of an epileptic attack. In spite of the difference in their ages and
temperaments, Dostoevsky found Solovyov's company extremely
congenial. This young man of twenty-five, the author of several
philosophical treatises, had already reached conclusions similar
to his own on such matters as the state of the West, the mission
of Russia, the moral maximalism of Christianity, the nature of
socialism. This last Solovyov condemned as the ultimate expression of the bourgeois spirit. The carefree mystic had a gift for
phrasing and organizing ideas with an easy grace that the novelist
may well have envied. Expansive in the company of those for
whom he cared, Dostoevsky must have talked freely on his
favorite themes to the young man. Solovyov recalled that on one
occasion he spoke of "the woman arrayed with the sun" who is
mentioned in Revelation, and of her crying out "in pain to be
delivered" of a manchild, declaring that the woman was Russia

and the child, the message she carried for the world. It was also to Solovyov that he confided the main theme and the plan of *The Brothers Karamazov*.

Theirs was not the traditional leisurely pilgrimage on foot, with halts by the wayside and nights under the stars. They made the long journey by train and carriage, cruelly jolted and sleeping in wretched peasant huts. It was only on the third day that Dostoevsky saw the white walls and blue cupolas of the monastery against the background of pine forest. He did not spend more than two days there. He had gone, as any simple person might go, in bereavement, to seek religious solace. But he went more particularly as a novelist in search of local color, his memories of pilgrimages made in childhood with his mother being insufficient for his purpose. What he saw at Optina Pustyn he used in the monastery scenes of his novel. Indeed, the consolation that was offered him by Father Ambrose he put into the mouth of Father Zosima, in the touching passage of *The Brothers Karamazov* in which the monk comforts the peasant woman for the loss of her child. The pitiful words of the woman herself echoed Anna's when her baby died. Dostoevsky's art had for him a religious significance, so that he could turn every part of his experience, no matter how private, how sacred, to its uses without any sense of immodesty or profanation. When Tolstoy underwent conversion, he rejected his art as belonging to that sinful life from which he had turned away. For Dostoevsky there was no division between his fiction and what he had of faith.

When, his pilgrimage over, he came back to Staraya Russa, where the family was summering as usual, he could concentrate on his book. Since the apartment in town held too many painful memories of little Alyosha, in the early autumn there were the distractions incident to moving into a new flat, Kuznechnyi Lane, No. 5—this was to be Dostoevsky's last home. By November he had completed the opening chapters of the novel. Indeed, the first installment of *The Brothers Karamazov* was published in the January issue of *Russky vestnik* for 1879, and further installments continued to appear during the subsequent months.

In order that the novelist might suffer fewer distractions, the family went to Staraya Russa that year at the end of April—earlier than was customary with them. They found the town buzzing with whispered comment on the hanging of an officer of the regiment stationed there. Vladimir Dubrovin had been suspected of being a member of a terrorist organization and had offered armed resistance to arrest. Executions of militant revolutionaries were then common, occurring on the average about once a month.

The previous year the novelist had attended the public trial of Vera Zasulich, who had fired at the brutal Governor General of Petersburg. Dostoevsky was rather glad of her unexpected acquittal, but was afraid that she would be made a heroine. If only there were some legal formula equivalent to the Scriptural admonition: "Go, and sin no more!" This kind of Christian extremism was not to the taste of Pobedonostzev who, upon the assassination of Alexander II, wrote to his pupil, the Emperor's successor, urging him to show no clemency toward the regicides. Dostoevsky's attitude toward the Dubrovin case was not one of horrified indignation but of wonder over the terrorist's state of mind. Dubrovin, he wrote to his eminent friend, lived in the firm belief that his entire regiment would yet come round to his way of thinking. "We say," he went on, "they are insane, nevertheless these lunatics have their logic, their doctrine, their moral code, yes, their God, and all this is firmly rooted in them." Did it occur to Dostoevsky that "these lunatics" might have their way with his country? "Sometimes," he wrote to Pobedonostzev a few months later, "a silly and sinful thought occurs to me: what will become of Russia when we, the last of the Mohicans, die?"

As was his habit he worked at night, stimulated by cup after cup of strong tea, bitter as beer. What with the backbreaking strain under which the novel put him, the trying weather—he wrote to the sound of trees crashing in the storm—the serious illness of both children, not to mention the distress of watching, even from a distance, what he called "the insane antics of the press and the intellectuals," by midsummer he felt badly in need of the cure.

It was to be his last trip to Ems. He found the place more execrable than ever. Nothing but "repulsive Yid mugs to be seen everywhere," he complained to Anna. Further, the room adjacent to his own was occupied by a rich Jewess and her grown son; they made it impossible for him to work and robbed him of sleep by talking ceaselessly at the top of their voices, "with the vilest Yid modulations," from morning till late at night. "The Yids," he told Anna, "have taken over everything, and there is no limit to their swindling." In the same vein he wrote to Pobedonostzev, declaring that Germany, certainly Berlin, "was becoming Judaized," and thus imbued with "the spirit of commercial realism," and that unbelievable cheating was ubiquitous.

True, the landscape was ravishing; how he hated every stone in view! At the concerts they rarely played Beethoven and Mozart, chiefly Wagner, "a most tedious German blackguard," and all manner of garbage. Hard labor in Siberia had been better. His loneliness was abysmal. He wrote to Anna that for nearly a month he had not heard his own voice. He didn't know how he stood it without her. After twelve years of married life she attracted him more than she had as a girl of nineteen. She filled him with an inexhaustible rapture and enchantment, which was increasing as time went by. "You will say," he wrote to her, in stressing the importance of the physical basis of marriage, "that this is only one side, and that the grossest. No, it is not gross, and besides, at bottom, everything else depends on it." Again, he wrote that the only thing she lacked for wifely perfection was frankness. His own outspokenness was so complete that she reminded him jestingly that his letters might come under the eyes of strangers. "So what?" he responded. "Let them be envious." In later years, before allowing the letters to be published, with anxious modesty she expurgated the most intimate passages.

The worried father was not lost in the passionate husband. He was a prey to nightmares and gloomy thoughts. He kept brooding over his death. Men were selfish. The world was a cold place. The children? What would become of them when he was gone? Something must be laid aside for them, he insisted, as his father had before him. He must finish the *Karamazovs,* establish his reputation with it, then resume the *Diary,* and with money from the subscriptions buy a place in the country. By the time the children are grown, it will have trebled in value, and with a stake in the land they will be substantial citizens. Apparently he had not yet received his share of the land bequeathed by Aunt Kumanina to her heirs.

For the time being, he was not saving; on the contrary, he was spending money. His letters bristle with the figures of his outlays. He drops the glass he used at the spring; it costs him five marks, and he buys another for four; he sighs over the loss, which he sets at nine marks, and besides, it is a bad omen. In spite of the demands of the cure, his boredom, and his anxieties, he manages to do a little work, about two hours a day, and sends off the section devoted to Father Zosima. Good riddance! The old man had been sitting on his neck long enough.

Letters from home are infrequent and not always reassuring. Anna has gone off on a long journey to inspect, at long last, the land left by Aunt Kumanina. She has hopes of coming to an agreement regarding the division of the property with the co-heirs, those "pickpockets, cheats, and sharpers," as Dostoevsky calls these kinsfolk. He is worried about the indignities to which Anna will be exposed, and the hardships that the children, whom she has taken with her, will suffer. They will have to stop in a dirty peasant hut where they will be starved and their belongings will be stolen (alas for the virtues of the Russian masses on which he harped so persistently!). He is better pleased with the news that the family is planning a visit to a monastery. They must pray for him—he is a great sinner. One letter brings word of the death of Emilia Fyodorovna. Curious, that on the eve of her passing he had had a dream—he had set it down the next day as was his habit—of Mikhail bleeding to death.

# ( III )

Dostoevsky had obligated himself to complete the novel within the year 1879. A little more than half the year had gone by when he discovered that, as usual, he could not keep his promise. He had overestimated his strength, he was writing more slowly than he used to, and he was more self-critical. But surely the following March would see the publication of the last install-ment. When he came to write book Eight, which contains the great scene of revelry in the tavern, it grew beyond the bounds he had originally set for it and so the delivery of it was delayed. He had intended this Book to conclude Part Three, but sud-denly decided that the novel would gain if he added another book to this section. He refused to be hurried. Haste would ruin his reputation now and for all time. The thing was being read everywhere, by the younger generation, by high society. He must do his best. When he finally dispatched the additional chapters, he was dizzy with the strain. The winter months sped by, and the end was still far off.

The season held fewer anxieties than usual. Anna and the

children were well, and his own health had benefited by the cure at Ems. His epileptic attacks were now less frequent. There were two in 1879, and four in 1880. He believed, however, that as he grew weaker, his resistance to them was lessened and the aftereffects lasted longer. He would occasionally make jottings on his seizures. Of the next to the last one he noted that it occurred in the morning with a sharp change in the weather and was followed by a state of mind that he described thus: "Ragged thoughts, migration into the past, dreaminess, melancholy, feeling of guilt," adding that he must have dislocated a little bone in the spine or strained a muscle.

The family's material circumstances, too, were less of a worry. They had at last paid off the creditors, the novels—five of them had already been brought out—were selling steadily, it was no longer necessary to beg Katkov for advances. Not that their relations were altogether satisfactory. Sometimes there were delays in payment and Dostoevsky had to dun the office. Sometimes he was nervous, fearing that on visiting Katkov, he had not been sufficiently dignified. Again, he fretted lest Katkov should fall seriously ill, and the magazine fold. And then there were objections to his use of certain words. An instance was the Devil's reference to the "hysterical squeals" of the cherubim. Dostoevsky argued that this was how the voices of the cherubim would sound to the Devil, and suggested that the phrase "joyous cries" be substituted. The editor compromised and the cherubim were allowed to utter "joyous squeals." On the whole, however, matters were looking up.

Since the beginning of 1880 there had been an additional source of income, however modest: the practical-minded Anna had set up as a bookseller on a mail-order basis. What with Dostoevsky's increasing age, his failing health, and his careless generosity to whoever held out a hand, be it a professional panhandler or the equally importunate Pasha, Anna felt that she must think of the future. The eight hundred and eleven rubles that the business netted her the first year promised well. When her husband died, however, she discontinued the enterprise, nor would she sell the good will of the firm—to attract customers, it had been established in Dostoevsky's name—lest the new owner bring that name into disrepute.

Meanwhile, the successive installments of *The Brothers Karamazov*, as they appeared in *Russky vestnik*, were finding an increasingly enthusiastic audience and rolling up the novelist's fame. He was more and more in demand when a literary evening was to be held for the benefit of the Fund for Needy Authors on which he himself had drawn twice. He read not only from his own works but from his favorites among the Russian masters— Pushkin, Gogol, Nekrasov. If as a reader he lacked Dickens' dramatic quality, he had the power of hypnotizing his listeners with his low cracked voice and passionate delivery, so that those who heard him once long remembered the experience. A lady who attended his recital of an unpublished passage from *The Brothers Karamazov* recalled that the audience was reduced to tears and thrown into "a kind of moral rapture." The chief attraction at a literary-musical soirée given by the Marquesa Paulucci for the benefit of a charity organization, he looked rather out of place in his ill-fitting frock coat among the gentlemen in full dress and the ladies *en grande toilette,* but he smiled, bowed, shook hands, all the while giving the impression that his thoughts were elsewhere. At these public appearances he was accompanied by Anna, his "faithful squire," as he called her. She would bring up the rear, carrying the book, the cough lozenges, the extra handkerchief, the scarf in which he was to wrap his throat when the reading was over. Her presence was a comfort and he made a practice of starting to read only after he had assured himself that she was in the audience. On the other hand, what with so many cavaliers about, kissing her hand and paying her polite attentions, his jealousy would often get the better of him. There was no telling to what extent Anna, in her early thirties, was sufficiently attractive to justify his jealousy. In Dostoevsky's last year a young admirer was in the habit of dropping in on him to hear him hold forth on various topics, including sex. If, when he called, the master was out, he did not wait. He disliked talking to Anna Grigoryevna. "She reminds me," he wrote in his diary, "of Mienich, the strict supervisor at my school who seemed always to be watching you. And she has a disgusting grin."

More than ever was he being lionized by the aristocracy. Not infrequently he was seen in the drawing rooms of titled hostesses. A young woman, meeting him for the first time at an evening party, saw "a grayish face, a thin, grayish beard, a distrustful, cowed gaze, and shoulders hunched as if with chill. He looked shrunken, meek, and, as it were, guilty." One could not be sure of his mood. Sometimes he was reserved and behaved conventionally, and only the perspicacious discerned that this was a mask. Again, he might march in, sullen and touchy, looking as if he expected to be insulted at any moment. He would retire to a corner, eyeing every newcomer suspiciously and simmering with malice—the crotchety, subtle old man. Alone the place and the company would restrain him from making himself unpleasant. He would sit, his head drooping, his look withdrawn, and not brighten up until he had managed to instill a drop of poison into a remark. Then he would smile and continue speaking. Otherwise, he might sulk all evening long. Occasionally, if the hostess coaxed him sufficiently, he would consent to give a reading. Then the sickly-looking, shrunken-chested man with the whispering voice would take on presence and "electrify" the guests.

Vicomte E. M. de Vogüé, the French diplomat stationed in Petersburg—he was related through his Russian wife to the princely Golitzyn family—often met Dostoevsky during his last three years. "A bear and a porcupine combined" was the Frenchman's impression of the novelist set down in his diary. In retrospect he is described thus: "a trim little man, all nerves, worn and bent by sixty bad years, withered rather than aged, having the ageless look of the sick, with his long beard and still blond hair, and in spite of everything, possessing the vitality of a cat, of which he once spoke." The Vicomte saw the stamp of the *mouzhik* on the novelist's features: the flat nose, the small eyes blinking under arched brows, the broad forehead dented by wrinkles and bulges, the temples hollowed as if beaten in by a hammer, the mouth of a sufferer, all the muscles of the face twitching. "Everything in this man was of the common people, an indescribable mingling of grossness, shrewdness, and gentleness—and something disturbing, perhaps the concentration of thought on this proletarian mask."

The Frenchman recalled that speaking before a circle of fashionable ladies, Dostoevsky might say: "You are not worth the least peasant." He would quickly put an end to literary discussions with the foreigner. "He would stop me," the Vicomte writes, "with a word of haughty pity: 'We possess the genius of all nations in addition to our own; that is why we can understand you, but you cannot understand us.'" On one of his favorite topics he could vaticinate long and eloquently. "One evening," Vogüé writes, "in an access of inspiration, he spoke of Paris as Jonah must have spoken of Nineveh, with the fire of biblical indignation: 'A prophet will appear at night at the Café Anglais.

He will write on the wall three flaming words. It is from there that the signal will be given for the end of the old world. Paris will go down in all her pride, her theaters and her Café Anglais.' In the seer's imagination that inoffensive establishment represented the navel of Sodom, a cavern of infernal and seductive orgies that had to be anathematized so that one would not go on dreaming of them."

For some time Dostoevsky had had the privilege of a regular visit with Pobedonostzev, who in the spring of 1880 became Procurator of the Most Holy Synod. They would meet on Saturday evenings after Mass in the dignitary's residence and have a heart-to-heart talk, which lasted beyond midnight. It was probably through the Procurator that Dostoevsky gained the entrée to court circles. He made the acquaintance of the Czar's young nephew, Constantine, the only Romanov who was to become a man of letters. The Grand Duke was most courteous to the novelist and introduced him to other members of the Imperial family. It has been mentioned that Dostoevsky presented a copy of *The Devils* to the Crown Prince, the future Alexander III. In asking permission to place in his hands *A Writer's Diary,* the author offered assurance of his "reverential esteem" and "limitless affection" for His Imperial Highness. The Crown Prince and his consort graciously received the novelist when he called at the palace to present them with one of the first copies of *The Brothers Karamazov* in book form to come off the press. At the Czar's request the tutor of his youngest sons, Sergius and Paul, arranged meetings with Dostoevsky for his charges. After his first talk with the two youths their putative mentor found that they had "kind hearts and were of exceptional intelligence." As a matter of fact, Grand Duke Sergius proved to be an inept and brutal administrator who, early in 1905, died by the hand of a revolutionary.

The state of public affairs at this time may account for Dostoevsky's popularity with those in high places. The Russo-Turkish War, from which he had hoped so much, had ended in a diplomatic defeat that shook the prestige of the government. Conditions in the country favored the revolutionary movement. This had now taken a new turn. The attempt, made in the middle seventies, to propagandize the populace peacefully had failed completely, and so too had the feeble effort to rouse the masses to armed insurrection. Accordingly, terrorist tactics were adopted, first in retaliation for police brutality, then as a means of frightening the government into concessions and so demoralizing it as to enable the revolutionists to seize control.

The two years of shootings and dynamitings were beginning to have their effect. The feeling arose that the government was being besieged. At the reception held in the Winter Palace on February 19, 1880, to celebrate the twenty-fifth anniversary of Alexander II's reign, the Czar looked to the Vicomte de Vogüé like "a ghost," while behind him, "another ruin," the old chancellor, Prince Gorchakov, gave the impression of a mummy taken out for an airing on this solemn occasion. "I'm done for, I'm done for," he kept muttering, as he leaned against a console so as not to fall, like the empire he was directing. "We are disturbed by the spectacle of these ruins . . . in this palace that trembles," the diplomat wrote in his diary. He also noted that at the performance of Glinka's opera, "A Life for the Czar," the entire Imperial Family was present, save for the Czar himself, it being considered too dangerous for him to appear in public. There were many black holes among the loges, which were emptied by the subscribers' fear. Society in the capital was panic-stricken. To the numbers of gentlemen and ladies who were frightened by the threat of violent revolution, Dostoevsky's doctrine of mystic nationalism was a grateful one, and his enthusiastic endorsement of the autocracy a moral support. It was only natural that Pobedonostzev should hold the novelist to be a man who, as he wrote to a friend, "fitted the times" and was indeed "irreplaceable."

The distinctions and glories heaped upon Dostoevsky may have reminded him of those early social triumphs that he had retailed in his letters to Mikhail with such breathless zest. He was not as thrilled by it all now and was more self-assured, but even his less highly stationed hostesses recognized that he was not quite at ease in the fashionable drawing room, that without being vulgar, he belonged unmistakably to the middle class. While his official rank, owing to his father's services to the State as an army physician, was that of a *dvoryanin* (noble), and though on occasion he spoke up for the leadership of the aristocracy, he had the manners, the habits, the standard of living of an intellectual proletarian lacking elementary financial security and exposed to indignities and humiliations.

# ( IV )

In order to escape from dinners, soirées, concerts, society women looking for spiritual solace and young people in search of advice, Dostoevsky again left for Staraya Russa early in the season. But he was not to get as clear a space for work on the novel as he had hoped. On May 23 he found himself in Moscow, having been delegated by the Slavic Charitable Society to attend the festivities connected with the unveiling of a statue of Pushkin on Strastnaya (now Pushkin) Square. He was also invited by the Society of Lovers of Russian Letters, which was arranging the celebration, to attend the Society's sessions and at one of them deliver an address on the poet.

The unveiling proved a sensational attraction. Exorbitant charges were made for seats on platforms erected on the Square, and people paid as much as fifty rubles for the rental of a window affording a view of the statue. Among the delegates the writing profession was, of course, generously represented. Its most prominent member, however, was not on the scene. Tolstoy had refused the invitation on the ground that Russian literature merely offered pastime to the well-to-do and that Pushkin meant nothing to the masses. Having recently undergone a grave spiritual crisis, he had lost interest in writing novels, turned against Church and State, and was devoting himself solely to the problem of how to live in accordance with the teachings of Jesus Christ. Thus Dostoevsky lost his last chance of coming face to face with his great confrere. Only once had they been in the same room, at a lecture by Solovyov. But Tolstoy had stipulated that no one should be presented to him and his wish was respected.

Immediately on his arrival Dostoevsky was driven to the best hotel in town, and two days later, in keeping with Moscow's tradition of hospitality, a sumptuous banquet, attended by a score of his admirers, was given in his honor at one of the best restaurants. "It must have cost a mint of money," he wrote to Anna, "flowers, yard-long filets of sturgeon, yard-long boiled sterlet, turtle soup, quail, strawberries, wonderful asparagus, ice cream, rare wines." There were naturally innumerable toasts in champagne and, after the dinner, magnificent cigars at seventy-five rubles a hundred were passed around. As the unveiling was delayed by the death of the Empress, Dostoevsky spoke of returning home; he was worried about Anna and the children; he had to complete the next installment of his novel. His Moscow friends would not hear of it. They would send a delegation to his wife to beg her to let him remain; they would send a delegation to Katkov to plead for an extension of time.

He stayed on, but he was in distress: he was homesick and fretted by a dozen petty matters, including trouble with his denture. There were his expenses. True, they were not likely to be heavy, since the municipality paid for his room and board, but that was embarrassing: he felt constrained not to take his meals at the hotel so as to reduce the bill that would be presented to the Duma—they mustn't think he was a hog. It was bad enough that before he learned of the arrangement he had ordered stamps freely and had sent back the coffee, complaining that it was too weak. There was one outlay that especially weighed upon him—the two wreaths that he would have to place at the foot of the statue would come to fifty rubles (in the end it was only fourteen, without ribbons). And then suppose it should rain on the day of the unveiling, and he were to catch cold and cough in the middle of his speech. That speech! He had already half promised it to two different publications. He slept badly and had continual nightmares about Anna being unfaithful to him. And all the time he was thinking: my book, my book!

He took comfort in calling on some high Church dignitaries, who told him that they were honored by his visit. "So they value a man," he wrote to Anna, "who stands up for God." What was keeping him in Moscow above all was the feeling that he must fight for his cause. Some of the delegates were certainly on his side, but perhaps more of them belonged to the enemy camp: freethinking, Westernizing liberals, headed by Turgenev. A clash was unavoidable, and he could not run away from the battlefield.

At last the great day dawned. He was afraid of it. He would have to rise at an unearthly hour—the ceremonies were to begin at eight in the morning—and only in the evening, worn out by the exercises, heavy with the food and drink of the banquet given by the municipality for the delegates, he would have to read a passage from Pushkin that demanded particular poise and mastery. The unveiling and the arrangement of the wreaths at the statue went off smoothly, and Dostoevsky's reading of the chronicler's monologue from *Boris Godunov* was brilliant, but Turgenev, who also read, according to Dostoevsky, "very poorly," got the greater ovation. Obviously, the man had a claque, Dostoevsky concluded. He too was acclaimed warmly, but he was applauded "exclusively," he wrote to Anna, by people in the more expensive seats. The way he was received by the public the next day confirmed him in the opinion that his own followers had true enthusiasm, while Turgenev's were mere *claqueurs*. There was a public session of the Society of Lovers of Russian Letters at which Turgenev spoke, not too successfully. The short speech that Dostoevsky made at the literary dinner that followed was, on the contrary, met by a "roar of enthusiasm, literally a roar," he told his wife. And as he was leaving the hall scores of guests, both young and old, kissed his hands. But he was deeply troubled. He was to deliver his important address the next morning, and he was afraid that he would lose even more sleep than usual that night and would have an attack. This he was spared.

Dostoevsky delivered his speech on June 8, at the second session of the Society, which, like the first, and the banquets of the two previous days, was held in the high-ceilinged eighteenth-century hall with its double colonnade, where the nobility gave balls and received the Imperial Family and where, forty-four years later—the mansion was by then renamed the House of Trade Unions—the body of Lenin was to lie in state. Writing to Pobedonostzev several days before leaving for Moscow, Dostoevsky had said that his speech was in keeping with his convictions "at their most extreme." For Pushkin, he added, gave expression to "the idea for which all of us (as yet a handful) work." The speech is an ecstatic apotheosis of the poet, and also airs the views familiar to the readers of *A Writer's Diary* if alien to the spirit of Pushkin. Twenty years earlier, when he was starting his first periodical, Dostoevsky had eulogized the poet in almost the same terms that he now employed. He began his address with the declaration that the appearance of Pushkin was a prophetic sign, an earnest of the fulfillment of his country's high destiny. He was the first to portray the typical Russian as the restless idealist who dreams of happiness for all mankind. Alone among the world's greatest writers, he had the gift of miraculously identifying with people of alien races and cultures.

He was thus able to give body and breath to the quintessence of the Russian national character, which is a genius for universality and panhumanity. Russia may be a poverty-stricken, backward land. But was not the Savior born in a manger? So the Russians, rather than any other nation, are perhaps gloriously called to bring about the unity of mankind in obedience to the law of Christ. Touching upon a more proximate matter, the speaker held out the olive branch to the Westernists, announcing that the feud between them and the Slavophiles was the result of misunderstanding. Returning in his peroration to the object of his panegyric, he remarked that Pushkin, dying as he did at the height of his powers, "undoubtedly took with him to his grave a great mystery."

The address—Dostoevsky read it from manuscript—came at the end of three days of oratory, which, rather than tiring the audience, overstimulated it. There was something in the worn face, the tense voice, the smoldering passion of the speaker's utterance that cast a spell on his listeners. The message thrilled and flattered: it stirred generous, if ephemeral, emotions; it opened glowing vistas into the future; above all, it satisfied men's craving to be assured that they belonged to a chosen people. Small wonder, then, that the address formed the climax of the festivities. "No, Anya, no," Dostoevsky wrote, "you can never imagine, never picture to yourself the effect it produced." When he appeared on the platform, he went on, the hall shook with salvos of applause, his words were repeatedly interrupted by applause, and when he ceased "there was a roar, a shout of ecstasy." The ovation that he received approached that tendered Voltaire on his last visit to Paris. Strangers embraced, men sobbed and swore to love each other. Great ladies, statesmen, students—all rushed to the platform to embrace and kiss him. He tried to escape into the wings, but was pursued by the throng, particularly women. One student, after shaking his hand, collapsed at his feet. Another young man became hysterical, a girl fainted. He himself was ready to faint. Two old men told him that they had been enemies for twenty years, but that on this day they made up. "You are our saint, our prophet! We owe this to you," they said. "Prophet! Prophet!" cried people in the crowd. Was he at last being accorded the role that he had vainly essayed time and again?

At the end of the session a troop of ladies stormed the platform and presented Dostoevsky with a laurel wreath nearly five feet across. Truly, as an observer remarked wryly, Dostoevsky and Turgenev between them succeeded in usurping the honors intended for Pushkin. The exercises concluded with readings, and Dostoevsky's part was to recite Pushkin's "The Prophet," an assignment which, in view of the acclaim that he had received, seemed suddenly providential. Late that evening—so Anna tells us—after all the visitors had left his hotel room, he took a droshky to the site of the monument and, not without some difficulty, lifted the enormous wreath that he had been given, laid it at the feet of the statue, and made a low obeisance to the poet.

The enthusiasm that had greeted the address, though extraordinary, was not unanimous. Dostoevsky antagonized the radical-minded members of the audience the moment he opened his mouth. They resented his casual dismissal of socialism as a "fantastic" cause and were outraged by his enjoining the intellectuals to humble themselves. His harping on Russia's mission struck them as a deplorably fatuous variety of national self-vaunting. Some of the young women were disgusted by his encomium to the heroine of *Eugene Onegin* for remaining faithful to the man to whom she had been *given* in marriage, instead of following the dictates of her heart, which belonged to Onegin. What Dostoevsky had exalted was "a stupid, enforced sacrifice." Momentarily not a few liberals did succumb to the hypnotic effect of his rhetoric. In fact, Turgenev came up to press his hand. On second thought, however, he was to decide that the address was nothing but wrongheaded, mystical gibberish, "resting wholly on falsehood extremely pleasant to Russian conceit," as he wrote to a friend.

Ivan Aksakov, a leading Slavophile, after drinking in Dostoevsky's speech, was moved to exclaim that it was an "historic event," the dawn of a new era of reconciliation, of peace and good will between his own faction and the Westernists. As a matter of fact, it was only a pseudo-event, the peace proving but an ephemeral truce. As soon as the ardent words appeared in cold print—the oration was published on June 13 in the notoriously reactionary newspaper owned by Katkov—the two camps were again at loggerheads. His opponents, Dostoevsky wrote to a friend, were treating him as though he were a thief or a forger; they attributed the spell his words had wrought to the effect produced by the lavish dinners on a eupeptic public. His opponents were certainly critical but by no means rude. One reporter, writing in a journal that followed a line left of center, found the speech so self-contradictory that it added up to zero, but commended Dostoevsky for emphasizing the debt of the intellectuals to the masses. Other critics pointed out that the principle of "panhumanity" had no bearing on Russian realities; that the role of an apprentice to the West fitted Russia better than that of a leader of mankind; that the perfecting of the inner man, stressed by the speaker, was inseparable from a matter he did not touch upon, namely, the betterment of social and political conditions.

Be that as it may, when in August Dostoevsky devoted to the address an issue of *A Writer's Diary* (the only one for the year 1880), he provided the text with introductory remarks and a reply to his critics. He described this in a letter to Aksakov as so embittered and so clearly intended to break with his opponents for good and all that they were sure to curse him with bell, book, and candle. The prolix retort is a set of variations on his familiar themes. The note of doom-laden prophecy is also sounded: Europe will be overwhelmed by a "political war," perhaps within the next decade; the catastrophe will destroy the old order in the West and reveal to the world the soundness and the wholly separate identity of the Russian monolith.

By the time this issue of the *Diary* appeared, he believed that he was on the last lap of his work on the novel. There were a thousand interruptions. As soon as he woke up (at one P.M.), the doorbell began ringing. One visitor came to beg, another to demand, a third threatened to shoot himself on the spot if his insoluble problem were not solved for him. There were deputations from students, from charitable organizations eager to secure the novelist's participation in a literary soirée. Budding authors sent in manuscripts with a request to peruse and place them. There was no time left to think, to read, to be with the children, to live. Until the day, early in November, when he dispatched the final pages of the novel, he worked furiously. Sometimes, after having written a chapter for which he had been taking notes for three years, he had to discard it and rewrite it completely. Except for those few passages that wrote themselves, he found the task so hard that it made him physically ill. Ten, twelve hours he would be sitting hunched over his desk, and at six o'clock in the morning, when the city was beginning to wake, he had not yet gone to bed. And this when the doctors had warned him that he must have his night's rest. It was worse than hard labor in Siberia! But the whole of literate Russia was waiting for him to put a close to the novel; that he should end it fittingly was a debt that he owed to himself, to literature, to God.

# 26

# "HURRAH FOR KARAMAZOV!"

THE last of Dostoevsky's novels, *The Brothers Kara-mazov,* has a towering reputation. Like other major works of his, it is a crime novel. Its obvious appeal is that of a skillfully managed detective story, but this tale of murder contains elements undreamed of in the philosophy of purveyors of who-done-its. It has not only the tension that results from conflicts between the persons involved, but is also a drama of the mind. Though the design has the involutions usual with Dostoevsky, the plot, which centers on a case of parricide, is fairly simple, and the fact that the action occurs in one place—a provincial town—and in the main has to do with one family, helps to sustain its unity.

This is another highly irregular family, like that portrayed in *A Raw Youth.* Here, however, the three legitimate brothers, for all the divergence among them, have solicitude, indeed, affection, for each other. The protagonists, while complex creatures of flesh and blood, yield their symbolic significance more readily than is generally the case. The Moscow Art Theater staged a dramatization of the novel as a medieval mystery play. It is the eldest son, Dmitry (Mitya), who holds the center of the stage much of the time, yet each of the Karamazovs is drawn with a firmness, an insight, an imaginative power, that sets him among the most memorable characters in fiction.

The begetter of the Karamazovs, whose given name is that of the novelist, is a small landowner who, starting out as a clownish hanger-on, has become a shady, and successful, entrepreneur, without ceasing to be a mountebank. Scarcely capable of a moral scruple or an impulse of natural affection, he is little more than a bundle of appetites, a kind of vicious Falstaff, built upon lust as upon a rock. "I want to live in my vileness," he says, "to the end of my days." Yet the shrewd old sot, at once spiteful and sentimental, has moments of "spiritual terror" and when in his cups is not beyond discussing the existence of God and the chance of immortality. His shameless sensuality is almost appealing in contrast with the sanctimoniousness that some pages exude.

The father's carnality has been transmitted to the sons, but in a sublimated form. He was married twice, the first time to a spirited, pretty, and dowered girl, who used to beat him and who ran away from him, leaving three-year-old Mitya on his hands. Completely neglected, the child was first in the charge of a servant and then shifted from one of his mother's relatives to another. Karamazov's second wife was an indigent, meek, long-suffering orphan, who had hysterical epileptoid fits and whom he drove to her grave. She had borne him two sons, Ivan and Alexey (Alyosha). It was as though the finer substance of these women had purified and humanized in the sons the man's gross animalism, so that their children grew souls. At the same time they all shared, to a greater or lesser degree, the dark, earthy power that was the heritage of the Karamazovs, a name the first two syllables of which mean "black" in Turkic.

Dmitry has much of his father in him. He, too, is a man driven by his lusts, knowing no measure, no discipline. Yet this passionate man possesses an unreflective moral sense of adolescent acuteness. He may do low things, but he is conscious of it and sorry for it. He may do cruel things, but the rough, impulsive quondam army officer has a great gift of pity. For all his physical exuberance, he has a longing for spiritual grace, even at the moment of utter debasement. The time comes when he is distressed, somewhat less plausibly than many others among Dostoevsky's characters, by the question of the existence of God. Again, like others, he is wide-hearted. The contradictions within himself perplex him. "What to the mind is shameful, is beauty and nothing else to the heart." The fact that a man may cherish what he calls "the ideal of Sodom" and "the ideal of the Madonna" at the same time confuses him painfully. Though he sinks to the depths of degradation, he knows his own baseness and can rise to the peaks of generosity. He quotes Schiller's *An die Freude,* and it is as though Dostoevsky were introducing him with a musical motif, fitting enough because there is a kind of music in his heart, a gaiety singing in him.

Seductive Grushenka, the kept woman who is the object of his fierce desire—the very woman after whom his father lusts—was ravished when she was seventeen, only to become slavishly enamored of her ravisher; later she became an old man's "protégée," and finally fell in love with Dmitry. Made of simpler stuff than he, she is at bottom his feminine counterpart: a somewhat coarse, hot-blooded creature, capable of cruelties and of a craftiness altogether foreign to him, but having also much of his humanity. She plays with the idea of seducing Aloysha, but when he treats her as a human being, her feeling for him becomes one of sisterly devotion.

In Ivan, the second brother, the Karamazov vigor runs along another channel. He, too, has an intense zest for living and a more exacting conscience than he knows, but he is intended to be the pattern of the intellectual, the man who plays with ideas, the doubter. Not that he is a cold rationalist, dealing in abstractions. He is anguished by the problems that he fastens upon. Like all those characters of Dostoevsky's who succumb to the temptations of the intellect, he stumbles, he goes astray. The proud, headstrong, mercurial Katerina Ivanovna (Katya), to whom Dmitry is for a time betrothed, is another twisted soul, torn by conflicting emotions.

If Dmitry comprehends the life of the senses and Ivan that of the mind, Alyosha, the youngest brother, embodies the life of the spirit——faith, goodness, unstinted loving-kindness. All of them are also credible human beings who act and suffer where extreme situations predominate. Alyosha is another attempt on Dostoevsky's part to portray the ideal Christian, another character resembling Prince Myshkin. Indeed, in the notes for the novel he is referred to as "the idiot." It is the one effort of this kind in which the novelist comes close to success. Alyosha is a novice at the local monastery, under the tutelage of Father Zosima, a

*staretz.** It may have been of this novice that the novelist was
thinking when he chose as the epigraph for his book these lines
from St. John: "Verily, verily, I say unto you, Except a corn of
wheat fall into the ground and die, it abideth alone; but if it die,
it bringeth forth much fruit." In his Foreword Dostoevsky
called the youngest brother his "hero."

Alyosha is no wan ascetic, but a smiling youth whose red
cheeks and sturdy frame consort ill with his cassock. There is
something in him, too, of the dark Karamazov strain. His godli-
ness is not without weak spots. He is human enough to be drawn
toward the temptations of the flesh, at least on one occasion.
It is significant that Lise, whom he apparently plans eventually
to marry (he has been bidden by his religious superior to leave
the monastery for the world), is a hysterical, sensual teen-ager
with perverse whims and a perverse charm. During a conversation in which she parades her sado-masochistic impulses before
him, he drops the remark that everyone occasionally loves crime.
She twits him with being a monk, whereupon he says: "Perhaps
I don't believe in God." When he was writing the book, Dostoevsky observed that, taken together, these four characters epitomized the cultivated Russians of his day. However that may be,
it does seem true that in Ivan, in Dmitry, in the old Karamazov,
the novelist embodied his own mental conflict, his emotional disorder, his carnality. Through these characters he could give his
own dark impulses their freedom, because they were disguised,
like the elements that rise to consciousness in the dream. Alyosha, on the other hand, represented the man he would so
gladly have been: armored in faith, strong enough to overcome
temptation, rich in love, wise in compassion.

There is a putative fourth son, Smerdyakov. He is employed
by Karamazov as a cook. His paternity is uncertain. The infant
was born under uncanny circumstances in the Karamazov garden,
the mother, an idiot, a vagrant, an utterly selfless ascetic, dying
in childbirth. Rumor persistently pointed at Karamazov as the
father. Presumably he had begotten the baby while drunk, not
in the heat of lust but cold-bloodedly, deliberately, in the spirit
of an obscene practical joke. The grown man is like his supposed

---

* An elderly monk, usually a hermit, possessed of the powers of a spiritual
counselor and healer; one who chooses to serve his novitiate under a *staretz* is
bound to him by a permanent link of obedience and self-abnegation, purported
to result in perfect inner freedom.

father in his want of conscience, common pieties, and human attachments, but, unlike him, seems sexless. He detests everything Russian, and regrets that his native land was not conquered by Napoleon in 1812. His amusements include hanging cats and teaching a schoolboy to feed a stray dog a piece of bread with a pin stuck in it. A flunkey from the crest of his pomaded hair to the tip of his polished calf boots, he is as loathsome as a reptile or a slimy cellar growth. Always ready to besmirch reason, Dostoevsky endows this dandified monster with a logical mind and extraordinary shrewdness. Smerdyakov is a masterly parody of the intellectual, a distorted image, as it were, of Ivan, in which his finer features are thrown out of focus, his baser ones magnified. Remarkably enough, the soulless bastard, like the saintly Myshkin, is an epileptic.

The background of the novel is crowded with peasants, merchants, schoolboys, and, in the ample chapters devoted to the preliminary investigation and the trial of Dmitry, magistrates and lawyers. Through Alyosha, Father Zosima is brought on the scene and the monastic regimen becomes part of the picture. Dmitry's former guardian, Miyusov, exemplifies Dostoevsky's *bête noire:* the unbeliever with strong Westernist sympathies who spends much of his time abroad. Another character whom the novelist holds up to scorn is Rakitin, ironically enough a divinity student. Dostoevsky knew that the Russian seminaries were hotbeds of out-and-out atheism. "Mankind," the young man declares, "will find sufficient strength in itself to love virtue, even without faith in the immortality of the soul. It will find such strength in love of freedom, equality, brotherhood." An atheist leading a moral life was an abomination to Dostoevsky. He does not allow Rakitin any virtue, but paints him as a nasty-minded, scoundrelly careerist, a money-grubber whose chief ambition is to own a tenement in the capital.

The scatterbrained Mme. Khokhlakova furnishes a large part of the comic relief, as when, Dmitry having pleaded with her for a loan of the three thousand rubles he needs to pay off a pressing debt, she overwhelms him with the suggestion that he is sure to win a large fortune by prospecting for gold—whereupon he spits in her silly face. Comedy is also supplied by the schoolboy, Kolya. He compensates for his short stature by asserting his superiority through the performance of unusually daring exploits, leads yokels by the nose in a rollicking fashion, and mouths with amusing sententiousness the Nihilist doctrines that Dostoevsky loathed, but, reclaimed by Alyosha, the boy is ready to immolate himself for what is right (*pravda*). Then, too, there are the miserable Snegiryovs, a family of poor folk who suffer from Dmitry's violence and are comforted by Alyosha's compassion.

Some fifty men, women, and children move through the pages of the novel. They are rushed through at a speed not easily recognized by the reader. As in the other novels, the seven or eight days—spread over a period of two months—in which the action takes place is a time span too brief for the multiplicity of the events.

Here as elsewhere the novelist was at pains to check the accuracy of certain matters of fact, little and large, that had to do with the story. Thus, for the section devoted to children he made it his business to find out what uniform schoolboys were wearing at the time, and he inquired of a pedagogue what their patter, habits, beliefs, offenses were. He affirmed that every item in Ivan's collection of atrocities committed against children had actually occurred. All these things "happened, *were,* they are printed in newspapers, and I can show exactly where—I have invented nothing." He said further that in describing the Devil's visit to Ivan, he leaned on the assurance of physicians that the hallucination was within the bounds of possibility. To avoid errors in delineating Dmitry's trial, he went to the trouble of consulting a prosecutor.

There is more of the furniture of ordinary life in this novel than in most of Dostoevsky's works. There is, too, some slight awareness of the ryhthms of nature, and, at one high moment, the mystic sense of man's communion with the universe.

# ( II )

Early in the story one finds the Karamazovs, accompanied by Miyusov, in the cell of Father Zosima, to whom they have come for arbitration of a quarrel between the old man and Dmitry over the inheritance from his mother. While they await the *staretz,* the conversation turns upon a newspaper article by Ivan on the subject of the ecclesiastical courts, a live issue in the mid-sixties. He maintained that each State ought eventually be transformed into a Church and reject every purpose inconsistent with the aims of the Church. One of the monks present heartily approves the proposition, which, he declares, is in harmony with "Russian thinking." Father Zosima, on entering, also hails the prospect of replacing all bodies politic by "a single universal and regnant Church," and the same monk who had spoken earlier chimes in: "This star will rise in the East." Miyusov, smiling condescendingly, interposes with the remark that he has heard Ivan assert that love of one's neighbor, indeed, all morality, nay, every "living force," rests on belief in God and immortality; destroy those beliefs and "everything would be permitted," even cannibalism; crime would be sanctioned as the inevitable outcome of the atheist position. Ivan does not object to this summary of his opinions. "Virtue is impossible," he asserts, "without immortality." Father Zosima intuitively recognizes that the young man vacillates between the positive and negative answer to the question of God's existence and is dubious of the orthodox theses that he himself formulates so sharply.

Owing to Karamazov Senior's outrageous behavior and his willingness, along with Dmitry's, to wash the family's dirty linen in public, the gathering concludes with a scandalous scene, in the course of which the old buffoon cries out that if Dmitry were not his son, he would challenge him to a duel. The *staretz* puts an end to the uproar by kneeling to Dmitry and touching the floor with his forehead, in reverence, he explains later, for the suffering in store for the man.

The following day Ivan opens his heart to Alyosha in an often cited section of the novel entitled "Pro and Contra." Ivan's avowal is a deeply moving piece of confessional writing. The two brothers, who had had no contact for years, meet in a screened-off corner of a shabby tavern and talk about "the universal questions," to the popping of corks, the click of billiard balls, the shouts of waiters, and the drone of a mechanical organ. When Russian boys meet, Ivan begins, they will talk of the existence of God and immortality, and if they are unbelievers, they will discuss socialism or the complete reshaping of society —the same questions, "turned inside out." Alyosha agrees that for "real Russians" these questions "come first and foremost." The marvel is not that God exists, Ivan goes on, but that the idea of God should have entered the head of "the savage and vicious beast" that man is. For his own part, he accepts God "simply and directly" and even His inscrutable purpose in creating the universe, but he insists that he refuses to accept it. A. J. Ayer, the British logician, has pointed out that the only way one can reject the universe is by killing oneself. Ivan is indeed a prospective suicide.

He is even willing to believe, he explains, that all creation moves toward an ultimate harmony, which will make it possible not only to forgive but also to justify the crimes of mankind. He concedes that human suffering—the earth is soaked with tears from its crust to its center—may have been intended as the price paid for the sublime finale. In that case, his Euclidean mind tells him, "none is guilty," echoing King Lear's "None does offend, none, I say, none." What Ivan cannot bear is the thought that part of the price paid for the far-off divine event is the suffering of children, tortured by adults—"if the Devil doesn't exist, he must have been created by man in his own image and likeness." He proceeds to confront Alyosha and, implicitly, his unfathomable God, with specimens of such atrocities, from a collection he had made and which could, of course, have been monstrously enlarged, had he lived in the mid-twentieth century. Brutality inflicted on children, he insists, can be neither forgiven nor avenged nor atoned for. The tears of one tortured child are "too high a price for harmony." While not denying God, Ivan, unlike Spinoza and Leibnitz, cannot reconcile His existence with that of evil. He questions divine justice, as Job had done of old. Being an honest man, he respectfully returns Him the entrance ticket to the millennium, preferring to stay outside, "unforgiving, unreconciled, intransigent." (This is an echo of a passage in a letter of Belinsky's, dated March 1, 1841, in which he declared that he would hurl himself from the highest rung of the ladder of evolution if account were not rendered him of all his martyred brothers.)

"That's rebellion," Alyosha observes gently. Ivan objects that one can scarcely live by rebellion, and he wants to live, "in spite of logic," certainly at least until he is thirty. He confesses to "a frenzied and perhaps unseemly thirst for life"; the blue sky and the sticky little leaves of spring are dear to him. His youth, he feels, will triumph over his disgust with so botched a world, seen as a "damnable, perhaps diabolical chaos," and keep him going. The novice interposes with the reminder that there is a Being capable of forgiving everyone for everything and on Whose Gospel the final glorious edifice, that will mean ultimate atonement and harmony, is to be erected. No, Ivan assures his brother, he has not forgotten Christ, and he retells "a poem in prose" that he has put together though not written down—"The Grand Inquisitor."

The plot of "The Grand Inquisitor" may be traced to thirteenth-century stories, circulated by monks, in which Christ visits the Pope, who orders the guards to cast Him *"in tenebras exteriores."* In the "poem" Christ, returning to earth, appears in Seville in the sixteenth century, when the Inquisition was at its height, with heretics being burned at the stake every day. He walks the "torrid plazas" of the Spanish city, the people recognizing and adoring Him. As during His first stay on earth, He performs miracles, restoring eyesight to a blind old man, raising a child from the dead. The Grand Inquisitor sees all this; he orders his guards to throw Him into a dungeon. The crowd makes way for them and promptly bows down to the ground before the ninety-year-old prelate, who gives them his blessing in silence. At night he comes alone to visit the prisoner. He tells Him that He is hindering the work of the Church and therefore, on the morrow, will be burned at the stake. He adds that, at a sign from him, the same people who had kissed His feet will heap faggots for the fire.

A long discourse follows. In sum, the Grand Inquisitor accuses Christ of having committed the fatal error of giving man inner freedom, allowing him the choice between belief and disbelief, between good and evil. For fifteen centuries, he says, the Church had grappled with that gift; now it is done for. The Inquisitor complacently envisages an indefinite period of contentment and peace, under the aegis of the Pontiff of Rome. Again, he delineates a different future, but not before detailing his charge against Christ. Satan, he reminds Him, had warned Him that there is no heavier burden for man than freedom of conscience. Permanent domination over body and soul, the prelate continues, can be obtained by three means: Miracle, Mystery, and Authority. When Satan offered these to Christ in the wilderness, He rejected them as baited traps. When He was bidden to turn stones into bread, He declined, saying that man does not live by bread alone. True enough, but, had Christ given men earthly bread in addition to satisfying the other cravings of that ignoble race, they would have surrendered their freedom, and He would have secured a faithful, happy following as numerous as the sands of the seashore. Instead, He had offered men the bread of Heaven, and had won only a minority: the elect, who, in order to believe, do not require the evidence of things seen, but who heed the voice of conscience.

Now the Roman Church, solicitous for the well-being of the common people, has corrected this mistake. It accepted the Devil's offers, spurned by Christ. Though aware that nothing is hidden from Him, the Inquisitor chooses to declare that since the eighth century (*i.e.,* when the foundation of the Papal States was laid by Pepin the Short) the Church of Rome has verily been with Satan. It finds in Miracle a way of enslaving men's minds. Mystery encourages blind obedience; further, it hides from the people the secret of the élite: that God does not exist. Authority, the purple and the sword of Caesar, enables the Church to establish the earthly kingdom ruled by the Supreme Pontiff, and thus satisfy the human longing for a universal State. All this falsely, in the name of Christ.

Forthwith the Inquisitor assumes the role of seer. It appears that the freedom Christ had preached will not have ceased to produce dire results. Grave trials, he predicts, are in store for mankind. People will follow leaders who will absolve them of all moral responsibility, affirming that there are no sinners, no criminals, but only the hungry, who should be fed before virtue is asked of them (a proposition that had been advanced by Belinsky). Priests will be persecuted and tortured, houses of worship destroyed, and an attempt made to erect another Tower of Babel. Untrammeled thought, and faith only in the promise of material plenty, a faith held out by science, will bring about such unrest, confusion, and misery that people will kill one another or themselves. After centuries of anguish they will crawl back into the fold of the Church, desiring only to lay their freedom at its feet. The clergy will emerge from the catacombs, where they had been in hiding, and rule the regimented flock in the name of Christ, but using the means that He had scorned. The onus of freedom lifted from their hearts, knowing the contentment of a well-fed herd, men will rejoice in total submission. Assured of immortality and the rewards of Heaven, they will live serenely and die peacefully. The thousands that make up the governing élite will suffer the martyrdom of a free conscience, but millions will be happy. Such will be the ultimate, everlasting triumph of the Church, resting on Miracle, Mystery, and Authority.

The venerable churchman concludes with a word *pro domo sua.* There was a time when he, too, abode in the wilderness, with locusts and wild honey for his meat. But one day he deserted the ranks of the strong and the proud and, out of a love crossed with contempt for humanity, decided to minister to the weak and the humble. Finally, he announces once more that Jesus will be executed the next day.

Ivan is not content with this conclusion to his "poem" and offers another. Christ had not uttered a word during the Inquisitor's entire discourse. In the second version he waits for Him to speak. For all response, Jesus approaches His adversary and gently kisses him on his withered, bloodless lips. The stern old man opens the door and bids Him go and never, never return. The prisoner disappears in the darkness.

"My socialist," Dostoevsky wrote to his editor, referring to Ivan, "differs from our socialists in that they are conscious Jesuits and liars . . . while he frankly admits that he shares the Grand Inquisitor's views." An entry in the novelist's notebook declares Ivan to be a more extreme atheist than even Europe had produced. "Consequently," the note ends, "not as a mere boy do I believe in and confess Christ, but my hosanna has been tried in a great crucible of doubts." As a matter of fact, Dostoevsky greatly exaggerated his success in depicting Ivan as an example of arrant atheism. The novel presents not a callow blasphemer, not a cold skeptic, but a sorely troubled doubter, at war with himself.

In the subsequent exchange between the brothers Alyosha cries out: "Your poem is in praise of Christ, it does not—as you meant it to do—indict Him." Indeed, the reader agrees with Alyosha that indirectly it does express reverence for Him. The novice remarks further that the "poem" attacks Rome only, and does not touch upon Byzantium. Alyosha, alias Dostoevsky, overlooks the fact that miracle, mystery, and authority, the foundations of the alleged Judas Church of Rome, are not repudiated by the Orthodox Church, which, the novelist never tires of affirming, is the sole repository of Christian faith in its purity. To Alyosha's suggestion that the Catholic revisionists are unbelievers, who want nothing but universal serfdom with themselves in the master's seat, Ivan retorts that his Inquisitor and others like him are actually secret atheists, but may nevertheless be genuine humanitarians who seek to make life tolerable for the common run. "You don't believe in God," Alyosha tells Ivan sorrowfully. He laughs and assures the novice that he has no intention of joining the Jesuits and helping them correct Christ's work. "Dear little brother," he says, "I don't want to corrupt you . . . perhaps I want to be healed by you." He repeats that he has decided to kill himself, but not before he reaches thirty. Alyosha asks where he will find the strength to endure the next few years, with hell in his head and heart. Ivan replies that the strength will be provided by "the Karamazov baseness." He declares explicitly that he will cling to the principle: "Everything is permitted," and asks his brother if he will reject him on that account. Alyosha gets up and kisses Ivan on the lips. "Plagiarism!" Ivan shouts delightedly. Shortly afterward the brothers part, Alyosha going to the right, Ivan to the left.

In commenting on his fantastic fable, Ivan bids Alyosha not take it seriously: "It's only a muddled poem by a dunderhead of a student." When that student is visited by the Devil in a nightmare, of which more later, and the fiend mentions "The Grand Inquisitor," Ivan, "crimson with shame," forbids him to speak of the piece. It is certainly flawed by incoherencies disconcerting in one who represents the intellect. Yet "The Grand Inquisitor" is indubitably arresting in its exploration of matters of major import.

Clearly the "poem" is a dramatization of Dostoevsky's conception of the Catholic Church as anti-Christian. This had been an obsession of his since the late sixties, when, during his stay abroad, he had followed with malicious attentiveness the efforts of the Roman hierarchy to preserve its territorial possessions and augment its political influence, while claiming the infallible pontiff's supremacy over secular rulers. It has been seen that this view of Catholicism is expatiated on in *A Writer's Diary*. There it is foretold that in a crisis the Church of Rome, to advance its interests, will enter into an alliance with militant socialists. As the "poem" is laid in the sixteenth century, these can be referred to only by innuendo and allegory.

Not to this does "The Grand Inquisitor" owe its enduring relevance. Here in sharp contrast are two evaluations of man's moral nature, one exalting, the other emphatically denigrating it. The serenity offered by inner freedom as well as its vexations, dangers, agony, are underscored. Further, the heart of Christian ethics is compellingly, if indirectly, conveyed. What heightens the effect of this chapter of the novel is that the venerable churchman, to whose denunciation Christ answers not a word, has about him a pathos that almost suggests tragedy.

The theocratic regime that the Inquisitor outlines as already attained in part and ultimately to be fully so, aims, he repeats, at achieving the greatest happiness of the greatest number. It is not, however, the happiness of those who are a little lower than the angels, but rather of babes and of the vile, weak creatures, "turned out as a practical joke," who, in the Inquisitor's eyes, make up the majority of mankind. For them, nothing but misery can come of inner freedom. Not its restriction, but the complete regimentation of all in every walk of life, will assure them the contentment that they crave. Sexual relations and family planning, too, will be under control. "We shall allow or forbid them," says the Inquisitor, "to live with their wives or mistresses, to have or not to have children." Alone a ruling élite, as has been noted, will have a monopoly on a free conscience and the concomitant possibility of unbelief. And as has also been noted, the prelate insists that love of humanity is the sole motivation of the Catholic Church in sponsoring that delightful scheme of things in the name of Christ. Clearly, Ivan's "poem" elaborates Shigalyov's blurred blueprint for Utopia in *The Devils*. It is a remarkable anticipation of the yet unborn totalitarian States established after the First World War, such as the Soviet Union and the Nazi *Reich*. The projected regime even shares with them the secrecy which is the mask of dictatorship. In a sense, "The Grand Inquisitor" is a tract for the twentieth century.

# ( III )

The father-son relationship is the major theme in *A Raw Youth*. There the author is concerned with a teen-ager's search for and discovery of his father. In *The Brothers Karamazov* he shows two of the sons possessed by a murderous hatred for their unnatural parent, and builds the novel on the murder of the old man by his bastard, with the tacit connivance of one of his legitimate sons. Here Dostoevsky was driving home the same moral lesson that he had sought to point in *Crime and Punishment*: that the mind, having abandoned the religious attitude toward life, may not be able to return to that haven save by the road of crime. It is mere conjecture that in fashioning the plot he was influenced by Fyodorov's philosophy, in which filial devotion is the sum and substance of piety, and, by the same token, parricide the archcrime. The psychoanalytic view has it that what

Dostoevsky in essence did in this novel was unconsciously re-enact the murder of his father by the outraged serfs and his own reaction to it. This was allegedly, as has been indicated in an earlier chapter, an overpowering sense of guilt, due to the fact that the assassination fulfilled the boy's unconscious wish. The tragedy, with its emotional repercussions, had, it is held, brought on his epilepsy, had informed his thinking, and had strongly affected the play of his imagination. It is his last novel which is his fullest confession; it is here that the whole complex, which had shadowed his life for forty years, is seen less darkly than in any other of his works. Those who read this meaning into *The Brothers Karamazov* are bound to put special emphasis on whatever points to an identification of the author with the two most deeply involved in the murder: Smerdyakov and Ivan. What seems to support the psychoanalytic hypothesis is, as will be seen, Ivan's outburst in court, when he cries out: "Who doesn't desire his father's death?" Much has been made of the fact that the novelist afflicted the actual assassin with his own disease. Freud went so far as to say that he did so "as if he were trying to confess that the epileptic, the neurotic, in him was a parricide." On the other hand, the gentle Alyosha apparently suffers from hysterical epileptoid fits inherited from his mother.

It is Smerdyakov who actually kills the old man and robs him of the three thousand rubles he had put aside to buy Grushenka's favors. But it is upon Ivan that the burden of guilt lies most heavily. He had given himself license to desire the death of his horrible old father. Yet since he held his wish to be inoperative, it was possible for him to believe himself beyond reproach. Smerdyakov, being of coarser fiber, interpreted crudely what he knew to be Ivan's feeling. Having heard him put forward the theory that to a man without faith in God and immortality "everything is permitted," and attributing to him his own mer-cenary motives—every member of the family stood to gain by the old man's death—Smerdyakov decided that he had Ivan's tacit consent to the murder. Ivan's irresponsiveness to his in-nuendoes he took to be the caution of a shrewd man who wished to furnish no evidence of his connivance, and when Ivan left for Moscow after Smerdyakov's hints of what might occur in his absence, the bastard believed that he had the other's mandate to go ahead. He was not wholly mistaken: even before his departure Ivan felt the claw of conscience.

If he bears the brunt of responsibility, his two brothers are in a way implicated in the crime. Dmitry wanted to kill his father and would have been able, in a fit of rage, to carry out the murder. Indeed, suspicion falls on him and he is arrested in a tavern at the height of a delirious orgy, when Grushenka, drunk, vows to be his slave for the rest of her life. She has just sent her first lover packing—a contemptible little man in a wig, a Pole, of course, accompanied by a compatriot, a cardsharp. As for Alyosha, he certainly did not wish the death of his father, for whom he actually had an affection. His sin was wholly one of omission: he had failed to draw Smerdyakov into his spiritual orbit by loving kindness.

Having been apprised of the catastrophe, Ivan returns to the city posthaste. Without delay he goes to see Smerdyakov, and visits him again several times thereafter. The bastard accuses Dmitry of the killing. This does not allay Ivan's apprehension, particularly since Alyosha, whose opinion he prizes highly, insists that Dmitry is innocent. If that is so, Smerdyakov must be the murderer, and he, Ivan, shares the man's guilt. He does not hide this conviction from Katya. The two are "enemies in love with each other," an extreme instance of a typical Dostoevsky relationship. To put an end to Ivan's tormenting uncertainty as to who is the criminal, she shows him a letter she had received from Dmitry on the eve of the murder. He had written that the next day he would kill his father, who had robbed him, even if he is sent to Siberia for it, would take the money from under the old man's pillow and pay her back the three thousand that he owed her. (She had given him the money to remit to her sister, but he had carelessly appropriated and spent part of it, carousing with Grushenka.) Jilted by him for "that creature" and insulted by her to boot, Katya knew the fury of a woman scorned, but, given to swinging between two extremes, her detestation of her former fiancé was apt to give way momentarily to ardent love.

In the meantime Dmitry is undergoing a complete change of heart. It started during the preliminary investigation which was conducted in the tavern. At the end of the proceedings he fell asleep. He dreamed that as he drove past a burned-out village he saw along the road a row of peasant women, all thin and haggard, begging for bread. One of them had in her arms a tot who cried and cried, holding out his bare little arms and little fists blue with cold. A gust of pity that he had never known before swept Dmitry's heart. He wanted to deliver those poor people, indeed, all humanity, from suffering, and do it at once, "with true Karamazov unrestraint." He heard Grushenka's tender voice beside him, and was seized with the desire to live on and to hurry at once toward a new, summoning light. "I've had a good dream, gentlemen," he said as he woke. The crying baby became for him the image of human misery, which would continue to haunt him.

In the jail, awaiting trial, his transformation assumed the character of a spiritual rebirth. On the day preceding the trial he poured out his heart to Alyosha in a frantic, confused speech. The public disgrace and the baseless charge of parricide, he declared, was "a blow from Heaven" with a beneficent result: "A new man has risen in me." He had had a premonition that, though innocent, he would be found guilty, and the prospect of twenty years in the Siberian mines used to frighten him. Now he was no longer afraid of suffering. If he were condemned, he would accept his punishment as an atonement for his disorderly, wicked life, for the injury done to the baby he had seen in his dream, and the injuries done to all babies, because "all are responsible for all." On his way to the tavern where Grushenka had gone to meet her former lover, he had decided to kill himself if he found that he had lost her. Now his hunger for life was insatiable. Some men, certainly Rakitin, perhaps Ivan, believed that chemistry accounts for everything; they can dispense with the Creator. But a man in irons burrowing underground cannot live without God. Speaking for himself and his fellow convicts to be, he cried: "From the bowels of the earth, we will intone a tragic hymn to God, with Whom is joy. Hail to God and His joy. I love Him!"

He has scarcely uttered his frantic hymn when he blurts out that he is not free from doubt. He is yet another soul tormented by God. "What if He doesn't exist?" he asks. Then is everything lawful? And whom will man love, to whom will he be thankful? Above all, "How is he going to be good without God?" he cries out. The thesis that morality rests upon belief in God and immortality is, as has been noted, the burden of Dostoevsky's mature work. Reflecting on this proposition, one recalls a passage from Tolstoy's Confession, begun in 1880, when *The Brothers Karamazov* was being serialized. "Then and now the public profession and confession of Orthodoxy was chiefly met with among people who were dull and cruel and who considered themselves very important. Ability, honesty, reliability, good nature, and moral conduct were more often met with among unbelievers."

Tolstoy was speaking of his own time, but as one looks before and after, the thesis that only a man clinging to God is virtuous remains equally untenable.

Dmitry, turning to matters nearer home, speaks composedly about Grushenka. In the past, he confesses, only her "infernal curves" tormented him, but "now I've taken all her soul into mine and through her become a man myself. . . . We shall fight. But I shall love her, I shall love her infinitely." Dmitry also whispers to Alyosha a deep secret: Ivan has conceived a plan, to which Katya is privy, of having him escape en route to Siberia and then with Grushenka make his way to America. In fact, the details have been thought out and preliminary arrangements have been made. Dmitry is plagued by misgivings: Wouldn't his escape be a running away from his cross? But Ivan is firm, and Alyosha offers no objection. Before leaving Dmitry, he assures his brother that he had never for a moment doubted his innocence.

Later that day Ivan learns that Katya had called on Smerdyakov. The letter that she had previously shown Ivan he had taken to be "a mathematical proof" of his brother's guilt. It now occurs to him that Katya was not sure of it, or she would not have visited the bastard. Torn by doubts, Ivan goes to see Smerdyakov. This time the man, seriously ill, breaks down. He relates in great detail how he had carried out the murder, produces the three thousand rubles that he had stolen from the old man, and bids his visitor take the roll of bills with him when he leaves. This he does. Smerdyakov denies his responsibility, however. "You killed," he tells Ivan, "you are the real murderer. I was only your faithful servant, and it was at your word that I did it." The horrifying truth dawns on Ivan: his own criminal desire, which he had thought safely concealed, had guided the murderer's hand. The scenes, especially the first of them, in which Ivan and Smerdyakov are confronted, are among the subtlest of Dostoevsky's pages.

Ivan is in a state bordering on elation when he leaves the murderer. At last he is free from the torment of uncertainty. On the morrow the two of them will confess to it all in court, hand over the stolen money, and Dmitry will be exonerated. For some time Ivan has felt ill, and when he reaches his quarters he is almost delirious, on the brink of "white fever." He falls asleep and has a nightmare in which a devil appears to him, not for the first time. This demon is quite unlike "the wise and dread spirit" of "The Grand Inquisitor." The epitome of vulgarity, he is a shabby middle-aged gentleman, sporting an eyeglass and fond of broad stories. He is given to excesses of conciliatory and good-natured self-effacement, typical of the hanger-on. There are moments when Ivan feels that his visitor is real, which annoys the unbeliever in him, who knows that this devil is he, himself, his double, his mimic (as Satan, in Tertullian's phrase, is "the ape of God"), the embodiment of his baser self. During their conversation the fiend, who claims to be a philosopher of the Cartesian school, touches on a wide variety of topics, such as dreams, modern medicine, hell, paradise, belief in God, his own reputation, and his temperament. In commenting on his host's proposition that everything is permitted to an atheist, he asks why a Russian must have a moral sanction if he wants to swindle. Ivan is so outraged by this that he grabs a glass and flings it at his visitor. The latter exclaims in amusement: "He remembered Luther's inkstand! He takes me for his dream and throws glasses at it."

Suddently there is a loud knocking at the window. Ivan wakes from his nightmare and lets Alyosha in. He brings the news that Smerdyakov has just hanged himself. Thus *The Brothers Karamazov*, like the other novels, is provided with a suicide. Dmitry had predicted: "God will kill Smerdyakov." Was the suicide another example of the death-dealing effect of atheism? Was it, rather, because he had undergone conversion and been overwhelmed by contrition? As a matter of fact, in his last days he had been reading a pious tract. But like a proper Dostoevsky character, during his last interview with Ivan he both admits and denies having become a believer. In any event, his plan to make a fresh start with the stolen money had collapsed. Had that made life intolerable for him? His end is as obscure as his beginning.

The bastard left no note confessing his guilt. Would the defendant's innocence be established by Ivan's testimony? He goes from his sickbed to court. Called to give evidence, he at first declares that he has nothing to say and makes for the exit, but, like Raskolnikov in a similar situation, he returns. He hands a roll of bills to the court attendant and, turning to the judge, explains that this is the money on account of which his father was murdered. "I got it," he says, "from Smerdyakov, the murderer. It was he, not my brother, who killed our father. He did the killing, and I told him to do it." He adds: "Who doesn't desire his father's death?" and goes on to insist that people's horror at parricide is sham. Then his mind gives way, he becomes violent, throwing the court into confusion, and is removed.

The commotion has barely subsided when Katya has a fit of hysterics. She refuses to leave the court, declaring that she has important evidence to offer at once. In testifying previously, she had made every effort to present Dmitry as honorable and high-minded, without sparing her maidenly modesty. Now she has a sudden reversion. She hands the court the letter that she had received from Dmitry on the eve of the murder and which she had shown Ivan as "a mathematical proof" of his brother's guilt. Beside herself, she cries out that Dmitry is a "monster." As for Ivan's testimony, it is that of a great-hearted man intent on saving his brother and given to unjust self-accusations. Dmitry shouts that he wouldn't have written that letter if he had not been drunk, but the document makes a deep impression on the judges and the jury. Katya's outburst ends in another attack of hysterics. She is carried out, sobbing and screaming.

After the remaining witnesses have testified, the prosecutor has the floor, followed by the lawyer for the defense, a renowned pleader imported from the capital. The ample space accorded to the preliminary investigation is greatly swollen by the account of the court proceedings, owing to the prolific eloquence of the two lawyers. But this does not seriously lessen the dramatic tension inherent in the trial of a parricide. Irony tinges the report of the prosecutor's performance, which is marked by eager rhetoric and insistent psychologizing. The famous Petersburg legal light is characterized by the author as "a debaucher of thought." As has been pointed out, Dostoevsky had no liking for the reformed judiciary. He came to believe that the punishments doled out by Leviathan only increased and multiplied crimes. Alone the Church could assure the security of the body politic. Alone the Church, replacing the State, "would succeed," as Father Zosima put it, "in restraining those who plan evil, and in regenerating the fallen."

When, about midnight, the legal celebrity concludes his plea, he is certain that the acquittal of his client is inevitable and so is the majority of the public. Nevertheless, the jury, apparently relying on the letter presented by Katya, pronounces Dmitry guilty. As no attenuation of the sentence is recommended, he is sure to get twenty years of hard labor in Siberia. His last statement in court ends with: "Katya, I forgive you!"

It appears that he may be spared the lot of a convict. Shortly after the verdict has been pronounced Alyosha calls on Katya to discuss the final preparations for Mitya's escape. She is anguished at having informed on him. Her adored Ivan lies in the adjacent room, gravely ill. Before succumbing to "white fever" he had given her the necessary instructions regarding the arrangements for the escape, as well as half of his inheritance. Part of the money was to be spent on bribing the convoy, the rest was to be used by Dmitry for the trip to America and his settling there with Grushenka.

On leaving Katya, Alyosha goes to see Dmitry in the hospital where he occupies a cubicle in the prisoners' ward—since the end of the trial he had been suffering from "nervous fever." He accepts the plan for his escape. Alyosha agrees that bribing is wrong, but allows that there are cases when it is permissible. Grushenka would not be able to come to him in Siberia and convicts are forbidden to marry. In jail Dmitry had told Alyosha that he had unlimited strength; now he admits that he is not equal to his "cross." What further eases his conscience is the thought that he is not turning tail in pursuit of pleasure. America will be another kind of penal servitude, "perhaps as bad as Siberia." Thus he will hug his "cross" and also derive the spiritual benefits of suffering. "I hate that America already," he exclaims. "And though they may be wonderful at machinery, every one of them, damn them, they are not my kind, they are strangers to my soul. I love Russia, Alyosha, I love the Russian God, though I am a scoundrel myself." He plans many years later to return to Russia, so that he and Grushenka may die in their native land.

Suddenly Katya appears on the threshold of the cubicle. Alyosha had persuaded her to come, if only for a moment, out of pity for Mitya. After a brief exchange, she says, her face wet with tears: "You love another woman now, and I another man, and yet I shall always love you, and you will love me." He responds with: "So it will be, so it will always be." When he asks if she believes that he was the murderer, Katya answers that she had never believed it, yet when she was testifying for the second time she persuaded herself that she did, but only momentarily. Having repeated that she came to punish herself, she leaves.

Dmitry's regeneration, like Raskolnikov's, is promised but not presented. What Mitya feared, he confessed to Alyosha, was not suffering, but the possibility that the new man whom he felt stirring within him might be submerged by the ordeal in store for him. What sort of person he would become either in Siberia or, if his escape were successful, in America remains uncertain. As the novelist said of Raskolnikov's new life, that is "another story."

# ( IV )

"The blasphemy of my hero will be solemnly refuted in the next Book, on which I am now working with fear, trepidation and awe, for I consider my task—the defeat of anarchism [by which he meant the extreme form of militant socialism]—a civic exploit." Thus Dostoevsky wrote to the managing editor of *Russky vestnik,* having mailed the first half of Book Five, in which Ivan voices his rebellion. In another letter, accompanying Book Six, "A Russian Monk," which deals with Father Zosima, he said that although he had not succeeded in expressing one tenth of what he wanted to, he considered this the climax of the novel. (Three months earlier he had assigned the same distinction, with better reason, to the chapters "Pro and Contra.")

Pobedonostzev, having read the installment in which Ivan speaks out, wrote flatteringly to the novelist, but noted with regret that he had not, so far, countered the young atheist's propositions. To his illustrious correspondent Dostoevsky repeated that the answer to Ivan, though not indeed a logical rebuttal, point by point, was contained in the section devoted to Father Zosima. But would his readers understand? Had he made himself clear? He was anxious. He had to meet the requirements of the art of fiction while driving his lesson home. To some people certain passages would seem either too rapturous or absurd, but, more inwardly considered, they were deeply true. He had written those pages with great love. He would compel men to admit that a "pure, ideal Christian" was no abstraction, but an actual, tangible figure, and, incidentally, that Christianity alone would medicine all of Russia's ills. Here—he spoke as if he were not the author of *The Idiot*—was a subject of absolute originality. "For the sake of it," he concluded, "the entire novel is being written."

Father Zosima was introduced early in the narrative, the author seeking in more than one scene to illustrate the monk's acute intuitiveness, compassion, wisdom. But it is only in "The Russian Monk" that Dostoevsky attempted a rounded picture of the *staretz.* Like not a few of the godly, in his youth he had undergone an instantaneous religious conversion. Previously he had been leading the life of an army officer, "a cruel, absurd, almost savage creature." In the novel he is shown at the end of his days. This blithe spirit, faintly reminiscent of St. Francis, an example of meekness and serenity, is one for whom loving kindness is alpha and omega, and hell the inability to love. There is nothing stern or harsh about him. "Pray God for joy," he admonishes his flock. "Men were created for happiness. All the righteous, the saints, the holy martyrs were happy." Rapture and ecstasy are a blessing. "All of God's work," he affirms, "is beautiful and good." He sees the monastic regimen as intended to keep the image of Christ pure, so that in the fullness of time it would bring the worldly into the fold of the faithful.

His moral extremism is exemplified in his admonition that one should refuse to sit in judgment on a fellow man, and instead, take his crime on oneself, suffer for it, and let the criminal go without reproach. Yet he can also accept compromise. When the old Karamazov jestingly asks the *staretz* what he should do to inherit eternal life, the answer is: close your pothouses, if not all, at least two or three. Human beings, he would have it, are united by the bond of mutual responsibility: each is guilty of the sins and crimes of all. He admits, however, that a growing egotism is destroying this bond and that other kinds of corruption are spreading from above downward among the Russians. People have lost interest in their fellowmen and live in isolation. "The number of things they have accumulated is greater, but there is less joy," says the *staretz.* Fortunately, the lower orders at least, though steeped in sin, "believe in God and weep tears of devotion," and this will be Russia's salvation. Father Zosima is sanguine for yet another reason: class conflict is impossible in Russia. "The time will come," he predicts, "when even the most corrupt rich man will end by being ashamed of his riches before the poor, and these, seeing his humility, will respond joyously and kindly."

The *staretz,* it will be remembered, also predicted—he is given to prophecy—that Christian society, now almost a heathen body, by Divine ordinance will eventually be transformed into the universal Church. Indeed, Dostoevsky had told Solovyov that the central idea of his novel was that the ideal toward which society should move must be the Church, as Solovyov himself believed. The novelist's ultraconservative friends were doubtless reassured when they realized that the transfiguration of the State was a millennial vision, not a practical program. What would become of the established order if that hope were fulfilled? Dostoevsky was an untrustworthy ally. His evangelical Christianity was tinged with anarchism in the conventional sense of the word. He harbored an instinctive animus against the State, conceived of as a soulless monster.

In a preliminary note for the novel Father Zosima counsels his flock thus: "Children, do not seek miracles, for miracles kill faith." This was a lapse into heresy: the Orthodox Church, no less than the Catholic, prizes miracle. Dostoevsky was certainly aware that the naïve faith of the peasant, which he was always crying up, fed on the miraculous. Evidently he came to recognize his blunder. The injunction of the *staretz* does not appear in the final text. On the other hand, in Ivan's "poem" much is made of the fact that Christ spurned miracle as diabolical. Father Zosima's death soon after Alyosha's meeting with Ivan was followed by an unnaturally rapid corruption of the body. This caused extraordinary agitation in the town. The clerics and some of the laity alike had eagerly expected that the remains of the saintly monk would manifest miraculous healing powers. Dostoevsky assured his editor that he had not invented the episode—such an occurrence had taken place in the revered monastery on Mount Athos. He would not have allowed himself, he wrote, inconsistent as he often was, to cast the slightest doubt on the miraculous healing power of holy relics. The incident was needed for the story: the scandal was a convenient way of testing Alyosha's faith.

For years, indeed, ever since he had conce'ved the grandiose project of *The Life of a Great Sinner,* Dostoevsky had wanted to enshrine in a novel, against a monastic background, the image of a saintly man, a rock of the Church. The unpublished chapters of *The Devils* contain a faint outline of such a character in such a setting. And now at last his dream was a reality. A reality? Scarcely. He believed that he had a firm grasp on the figure of Father Zosima, and stated with unintended humor that he shared the monk's ideas. Father Zosima is a mere shadow, a pale abstraction, compared to the solidity of a Karamazov. The novelist

wrote that the deathbed exhortations of the *staretz* were no
homilies. As a matter of fact, a hagiological odor clings to the
whole section in which the career and the teachings of Father
Zosima are retailed in a homiletic style. They are the work of
a preacher, no Savonarola. These pages are not a refutation of
Ivan's "blasphemy." The story of the monk's life opens with an
account of the last days of his brother, who died of consumption.
The youth had been led astray by a local atheist, but inexplicably
overcame the baneful influence and accepted his end with seraphic
joy. The situation somewhat resembles that of Ippolit in *The
Idiot,* but there the boy rebels against his outrageous fate. His
outburst has a savage thrust, carries a tearing grief, while the
history of the monk's brother is unconvincing and intolerably
mawkish. Dostoevsky failed to realize the *staretz* because, one
suspects, this character was derived from the surface of his
mind. The presentation of a perfect Christian, with no trace of
the human weakness to be found in Myshkin and Alyosha Karamazov, with no grain of the evil which the novelist regarded as
fundamental to human nature, was a task beyond the powers of
any novelist, and moreover foreign to his genius, however deeply
devoted to such an enterprise he felt himself to be.

He must have surmised that the section dealing with Father
Zosima was not an answer to Ivan. Dostoevsky made a jotting
in his notebook to the effect that the whole novel was an answer.
Of course, it was no more a logical rebuttal than the Zosima
chapters. But it is true that both Dmitry and Alyosha offer a
yea-saying to the world which triumphs over, though it does not
cancel, Ivan's doubts and negation. The passionate affirmation
of Dmitry, who most fully embodies the Karamazov *bezuderzh*
(unrestraint, impetuosity), is incomparably set forth. In a different way Alyosha exhibits the same attitude. What Albert
Camus called "the splinter of doubt" enters his faith, due to
the lingering effect of his talk with Ivan and to the scandal
attending the death of his *staretz.* But the splinter is removed,
and after his visit to Grushenka he returns to the cell where the
Gospel is being read over the body. As he listens, kneeling, to
the recital of the passage on the marriage at Cana of Galilee,
he falls into a gentle doze and dreams that his beloved *staretz*
and he are at the wedding feast, drinking "the new wine, the
wine of new great joy."

He wakes in a state of ecstasy, leaves his dead and goes into
the still, starlit night. "The hush of earth seems to melt into

the hush of the heavens. The mystery of earth touches the mystery of the stars. . . ." He stands gazing, and suddenly, his heart swollen with rapture, he drops to the ground, kisses the earth, and watering it with tears of joy, vows to love it "for ever and ever." It was as though threads from "God's innumerable worlds" joined in his soul and it vibrated with them. Writing even before he dispatched the chapter containing this scene, Dostoevsky declared it to be "the most essential" passage in Book Seven, perhaps in the whole novel (still unfinished).

To labor, once again, for the greater glory of God was his manifest intention in writing *The Brothers Karamazov*. Small wonder, then, that faith is allowed the final word in the novel, the faith of the simple folk. On the very last page Alyosha affirms his belief in the resurrection of the dead. In answer to the boys' question as they stand at the grave of little Ilyusha, he says: "Certainly we shall rise again, certainly we shall see each other and relate to each other with joy and gladness all that has happened." Carried away by love for their mentor and comrade, the children shout: "Hurrah for Karamazov!" The cry is more than an amen to Alyosha's pious affirmation. More than a promise to heed his parting admonition not to be afraid of life. Although the boys are expressing their devotion to Alyosha, the associations with "Karamazov" cannot be limited to this one bearer of the name. The reader may well hear the shout as a hosanna to all of life, its miseries notwithstanding. The hosanna seems to have behind it the force of the whole massive, inclusive book.

# 27

## "DO NOT DETAIN ME"

WHEN, on November 8, 1880, Dostoevsky sent the managing editor of *Russky vestnik* the epilogue of *The Brothers Karamazov*, he wrote: "So the novel is finished! It was three years in the making and it took three years to have it printed. . . . Permit me not to bid you farewell. I intend to live and write another twenty years." It appears from the brief Foreword to *The Brothers* that one of his projects was a sequel to the novel. In the work that we have Alyosha plays a subordinate part, but in the author's mind, we are told, he was the hero of the tale. The drama related in *The Brothers Karamazov* was a mere incident in his early youth, laid in 1867 or thereabouts, while his story proper was to be the substance of a second volume, the action to take place at the start of the eighties. Little is known of Dostoevsky's plans for this book and that little is doubtful. A contemporary has it that the boys mentioned in *The Brothers* were to figure as the chief characters in the sequel, which was to be called *The Children*. Dostoevsky told his friend A. S. Suvorin that Alyosha was to become involved in the revolutionary movement, take part in an act of terror, and be executed. According to Anna's more plausible version, he was to marry Lise, abandon her, go astray, and at last find his way back to the monastery, where he was to end his days, a beloved teacher, surrounded by a flock of children.

For the present, however, that work was not to be thought of. The enterprise to which Dostoevsky turned forthwith was *A Writer's Diary*. The thought of it had been with him while he was writing the novel. There were things that he felt impelled to say to his compatriots without the indirections of fiction. As early as August, 1879, he was writing to Pobedonostzev: "I have, I really have something to say, and just in the way in which you would have me say it." On resuming the *Diary,* he expected to appeal to this eminent friend for advice, as he had done previously. How gravely he regarded his task may be judged from the words he wrote to Aksakov just before embarking upon it: "Having decided to issue the *Diary* again next year, I have often prayed to God on my knees to grant me a pure heart, a pure, sinless word, spoken without irritation, without envy."

*The Brothers Karamazov* was still on the stocks when he began making jottings for the forthcoming *Diary.* Some of them were incorporated into the sole number that appeared in 1881. It is of a piece with its predecessors. There is the same rambling, muddle-headed, opinionated comment on the topics of the day, with excursions into political philosophy and occasional flareups of prophetic fire. The issue opens with an attempt, only half serious, to touch upon the financial questions which then occupied everyone's attention, but soon Dostoevsky leaves this difficult ground and turns to such familiar matters as the antinomy of Russia and Europe, the alienation of the intellectuals from the masses, the mission of the Russian people.

Here is once more the same medley of populist sentiment and monarchist faith, of Christian professions and jingoistic bluster. "Above all," he writes, "I stand for the masses, I believe religiously in their soul, in their great strength, which no one among us knows in its full scope and grandeur." Among his notes for the issue is the round statement: "The ideal of beauty is the Russian people." However lacking the masses may be in other ways, at least they have something to live by: their God and their Czar. The Orthodox faith is their one spiritual treasure. As for the bond between the people and the Czar, it is like that between a father and his children, a bond that is the adamant foundation of all Russian history, past, present, and to come. As a matter of fact the father of his people was just then hiding in his palace as in a prison, the object of a manhunt on the part of some of his children. One of the very men who were plotting against the Czar's life lodged just above the Dostoevsky flat and was arrested the very night that the novelist was taken mortally ill. In Dostoevsky's eyes the terrorists were the ultimate dreadful symbol of the division between the intellectuals and the people. That the simple-hearted believer in his monarch's good will was not free from skepticism may be seen from a jotting in his notebook to the effect that he would serve the Czar even more faithfully if the latter would come to believe that the people were his children. "Only," he adds wistfully, "he is taking too long to believe it."

The way for the Czar to show his fatherly confidence in the people, the novelist holds, is by inviting them to speak freely before him. It is the peasants, by no means the intelligentsia, who should be asked to tell their needs in a straightforward fashion, without resorting to any semblance of a Western parliament. The details of this happy scheme Dostoevsky is content to leave to the authorities. He says merely that "the inquiry may be conducted locally, by districts and cottages." At last the man of the soil will become vocal, and this will have momentous effects. For one thing, perhaps the old wall that has been standing between the classes and the masses will crumble. The honest utterance of the plain man—that will be Russia's salvation, that, rather than the "crowning of the edifice" of which so much talk is heard. The cryptic phrase referred to a constitution establishing parliamentary government. Any direct mention in the press of this consummation, which liberals had devoutly wished for generations, was taboo, and even the euphemism for it was used with circumspection.

Not everyone in higher government circles saw the salvation of the old order in bloody reprisals against the terrorists. There were those who favored liberal reforms along with a firm attitude toward subversion. They gained ascendancy when Count Loris-Melikov was appointed Minister of the Interior after heading a Supreme Commission for the Maintenance of State Order and Public Peace. He went so far as to propose the establishment of a consultative legislative Commission, which was to include elected delegates from zemstvo boards and municipal councils, in addition to functionaries and appointed experts. The plan, which was taken to be the first step toward representative government, was dubbed by a humorist "the bobtailed constitution."

Dostoevsky has nothing but scorn for the idea of a parliamentary regime. To the people this could only mean a change of masters, a change for the worse. He heaps contumely on "the white vests" (the prospective Russian M.P.s) and their "talkery." Their efforts, he writes in the *Diary,* are bound to be a failure. "They will only knock their heads against each other in the dark." In his notebook he abuses the constitution, the "European wench," in unprintable terms. What angers him above all is the notion of interposing anything between the people and their Czar. In Russia, he prophesies, freedom will be established "without revolutions, limitations [of the supreme powers], contracts"; for him freedom is the union between the autocrat and the populace. In essence what Dostoevsky wants is a dictatorship of the peasantry—a crowned dictatorship. And in the fullness of time this peasant empire will become an all-embracing Church, a spiritual union in Christ. This is what he calls "Russian socialism," contrasting it with the soulless materialistic socialism of the West. This transformation of State into Church, one reads in his notebook, will be the true "crowning of the edifice," but a couple of pages further on he observes realistically that the Church as a living institution has been in a state of paralysis since the time of Peter. It was that "Nihilist," he wrote to Pobedonostzev, who had uprooted the native culture.

Christianity versus socialism, the solution of the social problem by love or by reason—this dilemma vexed Dostoevsky to the last. He has no doubts as to which will prevail: "A sudden new spirit will blow." Certainly Russia has nothing to fear, although the future is fraught with danger. The end of the world is coming, he prophesies, falling into his apocalyptic strain. The close of the century will be marked by such a cataclysm as has never been seen before. But Russia must stand like a rock, and the waves will break on her shore. "No, we have no socialism, not at all," is his last word.

As though he needed to reassure himself on this point, he kept returning to his other favorite idea, namely that morality is rooted in faith. "Moral ideas," he jotted in his notebook, "spring from religious feeling. Logic can never justify them." And again: "Conscience without God is a horror; it may go astray to the point of immorality." The sole touchstone of morality is Christ. "But this," he goes on, "is no longer philosophy; this is faith; and faith is [as unmistakable as] the color red." As though not yet satisfied with his formulation of the idea, he stages a brief

debate with a utilitarian, which concludes thus: "To turn the
other cheek, to love another more than yourself, not because it is
advantageous, but because you like it to the point of its becoming
a fervent feeling, a passion. 'Christ was mistaken'—admitted.
This fervent feeling says: I would rather stay with the mistake,
with Christ, than with you." It is the conviction that he believed
he had acquired in prison a quarter of a century previously and
that he had then expressed in practically identical terms.

In the same breath he preaches turning the other cheek and
advocates, in his *Diary,* a public policy of shrewdness and violence. In Europe, he writes, Russia should lie low, all the while
working hard at home in secret preparation for the coming conflict. But in the East aggressiveness must be the order of the day.
"In Europe we were hangers-on and slaves, Asia we shall enter
as masters." Besides, the Russians, though Europeans, are also,
and perhaps more truly, Asiatics. Skobelev's victory over the
Turkomans on January 12, 1881, which completed the conquest
of Turkestan, seems to him of immense historic significance, since
Asia might play a decisive part in the future of the country.
With its vast expanses, the continent is perhaps destined to save
Russia from communism. Alexander I had made a capital mistake, he argues, in failing to come to terms with Napoleon after
driving him out: had he done so, the two might have divided the
world, France securing the West and Russia the East (a few
years earlier, it will be recalled, he had predicted that the world
would be divided between Russia and Germany). Napoleon
would have failed in the end, but Russia would have retained
the East and, as a sea power, could easily have defeated England. That old error must be rectified: Russia must face east.
"To Asia! To Asia!" Dostoevsky cries, and the last public utterance of this apostle of Christian love was a cheer for Skobelev's
conquering battalions.

# ( II )

The year 1881 opened auspiciously. The novel was a huge success in every respect—a staggering number of copies, fifteen
hundred in all, were sold within a few days after its publication
in book form. Furthermore, subscriptions to the *Diary* were

pouring in. Dostoevsky's health seemed better than usual, although it was clear that only his nervous energy sustained him. He went out a good deal and even consented to take part in private theatricals arranged by Countess Tolstoy, widow of the poet and playwright. As the month wore on, however, and the publication date for the first issue of the *Diary* approached, he was again in his customary hectic state. Would the censor pass the remarks on summoning the spokesmen of the peasantry? It was a matter of great importance to him, since he intended to return to the subject repeatedly in the course of the year. By Sunday, January 25, the entire copy for the issue was in the hands of the printer and Dostoevsky had received a reassuring word from the censor to the effect that the text would not be tampered with. The day found him, relieved at having the issue safely off his hands, in a good mood and the house was full of visitors. Before the afternoon was over, however, his irritability got the better of him and he had a little tiff with one of them over a trivial matter. At night he wrote a letter to the managing editor of *Russky vestnik,* pleading for immediate payment of a little over four hundred rubles owing him, on the grounds that he was "in extreme need of money." This was his last letter. The next summer, he had told Anna, he was planning to buy a piece of land near Moscow, and he may have been trying to scrape together cash for that purpose.

The following day his sister Vera, who had come from Moscow on a visit, was dining with the family. The meal began pleasantly enough, with jokes and reminiscences, but soon the guest steered the conversation toward that sore subject, the Kumanina inheritance. Indeed, she had come as an envoy of the other sisters, all of them incensed by Dostoevsky's having secured through litigation a share in the estate to which the will did not entitle him. Vera's mission was to persuade her brother to give up a part of it, and she did not mince words in denouncing his greed and cruelty. She ended by bursting into tears, and he, mortified beyond words, left the table before dinner was over and fled to his study. The ugly scene was destined to be the last in a long feud. As he sat at his desk, his head in his hands, he suddenly realized that they were wet with blood that was trickling from his mouth: he was having a hemorrhage.

Such is his daughter's account of what occurred. Strakhov's reminiscences lend some slight support to this story. On the other hand, Dostoevsky's widow says nothing in her memoirs of any family quarrel. According to her, the hemorrhage of the lungs came late at night and was caused by the strain of moving a heavy piece of furniture.

The doctor arrived, and in the course of the examination there was another flow of blood, which brought on a fainting spell. On recovering consciousness, the patient called for a priest, confessed, and received extreme unction. As soon as the priest left, Anna came in with the children to congratulate him upon having taken the sacrament. He gave the children his blessing and bade them love each other and take care of their mother. He asked her to read them the parable of the prodigal son. Then he bade them never forget what they had just heard, trust in God, and, should they fall into evil ways, remember that God's forgiveness was infinite and that He would rejoice in their repentance as the father had rejoiced in the return of his prodigal son. When the children left the room, he turned to Anna, thanked her for the happiness she had brought him, and begged her forgiveness for any unkindness he may have shown her.

On Tuesday he was cheerful, called in the children, spoke to them in a whisper, and even tried to amuse them by showing them a humorous weekly that had just come. Then the make-up man arrived with news that the issue of the *Diary* had been passed by the censor, but that the copy was seven lines too long and would have to be cut. With Anna's help the difficulty was ironed out and Dostoevsky was able to rest. Meanwhile the news of his illness had got abroad and expressions of concern began to pour in.

A quiet night followed. Waking while it was still dark, Anna, who had slept on a mattress beside the couch where he lay, found his eyes fixed upon her. She bent over him. He had been awake for hours, he whispered, and added that he knew he would die that day. He asked her to light a candle and give him his Bible. She handed him the copy of the New Testament which had been presented to him in Siberia and which he always kept by him. He was in the habit of opening it at random and telling his fortune by the passage upon which his eye lighted. He opened it thus now and bade her read. The words she read at the top of the page were these: "But John detained him, saying: I have need to be baptized of thee, and comest thou to me? But Jesus answering said unto him: Do thou not detain me, for thus it becometh us to fulfill all righteousness." " 'Do thou not detain me,' " Dostoevsky repeated; "that means I shall die." And he closed the book.*

He was calm and tried to comfort Anna, speaking of the children, reminding her of their happiness together, assuring her that in the fourteen years of their married life he had not been unfaithful to her even in thought (had he utterly forgotten Polina?). She tried to turn his mind to other things and begged him to rest. He obeyed her and was silent, but she knew by his expression that he was still brooding on death, though it held no terrors for him. Did she read his face aright? In her account of those last hours she is plainly intent upon painting a picture of a truly Christian passing. He was dying at the height of his powers, with his work unfinished and just when, for the first time, there was some hope of going on with it unhampered. Was he confronting his end with the submissiveness with which he had accepted his prison sentence, or was he relinquishing his hold with the reluctance of one who shared the Karamazov lust for life? Did he feel no shudder of dread, had he at last recovered that faith in which he could confidently murmur his childhood prayer: "All my hope I place in thee, Mother of God; shelter me under thy mantle"?

In the morning the bleeding became persistent, and all hope was abandoned. The one thought that seemed to oppress the dying man was that he was leaving Anna and the children without means. Certainly they could not depend on the income from his published works. Where would they turn? He kept whispering broken words of pity to Anna, as she sat beside him holding his hand. Several times the children came in for a brief moment, and he gave little Fedya his chief treasure: his New Testament.

As the day wore on the apartment filled up with friends and relatives. Pasha rushed in, demanding to be admitted to the sick-

---

* This account figures in the reminiscences of Dostoevsky's widow. She told an early biographer of her husband that the reading of the Bible took place in the afternoon of the day he died. The page in question bears the following inscription in her hand: "Opened by me and read at Fyodor Mikhailovich's request on the day of his death at 3 o'clock." The passage on which he lighted was Matthew III: 14-15. In the King James version it reads: "But John forbade him, saying, I have need to be baptized of thee, and comest thou to me? And Jesus answering said unto him, Suffer it to be so now: for thus it becometh us to fulfill all righteousness." This is somewhat different from what Dostoevsky's wife read. The book before her was a copy of the 1820 edition of the Russian New Testament. In later editions the text of verse 15 was corrected to bring it closer to the original and so to the English translation.

room, but was prevented from entering it. He was excited. He kept insisting that, as his stepfather had as yet made no disposition of his property, a notary should be summoned at once to draw up a will.

Toward seven in the evening Dostoevsky had a severe hemorrhage and sank into a coma. The doors of the sickroom were opened, and people filed into the shabby, gloomy chamber, the master's study. It was an added agony for Anna to share his last moments with these outsiders, some of whom were not even friends, but she was helpless. The motionless figure, fully dressed, lay on the couch, and there was no sound but the whistle of weak, difficult breathing. His head was thrown back upon the pillow, and a light nearby fell squarely upon the white forehead and cheeks and a smudge of blood on the chin. The two children knelt at the head of the couch, making the sign of the cross over and over in a frightened, hurried way. Anna clung to his hand. At last the priest came to murmur the prayer for the dying. It was eight thirty-eight when the doctor, bending over the body of Fyodor Dostoevsky, caught the last beat of that divided heart.

# POSTSCRIPT

URING his last years Dostoevsky's reputation owed not a little to his publicist writings. Death, retiring the journalist, advanced the novelist, but at the moment of his passing the tributes were paid to both. The loudest acclaim came from those who represented and upheld the established order. Grand Dukes sent the widow telegrams of condolence. The Czar granted her a pension of two thousand rubles.* The funeral expenses were paid by the Ministry of the Interior. Walking behind the coffin were the Minister of Education and Pobedonostzev. The latter was appointed guardian of the orphans. Church and State united to turn the stupendous obsequies into a quasi-official ceremony. To some the spectacle of the bishops eulogizing Russia's Marquis de Sade, as Turgenev put it, was food for irony. There was a handful of radicals who remembered that the dead man had once fought in the cause of freedom. A group of students among the mourners was restrained by the police from carrying fetters in memory of Dostoevsky's political martyrdom. But on

---

* Before the Revolution the bereaved family was prosperous, thanks chiefly to the income from the sale of Dostoevsky's books. Less than a year after the Bolsheviks seized power Anna died in Yalta, without a relative or friend at her side and almost destitute.

the whole it was as the religious zealot, the apostle of pity and love, the spiritual guide, that he was extolled.

A month later the capital was agitated by another funeral, that of Alexander II, who had been killed by a terrorist bomb. His successor pursued a policy of repression which postponed until the reign of Nicholas II the hour of reckoning and made it more terrible when it came.

The posthumous response to Dostoevsky's work can receive only brief consideration here. During the gray eighties the revolutionary turbulence subsided, and his popularity reflected in part the triumph of the forces of reaction. As the century drew to a close his writings found an increasingly receptive audience among intellectuals with an antipositivist bias. The decadent writers, so called by their detractors, declared Dostoevsky their forerunner. Tenderminded sophisticates in search of a comforting faith looked to him for support. After the abortive uprising of 1905–06, God-seeking and God-building became the fashion. The neo-Christians adopted him as their spiritual father and hailed him as the prophet of Russia's messianic destiny. Even in revolutionary circles he was valued not only as a novelist of genius. Lenin excoriated *The Devils,* yet wrote that the "unsurpassed" evocation of penal servitude in Siberia was also a picture of the "house of the dead" in which the Russian people lived under the Romanov czars.

At the fall of the empire the influence of Dostoevsky was in the air that literate Russia breathed. Although he had stood up for what was most odious to the Bolsheviks in the order that they had overthrown, early on, his prestige commanded the respect of the Soviet regime. He was second only to Tolstoy in the list of authors to whom monuments were to be erected, according to a decree signed by Lenin on July 30, 1918. In a speech made at the unveiling of Dostoevsky's statue in Moscow, he was declared to have been the harbinger of the Revolution. In 1921, on the occasion of the centenary of his birth, the Commissar of Education gave him a place of honor among Russia's "great prophets." To the émigrés he remained the seer of the Apocalypse.

Before long the encomia grew less frequent and a chilly note crept into the commentaries. Fledgling authors were warned against the influence of a writer who had failed to see that evil in human beings was the consequence of an evil social system.

Yet he had apologists who pointed to his high conception of the country's future, to his insight into the pathology of the soul of man under capitalism, to his abomination of the bourgeoisie abroad and his dread of its rise at home. At worst, they had it, one could pay him the tribute due a mighty adversary whom all the enemies of militant democracy must plagiarize. A permissive period lasting a little less than the first score of years under the hammer and sickle witnessed the appearance of the most complete edition of his works, with all the apparatus of scholarship. His papers in the archives were accorded publication, illuminating the gestation of the novels, and a large part of his correspondence was also brought out.

During the two black decades of terror that ensued, the novelist was in the bad books of the Party. Curiously enough, the Dostoevsky Museum was not closed and his works were not removed from the public libraries. Yet attempts to rehabilitate him were discouraged. Quoting Gorky to the effect that Dostoevsky was "the evil genius" of the Russian people, one critic declared that there was nothing more harmful than to try to lend "a pink glow" to that "reactionary countenance," the more so since he was widely read in the Soviet Union.

After Stalin's death in 1953 the official clouds lifted. An edition of Dostoevsky's collected fiction, including *The Devils,* was started with a printing of three hundred thousand copies. This was in commemoration of the seventy-fifth anniversary of the novelist's death. The occasion was solemnized on a large scale. An editorial in *Pravda* argued that "both the strong and the weak sides of his art should be neither over- nor under-estimated," and emphasized his having been "a humanitarian who told the truth about the life of the oppressed millions." The leader of nations had then been in the Mausoleum on the Red Square for three years.

By this time Dostoevsky's work had long been part of world culture. The West showed his performance a hospitality that, with other virtues, he had summarily denied it. Translations had begun to appear while he was still living. During the eighties they were welcomed in France. A decade after his death the bulk of his writings was accessible in German. Shortly before the First World War his collected fiction began to appear in English under a London, and, a little later, a New York imprint. It was during the war and the decade following it that his vogue in the West, especially Germany, reached its peak. The sadism fostered by the war lent this "cruel talent" a new relevance. Further, the atmosphere of his novels was congenial to men caught in the grip of catastrophe. Hermann Hesse saw him as the prophet of Europe's doom. To others he was the apostle of a revived Christianity or the keeper of the keys to the unconscious. A reaction against what amounted to a cult of Dostoevsky occurred in the English-speaking countries in the years immediately following the Second World War. Simultaneously his popularity waned in Germany under the impact of Nazi xenophobia.

The pendulum soon swung back in the opposite direction. Biographies, stimulating critical studies, new translations, multiplied. The last-named are not confined to the major languages of the West, indeed, of the world. *Poor Folk* can be read in Chinese. Dostoevsky's mark is said to be discernible in the recent fiction of India. Much of his work is available in Turkish and Persian. His influence is evident in the performance of certain Western writers, among them Thomas Mann, Franz Kafka, Rainer Maria Rilke, André Gide, William Faulkner. The Christian existentialists mention him as a predecessor. The *nouveau roman* group regards itself as his heir.

At home Dostoevsky has been officially restored to his place of honor in the hierarchy of the Russian "classics," a position that for the general reader he had never lost. While the commentators do not overlook his abhorrence of socialism and revolution, his public championship of the autocracy, his preoccupation with religion, stress is placed on his having been an ardent patriot, a detractor of the privileged and predatory classes, one who exalted the common people. Above all, he is seen as a major novelist in the hallowed native tradition of social-minded realism. To a limited degree he remained faithful to the basic precepts with which he had been indoctrinated in his youth: objective, truthful representation of the social scene, aimed at bettering the conditions under which men labored. His language, occasionally slipshod, his solicitude for the accuracy of factual details, are alike suitable to a workaday realism. Furthermore, the references in his fiction to current events and its concern with public issues testify to what he called his "thirst for contemporaneity," which Belinsky would have approved heartily. Yet he had an unusual conception of what realism entails.

If he did cast light on the Russian scene of his time, it was a refracted light. He averred that alone the writer's personal vision made for the most penetrating portrayal of what he observed. His "special eye" enabled him to see what others did not and, moreover, to gain foreknowledge of what only the future would reveal. When he was planning *The Life of a Great Sinner* he wrote to Strakhov: "I have my own peculiar view of reality (in art), and what the generality call almost fantastic and exceptional constitutes for me the very essence of the real." In fact, Dostoevsky was committed to *fantastic realism*. He was at pains to justify, to legitimize, as it were, this paradoxical concept. At its extreme, he ventured, the ordinary, the commonplace, borders on the fantastic. Furthermore, the life of people alienated from the soil and the folk could not be anything but weird. The same was true of individuals who were part of a society in which the family appeared to be vanishing, the start of the disintegration of the body politic. Russia, he feared, was in just such a situation. He wrote to a group of students, it will be recalled, that the country was tottering on the edge of an abyss. This did not keep him from repeatedly publishing his conviction that Russia was a monolithic empire and the mightiest power in Europe. Yet he had few equals in depicting what he regarded as disarray, disorder, chaos. This aspect of his work cannot but speak to men in our time. While his contemporaries, impressed by the triumphs of science and technology, looked confidently toward progress as inevitable, he was haunted by visions of war and revolution, of breakdown and collapse. Over his last three novels there could well be inscribed Yeats's well-known line: "Things fall apart; the centre cannot hold; . . ."

His confrères focused on figures who had taken on the solidity of the typical. He, on the contrary, chose as more grateful models aberrant individuals who were only potentially typical. Such individuals, imaginatively projected by exaggeration and intensification, abound in his fiction. They are passionate souls, often swinging between extremes, vainly reaching out for certainties, people not seldom sick in body and mind. Not a few of them are dominated by idea-feelings of a moral or metaphysical order, to the point of being, like the author, possessed by them.

What enhances the fantastic quality of Dostoevsky's narratives is the eerie atmosphere that pervades many of his pages. The narrator, whether the author or another, relies largely on hints, suggestions, glimmerings. In the telling, something is withheld. Even when a murder or a suicide is involved, the motivation may be left equivocal, obscure. If some dreams are inter-

preted, others remain oracular. Characters open their hearts to
intimates, occasionally to strangers, but confessions are partial
in more senses than one. Some of the protagonists are Rem-
brandtesque figures, molded by a light that struggles against the
enveloping dark.

Among the figures in his immense cast who move in a twilight
zone are saintly halfwits. Totally different from these is another kind of eccentric: grotesque characters, at once repulsive
and pathetic, and sometimes amusingly absurd. Not the least
gift of this novelist whose central concern was with ultimates
and absolutes, was a wry humor. It takes the form of caricature
or parody, with excursions into farce, bringing relief from his
lapses into the mawkish and the unctuous, as well as from his
extravagances.

In drawing grotesques Dostoevsky was working a vein that
Gogol had made the most of. But if he was in debt to this
master, he stood apart from the majority of his contemporaries.
Most nineteenth-century Russian fiction was largely written by
and for members of the landed gentry. It often breathes an air
of provincial indolence, and the rural scene that is likely to be
the background of the action lies in friendly daylight. Although
two of his most massive narratives unfold in a town remote from
the capital, his work is that of an urban writer. Feverish with
crisis, upheaval, catastrophe, it harbors the sense of tragedy and
is cast in a semidramatic form. The stage, illuminated of course
by artificial light, is the city, often Petersburg, with its glaring
contrasts, "its sick hurry, its divided aims." The main events
occupy a few days, with gaps equivalent to intermissions between the acts. The dialogues and confessions have mass scenes
as a foil. Dostoevsky's longer narrations were first serialized,
the installments appearing at long intervals. To keep the reader's
interest he made use of the shopworn stock-in-trade of melodrama, the thriller, the detective story. He did it sometimes
clumsily and apparently without compunction—he may even have
taken pleasure in it. The only plays he wrote were three youthful
productions of which no trace survives save the evocative titles
of two of them: *Maria Stuart* and *Boris Godunov.* Yet plainly
he found the theater congenial. Practically all his novels and
some of his stories have been adapted for the stage.

His narratives are, however, poles removed from the tight-
ness of drama. When he was at work on *The Devils* he confessed that his chief deficiency was that he had not learned how

to control his material. "Many novels and stories," he wrote to Strakhov, "squeeze themselves together into one of my novels, so that there is neither measure nor harmony." As a matter of fact, the symmetry of *The Idiot* points to a careful design. Nor is there lack of "measure and harmony" in *Crime and Punishment*. Indeed, the profusion of characters helps to give the novels their dynamism. This is paramount in *The Brothers Karamazov*, rich in gusto as that tumultuous work is.

Before he had composed any of his major novels, he wrote to Turgenev, as may be remembered, that literature should express things that "total consciousness, not *reason*, has yet to grasp." Total consciousness includes, of course, the subconscious. He did not discover it, but his performance shows him remarkably attuned to that latent mental activity and its role in human behavior. Among those manifestations of it which have a place in his narratives, dreams play a prominent and important part.

One feature of the psyche that his work repeatedly and emphatically exhibits is what he called "duality": the simultaneity of two opposed drives. It is the ambivalence that has since come to be regarded as fundamental to human nature. Here he was unquestionably leaning on introspection. His art was not a flight from himself. His was the antithetical mind that Byron attributed to Burns. It was epitomized by Montaigne thus: "We are, I do not know how, double in ourselves; so that what we believe we disbelieve, and cannot rid ourselves of what we condemn."

Toward the end of his life Dostoevsky made an often quoted entry in a notebook, which concludes: "They say I am a psychologist. Not true. I am a realist in a higher sense, that is, I depict the depths of the human soul." It is a truism that, *pace* his disavowal, he brought to his task extraordinary psychological insight. Nietzsche spoke for others beside himself when he called Dostoevsky "the only psychologist" from whom he "had anything to learn." The self that the novelist's explorations disclosed is a complex of ambiguous, contradictory impulses and responses, less subject to the control of reason than had been generally believed. He anticipated the findings of later, more scientifically oriented students of the mind. In defining himself cryptically as "a realist in the higher sense" he may have meant that his business was in part with man as belonging to the transcendental order of being. Indeed, in "the depths of the human soul," including his own, he found aspiration toward absolute good, ultimate harmony, the ideal of moral beauty which was for him the core of Christianity. He had been nurtured, however, in the belief that man is a fallen creature. Furthermore, experience as well as self-knowledge had strongly impressed him with human depravity. It has been pointed out that he was most effective in evoking brutality, perversities, demonic proclivities— the Devil is at home in these pages. Though he focuses on the inner life, the social setting is not overlooked. Dostoevsky was keenly aware that the secular, materialistic bias, that he regarded as destructive of intangible, precious values, was irresistibly spreading. And so, on the one hand, he envisaged mankind redeemed by Holy Russia under the aegis of a universal Church, and, on the other, harried by nightmares like the Inquisitor's Utopia. He was haunted by a vague premonition of dark times in store, of impending spiritual bankruptcy.

Dostoevsky, of course, has impressed himself upon generations less as a possessed visionary than as the novelist who, in greatly enriching world literature, deepened men's self-knowledge. In a letter, already quoted, he confided to Mikhail his adolescent discovery that "man is a mystery." He went on to say: "The mystery must be unriddled, and if you spend your whole life unriddling it, do not say that it was wasted time." That observation might serve as an epigraph to the bulk of his fiction, testifying to his steady concern with the baffling task that had beckoned to him in his youth.

# BIBLIOGRAPHY

THE most complete and textually reliable edition of Dostoevsky's writings is that issued in Moscow in 1926–30. Its scholarly apparatus comprises variant readings, lists of the editions that appeared during the novelist's lifetime, and information on the manuscripts extant, including preliminary drafts and notes. The amply annotated second Soviet edition (1956–58) contains, except for the Pushkin speech, his fiction only. The quotations from the stories and novels are taken from Constance Garnett's translations, first published in London, 1912–20, in twelve volumes, separately titled. In every instance the quoted passage has been collated with the original and in some cases altered. The Modern Library edition of *The Possessed* (*The Devils*) (New York, 1936) includes the suppressed chapter of the novel, translated by the present writer. He revised the Garnett translations of *The Brothers Karamazov* and *The Idiot* which The Limited Editions Club, New York, brought out in 1933 and 1956, respectively. David Magarshack retranslated *Crime and Punishment* (1951), *The Devils* (1953), *Best Short Stories* (1955), *The Idiot* (1957), *The Brothers Karamazov* (1958). *The Double* was rendered anew by George Bird (London, 1957). *The House of the Dead* was translated by Jessie Coulson, as was *Crime and Punishment,* which appeared with essays on it in a volume edited by George Gibian (New York, 1964). With the publication of *The Diary of a Writer*, translated by Boris Brasol (2 vols., New York, 1949), *Winter Notes on Summer Impressions*, translated by R. L. Renfield (New York, 1955), and *Occasional Writings*, edited and translated by David Magarshack (New York, 1963), the bulk of Dostoevsky's non-fictional work became available in English.

Some of the preliminary drafts of and notes for his stories and novels were lost, some he destroyed. Much of what is extant has been published. The material relating to *The Brothers Karamazov* was first issued in a German translation under the title *Die Urgestalt der Brüder Karamasoff* (Munich, 1928), the original appearing under a Leningrad imprint in 1935, when the notes for *The Devils* too were issued. By 1934 the volumes having to do with *Crime and Punishment* and *The Idiot* had seen the light. The papers relating to *A Raw Youth* were published in 1965. Under the editorship of Edward Wasiolek all of these works appeared in English (Chicago, 1966–71). In 1957 the Soviet Academy of Sciences published *Opisanie rukopisey Dostoevskovo*, a description of the novelist's manuscripts, listing all his papers down to the most trivial scrap, each item classified by subject, provided with its call number and the name of the library or archives where it is housed.

Aside from *The House of the Dead*, which is partly disguised autobiography, and certain passages in *A Writer's Diary*, Dostoevsky left no account of his life. The edition of his letters (4 vols., Moscow, 1928–59), with its abundant notes, is an indispensable repository of information about the novelist. There is a French translation of the letters (*Correspondence de Dostoevsky*, 4 vols., Paris, 1949–61) and an English rendering is in preparation. *Dostoevsky, a self-portrait* (London, 1962), by Jessie Coulson, contains copious excerpts from the letters. Some of the reminiscences affording glimpses of the novelist as seen by his contemporaries went into the making of the first biography, by N. N. Strakhov and Orest Miller, published in 1883.

To the devotion of the novelist's widow we owe a comprehensive catalogue of Dostoevskiana, published in St. Petersburg in 1906. There is an English translation (New York, 1928) of her diary for 1867, the first year the couple spent abroad, and a translation of her *Reminiscences*, abridged, is in *Dostoevsky, portrayed by his wife* (New York, 1926), edited by S. S. Koteliansky. She was also instrumental in founding the Dostoevsky Museum, located in his childhood home, the apartment in the wing of the Mariinsky Hospital for the Poor, later the Hospital for Social Diseases. In 1968 a list of the Russian-language editions of his works, and publications about them during most of the Soviet period (1917–65), appeared under the auspices of the Museum. The volume, which runs to four hundred pages, opens with a survey tracing in some detail the growth of the Dostoevsky bibliography over the years.

The titles listed below are a selection, chiefly in English, from biographies and critical studies. The numerous Russian works consulted have not been noted, since these are inaccessible to most of the readers to whom this book addresses itself. D. is used for Dostoevsky in all spellings.

Adler, Alfred. "D.," in his *The Practice and Theory of Individual Psychology,* translated from the German, London, 1925.

Ayer, A. J. "Philosophy at Absolute Zero," in *Encounter,* London, 1925.

Belknap, Robert L. *The Structure of The Brothers Karamazov,* The Hague, 1967.

Berdyayev, Nikolay. *D.,* New York, 1957.

Blackmur, B. P. "In the Birdcage. Notes on *The Possessed* of Dostoevsky," in *The Hudson Review,* vol. 1, no. 1, 1948.

Brodski, N. L. *The Plan of The Life of a Great Sinner,* London, 1922.

Camus, Albert. *The Myth of Sisyphus and Other Essays,* New York, 1959.

Capetanakis, D. *D.,* in his *The Shores of Darkness,* New York, 1949.

Carr, E. H. *D.,* Boston, 1931.

Curle, Richard. *Characters in D.; Studies from Four Novels.* New York, 1966.

D., Aimée (Liubov, the novelist's daughter). *A study,* London, 1921.

Ermiloff, V. V. *Fyodor D.,* translated from the Russian, Moscow, 195?.

Evdokimoff, Paul. *D. et le problème du mal,* Lyons, 1942.

Fanger, Donald. *D. and Romantic Realism,* Chicago, 1967.

Forster, E. M. *Aspects of the Novel,* New York, 1927.
Frank, Joseph. "Nihilism and 'Notes from Underground,' " in *Sewanee Review,* Winter, 1961.
──────. "The World of Raskolnikov," in *Encounter,* June, 1966.
Freud, Sigmund. "D. and Parricide," in *Art and Psychoanalysis,* William Phillips, ed., New York, 1957.
Gide, André. *D.,* New York, 1961.
Girard, René. *D., du double à l'unité,* Paris, 1963.
Guardini, R. *Religiöse Gestalten in D.s Werk,* Munich, 1947.
Harper, Ralph. *The Seventh Solitude; man's isolation in Kierkegard, D., and Nietzsche.* Baltimore, 1965.
Hingley, Ronald. *The Undiscovered D.,* London, 1962.
Howe, Irving. "D.: the Politics of Salvation," in his *Politics and the Novel,* New York, 1957.
Ivanov, Vyacheslav. *A Study in D.,* New York, 1960.
Jackson, Robert. *D.'s Underground Man in Russian Literature,* The Hague, 1958.
──────. *D.'s Quest for Form.* New Haven, 1966.
Kent, Leonard J. *The Subconscious in Gogol and D., and its antecedents,* The Hague, 1969.
Kovalesky, Sonia. *Sonia Kovalesky: Her Recollections of Childhood,* New York, 1895, chaps. 9–10.
Lavrin, J. D. *D., a study,* New York, 1947.
Levinson, A. *La vie pathétique de D.,* Paris, 1931.
Linnér, Sven. *D. on Realism,* Stockholm, 1967.
Lord, Robert. *D.: Essays and Perspectives,* Berkeley, California, 1970.
Magarshak, David. *D.,* London, 1962.
Matlaw, R. E. *The Brothers Karamazov: novelistic technique,* The Hague, 1957.
──────. *Notes from the Underground and The Grand Inquisitor,* New York, 1960.
Meier-Graefe, J. *D., the Man and his Work,* translated from the German, New York, 1928.
Mochulsky, K. V. *D.: his life and work,* translated from the Russian, Princeton, 1967.
*Modern Fiction Studies,* special number devoted to D., Lafayette, Indiana, Autumn, 1958.
Muchnik, Helen. *D.'s English Reputation,* in *Smith College Studies in Modern Languages,* XXII, 1939.
Murray, J. M. *Fyodor D.,* London, 1916.
Pachmuss, Temira. *F.M.O.,* Carbondale, 1963.

Powys, John Cowper. *D.*, London, 1946.

Rahv, Philip. "D. in *The Possessed*", in his *Image and Idea*, Norfolk, Conn., 1949.

———. "The Legend of the Grand Inquisitor," in *Partisan Review*, 1954, 3.

———. "D. in *Crime and Punishment*", in *Partisan Review*, Summer, 1960.

Randall, Francis B. *Chernyshevskii*, New York, 1967.

Reeve, F. D. *The Russian Novel*, New York, 1966.

Roe, Ivan. *The Breath of Corruption*, London, 1946.

Rosen, Nathan. "Chaos and D.'s Women," in *The Kenyon Review*, Spring, 1958.

Rosenberg, Harold. "*The Idiot*: Second Century," in *The New Yorker*, October 5, 1968.

Savage, D. "The Idea of *The Gambler*," in *The Sewanee Review*, Spring, 1950.

Shestov, Leo. *D., Tolstoy, and Nietzsche*, Athens, Ohio, 1969.

Simmons, E. D. *The Making of a Novelist*. New York, 1940.

Slonim, Mark. *Three loves of D.*, London, 1957.

Steiner, George. *Tolstoy or D., an Essay in the Old Criticism*, New York, 1959.

Stepun, F. *D., Weltschau und Weltanschauung*, Heidelberg, 1950.

Terras, Victor. *The young D., a critical study*, The Hague, 1969.

Trilling, Lionel. "The Fate of Pleasure: Wordsworth to D.," in *Romanticism Reconsidered*, ed. by Northrop Frye, New York, 1963.

Troyat, Henry. *Firebrand: The Life of D.*, New York, 1946.

Vivas, Eliseo, "The Two Dimensions of Reality in *The Brothers Karamazov*," in *The Sewanee Review*, Winter, 1951.

Wasiolek, Edward. *Crime and Punishment and the critics*, San Francisco, 1961.

———. *The Brothers Karamazov and the critics*, Belmont, California, 1967.

———. *D., the Major Fiction*, Cambridge, Mass., 1964.

Wellek, René, ed. *D., A Collection of Critical Essays*, Englewood Cliffs. N.J., 1962.

# INDEX